An Introduction to Education

SELECTED READINGS

Edited by Marjorie Mitchell Cann Ph. D.

Head, Department of Behavioral Sciences, Pensacola Junior College

Thomas Y. Crowell Company

NEW YORK • ESTABLISHED 1834

PREFACE

Learning Resources Laboratory — Room 331
School of Education
San Jose State University
San Jose, California 95192

THE BOOK you are about to read has been prepared as a result of a recent survey of college programs offered for future teachers. The survey was conducted by mail and by personal visits to colleges and universities. One of the first courses in the programs was the "Introduction to Education" course. In all colleges surveyed, this introductory course was more or less alike in scope and sequence, with the outlines and syllabuses reflecting a commonality of stated objectives. Yet despite the similarities, these objectives have not been satisfied by any available textbooks.

This finding prompted me to inquire further into the procedures for selecting textbooks and the reasons for their selection. In general, I found that the procedures were sound but not the reasons that underlay them. This was of great interest to me for I had begun the survey solely for the purpose of finding an appropriate textbook for my own students in their first education course.

Conferences with faculty members who were responsible for making the selection of a textbook for a beginning education course invariably gave the impression of utter disenchantment with the available texts. Comments of individual faculty members pointed out the fact that many of the books were so heavily weighted with readings on foundations of education that education as a distinct academic field with career opportunities was completely neglected. My review of other introductory texts frequently uncovered many that offered simple "how-to-do classroom teaching" procedures. None reflected the balance between the foundations of education and education as a distinct academic field that was desired by a majority of the instructors of this course. Consequently, the instructors were required to make a very real compromise when deciding which textbook to adopt for their students.

As a group, the instructors interviewed in this survey are representative of the best teachers in the field. All had been searching for a book that would meet the unique and special needs of a first course in the professional education sequence. The majority had found none. They unanimously agreed that they needed a book that presented education as a unique field of academic study and also as a professional vocation. The consensus was that foundations of education readings for an introductory course needed to be combined with readings on education as an academic field offering a multitude of career opportunities. On the basis of this consensus, *An Introduction to Education: Selected Readings* was planned to meet the needs identified in the survey.

Every selection in this book has been evaluated on the basis of appropriateness to the stated objectives in the course syllabuses obtained in the survey of programs. Being aware of the emphasis placed upon good teaching by a majority of the college instructors of our future teachers, it is with pride that the author shares this book of readings with them. The instructors strive to obtain the best instructional materials and to use the most effective teaching methods. They seek and deserve only the best in textbooks. It is with the hope that the readings in this book will meet the needs identified by many of the instructors that it is now offered to you. If it does this, it will interest and stimulate students who are studying education for the first time.

This book traces its beginning to a number of readings selected for my own students in an attempt to offer a well-balanced introductory course. A search, in which my students played an important part, was then undertaken to locate additional materials that would be informative, stimulating, and create a genuine interest in a career in education. Once the active interest in finding new readings had been created, the students sustained it by bringing many fine selections to my attention. These readings covered a wide range of reading materials from a variety of sources including professional periodicals and papers dealing with currently popular topics. Together, we determined the final selection of readings for the book.

The forty-two readings that comprise *An Introduction to Education: Selected Readings* examine in considerable detail three separate aspects of education: the foundations of education, education as an academic field, and career opportunities in education. They represent a diversity of authors from a wide range of academic fields. The book is designed for a one-semester or one-quarter course in the preprofessional sequence of a general education college program for either a two- or four-year college.

More readings are included than can usually be studied within any one semester to allow for a choice in selection from semester to semester. Another reason for this extensive offering is that it will give instructors ample opportunity to select readings and make assignments as their knowledge and teaching experience indicate is most appropriate for their students.

The book is divided into three parts. The selections in the first two parts deal with the basic areas of education—"Foundations of Education" and "Education as an Academic Field." Those in the third part, "Education as a Career," discuss the selection and preparation for a career in education; in addition, they also consider the professional teacher, his functions and responsibilities.

Many students in freshman and sophomore classes will complete two years or less of college. Those taking a pre-education course, therefore, may not pursue any formal learning beyond the first or second college year. Some will enter the paraprofessional occupation of teacher aide. This places a responsibility upon the instructor to make the course meaningful to these students as well as to those who will continue their education. In choosing readings for this book, I have kept this in mind. The readings are intended to give students an adequate understanding of the foundations of education and an awareness of educational career opportunities open to them. It should assist them in making a reasoned decision with regard to a career in education as well as becoming better informed citizens prepared to assume responsible leadership both within the profession and the community.

Every effort has been made to maintain a balance between selections in the foundations of education and those on the structure, functioning, and major developments in education as an academic field and vocation. In brief, it might be said that *An Introduction to Education: Selected Readings* is a survey of the field of education with a strong emphasis on stimulating interest in a career in the field.

Interpretative headnotes to each of the selections link the book together loosely but in a meaningful whole and indicate the educational significance of the selections. An especially distinctive and important feature of the book are the questions located at regular intervals, which are designed to encourage study, stimulate critical thinking, and facilitate self-evaluation of the learning process. Specific answers to each question can be found within the readings, thus providing the student with the feedback needed to indicate the status of his learning. Involvement in self-evaluation begins when the student prepares his answers without referring to the book. He is then to reread the selections to which the assigned questions refer, check his answers, and modify them where necessary. Thus, by immediate reinforcement and the elimination of possible fixations of errors, learning is increased and self-evaluation is achieved.

Instructors will find their own evaluative procedures strengthened by combining the student's self-evaluation with their own scheduling of tests. Ideally, answers to the questions found in the book will be submitted at regular intervals, with or without the student's own corrections indicated, to the instructor as the course proceeds. Progress can thereby be plotted so that the student may be advised on how he can improve his study habits. In this way, the most effective use of the evaluative process will be a combination of self-evaluation and evaluation by the instructor.

Some students may decide that the questions for self-evaluation may be fine for others but are not for them. This makes sense to the student who has learned by experience that he is held responsible only for what amounts to a summarization by the instructor of the textbook for the course. And almost any freshman knows that only a fool would incur the wrath of the nonintellectuals in his classes by asking for test questions on more than a summarization. He may also ask, "So why should I do any more than is necessary to pass?" The answer lies in his own reason for studying education. These evaluative procedures are designed for those who have a desire to learn as much as they can in an introductory course and who tend toward a love of learning and a zest for understanding. Every student must decide for himself whether he wishes this course to serve him simply as more college credits or as a genuine introduction to the field of education.

Having a custom-designed book of readings for a course that is essentially a reading course has one great advantage. When students are required to search through library references to do the readings assigned to them, one student frequently goes to the library for a group of friends. He summarizes the readings, has his notes duplicated, and shares them with the group. As a result, many students never read an assignment that requires a visit to the library. Making the readings readily available for student use is intended to encourage involvement by *all* students and study in depth by the more serious.

I wish to express appreciation to my students, colleagues, and friends who encouraged and assisted me in producing this book. I wish also to thank the many copyright holders who gave permission to reprint their works. A special thanks goes to those who gave their writings as gifts. Their generosity of spirit helps make it possible for me to share some of their thoughts and talents with students who will receive their first glimpse of education as a unique field of study.

M. M. C.

Pensacola, Florida

CONTENTS

PART ONE

Foundations of Education

The direction in which education starts
a man will determine his future life.

PLATO

The readings in this part will introduce you to some significant relationships between education and the fields of history, philosophy, psychology, sociology, and anthropology. The historical selections reflect the influence of various philosophies on education throughout America's history. The contribution made by psychology and sociology to education has increased greatly in the past fifty years, and much of this influence is seen in the four selections written by outstanding psychologists. In the past, anthropologists have shown a vital interest in education only on rare occasions. Their contributions, however, have provided and are now providing much to our perception of the part education can play in the context of society.

The first three selections in this first part survey the historical development of education in America. To appreciate the phenomenal growth of the American school system, it is necessary to have a knowledge of its history. A unique feature of the selections chosen for this introductory survey is the identification of men and women who have made our educational history. In fact, one of the major reasons for choosing James Frasier (Selection 1) as the first author is his talent for bringing history to life through some of the people who made it.

In "The United States of America," Robert Ulich (Selection 2) intersperses his historical account with his own philosophical views and beliefs. This strengthens rather than weakens the historical perspective and is intended to inspire students to contribute personally toward constructive development of education in America. Professor Ulich refers to the United States as "the country of immigrants." As an outstanding scholar and renowned immigrant himself, Ulich is in a better position than many writers to evaluate the state of American education. He shows his awareness of present conditions in his references to America's awakening from a state of complacency concerning its school situation in recent years.

A short history of teacher education by Paul Woodring (Selection 3) has been chosen to conclude the readings in the history of education. Woodring traces teacher education from the earliest normal schools to the present postgraduate programs. Historically, the earliest short courses were given at institutes held in the fall and the spring of each year. This was the only teacher training in the country at that time. The present trend, requiring a minimum of four years of college education, continues to meet with opposition from well-informed leaders in and outside of education. Many of these leaders advocate the study of professional courses for a nine- to ten-month period following a four-year liberal arts degree. This program is referred to frequently as the Master of Arts in Teaching (MAT), and it is supplemented by periodic refresher courses. This position assumes that until there is positive identification of the characteristics and competencies of successful teachers, there can hardly be an adequate program. The contrast is clearly made between the requirements for teaching then and the Master of Arts as a teaching degree today. This selection affords students ample opportunity for debate on whether short courses for teacher training or the four and five years in education programs are preferable.

"Philosophy of Education" is introduced in the selection by F. Bruce Rosen (Selection 4), in which the author shows the close relationship between history and philosophy. His position is that a knowledge of basic assumptions underlying educational thought contributes to an understanding of the philosophical aspects of education that have affected its history. Rosen presents some basic assumptions in his discussion of various philosophies of education and gives specific reasons for studying these philosophies. He relates current educational practices to the various philosophical systems in general and then, in turn, relates these to an individual's own philosophical system.

Next, Paul Woodring (Selection 5) discusses a wide variety of educational goals. He advocates devoting a greater proportion of the total time in high school to a liberal education rather than to vocational training. The wide variety of goals that Woodring discusses and the "eclecticism" that Rosen fears as a real danger appear to be relatively compatible at first glance. A reading of Rosen's philosophy, however, shows that he advocates a need to develop one's own philosophical system in order to view the educational program in its entirety. In contrast, Woodring advocates a more restrictive approach through an academic rather than an occupational emphasis. These selections provide opportunities for interesting comparisons and study.

Alfred North Whitehead's scholarly writing in "Aims of Education" (Selection 6) calls for education to prepare students for living in the present, since the present is the coming together of the past and the future or, in other words, the complete sum of existence. One outcome of Whitehead's philosophical approach is that his goal for education is very specifically stated, namely, that we should aim at producing men who possess both culture and expert knowledge in some special direction. Whitehead's philosophy is more complex than it appears at first reading and may be better understood by careful rereading. A study of his views will enable the student to appreciate how deeply convinced Whitehead is that "the race which does not value trained intelligence is doomed."

An introduction to the philosophy of education would not be complete without reading John Dewey and studying his philosophy. Oscar Handlin

(Selection 7) has written a very scholarly selection on Dewey's challenge to education.

The selection that follows Handlin's is "Personal Reminiscences on Dewey and My Judgment of His Present Influence" (Selection 8). The author, William H. Kilpatrick, was closely associated with Dewey for almost fifty years, initially as his student and later as his colleague in teaching. Thus, he is able to give the reader an intimate glimpse of Dewey both as a man and as an educator whose influence is still evidenced in American schools.

Each philosophy discussed in the five selections has contributed in some measure to American education. In American schools, evidences of each of them or variations of them may be found. An understanding of the philosophies and how they influence the educational process will enable you to appreciate the eclectic philosophical approach to education prevalent in America.

Psychology and education are closely related fields of study. In the first selection by William James (Selection 9), we have a definition of psychology as "the science of the mind's law." An introduction to the foundations of education would be incomplete without reading James's view on applying psychology in teaching.

John L. Phillips, Jr. (Selection 10), has written a provocative article on Jean Piaget, a zoologist turned psychologist. Piaget's psychology might be described as functional and applied. When he was a young man in Switzerland, Piaget proposed many of the ideas on the cognitive processes of children for which he is now renowned. He has since constructed a model of the development of the intelligence of children. Only in the past decade has there been any general acceptance of his theories; this, in part, is due to a lack of empirical data in his research findings. Despite the fact that individual cognitive processes are admittedly more subjective than objective in nature, Piaget's theories have now been further supported by convincing data and every teacher should be familiar with their basic tenets.

In "The Act of Discovery" by Jerome Bruner (Selection 11), we return once more to an American psychologist and scholar. Bruner, like Piaget, has conducted extensive studies on the cognitive processes, but he differs somewhat from Piaget in placing greater emphasis upon psychological experimentation. Bruner advocates testing his theories in the classroom. His insistence on testing and on direct application of his theories to methods of teaching make a study of Bruner exceptionally significant to teachers and future teachers.

The great teacher is the visionary teacher. He is capable of regarding teaching as a science and performing it as an art. The reader who shares this vision of teaching will be interested in comparing Bruner's "cumulative construction" concept of learning and Piaget's attention to attitude as a dimension of cognitive activity with Henry S. Pennypacker's (Selection 12) technique of "precision teaching." Pennypacker has studied teaching scientifically and places it firmly within the behavioral sciences. His technique is accompanied by a marked modification of the teacher's behavior and teaching style. This has provoked a great deal of critical academic discussion, particularly among traditionally oriented teachers. Teaching as an art requiring creativity and talent will undoubtedly remain, but if Pennypacker's psychological approach to teaching catches on, it holds great promise of making the products of teaching more measurable.

Sociology is one of the behavioral sciences most directly concerned with the study of human relations. It is imperative, therefore, that an introductory course in education include some sociology as part of the foundations of education.

The two selections presented for study both consider education from a national point of view. Henry Steele Commager, in "Free Public Schools—A Way to National Unity" (Selection 13), gives his ideas of the sociological implications for national unity which may be seen in the free American public school system, a theme that is clearly stated in the article's title. James B. Conant's "Toward a Nationwide Educational Policy" (Selection 14) is a natural companion piece to Commager's selection and students of education will find the ideas here quite provocative. Both selections also reflect the continuous concern of Americans about education.

The idea of free public schools as means to achieving national unity should raise as many questions as the idea of a nationwide educational policy in our pluralistic society. Doubtlessly, many of the questions that will arise have to be left unanswered in the selections. The review of past events relating to public schools and the projection of a future nationwide policy provides students with an excellent background of ideas from which to move into additional studies.

Only in recent years have anthropologists shown any real concern for the field of education. They have also been manifesting an interest in the application of anthropological principles and findings to the field. The two selections in this subject area delineate some of the possible as well as the actual contributions of anthropology to education.

Teachers and students reflect their individual cultures in every word and act of their lives. A teacher's culture influences what he does and how he conducts himself in his role as a teacher. In a similar way, the various cultures of his students affect what they do. The study and some understanding of cultural anthropology will assist a teacher to function more effectively in the overall education process.

George Spindler (Selection 15) points out that a teacher needs to approach his teaching with a sense of cultural relativity and an awareness of what Spindler calls the "total community." He also delineates relationships between changing cultural values and education. A careful look at these relationships will contribute immeasurably to your education as a teacher.

A "Redefinition of Education" (Selection 16) by the internationally famous anthropologist Margaret Mead is presented next. Her entire proposal rests upon the rapidly changing world in which we now live. Professor Mead's thesis is that all who are informed and share their knowledge with the uninformed, regardless of age differences, are teachers. The speed so characteristic of the modern world and the increasing proximity between all parts of the world have become major factors in acceptance of her thesis. These views should also convey to the reader a keen appreciation of teaching as an art of communication.

History

1

Historical Foundations
of American Education

JAMES FRASIER

Too often, a short historical account of education amounts to a listing of events, dates, and little or no identification with the great leaders who were responsible for the country's growth. The following selection presents educational developments through the lives of men and women whose contributions made possible the modern educational practices so unique in America. Frasier has named individuals, tabulated and discussed their contributions, which should add an interesting dimension to your study of this history.

HISTORICALLY, American education is an extension of the educational patterns of western Europe (especially that of Great Britain), just as originally American civilization was an extension of western European culture. Our forefathers were born into western European culture, and crossing the Atlantic ocean did not make radical changes in their patterns of living. In a very real sense, the institutions of the American colonies and later of the nation were built upon European foundations. It is true that the patterns have gradually changed in form and content, but even today there is a marked similarity between American culture and European culture, and between American schools and European schools.

The American colonists wanted their older culture patterns to change in a number of ways. Primarily, they wished to have the religious freedom that had been denied them in the countries from which they came. Political liberty

SOURCE: James E. Frasier, *An Introduction to the Study of Education* (New York: Harper & Row, Publishers, 1951), pp. 33–68. Copyright © 1961, 1965 by Harper & Row. Copyright © 1965 by James E. Frasier. Reprinted by permission of the publisher.

Presently professor in the College of Education at Arizona State University, from 1961 to 1963, Dr. Frasier was Director of Student Teaching at Oklahoma State University.

was another major objective they sought. The legal traditions of their old countries did not make provision for the people to be governed by statutes passed by lawmakers of their choice and enforced by magistrates of their own selection. It is significant to remember that the liberties most desired were not secured immediately. In fact, the Bill of Rights, which embodies the freedoms most sought by the new-world settlers, was not added to our Constitution until 1791, approximately 170 years after the original settlement at Plymouth, Massachusetts.

Achieving democratic patterns in education has also been an evolutionary process. It is important to note that democratic schools as the right of all children were not part of the new life envisioned by the new Americans. They were ready to fight for religious and political freedoms, but they did not seem interested in including children in the democratic pattern. Our early schools, from elementary schools through the Latin grammar school to the university, were patterned after those the settlers had left behind. It is true that the colonists did expand the elementary-school program to include a larger proportion of the population, but even the extended program followed the pattern, in materials and methods of teaching, that was common in Europe. In fact they used the same books and curricula and often imported the teachers from England and France. It was more than two centuries after the settlement of New England that the movement for democratic schools in a democratic society gained noticeable momentum.

The modern cultural pattern had its beginnings in the dawning of civilization—European culture was a product of all that had preceded it—and it has gradually developed since that time. The threads of that growth are many and complex. The history of education in our world, only one facet of the cultural pattern, is a thrilling story, but it is too complex to review here. Our text is concerned with the development of free, universal, public education in the United States, and this chapter is limited in scope to a summary of only those ideas and persons of significant influence on public education in America. Thus it is limited to mention of our western heritage and to review of some significant antecedents of European culture.

Greek Education

The earliest civilization having direct bearing on the educational pattern of Europe and later of America belonged to ancient Greece: to the citizens of Sparta and Athens. A study of the educational pattern of each of the two city-states is of particular interest today because across the modern world educational systems are still following in the general pattern of each. Politically Sparta exemplified the monistic culture of a dictatorship; Athens, with its more pluralistic society, strove towards a concept of democracy. Their beliefs about the proper functions of education and schools were also conflicting.

Education in Sparta

Education was of great importance to Sparta: its constitution reads more like a description of a military academy than an outline for a government. The life and interests of the individual were absolutely subservient to the public welfare. Every detail of conduct was carefully regulated, and even what little there was left of private and domestic life was utilized for the preservation of the state.

Spartan education, in a word, was concerned chiefly with the welfare of the state and, since welfare was thought of in terms of military superiority, it followed that Sparta was most interested in the development of warriors. Because of the supremacy of the state, the individual citizen was of importance only when he added to the military strength of his city; schools, of course, were organized in a manner reflecting the pervading objective of military superiority. The educational aims of Sparta later became those of Bismarck's Prussia, of Germany under Hitler, Italy during the time of Mussolini. In fact, in any dictatorial society all values are subjugated to the aim of the ruling class, group, or party.

In Sparta the city-state provided for the complete control of the training of the children by a system known as the "Spartan Agoge." The chief rulers had general authority over education, and every year a special educational officer was chosen from the highest leaders to supervise the training of the young. His authority was absolute. Under this superintendent were various types of assistants, including a number of official "whip-bearers," whose duty it was to administer punishment.

Spartan training, or *agoge,* began at birth. The newborn infant received a bath in wine on the theory that such a bath would kill the feeble but invigorate the healthy. Because children were the property of the state, the infant was immediately taken to the public council chamber. There the elders of the group decided whether it was worthy of being reared; if delicate or deformed, they decreed that the infant must be exposed on the mountain until death.

When the boys reached the age of 7 they were handed over to the state teachers who supervised their training until they emerged into full citizenship at 30 years of age. This period of training was not financed by the state; each citizen had to supply provisions for his sons. The boys were organized into bands or companies (of 64 students each) and were subjected to strict military discipline. The bravest and most prudent of the group was chosen as a leader; the entire group was placed in charge of a young man just above 20 years of age.

The program of living was designed to inure the boys to hardship and to prepare them to endure the severities of the life of a soldier. They slept on beds of reeds, without blankets, winter and summer. They wore only a tunic throughout the year, and always went barefooted. Their hair was clipped, so as to harden their heads to bear the heat of the summer and the cold of winter. The food was purposely kept in short supply, to teach them to bear hunger and to encourage resourcefulness in foraging for themselves.

At the age of 18 the young men were ready to take over the training of a group of youths of ages 7 to 18, who were embarked on the same program of barracks life. At age 20 the young men took the oath of loyalty to Sparta, and continued with their military training until they were 30. They became full citizens of Sparta, when they reached this age, and took their seats in the public assembly.

As is true in contemporary monistic cultures, the educational program of Sparta laid heavy emphasis on mind-training and memorization. The young men were taught to recite the laws of the state to music, and to sing from memory the grave and dignified chants of the old Doric style. Yet, as is also true in modern dictatorships, general intellectual education was considered unimportant.

The lack of intellectual training was the dark side of Spartan culture. Spartans had no interest in letters and taught neither reading nor writing. . . . The bare elements of mental arithmetic were acquired, but even for this they had little use. Of the great themes of human thought—history, geography, astronomy—we hear nothing. The drama was never admitted at Sparta. Rhetoric, studied so fervently in other parts of the Greek world, was frowned upon at Sparta. . . .[1]

Although in Spartan culture women were considered the equal and companion of men, and not their inferior, the education of girls was severely restricted. The main function of women was to bear children, and they were given gymnastic training, notably dance, to make them strong and capable of producing more acceptable children. No attempt was made to provide additional experience, and even the simplest home arts were ignored to a degree that Spartan women were noted for their lack of interest in the home.

Spartan education achieved its aims: Individuality was crushed out. Its people looked with disdain on others whose schools were not orientated militarily; and so did Sparta develop military men, but not a poet, philosopher, or artist, of note.

Spartans were exclusive, narrow, and arrogant. Their system was the resurgence of the primitive; all the more interesting because it synchronized with the birth of the higher civilization with which it stood in direct contradiction.[2]

[1] Frederick Eby and Charles Arrowood, The History and Philosophy of Education, Ancient and Medieval, Englewood Cliffs, N.J., Prentice-Hall, 1940, p. 211.
[2] Ibid., p. 241.

Education in Athens

The Greeks have made use of two terms to express education, *agoge* and *paideia*. (Both have influenced English words denoting teaching and learning: for example, "pedagoge" and "pedagogy.") *Agoge,* bearing the root idea of leading, discipline, oversight, applied especially to the type of education in Sparta. *Paideia* derived from *pais* meaning "child," usually signified the child's sport or play and formed the basis of Athenian education. Athenian culture was the result of the natural evolution of the activities of the play spirit and the outgrowth of child interest in songs and stories. Their culture contained no repressive educational traditions or prejudices, and, because a society mirrors itself more perfectly in its educational system than in any other social institution, the rearing of the child—both in and out of "school" —was natural. His growth in body and mind was as unhampered as the growth of the culture itself. Thus Athenian education, in sharp contrast to that in Sparta, can be characterized by the word "humanism."

Athenian boys started to school at about age six in a school far more adaptable to individual progress than most of our contemporary school systems. Artificial grading and grouping were de-emphasized, and music and literary education were given by individual rather than group instruction. The Athenian curriculum emphasized gymnastics and music, with the emphasis being shifted from one to the other in accordance with the growing capacities and needs of the child.

Gymnastics was offered for its military value, but also for its intrinsic value in building a strong body to house an alert mind. The greatest value of gymnastic training lay in its effect upon the moral life and sense of sportsmanship. All games and contests among the Athenians were played according to elaborate rules and "good form." It is significant to note that it is from Athens that our modern Olympic games come.

To the Athenian, music included all those arts that made for beauty and happiness as opposed to the drudgery of life. It began with melody, rhythm, poetry, dancing; later on, all literary instruction such as reading, writing, arithmetic, the learning of laws, the sciences and philosophy grew from a harmonic base.

It is obvious that Athenian educational patterns were designed to produce the well-rounded individual. According to Eby and Arrowood:

Education to the Athenians was a fine art, ranking with ceramics, sculpture, and oratory. The materials which they molded into form were different in each case, but the ends they sought were all alike—the products of the one idealizing, artistic spirit. Through a harmonious unfolding of the capacities of the individual, they aimed to produce a beautiful unity, a perfect human. . . . The old Athenian education produced the heroes of Marathon, and Salamis, and such men as Phidias, Pericles, Socrates, Plato, and all the other brilliant artists and thinkers of fifth-century culture. This artistic process of cultivating the native powers of the child in a harmony of personality is the true and original humanism.[3]

Table 1 provides summary comparison of education in Sparta and Athens, and has many implications for the modern monistic-pluralistic cleavages in conflicting contemporary societies.

TABLE 1.   *Comparison of Educational Programs in Athens and Sparta*

Basis of Comparison	Athens	Sparta
Purpose of education	To develop citizens	To develop soldiers
Type of development	Moral, social, and civic	Physical and military
Greatest emphasis	The individual	The state
Education, 7 to 16	In two private schools—physical education and music	In public barracks organized militarily and operated by state
By whom taught	Teachers—each boy accompanied at all times by slave called a pedagogue	Older boys and military personnel
Education, 16 to 18	Gymnasium—a public school—and civic training in assemblies and courts	Continued military life in barracks
Education, 18 to 20	Military training	Continued in barracks as captains over younger boys
After 20	Participation in community life	Army service from 20 to 30; citizenship at 30
Higher education	University of Athens; philosophy and rhetoric	None
Outcome of education	Philosophers, poets, scholars	Soldiers
Place in history	Great influence on philosophy and education throughout history	Little or no influence

Roman Education

The part played by Rome in the development of western culture is well-known, and admittedly great. Some students of education, however, have

[3] *Ibid.,* p. 285.

tended to depreciate the value of Roman contribution to educational history because Rome borrowed much of the pattern of its educational system from Greece, and added little that was novel. The truth is that Rome, in possession of most of the civilized world, was the teacher as well as the conqueror of the nations destined to become the centers of later western civilization. Imposing her language, political institutions, ethical code, arts, and approaches to living, Rome was notably a transmitter of culture.

Although Rome was for many years officially dedicated to stamping out Christianity, it was principally because Roman influence spread across Europe to the British Isles that the Judeo-Christian heritage spread to northern and western Europe. The ancient Christian church of Rome adopted Latin as its language of worship and (more significantly, here) also used classical Latin as the language of instruction in its schools. As Christianity spread among the Roman people, the church schools developed in influence and popularity. In 391 A.D. Christianity became the official state religion of Rome, and about a century later the Emperor Justinian ordered the closing of all other schools.

Finally, the Roman Catholic Church was the only group left to preserve the culture, learning, and education of Greece and Rome during the Dark Ages when education was at its lowest ebb in history. The Germanic tribes that overthrew the Roman Empire were simple, illiterate, barbaric people. Rather than fostering education and culture, they destroyed as far as possible all the culture of the newly conquered territory. During these times learning was found only in the Christian centers. It was not until the Middle Ages that there was a revival in learning and a new interest in education.

Education During the Renaissance

The countries contributing the most to the educational ideals and patterns of the United States were those in central Europe and the British Isles. Most of the men and movements discussed here belong to that part of the world.

It is necessary to go back to the latter part of the fifteenth century to find the beginnings of modern education. In the period of awakening called the "Renaissance," ancient learning was rediscovered and education took on new life. Along with it went a determined revolt against the narrowness of the culture of the Middle Ages; the development of a new literature, architecture, and art; and the beginning of scientific endeavor.

The revival of learning came first in Italy; from there it spread northward over Europe and the British Isles. Academies were founded for literary study in most important Italian cities, and libraries were established. There was much interest in Greek culture. Florence, which took the lead, in 1348 established a university for the promotion of the new learning.

The movement appeared much later in northern Europe than in Italy. It first became an important factor in educational, religious, and literary fields in the Netherlands. It was here that middle-class merchants had become wealthy through trade, and that much of the educational pattern that was to spread widely in Europe and England was first developed. It was here that Erasmus was born and contributed his first important work.

Erasmus

Desiderius Erasmus (1469?–1536) was perhaps the most famous man of letters and the most eminent educational theorist of the early sixteenth century. He was probably born in Rotterdam about 1469 and was educated first in his home country and later at the University of Paris and in Italy. He was ordained a priest of the Roman Catholic Church. His greatest influence on our American educational pattern came from his work in England, where he went during the reign of Henry VIII and remained for four years. There he assisted in the refounding of St. Paul's School, and taught Greek and divinity in Cambridge. More than anyone else he was responsible for the humanistic pattern of the curriculum at St. Paul's. This movement gave rise to many of the academies in England which later became the pattern for similar schools in America.

Erasmus wrote many books, particularly in the field of educational theory. His theories of education were far ahead of his time: he believed in universal education, condemned corporal punishment, and advocated the study of Latin and Greek. He believed that the teacher should not spend his time teaching too many rules of syntax—that a language was learned not by memorizing rules but by daily intercourse with those who could speak it.

The humanities as we know them today came into the educational pattern during this period. There developed two conceptions of the humanities. One was the narrow humanism which tempered the study of Latin with some attention to Greek in order to develop an elegant literary style. The broader conception called for the study of classical literature for a better understanding of the pursuits and activities proper to mankind. It required the study of all subjects dealing with man as a human personality. This broader conception of humanism was the forerunner of the present emphasis in education on the social studies, political economy, government, economics, sociology, psychology, and education. Unfortunately, narrow humanism too often dominated the schools during the revival of learning, and as time went on, many schools became more narrowly humanistic.

Importance of Printing

In discussing Erasmus, and later Luther, it is important to note the development of printing. Nothing that happened in this period was of greater importance. Prior to the invention of printing with movable type there were very few books, and these were hand-written. It was impossible for an ordinary person to own a Bible or a book of any kind. All teaching had to be done by word of mouth.

Printing with movable type had been in use in China for some centuries before it was invented in Europe, but the European who invented movable type had no information concerning printing in China, so he was an independent inventor. The time, the place, the exact date, and the inventor are all clouded in mystery, but this great event took place in central Europe, probably in Holland or Germany, about 1440. The inventor could have been Gutenberg, a German printer. It is known that he printed the earliest books of which copies remain. Gutenberg printed his first Bible in 1456, and from Holland and Germany printing rapidly spread to other countries.

For the first time in the history of the Christian religion Bibles were now available in some number. The reaction of church authorities was mixed: some welcomed the Bibles, others forbade their use by laymen.

Printing was well developed in central Europe before Luther was born, but it became one of the most powerful agencies for the dissemination of the doctrines of Luther and his followers. If movable type had not been invented, the Reformation might have been delayed for many years or might have had a very different outcome.

Martin Luther

Martin Luther (1483–1546) was born on November 10, 1483, at Eisleben, Germany, to a family of the free peasant class.

At the desire of his father, Luther began the study of law in 1503. However, two months later he entered a monastery—no one knows just why. His decision may have been the result of a vow he took, during a violent thunderstorm, to become a monk. Having entered upon his religious career he devoted his life to it with great seriousness.

This discussion is concerned only with Luther's influence on education, hence it will not deal with his pestuous career in the service of the church. Luther finally broke with the Catholic Church and in October, 1517, nailed his famous theses to the door of the church at Wittenberg. From then on he was an outcast so far as the established church was concerned.

It must be remembered that Germany had no lack of schools in Luther's time. By 1500 Germany boasted 13 universities and a great many lower schools, some of them very good.

The German people were extremely religious at the time of the Reformation. The Bible was a favorite book among the common people, and when it was made more easily available through printing its use became more general. What, then, did the Reformation have to do with the development of public schools? In the first place Luther placed a great stress upon the dignity of the individual. In his treatise on "The Christian Liberty" he wrote: "Nor are we only kings and the freest of all men, but also priests forever, a dignity far higher than kingship, because by that priesthood we are worthy to appear before God, to pray for others, and to teach one another mutually the things which are God." [4]

Secondly, Luther taught that the Bible was the ultimate source of religious truth, which made education a necessity. Man now had a reason for education. If he was to be his own priest and if the Bible was to be his guide, then he could not fulfill his life's mission unless he was able to read. This led to a great spread in education. Furthermore, Luther wrote many sermons, treatises, books, and pamphlets giving his religious views which were read by the multitudes as soon as they had learned to read.

Even before the coming of Luther a large number of Bibles and many other books had been printed in German, and these could now be read by more and more people. The student of education should not conclude that the Protestant Reformation was all Luther and all in Germany. Many other famous men, in many different countries, were a part of the Reformation. The groups they represented differed in numerous points of doctrine, but they did agree on the dignity of the individual, the importance of the Bible, and the need of universal education. It must not be concluded, however, that free public education sprang into being at this time, for this was not the case. Luther never did separate education from the church. Even the Puritans, after they had set up schools and churches in New England, always thought of them as a part of the same plan—in fact the weekday school and the Sunday church were usually held in the same building.

A great many different movements grew out of the Reformation—the various Protestant denominations were one result. These were developed in various countries under various important leaders. One small group, developed in Moravia, was fundamentalist so far as beliefs were concerned. Its members believed in a literal interpretation of the Bible. They were an interesting and very devout group, but they would not be mentioned at this time if it were not for an outstanding bishop of the church who was the first great modern in educational thinking. His name was John Amos Comenius.

[4] F. V. N. Painter, *Luther on Education,* Philadelphia, Lutheran Publication Society, 1889.

Comenius

John Amos Comenius (1592–1671) was born at Nivnitz in Moravia. He attended the village school and at the age of 15 entered the grammar school at Prerau. The schools of the day were very poor and Comenius was dissatisfied with them. He moved on to the University of Herborn to study when he was 18.

Four years later, after one year at Heidelberg, he returned to his native country, planning to be ordained a minister in the Moravian Brotherhood. However, this was not possible until he was 24, so he turned to teaching and became master of the school of the Moravian Brotherhood at Prerau. He became interested in education and wrote his first book, a textbook on grammar.

He entered the ministry at a time when there was a great struggle between the Protestants and the Catholics in Moravia. His home was twice plundered; his books and manuscripts were burned, and his wife and children were killed. The Moravian Brotherhood was driven into exile in Poland in 1628.

Comenius, who became a bishop in his church, lived for 79 years, mostly in exile. He gave all his thought and energy to the advancement of mankind through religion and education. He chose to be a priest but spent most of his life as an educator and wrote a great many books in both fields.

While in exile he was in charge of a school at Lissa, Poland. Here he worked out much of his educational program and wrote his great work on method. He subsequently went to Sweden to help reform the schools there. Later he worked in England, then went back to Sweden for eight years, thence to Hungary, and finally to Amsterdam where he completed his life's work.

Cotton Mather reported in 1702 that Comenius was offered the presidency of Harvard College, in 1654. Henry Dunster had resigned as president and Comenius was suggested as a successor. But Comenius did not accept the offer, and Cotton Mather noted, "But the solicitations of the Swedish Ambassador, diverting him another way, that Incomparable Moravian became not an American Citizen." [5] Much research has been done in an attempt to establish the truth of this report. No one has been able to uncover anything to substantiate this story published by Cotton Mather, and historians of Harvard seem to agree that the incident never happened.

Comenius was without doubt the greatest educator of his century. In fact, many of his ideas are incorporated in our present educational system. He proposed a grading system based on the growth and development of children. His plan called for a single-track educational program; it applied to the boys

[5] Will S. Monroe, *Comenius*, New York, Scribner, 1900, p. 78.

and girls of all classes. He rejected the idea of one school system for upper-class children and another and poorer one for the children of the lower classes. His plan was democratic.

Comenius wrote in the *Great Didactic,* "Everybody ought to receive a universal education and this at school." He was much ahead of his time in this respect. Although the single-track plan of education is basic to any democratic conception of education, it is just now being tried for the first time in most of central Europe.

The most important educational proposal made by Comenius concerned the organization of a school system. He proposed four levels of education. Each stage was to be a different kind of school, and each school was to be six years in length. Roughly the divisions corresponded to his conception of the four periods in the life of a growing child.

There should be a mother's school, in the home, for children from birth to age 6. There should be a vernacular school in every village for all children from 6 to 12. There should be a gymnasium in every city for children from 12 to 18. The gymnasium was to be followed by six years at the university. These divisions correspond quite closely to the present-day organization of education in America.

The child's mother was to be his teacher for the first six years. She would teach the child the beginnings of knowledge that would be useful to him during his life. Comenius put great emphasis on the teaching of objects and the development of the senses. Children were to be made acquainted with such things as water, earth, air, fire, rain, stones, iron, and plants to prepare them for the later study of the natural sciences. In the same manner the mother was to teach the children about the sun, moon, stars, mountains, valleys, and plains. Seeing, hearing, tasting, and touching were avenues through which children were to make contact with many natural things. Comenius wrote a book for the mothers called *School of Infancy,* in which he told them what to teach. He also prepared a picture book called *Orbis Pictus* for the children, to help them understand things that were not in their own physical environment. This type of book represented a new idea in education. The children asked questions which the mother answered, and they answered questions she asked, thus laying the foundation for reasoning.

Comenius had great faith in mothers, a faith that was not shared by most contemporary educators. He envisioned a mother who was well-educated and all-wise, but because there were few mothers of that kind, the first step in his educational pattern was not a great success. The nursery school is an outgrowth of the idea so well expressed by Comenius, but it depends upon specially prepared teachers instead of mothers for most of the teaching.

At the time of Comenius there were schools for the poor in which they were taught in the vernacular of the region. The children of more well-to-do parents were sent to schools where the language of instruction was Latin. Comenius considered this a bad plan. He thought that all children of all the people should go through the six years of elementary education together, for this would be good for the social development of all the classes. Moreover, he thought that using the vernacular in teaching those who were to be the country's leaders was valuable to them.

The subjects of the vernacular school were about the same as those taught in the early elementary schools in America. Comenius worked out a system of teaching whereby the pupils were grouped in six different classes. They studied the same subjects in each class but every year they went more deeply into each subject.

The third 6-year period was to be spent in the gymnasium or Latin school. Here again Comenius proposed the gradation used in the vernacular school. However, the offerings of this type of school were very ambitious, for here students were to achieve universal wisdom. They were to learn four different languages and get a suitable grounding in all the sciences and arts. He thought it best to approach the teaching of language by having the students read familiar material; grammar was to be taught later.

Comenius set down his educational beliefs in a book called the *Great Didactic*. Much of what he wrote is very modern even today. He believed that education should follow nature, and that it should proceed from the simple to the more difficult. Far from believing that proper education is circumscribed rote learning, he felt that children should learn to do by doing. He also put much emphasis on the teaching of practical things; he wished to eliminate all useless materials. He made a plea for gentle discipline in place of the brutal methods that were common in his time.

In spite of his pioneer work, education was little changed for centuries. Those with whom Comenius worked soon forgot both him and his educational philosophy. Not until much later did he take his place as a frontier thinker in education. Most of his plans in this field have influenced education in our time.

It is interesting to note progress and development in any field. One is impressed by the gap between the aspirations and ideals of the frontier thinkers and the achievement of their programs. Many of Comenius' ideals have not as yet been attained in the countries where he lived and worked.

A great many Moravians migrated to America in the eighteenth century. One group founded a community named Salem. It is now a part of Winston-Salem, North Carolina. Here they built the kind of houses they were familiar with in Moravia. They set up their church and organized a type of cooperative living.

Rousseau

Jean Jacques Rousseau (1712–1778), a political as well as an educational pioneer, rebelled against the religious, educational, social, and governmental conditions of his time. He attempted to circumvent the artificiality in religion and education and to curb the exploitation by government prevalent in France.

Rousseau's writings had great political influence. His book *The Social Contract* became the bible of the French Revolution. His influence was also felt in America; Jefferson and other American leaders knew and believed in his political teachings. In fact much that was written at the time of the American Revolution found its source in Rousseau's ideas. Rousseau believed that men were not bound to submit to a government against their own will. He advocated the overthrow of the existing autocratic government in France and the establishment of a republic. He believed in universal suffrage based on "liberty, fraternity, and equality." He was the prophet of both the American and the French revolutions.

In the field of education Rousseau's ideas were just as radical. He protested against the stern, unreal, artificial schools of his time, in which little boys were treated as small men. Education was meaningless, the methods were stiff and unnatural. There was excessive emphasis on religious instruction and book education. Like Comenius more than a century before, Rousseau preached the substitution of life amid nature, childish problems, ways, and sports.

Rousseau believed that education was the remedy for the ills of society and that in the processes of education the child should be the center of gravity. The nature of the child should determine the nature of the teaching rather than a logical order of subject matter suited only to an adult mind. According to Rousseau, the child was to be considered a child and taught as a child rather than as a miniature adult. His chief concern was to provide the child with real, vital, concrete experience.

Rousseau's educational program was concerned with the child's physical and mental life.

Do not suffer the child to be restrained by caps, bands, and swaddling-clothes; but let him have gowns flowing and loose, and which leave all his limbs at liberty, not so heavy as to hinder his movement, nor so warm as to prevent him from feeling the impression of the air. By keeping them dressed and within-doors, children in cities are suffocated. . . . I repeat it, the education of man begins at birth. Before he can speak, before he can understand, he is already instructing himself.[6]

[6] Jean Jacques Rousseau, *Emile*, New York, Appleton-Century-Crofts, 1898, p. 25.

Much of Rousseau's educational teaching is contained in his famous book *Emile*, which became as important in education as his *Social Contract* was in the world of politics. "All is good as it comes from the hand of the Creator; all degenerates under the hands of man." This is the opening sentence in *Emile*, a book in which Rousseau described the education of a boy, whom he called Emile, from birth to maturity. No one reading it now would take it as a serious discussion of the philosophy of education. It is a book of protest, its suggestions are extreme, but it contains a great many of the truths that are now commonly accepted by those who advocate modern and progressive schools.

Rousseau believed that we should treat the child instead of subject matter. He taught that present life is more important in teaching than a life to come later, and that authority should be replaced by reason. Education should take place through the senses rather than the memory; therefore, he felt that physical activity and health were of great importance. Education at each age should be suited to the activities normal for that age. Teachers should make use of the natural interests of children in education. All these statements are in keeping with good educational practice in America today.

Rousseau's writings may seem to the reader today to be filled with suggestions that are crude and impractical. However, when considered in the light of the conditions that prevailed in his time, these writings are of the greatest significance. *Emile* created interest in educational reform in France. Its influence soon spread to Germany and to other European countries. The torch of educational reform along humane and democratic lines that had been lighted by Comenius was rekindled by Rousseau and handed by him to the many men who were to follow him, both in Europe and in America. In particular, a young man in Switzerland by the name of Pestalozzi was greatly influenced and inspired by *Emile:* he picked up the torch and carried it much farther ahead.

Pestalozzi

Johann Heinrich Pestalozzi (1746–1827) was born in Zurich, Switzerland. As a young man he came under the influence of the teachings of Rousseau. Pestalozzi first tried out Rousseau's method of teaching on his own children, and discovered many shortcomings. In 1774 he established a school on his farm: 50 abandoned children were his pupils. Combining work on the farm with study of the ordinary subjects in the elementary curriculum, the children learned to make cheese while they learned to read. The school was conducted for two years and, when the family funds were exhausted, it was closed. But Pestalozzi still held to a firm belief in the power of education. He also saw many answers to the pressing educational problems of his day. In Europe at the close of World War II there were many orphan children needing homes and education, and a school was established in honor of Pestalozzi. Most of the money was raised in Switzerland and the school was built in the Swiss Alps. The school for orphans that Pestalozzi established lasted only two years but the new Pestalozzi School seems to be a permanent organization.

Locke and Rousseau took into account only the difficulty of dealing with one pupil. Their method was to shut up their solitary pupil, away from the contaminating influences of the world, to provide him with a tutor who was a marvel of discretion and wisdom, and to show how under these circumstances they might work their ideal of education.

Pestalozzi sought to reform education on more generous lines. He aimed at the regeneration of mankind. He lived for years among beggars, in order to learn "how to make beggars live like men." He dealt with the poor and outcast, and strove by means of education to give these neglected children self-respect and to raise them from moral degradation.[7]

After closing his school Pestalozzi turned his attention to writing. His most famous book, *Leonard and Gertrude,* was written at this time. The great success of this book made him an important figure. It is an unusually interesting novel, concerned with Swiss peasant life and practical home education, and it makes good reading even today.

Pestalozzi's many teaching positions took him from one place to another. For six months he had charge of a village school where he taught 169 orphans. His last and most important position was as director of the institute he established at Yverdon and conducted for 20 years. Here, he demonstrated with children the methods that were to make him famous.

His institute became so well-known that it attracted the interest of prominent friends of education from all over Europe. Teachers came from other countries to learn his methods, and ruling monarchs came to learn what they could do to provide better schools in their countries. Froebel, Herbart, and Sheldon, all of whom will be discussed later, came to Pestalozzi as students. Froebel remained for two years as a student and teacher. Herbart, the eminent German psychologist, visited the institute and was much impressed by what he saw. Recognizing that what the movement needed was an educational psychology, he returned to Germany and developed not only a psychology but a method of teaching.

Pestalozzi set forth his educational beliefs in a book called *How Gertrude Teaches Her Children.* This is his book of methods. Pestalozzi begins his teaching with nature and the five senses. But he does not trust nature as Rousseau did.

---

[7] Catherine I. Dodd, *Introduction to the Herbartian Principles of Teaching,* London, Swam, Sonnenschein and Company, 1898.

Even at the infant's cradle we must begin to take the training of our race out of the hands of blind, sportive Nature, and put it into the hands of that better power which the experience of ages has taught us to abstract from the eternal laws of our nature.[8]

The most essential point from which I start is this:—Sense-impression of Nature is the only true foundation of human instruction, because it is the only true foundation of human knowledge.[9]

All instruction of man is then only the art of helping Nature to develop in her own way; and this art rests essentially on the relation and harmony between the impressions received by the child and the exact degree of his developed powers. It is also necessary in the impressions that are brought to the child by instruction that there should be a sequence, so that beginning and progress should keep pace with the beginning and progress of the powers to be developed in the child.[10]

Pestalozzi also wrote a guide for teaching spelling, and another for teaching reading. Although he is well-known for his writings, perhaps his greatest contribution to education is embodied in the lives of those whom he taught.

Comenius worked out, in some detail, a system of education. Herbart developed detailed methods of presenting subject matter. Pestalozzi did neither. His contribution was largely his philosophy of education and the relationship of teacher to child. The best statement of his ideas was made by Pestalozzi himself when he contrasted, for his followers, the methods of the usual schoolmaster and those he recommended.

The teacher starts usually from objects, you from the child himself. The teacher connects his instruction with what he knows, in order to teach the child; you know in the presence of your child nothing else than himself and connect everything with his instincts and impulses. The teacher has a form of instruction to which he subjects the child; you subject your course of instruction to the child and surrender it to him, when you teach, as you surrender yourself to him. With the teacher, everything comes from the understanding, with you all gushes out from the fullness of heart. The child is childlike toward you, because you behave motherlike toward him; the more you are motherlike, the more childlike he is.[11]

To understand why this was a revolutionary doctrine at that time, it is necessary to be familiar with the kind of schools that were prevalent for the poorer classes. In the usual school, subject matter, most of it useless and uninteresting, was predominant. The schools were conducted in unsanitary and largely unequipped buildings. The methods of teaching were chiefly assignment, recitation, and punishment. The children were beaten much and taught little, there was no feeling of friendship between teacher and pupils.

[8] Johann Heinrich Pestalozzi, *How Gertrude Teaches Her Children,* Syracuse, N.Y., C. W. Bardeen, 1898, p. 249.

[9] *Ibid.,* p. 316.   [10] *Ibid.,* p. 58.

[11] Quoted by Tadaus Misawa, *Modern Educators and Their Ideals,* New York, Appleton-Century-Crofts, 1909, p. 127.

The teaching method of Pestalozzi spread first to Prussia. The king of Prussia, becoming very much interested in the new education, wished to visit Pestalozzi. When he arrived, Pestalozzi, although ill, insisted on being taken to see the king. As he was being lifted into his coach, he fainted, whereupon his friends urged him to give up his intended visit. But Pestalozzi said, "Let me go; for if by my humble intercession, I shall only cause a single Prussian child to receive better instruction, I shall be satisfied."

Pestalozzian schools were established in large numbers in Prussia. The new teaching methods spread largely from Prussia (instead of directly from Pestalozzi) to other European countries, and to England, and later to the United States.

In 1843 Horace Mann visited the schools of Europe and reported on his trip in his seventh annual report as secretary of the Massachusetts State Board of Education. The most interesting part of this report had to do with his observations on the schools of Prussia. Here Mr. Mann discovered what he thought to be the best type of elementary education he had seen on his trip. He was enthusiastic in his praise of the schools that had been set up by the followers of Pestalozzi. In these schools there was perfect harmony between teachers and pupils. The children were happy, no force or bribes were necessary to obtain the desired results. The report was widely read in America.

The schools in Oswego, New York, comprised the first public-school system in America to adopt the Pestalozzian method. The superintendent of schools, E. A. Sheldon, was dissatisfied with the methods in use. He was looking about for something better. He found it in the Normal and Training School at Toronto, Canada, which he visited in 1859. On his return to Oswego, Mr. Sheldon obtained from England the plans for the new type of education and introduced it into the Oswego schools. The teachers met once a week to learn about the new method and to ask questions. The experiment was so successful that soon people were coming from a distance to find out about the Pestalozzian method.

Because of the great popularity of the new method of teaching and the desire on the part of so many people to study it, the Oswego Normal School, a state institution, was set up in 1865 under the direction of Mr. Sheldon. The spread of Pestalozzi's teachings in America stemmed in large part from this normal school, which became nationally important almost immediately. Teachers came to it from more than half the states in the Union. Normal schools as far west as San Francisco obtained teachers from Oswego so that they too might learn about and teach the new method.

So the influence of Pestalozzi spread. He took the torch from Rousseau and carried it far in his lifetime. With it he kindled torches for Herbart, Froebel, and a host of other educators to carry forward.

Froebel

Friedrich Froebel (1782–1852) was the son of a pious, poor, orthodox Lutheran minister who never understood the dreamy, troublesome child. His mother died when he was an infant. His father married again, but his stepmother was unkind to him. A mother's love and a happy home life thus denied him, he left home to live with an uncle. He attended the village school but was not a successful pupil, so he apprenticed to a forester. It was in the forest that he developed his lifelong love of nature. There also he attained some of the sense of the unity of nature that was to pervade his philosophy. Froebel studied at Jena, the foremost university in Germany, with little success. His university career ended in disgrace when he was jailed for two months for a very small debt that he could not pay. The circumstances of Froebel's early childhood and his experiences in the forest give us a key not only to his whole life pattern but also to his educational philosophy.

The most important thing that happened to him was the opportunity to work with Pestalozzi at Yverdon. In him Froebel found a kindred soul. He understood Pestalozzi's passion for little children and desire to build an education that would be a part of life. Froebel remained at Yverdon for two years, first as a pupil and later as a teacher. His educational philosophy was profoundly affected by Rousseau and Comenius as well as by Pestalozzi.

In 1837 Froebel opened his first kindergarten in Blankenburg. This type of school was his greatest contribution to education. He was influenced, no doubt, by the plans for a mothers' school advocated so ably by Comenius. But mostly the kindergarten was a result of his passionate love for little children and his desire to do something for them. Pestalozzi's teachings and his own unhappy childhood also contributed to Froebel's wish to make life better for them.

Froebel said that the object of the kindergarten was

. . . to give the children employment in agreement with their whole nature, to strengthen their bodies, to exercise their senses, to engage their awakening minds, and through their senses to bring them acquaintance with nature and their fellow creatures; it is especially to guide aright the heart and the affections, and to lead them to the original ground of all life, to unity with themselves.[12]

This statement is a bit vague. Froebel's desire for unity, which is found in all his writings, is not always clear. His philosophy is filled with religious mysticism. Whatever he said about his philosophy, we know him best by what he actually did for the education of the little children.

---

[12] Ross L. Finney, *A Brief History of the American Public Schools*, New York, Macmillan, 1925, p. 99.

Froebel devoted the last years of his life to his kindergarten, and established a special school for kindergarten teachers. The rapid spread of the kindergarten movement over the educational world was due largely to the teachers who received their inspiration and the preparation for their work directly from Froebel and then went to other countries to establish these institutions.

Only in its home country, Germany, did the kindergarten movement die. The Prussian government under Bismarck desired to stamp out everything that looked like democracy. The kindergarten was, of course, almost pure democracy, so kindergartens were forbidden by edict of the Prussian government. Froebel, it is said, died of a broken heart.

Froebel's two main principles were self-activity and social participation. Music, supervised play, handwork, dramatics, dancing, drawing, group work, singing, and many other activities in the modern school were part of the school for little children planned so well by Froebel more than a century ago.

Froebel set down his educational beliefs in a book entitled *The Education of Man*. He wrote a great many other books in this field, including *Songs for Mother and Nursery*, a songbook for little children.

Herbart

Johann Friedrich Herbart (1776–1841) was a German professor and a contemporary of both Pestalozzi and Froebel. He was a very different type of individual, however. He was born into the important professional class and was given an excellent education, graduating from the University of Jena. He spent most of his life as a university professor of philosophy and education. Herbart was first of all a scholar, he did not share with Pestalozzi and Froebel their passionate desire to help the poor and needy. He established the first demonstration school in connection with a university, and taught a small selected group of children. His teaching and writing were done at the Universities of Gottingen and Konigsberg.

Herbart based his educational theories upon ethics and psychology, and he emphasized at the outset that the one supreme aim of education is the development of moral character. He rejected the theory of the mind's division into "faculties," and believed that the mind functions as a unit. For many years Herbart was hailed as the father of modern psychology and modern method. However, his concepts were not of great lasting value; on them have been built a much more usable psychology and theory of method. It should be said, nonetheless, that Herbart was the first to take teaching methods out of the realm of the accidental and build a scientific approach to classroom problems.

Herbart worked out a scheme to make teaching an orderly and scientific process. The scheme included five formal steps: (1) preparation, a review of related material that had been previously learned; (2) presentation, in which the teacher presented the new material to be learned; (3) comparison, in which the new facts were organized under the teacher's direction in preparation for the development of any general truth that should be arrived at in comparing the old and the new; (4) conclusion, a generalization from the old and new facts presented (this was the climax of the lesson); and (5) application, of the general principles learned. This final step was added later by the followers of Herbart.

It is apparent that the above plan involves the process of inductive thinking. Herbart's mistake was in assuming that all teaching could be made to fit this pattern. Those who followed his plan soon found that teaching in accordance with it was often sterile, formal, and not of any great value. From the standpoint of modern educational philosophy, the plan's greatest fault is that it is always text problems that the children are solving. Life and learning are seldom made up in such handy packages.

Herbart's real influence came after his death. Many of his followers carried on the work in German universities, particularly at Jena. The most important of these "Herbartians" was Dr. Wilhelm Rein, professor of pedagogics at Jena. Herbartianism spread far beyond Germany. It had great influence in England. Many American educators studied with Rein, at Jena. Enthusiastic Herbartians on their return to America organized the National Herbartian Society in 1895. In 1902 the name was changed to the National Society for the Study of Education. This is still a very important educational organization in America.

The Beginnings of Education in America

During colonial days education was scattered, fragmentary, and largely unsatisfactory. Each group of settlers brought with them not only their language, customs, and religion, but also their ideas of education. Thus many very different patterns of education were attempted in the various colonies. Three of these patterns are important: those in (1) the southern colonies, (2) New England, and (3) the middle colonies.

The Southern Colonies

The southern colonies developed their own peculiar kind of education based on their English background. Virginia and the other southern colonies were largely settled by Englishmen, most of whom came from the ruling class. They brought the English ideas of class with them. The colonists settled on large tracts of land and developed great plantations, and an aristocratic society. The owning and ruling class hired tutors to teach their children until they were old enough to be sent to England to complete their education. The work on the plantations was done by slaves, indentured servants, and convicts brought over from England. The children of these groups received no education. The Virginians were simply following the pattern of the mother country, for in England the official position at the time was that the laborers should be kept ignorant as well as poor; the business of the poor was to work, not to think. The southern colonists believed in authority—the authority of the Church of England over religious affairs, the authority of the owners over those who worked. It was the royalist pattern so common in England and in other European countries at the time. No organized attempt to promote public education in the South was made during colonial days.

It should be noted that one lone voice was raised in Virginia for general education, it was the voice of Thomas Jefferson. But no other effort followed Jefferson's, hence Virginia had to wait until the middle of the nineteenth century for the establishment of anything resembling a school system.

New England

While aristocratic Englishmen were planting their class system and their ancient ideas of man's relationship in Virginia, other Englishmen were establishing a far different type of colony farther north, on the rockbound coast of what was to be called New England. To this place came men with a dream of freedom and a desire to make a new kind of society in the New World. They left class system behind them, for it had no part in their plans. They left England and her autocratic civil government to establish a colony where men would be free to govern themselves. One would expect such a group to establish something new in education, and they did. They established that education was universal, and taxed themselves to pay the bill. Both ideas were different from those held in the mother country. Nevertheless, they patterned their schools after those they had known; their Latin grammar schools and universities were all faithful copies of similar schools in England.

The ideas of education held by the settlers of New England grew more out of religious than out of political considerations. The Puritans believed that the Bible was the guide of life and that the right to read and interpret it was a test of religious liberty. It was very necessary, therefore, that every person should learn to read the Bible for himself. The Pilgrims in Massachusetts, the Quakers in Rhode Island and Pennsylvania, the Dutch in New Amsterdam, the Swedes in Delaware, and the Germans in Pennsylvania were all motivated by the desire to read the Bible. This great religious urge led to the establishment of schools.

Whereas the South developed an educational pattern based upon the tutorial plan in the home, in New England the educational center was the community. The wealth of the community was taxed to pay the bill. In the South the poorer classes were disregarded; in New England education was for all since it was motivated by the desire to read the Bible. There was no question of religious freedom in the New England schools because the early colonists settled among groups with the same religion. Hence the public school in a Massachusetts town could teach the children to read and write at the same time that it taught them the faith of their fathers.

The Middle Colonies

In the middle colonies we find a different plan of education. They too were motivated by a desire to read the Bible. However, their schools were organized by the churches and not by the local civil government.

The situation in the middle colonies is well stated by Cubberley in his *Public Education in the United States.*

In New England the Puritan-Calvinist had had a complete monopoly of both Church and State. Into the Middle Colonies, best represented by New Jersey and Pennsylvania, there had come a mixture of peoples representing different Protestant faiths, and no such monopoly was possible there.

Unlike New England, though, no sect was in a majority. Church control by each denomination was, as a result, considered to be most satisfactory, and hence no appeal to the state was made by the churches for assistance in carrying out their religious purposes. The clergymen usually were the teachers in the parochial schools established until a regular schoolmaster could be had, while private pay schools were opened in a few of the larger towns. These, as were the church services, were conducted in the language of the different immigrants. Girls were educated as well as boys, the emphasis being placed on reading, writing, counting, and religion, rather than upon any form of higher training.

The result was the development in Pennsylvania, and to some extent in the other Middle Colonies as well, of a policy of depending upon Church and private effort for educational advantages. As a consequence, the provision for education, aside from certain rudimentary and religious instruction thought necessary for religious purposes, and aside from the apprenticing of orphans and children of the very poor, was left largely for those who could pay for the privilege.[13]

The tax-supported school came out of the New England colonies, the private institution-supported school was a product largely of the South, while the middle colonies developed private church-supported schools. It required two centuries for universal, free, nonsectarian, tax-supported education to become the national pattern.

[13] E. P. Cubberley, *Public Education in the United States,* Boston, Houghton Mifflin, 1934, pp. 20–21.

Education in the Young Nation

In 1776, when Thomas Jefferson wrote the Declaration of Independence declaring that all men were created free and equal, there was no equality of education and no general freedom of educational opportunities in the new nation. It became one of the great tasks for the new nation to develop an adequate plan for public education.

When this nation was established, Pestalozzi was conducting his important educational experiments in Switzerland, and men from many lands were journeying to his school to sit at his feet. Rousseau was just completing his great work in France as the philosopher of the French and American revolutions. These two men had a profound influence on the educational thinking of our country. Froebel and Herbart came later—both of them were born at about the time our nation came into being.

Thomas Jefferson

A great liberal, Thomas Jefferson (1743–1826) was born in Virginia and lived there on a large estate—except for the years he was away in public service—until his death.

Jefferson had great faith in democracy and in the rights of the common man. It naturally followed that he had great interest in public education. He believed that man was created to govern himself. He also believed that education was necessary in a democracy, for how could man govern himself if he could not understand the economic and political problems around him? In a letter to George Washington, Thomas Jefferson wrote on January 4, 1786: "It is an axiom in my mind, that our liberty can never be safe but in the hands of the people themselves, and that, too, of the people with a certain degree of instruction."

In 1779, while a member of the Virginia legislature, Jefferson introduced a bill providing for free public education in his state. This bill, which he called "A Bill for the More General Diffusion of Knowledge," was the first definite proposal in America for the establishment of a state system of public schools. It is amazing that such a plan should have been proposed by a southern planter in Virginia, a state that believed not at all in free or public education: if the proposal had been made in Massachusetts it would not have been so startling. But Jefferson's fellow planters who made up the legislative body in Virginia would have none of this educational plan. It remained for other states to establish public-school systems, and in fact it was not until 1860 that any public educational system was adopted in Virginia. Jefferson did live to see the University of Virginia established, but his plan for separating the state from the church had no success.

In the light of what is now known about state systems of public schools, it is interesting to examine Jefferson's plan. The counties of Virginia were to be divided into hundredths (these divisions correspond to the school districts of today) and the qualified voters were to elect three county aldermen who were to build, have charge of, and maintain schools where both boys and girls were to be educated. The plan provided that all children should have three years of elementary education free. If children attended the elementary school for a longer time, their parents were to pay tuition.

The Jefferson plan provided for the appointment by the aldermen of a superintendent of schools. He was to be a man of "learning, integrity and fidelity to the commonwealth." Each superintendent was to have charge of ten schools, and his duties were to be much like those of the modern superintendent of schools. He was to hire teachers, examine the pupils, visit the schools, and have general control of them. The schools were to be financed in the same manner as other county activities.

Jefferson's plan also made provisions for the establishment of secondary schools. High school districts were to be made up of several elementary school districts. The high schools were to be built on plots of 100 acres; the buildings and their maintenance were to be paid for out of public funds. Boys were to be selected from the elementary schools on the basis of their promise, and they would then get free education at the secondary school level. Outstanding graduates of the high schools were to be sent at public expense to the College of William and Mary.

Jefferson was not a professional educator. However, he set up the ideals and a pattern for public education. His own state had no middle class—the large landowners had already provided for their own children and had no interest in the education of the people who worked on their plantations. Hence the Jefferson plan did not have a chance in Virginia; it remained for other states to lead the way.

It is interesting to speculate on what might have happened if Jefferson's plan had been adopted in Virginia. It might have speeded up the establishment of free public education by at least a century.

Benjamin Franklin

Benjamin Franklin (1706–1790) was a man of many talents. He is best known as statesman, scientist, and philosopher, but he was also interested in education.

Although Franklin was born in Boston and received what schooling he had in that city, he did not share the educational philosophies of Horace Mann and John Adams. These men believed that education was a state function; Franklin held that it was an individual function. Adams and Mann would tax property owners to raise money to educate the children of all the people; Franklin believed that the money should be contributed by individuals interested in organizing and maintaining schools. He thought that plans should be made, if necessary, for the education of the poor, but that if public money was to be used, it was for pauper education. A great many people in Pennsylvania held the same opinion as Franklin, and Pennsylvania for years looked upon public education as education for the poor.

Franklin proposed no system of education. He was instrumental, however, in founding an academy in 1749. Included in the chapter on secondary education is the story of the academy founded by Franklin which later became a great university.

Franklin did not attend college. He was self-educated, and he was one of the best-educated men in the early days of our nation. It is little wonder, then, that he looked with disfavor upon those colleges teaching Latin and Greek but no useful information.

Believing that education should be practical, Franklin did not hold with the Latin and Greek of the Latin grammar schools: he maintained that all education should be conducted in English. Furthermore, he felt that the subject matter of the schools should be such as to prepare youth for an occupation. It is understandable that in writing out the plans for his academy, Franklin should put so much stress on English—he was a master of writing simple, understandable English, and his students were to learn to read, both silently and orally, and to write English. The pupils should learn arithmetic, too, and how to keep accounts—Franklin mentioned many times in his writings that keeping accounts was very important.

In his plan for the curriculum for his newly established academy, Franklin suggested the wide use of prizes. He suggested that two "scholars" be paired in spelling: each was to ask the other to spell ten words each day; the one that spelled the most words correctly to receive a prize—"a pretty, neat book of some kind."

Did Franklin have any influence in education? Yes. The type of academy he planned spread very rapidly over the country, crowding out the Latin grammar schools that had been common before his time. But most of the academies never did fulfill Franklin's dream. Even his own academy, falling into the hands of a board of trustees, made up largely of members of the Church of England, added Latin and Greek to the curriculum. Eventually his academy took on more and more of the college-preparatory aspects of secondary education, which was not as Franklin planned it. Even with his great prestige, he could not establish and run the kind of school he dreamed of. It was not until a century later, when the public high school came into being, that Franklin's plan for a secondary school taught in English and teaching useful things became accepted.

Franklin's plan for individual self-education also had an enormous influence on the youth of his time. You must remember that in Franklin's time there were no free public schools in Pennsylvania. The rate of illiteracy was very high. If a young man wished to get an education he had to do it largely for himself, particularly if he was too poor to pay tuition. Franklin's example was followed by a great many young men.

Horace Mann

Horace Mann (1796–1859), often referred to as the father of our public schools, was educated as a lawyer and practiced law with great success for 14 years. He was elected to the Massachusetts House of Representatives in 1827 and served as a member of it until he transferred to the Senate in 1833. While a member of the legislature he was instrumental in securing the passage of a law setting up a state board of education. Mann left the legislature and the practice of law at a great financial sacrifice to become the first secretary of the newly created state board of education. He did not return to politics until 1848, when he resigned as secretary of the board of education and took the place in the Congress of the United States vacated by John Quincy Adams.

Why did Horace Mann give up law and politics for education? He said that "the interests of a client are small as compared with the interests of the next generation." He was determined to do something for the schools of Massachusetts, for the need for school reforms there was great at that time. The schools lacked adequate financial support, the terms were very short, there was a scarcity of textbooks, the buildings and equipment were inadequate, and there were few properly prepared teachers. In fact there was no provision for the preparation of teachers in Massachusetts—or in any other state, for that matter. There were no superintendents of schools, and no one to supervise and advise with the teachers. A great many children were growing up without going to school. Horace Mann threw all his energies into this problem.

Through his efforts the first public normal school was established in Lexington, Massachusetts, in 1839. In his address at the dedication of the first building Mann painted a glowing picture of the importance of such schools for the education of teachers. He more than anyone else started the movement that provided America with normal schools, teachers' colleges, and colleges of education for the adequate preparation of those who teach our children.

Horace Mann's greatest contribution to the literature of education lies in the 12 annual reports he made as secretary of the Massachusetts State Board of Education. In them he wrote on the conditions of education in his state and elsewhere, and discussed the aims and purposes of public education. He believed and taught that education should be nonsectarian, universal, and free, and he set up a system of education in Massachusetts to facilitate meeting these goals. Students of education who are interested in his work will find much valuable material in these reports.

In 1853 Horace Mann was instrumental in the founding of Antioch College at Yellow Springs, Ohio. He became its first president and remained there until his death. Thus he influenced college and on a lower level public education as well. Having fought for free public education in Massachusetts with great success, Mann became interested in extending some of his reforms to the college level, and in Antioch set up a college that was nonsectarian and coeducational. Both of these ideas were revolutionary a hundred years ago and occasioned bitter criticism by other college men of the time. His most quoted statement was one he made to his students in a baccalaureate address delivered shortly before he died: "Be ashamed to die until you have won some victory for humanity."

The influence of Horace Mann reached not only to the other states in this country but also to South America. He was well-known in Chile and Argentina by reason of a man named Domingo Faustino Sarmiento, a native of Argentina who had been exiled from his country. During his exile Sarmiento lived in Chile and became a very important citizen of that country. Commissioned by the government to visit the United States and make a report of the school system, he spent considerable time with Horace Mann. Upon his return to Chile he wrote a book reporting his trip. It contained a great deal about Mann's ideas on education and it also included sections of the school laws of Massachusetts. His report, however, had little influence on the educational practices in Chile.

Sarmiento later returned to Argentina, whence he was sent by his government to the United States as Minister. Once again he turned his attention to our system of education. In 1868 he was recalled to Argentina to become President. With an opportunity at last to do something for the schools of his country, he remade the school system largely on the American pattern he had learned so well from Mann. Horace Mann is still remembered and much revered in Argentina.

Henry Barnard

Henry Barnard (1811–1900) followed closely in the footsteps of Horace Mann. He too studied law and was admitted to the bar; he too deserted law to dedicate his life to the cause of public education. Barnard spent two years in Europe making a study of education, devoting most of his attention to the work of Pestalozzi's disciples in Germany and Switzerland. His mind was enriched by valuable observations of social and educational conditions, but he appreciated more than ever the institutions in his own country and was convinced that hopes of permanent prosperity depended upon universal free public education.

After his return Barnard was elected a member of the Connecticut legislature. He promptly proposed and secured the passage of a bill setting up a state board of education—the same sort of educational program that Mann had established in Massachusetts. Again following Mann, Barnard left the legislature to become the first secretary of the board. He carried on in Connecticut the same intensive program that Mann had carried on in Massachusetts. His salary was low—three dollars a day and traveling expenses—but he held the office from 1839 to 1842 and accomplished great reforms in that time. The members of the legislature, however, did not support Barnard and his program and they abolished the office in 1842.

Going to Rhode Island, Barnard there carried on a campaign for better public education. He talked to the Rhode Island legislature and was instrumental in having it enact a law similar to the one he had proposed in Connecticut. He became the first commissioner of education for Rhode Island and again did pioneer work for education, vastly improving educational conditions in the state.

Barnard held many other important offices in the educational field. He returned to Connecticut later as president of the normal school and ex-officio secretary of the state board of education. Still later he became president of the University of Wisconsin. His last position was United States Commissioner of Education. The first to hold this office, he served with distinction, setting the pattern for many succeeding commissioners.

Barnard's greatest contribution to the literature of education was the *American Journal of Education,* which he founded in 1855 and edited until 1893. During these years it was the outstanding educational journal and did much to help shape the educational pattern in America. Barnard also edited and published, in 1852, a book on normal schools. It is filled with material of great educational and historical value.

Other Early Leaders

While Mann and Barnard were doing pioneer work in Massachusetts, Connecticut, and Rhode Island other great pioneers were making educational history in other states. One of them was Calvin H. Wiley, a native of North Carolina. Like Mann and Barnard he was a college graduate; he also followed the same pattern by becoming a member of the North Carolina legislature, where he worked for the passage of a bill to set up a state educational organization headed by a state school officer. When the bill creating the office of state superintendent of schools became law Wiley too left the legislature to assume that position. He published a state educational journal, organized a state educational association, wrote textbooks, and traveled about the state talking in behalf of better schools.

John D. Pierce, a Congregational minister, came to Michigan in 1831 and remained there for the rest of his long life. He was instrumental in setting up the Michigan state school system and was the first superintendent of public instruction. Caleb Mills was a pioneer educator in Indiana; and Samuel Lewis was the first superintendent of public instruction in Ohio. The list of state school pioneers should also include Robert J. Breckinridge, Kentucky's first state superintendent, and Ninian Edwards, who was the first to hold that office in Illinois. Thaddeus Stevens should also be mentioned, for as a member of the legislature of Pennsylvania he fought, almost alone, to set up a system of free public education in his state.

The Education of Women

The educational patterns brought from Europe by our forefathers did not contemplate formal education for women. The relative position of women's education in the seventeenth and early eighteenth centuries was similar to the civil and political rights held by women at the same time. Equal educational opportunity for girls was secured by an evolutionary process which closely parallels the general struggle for a free, nonsectarian, tax-supported public school system.

In colonial days women had almost no civil or political rights. A married woman's property belonged to her husband, even if she owned it before they were married; and she could not "will" property at her death. In all matters women were subject to their husbands. In such a society it was little wonder that no provision was made for the higher education of women and that only the minimum elementary education was provided. In colonial times girls were admitted to the public elementary schools where they were taught the rudiments of learning; however this seldom went beyond reading, writing, and a little arithmetic.

The colonial colleges did not admit women as students. Most of the early grammar schools and academies, following the European system of education, also excluded girls. Girls were destined to become homemakers and mothers, and they learned all the many skills needed to manage a home successfully from their mothers. Young women were constantly discouraged from seeking academic education. Even intelligent and educated men believed that it was a mistake for women's education to go beyond the barest fundamentals.

During the time our great educational pioneers were fighting for free public schools, a group of determined women were fighting a great battle for adequate higher education for their own sex. A brief sketch of the work of three of these women will exemplify some of the prevailing attitudes and problems. Emma Willard, Catharine Beecher, and Mary Lyon did not work for equal property rights or for political rights, but each insisted on a program of education that would make women the educational equal of men in their own sphere.

Emma Willard

Emma Willard (1787–1870) was born in the village of Berlin, Connecticut, the sixteenth of 17 children. She attended the public school until she was 15 and then entered the town academy where she studied for two years. At the age of 17 she began her educational career as a teacher in a district school during the summer term.

When Emma Hart Willard started teaching, little education was available for women, though the New England states provided public education on the elementary level for girls as well as boys. There were many "female seminaries" that provided a scanty education for girls, but they were generally on a low educational level.

Emma Hart had a great dream. She wanted to organize a system of education for women that would offer the same permanence, uniformity, and respectability as educational institutions for men and yet would be adapted to the needs and interests of women.

From 1804 until 1821 Emma Willard (she married Dr. John Willard in 1809) held many educational positions. She taught in a country school, and she taught in the academy at Berlin. The following year she went to Westfield, Massachusetts, to teach in an academy for girls that had been established in 1800. From there she went to Middlebury, Vermont, to teach in another female academy.

In 1814 she opened a boarding school for girls in Middlebury. Although this was a success, she dreamed of a publicly supported institution of higher education for women. So she turned her attention to the state of New York where with the assistance of Governor De Witt Clinton she presented her plan for female education to the state legislature. She was successful in getting an act passed granting a charter for the establishment of an academy for young ladies. She was unsuccessful, however, in securing the financial support she so much desired. Back in Middlebury again, she published her plan for the education of females. It attracted a great deal of attention and was widely read both in this country and in Europe.

After the disappointing experiences with the legislature of New York Emma Willard was delighted when the common council of Troy, New York, decided to raise $4000 to purchase a building for a female academy. The money was raised and the building was purchased. More money was raised by subscription, a board of trustees was appointed, and in the spring of 1821 Emma Willard opened what was to be her most famous school. At first it was called the Troy Female Seminary, the name being changed later to the Emma Willard School.

In many ways the opening of the Troy Female Seminary marked a new milestone in the education of women. The school was popular and prosperous from the beginning. The leading families of the country sent their daughters there to be educated. Emma Willard turned her attention to the education of teachers, and several years before the first normal school was established she had prepared several hundred girls to become teachers. Many graduates of her school went to the southern and western states and did pioneer work in establishing educational institutions for women.

In 1843 Mrs. Willard became closely associated with Horace Mann and Henry Barnard in a great agitation for normal schools. She wrote several books, including a history textbook, and collaborated with W. C. Woodbridge on a geography that was widely used in the schools for many years.

Catharine Beecher

Catharine Beecher (1800–1878) came from a distinguished family. Her father, Lyman Beecher, was the eminent Congregational minister, her brother the famous Henry Ward Beecher, and her sister the even more famous Harriet Beecher Stowe.

Catharine Beecher grew up in a parsonage. Her young life was very busy because there were 13 children and she was the oldest girl; thus she learned at an early age to perform the many tasks that had to be done in a New England home. The training her mother gave her in caring for children and keeping house was of great value in her later life as a teacher. She did not attend school until she was ten, her mother teaching her in the meantime to read, spell, write, and do a little arithmetic, geography, and art. She entered an academy in 1810, but it provided little that her mother had not already taught her. She began teaching in a girls' school in New London, Connecticut, and in 1828 founded the Hartford Female Seminary, which was long one of the important institutions of its kind in America.

Catharine Beecher was a great pioneer spirit. Like Emma Willard, she had an ardent desire to do something about the education of women in this country, but again—like Mrs. Willard—she expressed no interest in political equality for women. She dreamed of a system of higher education that would provide women with the same educational opportunity the men enjoyed. She was not interested in training women for the professions usually occupied by men. She thought that women should be educated for teaching, nursing, and homemaking; and her ideas concerning the place and work of women dominated her educational planning. She was interested in suitable physical education for women, and she developed courses in her schools that taught them how to be graceful and "to sit, to stand and to walk properly." She also developed the first courses ever taught in home economics and wrote several books for her classes and for housewives.

In 1838 Catharine Beecher moved with her family to Cincinnati, Ohio, and here she continued her interest in the education of women, particularly in their preparation for teaching. She organized and conducted the Western Female Institute, and from it she sent a great many young women into the teaching field; many of them went to the South and to the West.

Miss Beecher organized the Woman's Education Association and traveled widely over the country in its behalf. She raised funds and was instrumental in establishing schools for women in Milwaukee and other western cities. She wrote books and gave a great many lectures, and until her death in 1878 she devoted her time and energy to advancing the cause of education for women.

Mary Lyon

Mary Lyon (1797–1849) was another pioneer who devoted her life to the advancement of education for her sex. She did for college education what Emma Willard and Catharine Beecher had done at the less advanced level in establishing seminaries and institutes. She envisaged a college for women that would be comparable to the colleges already established for men. There was no such college at that time and coeducation had not been thought of.

In 1836 Mary Lyon founded Mount Holyoke Seminary (later Mount Holyoke College) and became its first president. This was not accomplished easily at a time when it was unfashionable for a woman to be interested in higher education. Miss Lyon and her friends went from town to town and from door to door explaining her project and soliciting funds for the new seminary. Finally, after the funds were raised and a building was constructed, America's first higher institution for women opened its doors to a group of eager students in the fall of 1837. Girls who were at least 16 years of age and who could pass a written examination in certain fundamentals were accepted as pupils.

Mary Lyon did not create the demand for higher education for women, nor was she the first to voice it. The founding of Mount Holyoke, however, marked the initial appearance of the great institutions which are today devoted to higher education for women. Wesleyan Female College at Macon, Georgia, was chartered and legally authorized to confer diplomas on its graduates in the year of 1837. Vassar, Smith, and Wellesley, which were founded later, owe much to Mount Holyoke and to the work of Mary Lyon in breaking down the wall of prejudice against the education of women. Mount Holyoke also prepared teachers who later became leaders in establishing other colleges for women.

The Ascendance of Democratic Education

So far this brief summary has been concerned mostly with the men and women who were instrumental in beginning the movement towards our system of free public education in the various states and in advancing education for women. In the context of their time the contributions of these persons was of greatest significance. By 1870 elementary education was available to almost everyone who wished it. The ideal of free universal education had not yet been applied to secondary schools or to colleges, however. Professor R. Freeman Butts has noted that during the century 1770 to 1870 the idea was to provide some education for all and much education for a few.[14] From 1870 to 1960, according to Professor Butts, the keynote of a century of democratic education was "more education for more people." [15] American education has made much progress towards this objective since 1870.

In 1870 a majority of elementary-age students were enrolled in school, but by 1960 more than 99 percent were in attendance. In 1870 approximately 8 percent of children aged 14 to 17 were actually in secondary school; by 1960 nearly 90 percent were attending. These facts show our current approximation of universal elementary and secondary education.

The increase in higher education enrollments have been even more marked. In 1900 approximately 4 percent of all youth aged 18 to 21 were attending posthigh-school institutions; by 1960 almost 40 percent of this population were enrolled in colleges and universities. In 1870 adult education was almost universally limited to our largest metropolitan centers where "Americanization Education" courses were offered to those immigrants preparing for citizenship. By 1960, courses in general, vocational, and avocational education were available to millions of adults.

The movement towards a more democratic education had not been limited to concern for the quantity provided. Important progress has also been made towards improving the quality of American education. Advances in quality, however, are more difficult to effect than are quantitative changes. Different experts have different ideas as to what constitutes quality in any given area,

[14] R. Freeman Butts, "Search for Freedom—The Story of American Education," *NEA Journal,* March, 1960, pp. 37–42.
[15] *Ibid.,* p. 42.

and achieving the consensus level necessary to make progress on a broad scale is a formidable task! The struggle towards quality in education is too complex to discuss in a brief review, but a few of the significant happenings must be noted.

Even before universal elementary education was an accepted idea, necessary reforms were being urged on the existing schools. The colonial objective of literacy for all was shown to be narrow and constricting, and schools were asked to broaden their offerings and to add courses ranging from art and history to physical education and natural sciences.

Secondary education has also undergone much reform since 1870. The most important changes necessitated by the acceptance of the comprehensive secondary school attendance for virtually everyone accentuated the problem of proper course offerings in junior and senior high school. Since 1900 there have been at least three noticeable trends in curricular emphasis in secondary education. From the earliest times a very rigid set of college-preparatory requirements dominated our high schools. In the period loosely bounded by the end of World War I and the beginning of World War II college preparation gave way to life-adjustment and personal development as major emphases in secondary education. Since the close of World War II a new wave of reaction has affected junior and senior high schools. Academic excellence, particularly in the areas of science, mathematics, and foreign languages has become the prime objective of many schools. This later trend can become nothing more than a return to the college-preparatory program of our schools in 1900; it can also, however, lead to a program of secondary education which does a better job of academic preparation while it continues to meet the needs of all students whether or not they are college-bound.

The efforts towards freedom in American education are continuing. Progress will not be easily achieved, nor will it occur universally, but it is encouraging to know that most Americans are aware that improved and improving education is imperative. The ultimate goal is to build an educational enterprise which will free the minds of people and equip them as free citizens and free persons.

2

The United States of America

ROBERT ULICH

*Here we have an observation of American education and its uniqueness from a
different point of view than that of Frasier. Ulich presents a history of education in a way that gives the reader an opportunity to study the nature of American history on the basis of cultural values. This adds the dimension of an historical and cultural perspective that closely relates the growth of the United
States to the cultural values of the reader. Ulich pleads for the "now generation"
to understand the proper relationship of educational learning to the future of
all men everywhere. His praise of our nation's great achievements in education
is doubtlessly one of the reasons for his concern with the concomitant challenge inherent in these achievements.*

THE UNITED STATES has often been called the country of immigrants.
This explains the fact that there is no sovereign country belonging to Western
civilization that, seen from one point of view, has been so dependent on influences from abroad as the United States, but that, seen from another point
of view, has produced so indigenous a political and educational system.

To speak of the influences first: Massachusetts or the Bay Colony, the most
educationally minded of the early provinces, developed its school system on
the Protestant conviction that every Christian should live in an immediate
and personal relation with his Lord. Consequently, he should not remain ignorant of God's plan concerning the nature and purpose of man. Rather, he
should have access to God's word, contained in the Bible, without a hierarchy
of priests standing between him and divine grace. This, of course, as in Protestant Germany, involved the creation of a broad elementary school system,
for in order to escape eternal damnation people had to be able to read. The
Massachusetts Law of 1647 ordered that every township of fifty or more

SOURCE: Robert Ulich, *The Education of Nations* (Cambridge, Mass.: Harvard University Press, 1961), pp. 225–254. Copyright © by the President and Fellows of Harvard
College. Reprinted by permission of the publisher.

The author was, for many years, a professor and distinguished scholar of education
in the Graduate School of Harvard University, where he held the position of James
Bryant Conant Professor of Education. He received his formal education in Germany,
which culminated in the Ph.D. from Leipzig University. For more than thirty years,
he has been an outstanding author. Among his many works in the fields of history, philosophy, and education are *Philosophy of Education, History of Educational Thought,*
and, most recently, *Progress or Disaster.*

householders should appoint a person "to teach all such children as shall resort to him to write and read" and that every town of more than one hundred
householders should set up a grammar school in order to fit youth for the
university.

In addition, just as Calvin in Geneva insisted on a close relationship between church and state, so also colonial Massachusetts developed during the
seventeenth century a kind of theocratic system, with the community of the
saints or the elect forming at the same time the church and the body politic.
This was no democracy in the modern sense of the word, nor did the Puritans
differ from any other Christians of the time in their assurance that they alone
knew what the Lord had meant with the creation. Yet, through the common
deliberation in the town meetings and through the early legislation on a public tax-supported school system, Massachusetts prepared the ground for later
democratic developments—just as little intended by the founding fathers as
European democratic development by Luther and Calvin.

As a matter of fact, the Virginia Colony, the founders of which had settled
at Jamestown in 1607, thirteen years before the Mayflower landed at Plymouth and twenty-three years before the Arabella arrived at Boston, has a
much truer claim to being the cornerstone of American liberty than the Puritan settlements. Unlike the North, Virginia granted religious freedom to
members of all faiths who would take the oath of allegiance to the British
crown (though Sir William Berkeley, Governor after 1642, persecuted the
Puritan minority). Virginia had a charter that granted representative government, and except for some few critical years (1611–1616) it had trial by
jury. But Virginia was largely Anglican and therefore less interested in the
education of the common man than were the Puritans; it soon had a plantation and slave system with wide geographical distances between the inhabitants. The wealthy families preferred small private schools with tuition, or
the tutor, according to the advice given by John Locke in his *Thoughts Concerning Education*. Some of them sent their sons to England for a gentleman's
education. Only at a few places did parish schools provide a degree of literacy for the poor.

Without much difficulty the more privileged part of the population of early
Virginia could have resettled in monarchical England, whereas the Puritans
would have been a dangerously alien element. Even for Cromwell, with a nation behind him that felt the first lure of world power, the concept of a commonwealth as developed by his Puritan brethren of New England would have
been too stiff, too moralistic, too antiquated.

Yet, in order to survive mentally and physically in the wilderness, the Puritans needed the same sense of being chosen or elect that helped the Jews to
survive under the persecution of ancient and modern nations. As a matter of
fact, for few Christian sects was the Old Testament with its idea of a cove-

nant between Jehovah and his people so much of a reality as for the New England Calvinists.

There was still another element of cultural strength in the Puritans. Like Milton, they lived not only in and with the Bible, but also in and with the heritage of Greece and Rome. Hence their emphasis not only on a broad elementary school system of Christian character, but also on a classical training for the prospective leaders of their society. Boston Latin School was established in 1635, and Henry Dunster, the first president of Harvard, formulated in 1642 the following entrance requirements.

When any Schollar is able to understand Tully, or such like classicall Latine Author extempore, and make and speake true Latine in Verse and Prose, *suo ut aiunt Marte;* And decline perfectly the Paradigm's of Nounes and Verbes in the Greek tongue: Let him then and not before be capable of admission into the Colledge.[1]

If, then, religion and the classics were the pillars of education, science was by no means foreign or suspect to the Puritans. Rather than being afraid of its mechanistic implications, they considered its discoveries new revelations of God's grandeur. The fact that at the same time they would have witches was not unique with them. There were many men in the sixteenth and seventeenth centuries, among them the great French political philosopher Bodin, who combined a high degree of rationality with the crudest belief in magic.

We do not know exactly to what degree the rather impressive school laws of early New England (1642, 1647, 1650) really brought all children into schools. To conclude from the number of later injunctions, many of the pioneer families believed more in the training of youth through family life and hard work than through schoolmasters. The quality of these decreased, moreover, after 1700, when the Puritan hierarchy had to yield to a more worldly government.

The old Latin grammar school was the pattern for secondary education all over the American colonies. It continued a classical tradition that, as the letters of Jefferson and the Adamses show, still produced in sensitive minds a grand style of writing, thinking, and living. Nevertheless, just as in other countries, it became increasingly pedantic and remote from the interests of the majority of even the more privileged youth. Thus, after 1700, private schools were opened which catered to the interests of trade and commerce by teaching not only the traditional subjects but also navigation, applied mathematics, surveying, and other topics of interest to the emerging class of merchants. And in 1749 Benjamin Franklin wrote his *Proposals Relating to the*

[1] *New England's First Fruits* (London, 1643). Fully reprinted in Samuel Eliot Morison, *The Founding of Harvard College* (Cambridge: Harvard University Press, 1935), pp. 419f and especially p. 433.

Education of Youth in Pennsylvania, in which he recommended two main innovations: one, emphasis on English and modern foreign languages (French, German, and Spanish); the other, emphasis on mathematics and "natural and mechanic philosophy." Thus, besides a Latin department, his proposed "Academy" was to contain an "English" and a "Mathematical School." The methods of instruction should lead the student to scientific experimentation, observation, and application.

> While they are reading natural history, might not a little *Gardening, Planting, Grafting, Inoculating,* etc. be taught and practised; and now and then excursions made to the neighboring plantations of the best farmers, their methods observed and reasoned upon for the information of youth? The improvement of agriculture being useful to all, and skill in it no disparagement to any.[2]

Though Franklin's idea of a more utilitarian education preceded the spirit of the time because of, to use his own words, mankind's "unaccountable Prejudice in favour of ancient Customs and Habitudes," [3] it nevertheless prophesied a new era. Between 1759, the year when Franklin's Academy opened in Philadelphia, and 1850, academies, all fashioned according to a variety of practical purposes, increased to more than six thousand in number.[4]

Franklin's life and thought themselves are the best source for discovering the new spirit that permeated the colonies during the era of the Enlightenment. Religiously, what a difference from the diaries, sermons, and the pedagogy of the Mathers of the seventeenth century! Throughout the original states during Franklin's life the old religious "establishments" began to be shaken, partly because the population became more and more heterogeneous, partly because widening contacts with different cultures undermined dogmatic assumptions held absolute so far, and partly because the ideas of natural law and freedom of conscience—both so important for the understanding of the American Constitution—required tolerance and respect for the serious opinions of one's fellow man.[5]

In Franklin's and his friends' minds, all influenced by Locke, Hume, and the French *philosophes,* there no longer live the ideas of original sin, of total depravity, of predestination, and of the unquestionable authority of the Scripture, but a courageously illogical mixture between a somewhat mechanical

---

[2] *Benjamin Franklin: Representative Selections,* ed. F. L. Mott and C. E. Jorgenson (New York: American Book Co., 1936), pp. 205–206. See also *Writings of Benjamin Franklin,* ed. A. H. Smyth (New York: Macmillan, 1905–1907), II, 395; Robert Ulich, *History of Educational Thought* (New York: American Book Co., 1945), pp. 225–241; Ulich, *Three Thousand Years of Educational Wisdom,* pp. 426–462.

[3] *Writings,* X, 30.

[4] See J. D. B. De Bow, *Statistical View of the United States . . . Being a Compendium of the Seventh Census* (Washington, D.C.: B. Tucker, 1954).

[5] See R. Freeman Butts, *The American Tradition in Religion and Education* (Boston: Beacon Press, 1950).

deism and the conviction that the Lord will personally look upon those who first of all try to help themselves. A moral life is more important than theological and metaphysical speculations concerning an ultimate world about which we know little anyhow. But God, or Nature, or "Nature's God," gave us the wonderful gift of reason, of observation and experiment. Yet, there is no arrogant scientism in Franklin's mind. In a letter to Peter Collinson of the year 1747 he writes: "If there is no other Use discover'd of Electricity this however is something considerable, that it may *help to make a vain man humble.*" [6] Franklin possesses a wise and earthy humor, but he refrains from the cynicism of a Voltaire. Rather he is Newtonian in his respectful attitude toward the laws that the divine Creator has planted into the universe, and, to a degree, in the soul of every human being.

There is much difference between Franklin and the other great statesman and educational figure of the Revolutionary period, Thomas Jefferson. [7] The first is the self-made man, looking for the useful and the moral in things and people, an astute and successful businessman, systematic in behavior and in thought (which made him one of the fine scientists of the age), the best exemplar of the new Northern middle class. The other, a landowner without real interest in the rising business class, enchanted by "the precious remains of antiquity" (not only in architecture, but also in thought), by the beauty of men, buildings, sculptures, and gardens, a potential architectural and scientific genius who nevertheless preferred accomplished amateurship to specialization, interested in increasing his plantation, but spending money easily, is the true example of the old aristocrat from the South.

Yet, there is also much similarity in the two. Mysticism, even of the great type, is foreign to them. They hate dogmatism in matters of faith, as they hate tyranny in matters of state. Their religion, though an essential part of their personalities, is unsentimental. Jesus represents one of the revelations of divine wisdom, but they refuse to argue about his being the Son of God. Locke, Hume, and Newton are much nearer to them than Plato; Jefferson writes to Benjamin Rush on April 21, 1803: "I name not Plato, who only used the name of Socrates to cover the whimsies of his own brain." [8] Rousseau had no influence on either of them; he was for them too romantic. Both loved books. Jefferson had a library of six thousand volumes. But for both ideas were only as good as they proved themselves in action. On the other hand, fact and action were only as good as they appeared before the tribunal

[6] *Representative Selections,* p. 194; *Writings,* II, 325.

[7] See Ulich, *History of Educational Thought,* pp. 242–257, and *Three Thousand Years of Educational Wisdom,* pp. 463–479. For a selection of Jefferson's educational writings, see *Thomas Jefferson and Education in a Republic,* ed. Charles F. Arrowood (New York: McGraw-Hill, 1930).

[8] *The Writing of Thomas Jefferson,* Definitive Edition, ed. A. E. Bergh (Washington, D.C.: Thomas Jefferson Memorial Association, 1907), X, 383.

of reason. Both were willing to sacrifice their personal existences for the freedom of their country, but both were also sufficiently familiar with the human race to know that in the hands of unworthy and uninformed men freedom will soon be lost, turning either into chaos or into tyranny.

Hence, just as we can observe in the newly emerging nations of today, so also in the new United States the minds of the great statesmen turned to education as the best protector of the republic. Washington said in his Farewell Address of 1796:

Promote then, as an object of primary importance, institutions for the general diffusion of knowledge.—In proportion as the structure of a government gives force to public opinion it is essential that public opinion should be enlightened.[9]

And Jefferson wrote in his beautifully terse prose:

It is an axiom in my mind that our liberty can never be safe but in the hands of the people themselves, and that, too, of the people with a certain degree of instruction.[10]

Whereas Franklin's interest in education begins before the middle of the eighteenth century, Jefferson's writings on the same great national issue coincide with the fight for, and the initial struggles of, the new republic for its existence.[11] It is characteristic of Jefferson's whole personality that his "Bill for the More General Diffusion of Knowledge" of 1779 builds, on a broad and democratic foundation of elementary schools for all, a selective system of advanced grammar schools and of higher education. The selection becomes more stringent the higher up the publicly supported student (for stipends will be necessary if he comes from poor parents) intends to climb on the educational ladder.

Jefferson's bill was finally passed by the Virginia Assembly in 1796, though in effect defeated through amendments that gave the power into the hands of the individual communities. Like Franklin's "English School," Jefferson's scheme was ahead of its time. It has been called aristocratic in the sense of being against the spirit of democracy. This is correct if democracy is mistaken for equalitarian mediocrity, but many of us will believe with Jefferson that democracy particularly needs high and rare quality to avoid the cult of the mass man. Rightly he says in a letter to John Adams of October 28, 1813:

[9] *Washington's Farewell Address . . .* ed. Charles R. Gaston (Boston: Ginn & Co., 1906), p. 12.

[10] Letter to Washington, January 4, 1786, in *Writings,* XIX, 24.

[11] "Bill for Establishing Religious Freedom," 1779; "Bill for the More General Diffusion of Knowledge," 1779; "Bill for Establishing a System of Public Education," 1817.

For I agree with you that there is a natural aristocracy among men. The grounds for this are virtue and talents . . . The natural aristocracy I consider as the most precious gift of nature, for the instruction, the trusts, and government of society . . . May we not even say that that form of government is the best, which provides the most effectually for a pure selection of these natural aristoi into the offices of government? [12]

Franklin, who died twenty-three years before this letter was written, would have agreed with it. The only difference between him and Jefferson might have been that Jefferson considered classical studies, and among them Latin more than Greek, the cornerstone of Western civilization. "It would be very ill-judged in us," so he said in the *Notes on Virginia,* if we followed the examples of Europe where "the learning of Greek and Latin, I am told, is going into disuse." [13] No diploma, from his point of view, should be given to a graduate of the University of Virginia

who has not passed such an examination in the Latin language as shall have proved him able to read the highest classics in that language with ease, thorough understanding and just quantity; and if he be also as proficient in the Greek, let that too be stated in his diploma. The intention being that the reputation of the University shall not be committed but to those who, to an eminence in some one or more of the sciences taught in it, add a proficiency in these languages which constitute the basis of good education, and are indispensable to fill up the character of a "well-educated man." [14]

But even here Franklin might have agreed with Jefferson, for he protested only against the monopoly claimed by the ancient languages in advanced education, not against the languages as such. And Jefferson himself wrote in a letter to John Brazier of August 24, 1819:

For the merchant I should not say that the languages are a necessary. Ethics, mathematics, geography, political economy, history, seem to constitute the immediate foundations of his calling. The agriculturist needs ethics, mathematics, chemistry and natural philosophy. The mechanic the same. To them the languages are but ornament and comfort . . . [15]

And both would have buried their differences under the supreme principle of education stated by Franklin when he said:

With the whole [process of instruction] should be constantly inculcated and cultivated, that *benignity of mind,* which shows itself in *searching* for and *seizing* every opportunity to *serve* and to *oblige;* and it is the foundation of what is called GOOD BREEDING; highly useful to the possessor, and most agreeable to all.[16]

[12] *Writings,* XIII, 396.   [13] *Ibid.,* II, 205.
[14] From the Minutes of the Board of Visitors of the University of Virginia, October 4, 1824, in *Writings,* XIX, 444. See also Jefferson's letter to John Brazier of August 24, 1819, in *Writings,* XV, 207–211.
[15] *Writings,* XV, 211.   [16] *Ibid.,* II, 396; *Representative Selections,* p. 206.

In view of the enormous changes the United States and its schools have undergone during the nineteenth and twentieth centuries, is it still even worth while to recall the memory of a Franklin and Jefferson? The answer is "yes," and for the following reasons.

First, both men are not merely historical figures who have done their work in helping to give the American people its political independence and Constitution and in reminding them of the educational foundation of democracy. Today Franklin is still the symbol by which to illustrate certain features of the American character: it is utilitarian, not in an egotistic sense of the word, but willing to sacrifice personal interest for the usefulness of the whole. There is no country where a rich man would be so criticized for keeping all his earnings for himself as the United States. A great number of universities, schools, museums, hospitals, as well as the whole religious life of the communities, are supported by voluntary gifts. It would be advantageous for international understanding if the many critics of "American materialism" in other countries knew of this situation and imitated it. Franklin is also characteristically American, or, as one could say, the American is also characteristically Franklinian, in his desire for action, for trial and experimentation, and in his belief in the possibility of progress, provided men behave rationally. Many Americans, as perhaps Anglo-Saxons in general, resemble Franklin also in their distrust of absolutes and in their willingness to compromise in matters philosophical. The logic of a good and successful life, individually as well as communally, may not always be the same as the logic of the thinker; yet both may be right. The pragmatic humanism of William James and John Dewey has its origin in the thought of such men as Benjamin Franklin.

Difficult though this may be for the Continental European to understand, this pragmatic attitude, with all its shades over into relativism, is by no means unprincipled. It represents a form of faithful idealism. It rests essentially on the eighteenth century's concept of natural law, which, if traced back to its origin, appears to be rooted in both the Greco-Roman and the Christian interpretations of the rights of man. The Declaration of Independence, after referring to the "Laws of Nature and of Nature's God" contains the following sentence:

> We hold these truths to be self-evident, that all men are created equal, that they are endowed by their Creator with certain inalienable Rights, that among these are Life, Liberty, and the Pursuit of Happiness.

It is the peculiar fortune of the American nation, one which penetrates its political consciousness more than any verbal schooling could do, that, though blessed with great leaders in the period of the Revolution, it considers its birth, its Constitution, and its government as the work and expression of the whole people. What a difference from the life of nations whose forms of government carry with them the memory of warring monarchs, of defeat, of the imposition of a ruling caste, or even of conquest by a foreign power!

Besides Franklin and Jefferson, it is Lincoln to whom the American citizen of some intellectual standard feels admiringly related. To the people of Sangamon County Lincoln said:

> Upon the subject of education, I can only say that I view it as the most important subject which we as a people can be engaged in . . . For my part, I desire to see the time when education, and by its means, morality, sobriety, enterprise and industry, shall become much more general than at present, and I should be gratified to have it in my power to contribute something to the advancement of any measure which might have a tendency to accelerate the wider education of our people.[17]

There may be differences of opinion whether George Washington, the great general and statesman, plays as great a role in the hearts of the nation as the men just mentioned, despite his prominent role in the textbooks and the stories for children. Somehow he lacks the popular common sense of Franklin, the intellectual charm of Jefferson, and the mixture of deep humaneness and religious transcendence that radiates from the life and face of Lincoln. Take these three, or, if you want, include Washington, as the fourth, and you have the ideal of the good American, his real and great educators. They have provided the ethical foundation without which America would hardly have been able to maintain its moral and national identity.

Though in the following section I will relate the growth of the American school system to the increase of the population and to the change from an agrarian to an industrial society, it would be wrong to overemphasize these material factors. Unless a nation's vitality is gone, it creates ever-new situations and responds elastically to them. In the middle of the nineteenth century America was no longer the country of the Puritans (which it never had been entirely); nevertheless, the high aspirations remained. Often without the loss of religious zeal, indeed, still Christian in a sense, Americans engaged in all kinds of humanitarian movements, from prison reforms to lyceums, from antislavery societies to back-to-nature appeals. In essence, they tried to find out how much of the promised supernatural millennium could be realized within the realm of nature. From the Constitution to Franklin D. Roosevelt's New Deal, the transcendental and the secular always joined hands in the struggle for man's freedom, however differently understood. Inevitably, the schools and the training of teachers had to be included.

[17] Abraham Lincoln, "Address to the People of Sangamon County, March 9, 1832," *Complete Works,* ed. J. D. Nicolay and John Hay (New York: Francis D. Tandy Co., 1905), V, 7.

The School System in a Growing Nation

So much happened in the U.S.A. between the formative years of the republic and the two world wars that it might have been too severe a challenge for the integrating power of any other nation. Whereas in 1790, the year of Benjamin Franklin's death, the population was almost entirely rural, today only about 30 per cent live on the soil. Even they work under mechanized conditions that set them farther off from a Jeffersonian landowner than the latter is from a Roman farmer or a man who today plows his fields in the valleys of the Himalayas. The nation has expanded from the thirteen original states to the fifty states reaching from the Atlantic to the Pacific; it has increased from about four million in 1790 to about one hundred and fifty million in 1950.[18]

After the middle of the nineteenth century waves of population rolled toward the Middle West and the West. In 1840 Chicago had forty-five hundred inhabitants; in 1880 it had half a million; in 1890, a million. Some cities almost doubled their population every year. The railroad mileage was 23 in 1830, 2,818 in 1840, and 30,626 in 1860. In 1869 one could travel on rails from the East to San Francisco.

This process of opening up a continent was accompanied by a second factor, which probably more than anything else changed the character of the American population and its school system, namely, foreign immigration. Until 1830 immigration did not add significantly to the growth of the population. But in the decade between 1841 and 1850 the total immigration rose to 1,597,604 as compared with 495,736 during the preceding decade, the increase being largely due to the famine in Ireland and the political unrest in Germany.

In 1930 slightly less than one fourth of the entire population was foreign-born or native inhabitants with one or both parents foreign-born. In 1790, the year of the first official census, 90 per cent of the white population was of British (including Scotch and Irish) stock; the Germans were near 6 per cent.[19] The number, however, may not be correct, since many immigrants, especially Germans, had adopted Anglicized names. In 1850 the Irish formed nearly half the foreign-born. In 1900 the northwestern Europeans, with Irish included, represented only 66.4 per cent, and after 1880 Italians, Russians, Poles, Austrians, Bohemians (the latter two mostly of the Slavic part of the population), and Hungarians entered in ever-greater numbers. From 141,132,

---

[18] Clifford L. and Elizabeth H. Lord, *Historical Atlas of the United States,* rev. ed. (New York: Henry Holt, 1953), pp. 198–199.

[19] U.S. Bureau of the Census. *A Century of Population Growth* (Washington, D.C.: Government Printing Office, 1909), p. 117.

in 1919, immigration increased to 805,228, in 1921.[20] There was no free land and no frontier so that many of the poorer immigrants were forced to crowd in the growing slums of the big cities. The ports of arrival were the larger cities, and some kind of living could more easily be secured there. The dispersion of foreigners to other parts of the country, therefore, was a slow process.[21] At the same time employment became increasingly difficult, even for returning veterans. Thus, after some initial legislation Congress passed the Act of 1924, which introduced a highly reduced quota system and which, because based on the population census of 1890, practically excluded all immigration from Asia and Africa.

The increase in population from other than Germanic stock changed the mentality of the nation. The United States of today is pluralistic and even full of contradictions in its spiritual structure. The optimist-rationalist strain of thought that comes from Franklin and Jefferson and, despite his profound transcendentalism, also from Lincoln, still remains. But one may ask whether it is still dominant among the educated.

According to the 1958 Yearbook of American Churches, published by the National Council of Churches, church and synagogue membership had risen to more than 103,250,000 in 1956. It has doubled during the past thirty years and is constantly rising, while the population has risen 40 per cent. At the present, sixty-two out of one hundred Americans of all ages are members of a church or a synagogue. The Protestants in their totality number more than 60,000,000; the Roman Catholics, more than 34,500,000 members.

Parallel with the stronger interest in religious institutions (which does not necessarily indicate a correspondingly genuine interest in religion) there can be found all kinds of mental patterns shading from indifference and agnosticism to the most multifarious modes of superstition. This variety of views exists in all modern countries, but there is probably none with such vital sectarianism as the United States.

Boston, once the citadel of the Puritans, is now, like New York, one of the foremost Catholic world centers. The Protestant churches of the United States taken together still embrace almost two thirds of registered Christians with an ever-fresh sectarianism constantly agitating the minds of religious seekers. In 1956, on one of the historical residential streets of Cambridge, a Mormon church was erected, directly across the street from a Quaker meeting house, and not far away from Harvard University, from the various old Protestant churches and theological schools, from a Christian Science church, and from the domicile of the Catholic Father Feeney, who was defrocked because of

[20] U.S. Immigration and Naturalization Service, *Annual Report*. Table I: "Immigration to the United States, 1820–1948."

[21] William S. Rossiter, *Increase of Population in the United States 1910–1920* (Washington, D.C.: Government Printing Office, 1922, Census Monographs No. 1).

his dogmatic fanaticism. All over the country one finds Russian and Greek Orthodox churches, and in the city of Washington, D.C., a voice from the minaret of a mosque will admonish the faithful to observe the holy month of Ramadan.

All these changes in industry, population, and religious outlook went on in a country whose path toward prosperity was all but steady. The incorporation of new territory and the conquest of the West were not always accomplished by peaceful and morally dignified means; the Civil War from 1861–1865 was one of the most severe inner crises any modern nation has been able to survive. Perhaps the reconstruction immediately after this war left deeper wounds in the souls of the Southern citizens than the war itself. Finally, the participation in two world wars placed the nation in a position of international responsibility never dreamed of and even undesired in earlier times. Thus waves of liberalism and internationalism changed to waves of political phobia and isolationism, which, though going under the name of democracy, often revealed a frighteningly totalitarian spirit. The panics of 1837, 1873, 1893 and the stock-market crash of 1929, each with years of unemployment in its wake, brought the country close to financial ruin. And, as can hardly be astonishing with a people of such wild and gigantic growth, speculation and corruption undermined the nation's self-confidence and moral quality from time to time.

How did education—this is now the main question—adjust itself to these vicissitudes? During the 1830's it became increasingly clear to the socially minded that the prevailing educational system of elementary schools with incompetent teachers, the Latin schools in the larger cities, and the academies for the mostly nonprofessional middle class were inadequate to cope with the tasks of the growing nation. Americans looked for patterns from abroad and found them, especially in the German elementary, secondary, and higher schools. Many reports were written, and, deploring the state of teachers' education in his county, the Reverend Charles Brooks (1795–1872) began his public lectures on the Prussian system of normal schools in 1835. Two years later, Horace Mann, often called the father of American public education, took office as secretary of the newly established Massachusetts Board of Education. He found the common school system "degenerated in practice from the original theoretical view of the early Pilgrim Fathers" and criticized a generation that through

the opportunities unparalleled in the world's history, which the establishment of the Federal Union had opened to all classes of men to obtain wealth, had lost sight of the idea of having the rich and the poor educated together.[22]

[22] Massachusetts Board of Education, *Reports 1838–1848*. 3 vols. (Boston, 1839–1849). Contains Reports 1 to 12 by Horace Mann. Robert Ulich, *A Sequence of*

Whatever the influences from other countries—and they increased during the nineteenth century, especially those from Germany in regard to higher education—the idea "of having the rich and the poor educated together" was in that time uniquely American. Despite rising discrepancies between the emerging social classes it was part and parcel of the creed that Franklin and Thomas Jefferson had bequeathed to a new republic, that "liberty can never be safe but in the hands of the people . . . with a certain degree of instruction."

At the end of his Twelfth Annual Report Horace Mann formulated his final credo of public education in its various religious, social, and moral aspects. He writes:

Such, then, in a religious point of view, is the Massachusetts system of Common Schools. Reverently, it recognizes and affirms the sovereign rights of the Creator; sedulously and sacredly it guards the religious rights of the creature; while it seeks to remove all hinderances, and to supply all furtherances to a filial and paternal communion between man and his Maker. In a social and political sense, it is a *Free*-school system. It knows no distinction of rich and poor, of bond and free, or between those who, in the imperfect light of this world, are seeking, through different avenues, to reach the gate of heaven. Without money and without price, it throws open its doors, and spreads the table of its bounty, for all the children of the State. Like the sun, it shines, not only upon the good, but upon the evil, that they may become good; and, like the rain, its blessings descend, not only upon the just, but upon the unjust, that their injustice may depart from them and be known no more.[23]

Beautiful and sincere as these words were, they differed shockingly from the real situation. In 1857, the year that the National Teachers Organization was organized in Philadelphia, two thirds of the teachers of Pennsylvania were under twenty-five years of age, two fifths had taught less than three years, two thirds were probably only temporarily appointed. The salaries over the whole country were barely on a living standard.[24]

Yet, the years of "degeneration" as Horace Mann himself had called them, in comparison to the prestige that education had enjoyed during the period of the Pilgrim fathers, were also the years of regeneration. For in the middle of the century state departments of education and normal schools were founded; the teachers became conscious of their profession, began to read journals, and assembled in associations and institutes; textbooks were improved; instead of

Educational Influences (Cambridge: Harvard University Press, 1935). See also *Reports on European Education by John Griscom, Victor Cousin, and Calvin E. Stowe*, ed. Edgar W. Knight (New York: McGraw-Hill, 1930).

[23] Horace Mann, "Twelfth Annual Report of the Secretary of the Board of Education," in *Massachusetts Board of Education, 12th Report* (Boston, 1849). p. 140. See also *The Republic and the School. Horace Mann on the Education of the Free Man*, ed. Lawrence A. Cremin (New York: Columbia University Teachers College, 1957). Contains extracts of Mann's *Twelfth Report*.

[24] Edgar D. Wesley, *NEA: The First Hundred Years* (New York: Harper, 1957).

the old and sometimes incredibly filthy houses new school buildings were erected, and they harbored more and more children, organized in grades, instead of crudely lumped together, as before. Perhaps the deplorable state of schools at the time of Horace Mann had, historically speaking, even its positive side. The people themselves could, and had to, build their schools—from scratch, so to speak. This, together with the ideal of social justice, may have been the reason for the rejection of the European system of separate elementary and secondary schools in favor of a single-ladder, universal, and tax-supported public school in which, ideally at least, every sufficiently talented child has the same chance to climb from one rung to the next.

There was, needless to say, opposition on the part of the well-to-do. Why should they be forced to pay local taxes for schools that the children of the poor could attend without any contribution on the part of their parents? The matter was finally settled (1874) by the Supreme Court of Michigan in the so-called Kalamazoo case, in which the Court granted the community the right to tax itself for the maintenance of its secondary schools.

It was also in the seventies that the National Education Association (founded in 1857 as the National Teachers Association by various state teachers societies for the purpose of effective national representation) began to exercise a growing influence on general educational policy. Out of this endeavor grew in 1880 the National Council of Education. It soon started an era of reports and inquiries that had more influence on American schools, from the elementary to the tertiary level, than similar documents in other countries. Certain reports of England are comparable because of the fact that both countries had to replace the missing central educational hierarchy by self-initiative and self-government. In the United States, however, the cooperative attempt by interested men at improving the schools was by necessity still more important. For, first, America lacked the long and somewhat hierarchical social tradition of England; second, it had no schools that, liked or not, nevertheless set the pattern, like the old public schools in England; and, third, it had to adjust its schools to a people with cultural differences unknown to other countries.[25] The constitution of the Council stated as its objective "to reach and disseminate correct thinking on educational questions." For this purpose, so the statement continues, "it shall be the aim of the Council, in conducting its discussions to define and state with accuracy the different views and theories on the subject under consideration, and secondly to discover and report fairly the grounds and reasons for each theory

[25] The following considerations are largely based on the *Proceedings of the National Education Association* and on a report entitled "On the Conflict between the 'Liberal Arts' and the 'School of Education,'" submitted to the American Council of Learned Societies by Howard M. Jones, Francis Keppel, and Robert Ulich. Reprinted in *The ACLS Newsletter,* Vol. V, No. 2 (1954).

or view, so far as to show, as completely as possible, the genesis of opinion on the subject."

Of the various reports issuing from the Council's activities three became landmarks in the history of American education, the Report of the Committee of Ten on Secondary School Studies (1893), the Report of the Committee of Fifteen on the Training of Teachers and on the Correlation of Studies in Elementary Education (1895), and the Report of the Committee on College Entrance Requirements (1899).

I am here especially interested in the Report of the Committee of Ten, which worked under the chairmanship of President Charles William Eliot, of Harvard University. This document represents, so to speak, the end of the four-year high school as an academic and selective institution. Up to 1890 this school, though organically linked to the eight-year elementary school, had nevertheless remained the training ground for the more privileged of the nation who aspired at some sort of professional education. According to the Annual Report of the Federal Security Agency (1952), [26] in 1890, only about 7 per cent of the eligible youth of a total population of sixty-three million were enrolled in secondary schools, that is, in terms of percentage, less than there are now enrolled in the academic secondary institutions of bifurcated European systems. The Report of the Committee of Ten shows that the teachers of the ancient languages, and of the liberal arts in general, still claimed the high school as their old and proper domain. However, they were already on a polite defensive against all kinds of undesirable newcomers such as the natural sciences and the more applied subjects of learning.

Indeed, the great change came soon. After 1890 the high-school population doubled every ten years until the maximum was reached in 1940 with an enrollment of more than seven million. Then, in consequence of the lower birth rate in the economically troubled thirties, the school population declined for some years. Since 1954 the number of pupils again has increased by leaps and bounds. In 1957, eight million were in high schools, and in the early 1960's the number may rise to ten million. No longer 7 per cent as in 1890, but 80 per cent of the eligible boys and girls are now in some form of secondary education, and, though with great differences in various localities, between 50 and 60 per cent of the pupils graduate. Since, together with the growth of the population in an increasingly technical society, the tendency toward prolonging the years of professional preparation also grows, the colleges will become more and more inundated. Currently, slightly more than 30 per cent of the college age group are in colleges of some kind or in universities (about two and a half million), whereas in England, to use it as an example of other European countries, about 5 per cent of the total age group attend

[26] *Annual Report, 1952* (Washington, D.C.: Office of Education, Federal Security Agency), p. 14.

institutions of higher learning. Around 1960 four million students may be in our colleges, and before 1970 there may be six million or more.

No longer is there any semblance of Jefferson's selective scheme, or of anything that Franklin, who by himself learned several languages, would have considered an advanced education. And how can it be otherwise since the measure of intelligence of the high school students ranges from those close to the moron up to the highly talented? In other words, the American secondary school has become a school of and for the people, and attending college will for the American middle class change more and more from a privilege into a requirement or a matter of custom.

The socialization of the high school, or its function of educating the rank and file citizen without much claim to scholarly pursuits, became evident in the Report on the Cardinal Principles of Secondary Education of 1918.[27] It defines the goal of education in the following terms:

> The purpose of democracy is so to organize society that each member may develop his personality primarily through activities designed for the well-being of his fellow members and of society as a whole . . .
> Consequently, education in a democracy, both within and without the school, should develop in each individual the knowledge, interests, ideals, habits, and powers whereby he will find his place and use that place to shape both himself and society toward ever nobler ends.

The high school is to achieve this noble goal by instilling in pupils (1) health, (2) command of fundamental processes, (3) worthy home membership, (4) vocational training, (5) citizenship, (6) worthy use of leisure, (7) ethical character.

In comparison with the Report of the Committee of Ten, this means a complete shift in emphasis from the earlier scholarly interest in subjects toward a social interest in producing a normal, physically and morally healthy individual. Values that the older selective high schools could take more or less for granted because they were taken care of by the family are now placed into the foreground. The scholarly purpose has receded before the aim of normalcy and adjustment to life.

This change was supported by both a philosophical and a psychological trend. Philosophically and methodologically during the main part of the nineteenth century, American education took its principles from the Pestalozzian movement, from Froebel, from Hegelianism, as represented by William T. Harris and his friends, with their center in St. Louis, and from Herbartianism, as taught by the brothers Charles and Frank McMurry. Each of these European, especially German, movements of thought received a specific na-

[27] *Cardinal Principles of Secondary Education.* Report of the Commission on the Reorganization of Secondary Education (Washington, D.C.: U.S. Bureau of Education, 1918).

tional hue in America. St. Louis Hegelianism took the more optimistic and activist sides from the master's dialectic, and the Herbartians cared more for Herbart's psychology and theory of learning than for his complicated metaphysics. The prevailing tenor was still idealistic, and the specific dignity of man was understood to lie in his capacity to think and act in harmony with the inner laws of a rationally understood universe. The critically minded were already attracted by Herbert Spencer's *First Principles* (1862), *Principles of Sociology* (1877–1896), and *Essays on Education* (1861).[28] In the latter he protested against the uselessness of the typical classical studies and the harsh discipline in the English public schools, thereby giving support to the democratic trends in American education. And, as in every country, so also in the U.S.A. the work of Darwin created both fury and admiration. By jumbling the ideas of these two Englishmen, every group could read out of them whatever justification it needed for its particular propensity: rugged individualism for the entrepreneur, collective action for the socially minded and for labor, the appeal to will for the voluntarist and the idea of immutable law for the determinist, a new gospel for the atheist and the hope of eternal progress for the secularist Christian.[29]

After 1900, the pragmatism of William James and especially of John Dewey became the guiding force for the progressive American teacher, though one must be cautious with generalizations. The bulk of professional literature does not always indicate the actual disposition of men's minds. Much more than the theoretician may think, American teachers still cling to the old religious or idealist traditions, and an increasing number of them are Catholic.

However, especially in the field of education, John Dewey became the foremost spokesman of the *Zeitgeist* of the first four decades of the twentieth century. He combined in his thought Hegel's idealist evolutionism and respect for institutions (which he transferred to democracy) with Darwin's theory of natural evolution, with scientific experimentalism, with the pioneer spirit of a society that had shifted from agriculture to industry and labor, and with the missionary zeal of American democratic nationalism. As a philosopher, Dewey was of minor rank if compared with the really great men of thought; as a cultural apostle, he had an immediate influence on his environment that only a few university professors have ever had.

Unfortunately, like all men who think of thinking as a way of action and consequently wish to influence other people, he tolerated too benignly a kind of discipleship that spread his name into groups generally impervious to difficult abstractions, but that at the same time oversimplified his ideas and thus

[28] *Education: Intellectual, Moral, Physical* (1861).
[29] See Richard Hofstadter, *Social Darwinism in American Thought* (Boston: Beacon Press, 1955).

perhaps did them more harm than good in the long run. And, whatever the merits of his philosophy, in his opposition against the old metaphysics he failed to make explicit the metaphysics inherent in his own system of thought and thus allowed the isolation of the surface from the depth of his ideas. Certainly, under the name of progressive education, child-centered schooling, creative teaching and learning, modern and, on the whole, better pedagogical methods were advanced, from which even conservative schools profited more than they like to admit. At the same time such noble and perennial requisites of civilization as duty, authority, devotion to ideals even if connected with sacrifice were dimmed by the vague use of such theories as growth for its own sake, experience, activity, learning by doing, self-development, and democratic living. Whoever carefully reads Dewey's main educational work *Democracy and Education* will find that, by centering ideals like discipline and duty around the concept of interest, he does not intend to belittle their importance, but to create a more dynamic conception of human development. However, recommendation of educational subjectivism can easily be read out of his statements, and that was the danger. Hearing the protest against false authoritarian methods, men forgot that there must not only be process and activity, but also an aim; not only interest (which so easily glides over into mere self-interest), but also the willingness to learn and work even under difficulty; not only an understanding for the specific conditions of childhood, but also an understanding for the conditions of the civilization into which the child has to grow; not only freedom from false authority, but also respect for rightful authority.

The other disintegrating influence on a clear conception of what youth can and should learn in school came from the controversy between the traditionalists in education and the findings of modern psychology. Needless to say, the whole issue is closely related to John Dewey's philosophical criticism of conventionalism in education. It is the American version of the struggle between the humanists and the progressives we encountered especially in French and German history. Unfortunately, many conservative advocates of the old liberal arts, especially the teachers of the ancient languages, rather than simply and proudly referring to the inherent values of a great heritage, attempted to bolster up their vanishing prestige and self-confidence by a most doubtful theory of universal transfer. According to this theory, the learning of grammar, particularly of Latin grammar, was supposed to strengthen miraculously all "the muscles of the mind" and to be, therefore, of most general value and utility. Against this essentially materialistic concept of human intelligence, Edward Lee Thorndike, who had begun his experiments in 1901, could assert in his comprehensive work on *Educational Psychology* of 1913–1914:

The notions of mental machinery which, being improved for one sort of data, held the improvement equally for all sorts; of magic powers which, being trained by exercise of one sort to high efficiency, held that efficiency whatever they might be exercised upon; and of the mind as a reservoir for potential energy which could be filled by any one activity and drawn on for any other—have now disappeared from expert writings on psychology. A survey of experimental results is now needed perhaps as much to prevent the opposite superstition; for, apparently, some careless thinkers have rushed from the belief in totally general training to the belief that training is totally specialized.[30]

The last sentence in this statement is revealing. Just as Dewey's ideas were often falsely applied by his disciples, so were Thorndike's. There is no evidence that he directed his critical inquiry into the prevailing theories of learning in a spirit hostile to good standards in the liberal arts and related school subjects.

Yet, by some modernists, if we may call them this, experimental psychology was used to disparage any hierarchy of the intellectual disciplines. Unfortunately, this tendency is still with us. It leads to an atomistic education, which, sadly enough, had already been introduced into the American high school by the Report of the Committee of Ten and the Report of the Committee on College Entrance Requirements. For, in order to create some regularity in face of the threatening chaos of high-school subjects, these committees had postulated that a respectable college should admit only those candidates who could show a record of credits for sixteen courses. But, while in the 1890's there was still some reason to assume that sixteen courses would form an organic body of knowledge, after World War I this assumption proved to be illusory. Except for some basic subjects such as American history and English, the sixteen credits now can refer to the most scattered congeries of subjects. It apparently makes no difference to some educators whether the mind of the student has been nourished by material worth learning from a scholarly and humane point of view, or whether it has just been kept busy with something, no matter how trivial.

Thus serious complaints accumulate that the American high schools offer a "grab-bag" education ranging from physics and Latin to basket weaving, mountain climbing and automobile driving, while the colleges turn out a growing proportion of youth who despite sixteen years of exposure to teachers show few signs of academic discipline and learning.

The mechanical reliance on credits, from the high school to the graduate schools of the universities, without due respect for coherence and standard, is the curse of American education. No real reform will be possible unless the program of study is brought into harmony with the development of human in-

[30] *The Psychology of Learning* (New York: Columbia University Teachers College, 1913), II, pp. 364–365.

telligence, which requires steadiness, concentration, courage in overcoming difficulties, and a sense of the relation between a single subject and the wider context to which it belongs.

To a degree, since the time when the public high school changed from a selective into a more or less universal national institution, educators have tried to meet the arising difficulties by two measures. First, in order to allow more specialization according to talent, they have divided the high school into a college-preparatory, a commercial, a technical, and, if feasible, in a general division. Secondly, many communities have changed the original structure of eight elementary and four secondary-school years into a six-year elementary, a three-year junior high, and a three-year senior high school program. This structure allows, on the one hand, for greater flexibility in discovering and cultivating the interests of the student and, on the other hand, for his greater concentration on a group of subjects arranged according to his purpose, ability, and interest. As will be shown in one of the next sections, with these measures the American school approaches somehow the more compartmental character of the European system. However, the totally unselective admission to the high school as well as extreme decentralization, which often allows the community to control the school administrator and his teachers without any admixture of scholarly standards, does not permit sufficient insistence on good performance. Hence the waste for many talented students who during the most malleable years between twelve and eighteen could easily have learned one or two foreign languages and more mathematics and science in addition.

Despite sometimes hard, though by necessity rather mechanical, entrance tests, the colleges and universities have been unable to stem the high school's trend away from academic subjects. Hence, in contrast to Europe where the student at a university is given a considerable amount of freedom because one may trust that he has received some intellectual discipline in his preparatory school, the American college and even the university believe they must impose on the young scholar a rigorously regulated schedule, class attendance lists, examinations during and after each course, and all kinds of guidance procedures. There reigns a pedantic and unacademic climate. Would it not be more conducive to a person's development if he were more free when he could profit from his freedom, namely, as a young man, or woman, and more controlled when control might be at the right place, namely, as an adolescent? But these are things about which it is hard to argue with an American. As things stand, the first two of the four years of undergraduate work become increasingly filled with subjects that could well have been mastered in high school. This is especially the case in regard to languages.

No wonder that Americans are now frightened by the unexpected efficiency of Russian schools. The missionary enthusiasm that especially after the two great wars made American educators believe they had the key to democracy in their hands has now given way to a more sober attitude of self-examination.

The Tasks of the Future

No people can rest on the achievements of the past. The United States is now one of the great world powers in an extremely competitive situation, and this position will be lost unless it is based on inner as much as outer wealth.

What the American school now needs is, first, a combination of the principle of equality and of justice to all with the principle of quality. As the American schools operate now, they neglect not only the theoretically gifted but also the practical students. The correction of this defect need not endanger the unity of the American high school; in the future it should still keep together the nation's youth up to the age of eighteen. Unity and diversity do not necessarily contradict; they can even support each other. Separate schools for the young intellectuals and vocational or trade schools for the practical are against the tradition of the country. There should be just as much dignity, humaneness, and satisfaction in helping the practically minded pupil toward his kind of productivity as in helping the theoretically talented toward his form of creativeness. Unless we succeed in this twofold task we will end on a level of verbalization too low for the gifted and too high for the practical.[31]

The second task incumbent on the American school is an organic rather than a mechanical concept and method of organizing both the program of studies and the process of examination and selection. As has already been said, mere credits acquired by the most disparate and incoherent kind of activity do not form a mind, but confuse it.

Third, America needs a combination of the traditional decentralization with concerted national and professional leadership, as it existed to a high degree between 1840 and 1900. Political and administrative centralization in Washington, similar to the kind France has in Paris, is impossible in the United States, and if possible, it would be disastrous. For there exists neither the well-trained officialdom, stemming originally from the old monarchical hierarchy, nor the cultural unity, which, despite all internal differences, still characterizes France, nor the willingness of the people to receive and obey orders from above. But all this is no excuse for managerially minded school administrators or politicians on school boards to exercise their power over better-educated teachers and parents.

Fourth, there must be brought about a closer coordination and cooperation

[31] See Robert Ulich, *Crisis and Hope in American Education* (Boston: Beacon Press, 1951).

between the colleges and universities, on the one hand, and the secondary schools, on the other. It is paradoxical for a country to have a single-track system and, at the same time, so little mutual attention, interconnection, and sometimes even mutual esteem as exists in the United States between the secondary and tertiary institutions. The result is a situation that sometimes borders on chaos. The state teachers colleges also, which, though belonging to the higher level, now lead an almost isolated existence, must be included in the intellectual blood stream. Otherwise one third of the teaching profession will lead an intellectually isolated existence. Generally, a broader humanistic rather than a primarily technical training of teachers must be aimed at in the various schools of education. But by no means should this lead, as some people advocate, to an absorption of the professional preparation of teachers by other departments, such as psychology, philosophy, sociology, and history. Education has become too complicated and demanding a responsibility, both from the scholarly and the national point of view, to be administered in a scattered, left-handed, and consequently more or less amateurish fashion. Certainly, some people are by nature, as it were, good teachers, and others are not. But a born teacher exists as little as a born lawyer or a born physician. In addition, the conditions of modern civilization are such that our schools, whether they like it or not, have to include a number of social obligations that in earlier times were discharged by family, church, and community. They demand much more from the teacher than just the instruction of this or that subject matter, however paramount this purpose is. Therefore, though education in the wide sense of the word is the responsibility of every college or university in its totality, there must be in both central agencies in which the various scholarly and social tasks of the teaching profession receive unity and clear focus. This agency can only be a highly developed department, or school, of education.

There are other aspects worthy of discussion, which, though perhaps external at the first glance, nevertheless determine the spirit of teaching and learning. American youth are one-sidedly educated by women, who form more than 72 per cent of the teaching staff. This is no wonder if one considers that the living conditions in the United States are such that teachers' salaries, though comparing favorably with the profession's income in other countries, are nevertheless too low in purchasing power. If 73 per cent of the male teachers are forced to look for outside occupation to keep their families on a decent standard, other professions will be more attractive. Furthermore, the majority of instructors in secondary schools have a teaching load that exceeds that customary in other countries. There is little if any, awareness on the part of the American public that a bad scholar cannot be a good teacher, and that the latter needs a private library and time to read in order to escape the ever-threatening danger of routine and incompetence. Finally, the enormous contrasts in the quality of teaching in the various states much be corrected by federal aid without interference in the freedom of the teaching profession. This rich country has, besides school palaces no other nation could afford, still some ten thousand high schools with less than two hundred students. Naturally, they cannot give even the minimum of diversified education that young people of the ages between fourteen and eighteen have the right to expect.

The shock the United States has received from the sudden realization of Russia's advances in the field of education, especially in science, has uncomfortably awakened the nation from its complacency concerning its school situation. Congress has granted considerable sums to be spent in the form of federal aid to schools and universities, and the states will have to match most of the funds; newspapers and journals abound with articles dealing with the best possible training of the considerably more than forty-one million persons enrolled in schools and colleges (an increase of 27 per cent over the past five years); and all the institutions of learning, from the elementary schools to the graduate schools of the universities, are frantically looking for funds in order to attract better teachers. In view of all the one-sided statements issued by an innumerable number of more or less competent individuals and organizations, it was encouraging to read the balanced report of the Educational Policies Commission, prepared under the chairmanship of the President of Indiana University, Herman B. Wells, and published January 3, 1958. Fully recognizing the merits of the American schools, it nevertheless urges a more responsible participation of the American public in the affairs of its schools; a better preparation, higher payment, and increased recognition of the role of the teacher; better counseling; better opportunities for the gifted student; improvement of instruction not merely in mathematics and the sciences, but in all subjects, including languages; better-equipped schools and college buildings; and "a substantial breakthrough in educational finance." Of considerable value also is the Rockefeller Brothers Report on education with the descriptive subtitle: *The Pursuit of Excellence: Education and the Future of America.*[32]

These reports have now been overshadowed by the so-called Conant Report.[33] After examining a number of comprehensive high schools in eighteen states, Dr. Conant, former president of Harvard University, affirms his belief that the pattern of these schools—critically looked at by the English and other European nations—is capable of satisfactory reform without fundamental changes, under the condition that provision is made for proper size, for a

---

[32] Report V of Special Studies Project, Rockefeller Brothers Fund, in *America at Mid-Century Series* (New York: Doubleday, 1958).
[33] James B. Conant, *The American High School Today* (New York: McGraw-Hill, 1959).

competent staff of teachers and administrators, for a better guidance program, for a better balance between individualized, general, and certain forms of vocational education, for a richer and stiffer curriculum for the gifted, especially in science and languages, and for several other improvements.

Dr. Conant's report is sufficiently empirical, realistic, and at the same time demanding to be a challenge to the school administrators. They should, however, not forget that, according to the author, "the study has made no attempt to answer such questions as 'How satisfactory is the typical American high school?'"

Certainly, even if the author's recommendations in regard to the advanced academic courses were fulfilled, the so-called "college preparatory divisions" in the American comprehensive high schools would still lag behind the standards of those secondary schools in Europe that prepare a young person for higher studies. Dr. Conant remarks:

> In the European pre-university schools an eight- or nine-year rigorous course in languages, mathematics, science, history, and literature prepares the student to pass a state examination for a certificate which admits him to a university. The failures during the long course are many, and a considerable number fall by the wayside, but those who succeed finish with a mastery of two languages, a knowledge of mathematics through calculus and of physics and chemistry at the level of our sophomore college courses.[34]

But Dr. Conant rightly points at the incomparability of the American high school and college with the European preuniversity secondary school and university.

In consequence of their specific purpose, most of the reports written during the past decades give little or no attention to certain questions for which there may be no clear-cut answer, but which, nevertheless, have to be kept alive if education is not to degenerate into routine. What are the basic criteria according to which to judge the education of a nation? As this book has shown, there are many. However, one criterion is paramount, namely, whether a school system creates among its youth a feeling of national belonging within a general climate of universal human values such as decency, respect, and cooperation. Instead of condescendence on one side and servility on the other, does every good citizen feel a sense of equality among the lawful members of the nation? In the light of this criterion one can only agree with Henry Steele Commager, who affirms in his book *Living Ideas in America:*

> No other people ever demanded so much of schools and of education as have the American. None other was ever so well served by its school and its educators.[35]

[34] *Ibid.*, p. 2. At certain schools three to four languages are required, but generally with a reduction of science.

[35] New York: Harper, 1951, p. 546. See in this context also G. Z. F. Bereday, *Equality in Education—Its Meaning and Methods* (New York: Harper, 1960).

But one has to go further. America is proud of the mobility of its population and, relatively speaking, of the absence of tight social classes (though there exists, as the vengeful heritage of older times, the problem of segregation). The nation is also proud of its universal school system and of the fact that abundance of living is not merely a privilege of a few. The American industrialist and engineer excel through their technical knowledge. Finally, this country has been given the role of leadership among the noncommunist nations.

These are certainly great achievements, but they also involve great obligations. Whither will all this mobility lead? For there is no blessing in mobility, unless it creates deeper forms of happiness than a mutual race and scramble. Does the universality of the school system produce not only more widespread knowledge, but also better taste and more courageous individualism within a framework of worth-while loyalties and a deeper faith in man and the ultimate sources of his existence? Does abundance express itself primarily in the sale of automobiles, or in the greater appreciation of the finer arts of living? Are industrial energy and production merely means for a higher quantity of production, or for a qualitative culture that makes American leadership a matter not only of bigness, but of truly deserved respect among the family of cultured nations? This is a challenge of a magnitude rarely faced by any other nation. The future of humanity will depend on the answer.

3

A Short History of Teacher Education in the United States

PAUL WOODRING

The following account of education in the United States and its historical antecedents reflects the dominant philosophies and changing socioeconomic conditions that have determined the continuous commitment of the American people

SOURCE: "A Century of Teacher Education," *School and Society,* Vol. 90 (May 5, 1962), pp. 211, 236–242. Reprinted by permission of the publisher.

Presently a distinguished service professor on the faculty of Western Washington State College, Dr. Woodring has been a prolific writer in the field of education for more than thirty years and has served as education editor for a number of years for *The Saturday Review.* He has received national recognition for his dedication and exceptional contributions to education and has been an officeholder in many professional organizations.

*to support free schools in a free society. To students in education, the
requirements for teaching in our schools are of primary importance. The major
changes that have occurred in these requirements during the past hundred years
are presented by Woodring. He critically analyzes the organization and content of teacher education programs and proposes that teacher education become a part of the mainstream of higher education.*

. . . ONE HUNDRED YEARS AGO there were no teachers colleges; universities had not yet established schools or departments of education; and the subject of "education" would have been difficult if not impossible to find in the
course listings of American colleges. Edgar Wesley has observed that, in
1859, "Colleges, academies, and upper schools of various kinds had existed
for two centuries in America without making any noticeable contribution to
the training of teachers."[1]

After the Civil War, a few universities and colleges, mostly in the Middle
West, established chairs of "pedagogy" or "didactics." Usually, these were
found within the department of philosophy, which at that time also included
whatever psychology was taught. But the state universities of Iowa and Michigan created departments of education during these years, and Teachers College became a part of Columbia University in 1892. Most of our university
schools and departments of education, however, did not come into being until
after the close of the century.

Throughout most of the nineteenth century, it was the normal schools and
institutes that carried the responsibility for teacher education and both focused their attention on preparing teachers for elementary rather than secondary schools. Neither was a part of *higher* education. The nineteenth-century
normal school usually accepted students with only an elementary education
and institutes often had no admission requirements. Yet, both these institutions made very important contributions to teacher education and they set the
pattern for much that was to follow.

Institutes offered short courses of a few days or a few weeks, taught by
itinerant speakers or local school administrators who gave instruction in
schoolkeeping and inspirational lectures. The poorest institutes were probably
better than none at all because they brought teachers together for discussion
of mutual problems; and when Horace Mann came to speak, or when William James came to deliver his "Talks to Teachers," as he did in many parts
of the country in the 1890s, the institute must have reached a high peak of
excellence.

Before the Civil War, normal schools were established in at least 10 states,

[1] Edgar Wesley, *NEA: The First Hundred Years,* New York: Harper & Row, Publishers, 1957, pp. 79–80.

but enrollments were small and it is doubtful that more than two or three per cent of the teachers had attended them. During the last third of the century, however, normal schools spread rapidly across the country and enrollments rose dramatically. . . . Wesley estimates that normal school enrollments grew from 10,000 in 1870 to nearly 70,000 at the end of the century . . .[2]

Since their founding, there has been a great deal of debate about the quality of education provided by the normal schools. Perhaps the reason is that there was a tremendous range in quality among the different institutions and the debaters were not talking about the same schools. At its worst, the normal school was a shabby little institution with a single teacher who taught courses in pedagogy with perhaps a little time for a review of the elementary subjects. At its best, however, it was a very substantial professional school, headed by an able educator who was assisted by a devoted faculty. In addition to courses in pedagogy and a period of supervised practice teaching, the best of the normal schools offered an academic curriculum comparable to that found in the better academies of the day and probably not greatly inferior to that found in the first two years of the liberal arts colleges. . . .

After the turn of the century, the number of private normal schools declined because these institutions were unable to face the competition from publicly supported ones that charged no tuition. The number of state normal schools continued to increase until about 1920 and their enrollments grew rapidly. By 1900, the growth of public high schools made it possible for many normal schools to require a high school diploma for admission. This enabled them to reduce their attention to secondary school subjects and to take steps toward transforming themselves into four-year degree-granting teachers colleges. Nineteen state normal schools made this transition between 1911 and 1920, sixty-nine between 1921 and 1930, and most of the others did so between 1931 and 1950,[3] by which time the normal school had become almost obsolete.

The state teachers colleges, however, had a short life. Within twenty years after they had emerged out of the normal schools, they began transforming themselves into general state colleges or state universities which granted liberal arts and other degrees, as well as the B.S. in Ed., which was usually the only degree offered by the teachers college. This change came first in the Middle West and the Far West; it came more slowly in the northeastern section where powerful private colleges and universities bitterly resisted the efforts of the teachers colleges to take on new responsibilities.

In California, the state normal schools became teachers colleges in 1921 and general state colleges in 1935. . . . In New York, the normal schools did

---

[2] *Ibid.*, pp. 82–83.   [3] Wesley, *op. cit.*, pp. 88–89.

not take the next step until 1961. At the end of 1961, public teachers colleges were found in only fifteen states.*

The changes have not been in name only; a new kind of college has emerged which continues to prepare many teachers but also provides a general or liberal education at modest cost for many who do not plan to teach. The academic courses offered in these colleges and the professors who teach them have the same strengths and weaknesses as are found in other undergraduate colleges, both public and private.

Since 1900, universities have accepted a growing proportion of the responsibility for teacher education. During the first two or three decades of the twentieth century, most of the major universities established schools or colleges of education and the others established departments of education. The number of professional courses offered for teachers and administrators in a typical university grew from two or three in 1900 to several hundred in 1960, and this led to charges that the courses had proliferated beyond the available intellectual content and that there was much duplication of content in courses with different titles and numbers. The reply that proliferation could be found in other departments, too, was true but was not accepted as a sufficient justification.

In 1958, 25.3 per cent of all beginning teachers came from public universities and another 10.3 per cent came from private universities. Many of those who attended other colleges as undergraduates later went to universities for graduate work.

Today, all the major state universities and many land-grant colleges and municipal universities maintain large schools or colleges of education. Most of them offer courses at both the undergraduate and graduate levels and grant bachelors' degrees for beginning teachers and masters' and doctors' degrees for teachers, supervisors, specialists, administrators, and college teachers of education.

In some state universities, all undergraduates planning to teach are encouraged to enroll as freshmen in the college of education. In many others, the college of education enrolls only those who plan to teach in elementary school and those who plan to teach physical education, home economics, agriculture, etc., in high school, while those who plan to teach the academic courses at the secondary level enroll in, and earn their degree from, the liberal arts college of the university, taking only such professional work in the school of education as is required for certification. But even when the prospective teacher is enrolled in the college of education, he usually takes the

---

* Historically, this date is incorrect. In 1938, a four-year college course was established at state normal schools, and in 1942, the granting of the bachelor's degree was authorized by the New York State Board of Regents. In 1947, the master's degree was offered.—Ed.

major portion of his academic work from professors in their liberal arts colleges; and if our teachers today do not know their subjects, or are not liberally educated, the responsibility must be accepted by the academic professors who failed to teach them properly.

Some large private universities maintain undergraduate and graduate schools of education similar to those found in state institutions. Many, however, including such renowned institutions as Harvard and Chicago, have graduate schools of education only, while Princeton and Yale have neither schools nor departments of education. Teachers College of Columbia University has become in recent years almost entirely a graduate school.

American teachers are prepared, to the point of initial certification, in more than 1100 different colleges and universities, and, inevitably, the range in quality among these varied institutions will be enormous. Unfortunately, the colleges with the highest entrance standards and the highest standards of instruction do not turn out their fair share of teachers because they draw their student bodies from socio-economic classes in which parents as well as students do not look upon teaching as a sufficiently satisfactory, remunerative, and "prestige" profession, particularly for men.

But, although the talents of the students and the quality of instruction varies greatly among the colleges that educate teachers, there is a fair amount of uniformity in the courses studied—a uniformity resulting in considerable part from state certification requirements.

Of the 52 certification authorities (50 states plus Puerto Rico and the District of Columbia), 51 now require the bachelor's degree for beginning high school teachers and 44 require it for elementary teachers as well. Nine states require high school teachers to complete a fifth year of college during the period of initial certification and three require a fifth year for beginning secondary teachers.[4]

The required course nearly always includes a period of general education approximately two academic years in length, plus two more years during which the time is divided between a major in an academic dicipline (or, in the case of elementary teachers, a "field" major which may include several disciplines) and a sequence of professional courses. For elementary teachers, the professional requirements range from 16 to 36 semester hours in the different states, with a median of 21 hours. For secondary teachers, the range is 12 to 29 hours, and the median is 18. Many colleges, however, require more professional hours than the state requirement for certification. . . .

An important departure from the standard or conventional program for teachers is that which leads to the Master of Arts in Teaching degree. This newer program was originated at Harvard in 1936 at the suggestion of

[4] W. Earl Armstrong and T. M. Stinnett, *A Manual on Certification Requirements for School Personnel in the United States*, Washington D.C.: NEA, 1961.

James B. Conant, who then was president of the University. Dean Keppel of the Harvard Graduate School of Education estimates that today "at least thirty AMT (or MAT) programs are known to be in existence, plus fifty other programs that award different degrees but try to solve the same problems in the same way." [5]

The MAT program selects liberal arts graduates who have strong majors in the academic disciplines and offers them a year (or more) of instruction at the graduate level. In a typical program, the student takes a summer's work in educational psychology and educational philosophy, followed by a semester's internship in a public high school. During this semester, he takes part in a weekly seminar on the methods and materials for teaching his subject and his teaching is closely supervised; in some cases he participates as a member of a teaching team. During the second semester, he returns to the university for graduate-level courses in his teaching field and, sometimes, an additional course or semester in education. Many of those who have worked with this program are convinced that it should and probably will become the standard program for the preparation of secondary teachers of the academic subjects. . . .

Today . . . there is widespread agreement that any sound program for teacher education must include: a substantial program of general or liberal education, representing not less than two years of work beyond high school; a knowledge of the subject or subjects to be taught, which, in the case of the secondary school teacher, should be provided by a strong academic major at

[5] Francis Keppel, "Master of Arts in Teaching," *Saturday Review,* 44: 53–65, June 17, 1961.

Editors' note: Compare the following 1963 news report: "The 'education major' is doomed in California. In what Thomas W. Braden, president of the state board of education, calls a deathblow to 'educationese,' the state is drastically upgrading its teacher certification requirements. Ultimately, California will turn down all applicants whose sole or chief training is in the methodology of teaching. Instead, it will demand degrees in academic subjects, stressing substance over technique.

"So sweeping is the change, says Braden, that if used to gauge California's current teachers, the new standards would disqualify 20 per cent of high school teachers, 75 per cent of junior college instructors, and 90 per cent of elementary school teachers. 'Professional education' is no longer an acceptable major. Would-be administrators will have to major in academic fields, from science to humanities. New teachers must minor or major in those fields, although they may also take degrees in nonacademic subjects such as home economics or industrial art. All must have a working knowledge of a foreign language.

"*Extra Schooling.* A fifth year of college will be required of all school teachers, although elementary teachers can take it while working. In contrast to past practice, schools will not let teachers teach outside their academic fields—will no longer plunk an English teacher in French class to save money, for example. The so-called 'Einstein clause' is in full force; able artists or writers are welcome to teach in California public schools even if they never had a day's formal education. . . ."—"We Want Teachers Who Are Educated," *Time,* 81:74, May 10, 1963. Courtesy *Time;* copyright Time, Inc., 1963.

the undergraduate level plus some graduate work in an academic discipline; a knowledge of the contributions of philosophy, history, psychology, and the other social and behavioral sciences to an understanding of the place of the school in the social order and the processes of learning; and a period of prac-.ice teaching or an extended internship during which time the prospective teacher tries out various methods of teaching under competent supervision.

There is still, in 1962, widespread disagreement about the proper organi-zation and content of professional courses for teachers and about the place of these courses in the curriculum. There is also disagreement about whether the internship should come during the undergraduate years or after the student receives the baccalaureate. It seems clear, however, that in the years ahead, teacher education will not be a thing apart, provided by separate institutions for teachers, but will be a part of the mainstream of higher education in America.

EVALUATION

JAMES FRASIER, **Historical Foundations of American Education**

1. (a) What does Frasier regard as the historical model on which the American educational system is based?

   (b) Name and briefly explain any exceptions the author indicates to this model.

2. Frasier divides the history of American education into five historical periods. Name these and within each identify some of the unique contributions and at least two outstanding persons.

3. What facts about education does Frasier specifically report as marking the ascendance of democratic education in America at the following times?
   1. 1770–1870
   2. 1870–1960
   3. 1870
   4. 1960

4. Colonial America was comprised of three major regions: New England, the Middle States, and the Southern Colonies. Outline the major patterns of education in each of these.

5. (a) In America's educational history, what has been the ideal for which the people have struggled?

   (b) What does Frasier give as the ultimate goal of American education?

ROBERT ULICH, **The United States of America**

6. (a) What explanation does Ulich offer for the fact that there is no sovereign country belonging to Western civilization?

   (b) How does Ulich describe Massachusetts?

   (c) How did the Protestant conviction that every Christian should live in an immediate and personal relation with his God affect the development of education?

7. (a) Identify two factors that prepared the ground for the later democratic development of education in Massachusetts.

(b) Why does Ulich believe that Virginia has a truer claim to being the cornerstone of American liberty than has Massachusetts?

(c) Other than religion, what is the second pillar of Puritan education?

8. How did the Puritans regard science?

9. (a) What school was the pattern for secondary education in Colonial times?

   (b) What was its emphasis?

10. (a) Between what years did the private academies prosper?

    (b) How extensive were they in number?

11. List a number of marked distinctions between Benjamin Franklin and Thomas Jefferson.

12. List the similarities between these two men.

13. What supreme principle of education was stated by Franklin?

14. Outline Ulich's reasons for justifying a study of Franklin's leadership in early American education.

15. Identify two factors that Ulich holds to be directly related to the growth of the American school system.

16. What single distinction does Ulich attribute to the personalities of Franklin, Jefferson, and Lincoln?

17. Briefly outline Horace Mann's final credo of public education.

18. How close to reality was this credo in Mann's time?

19. What special significance does Ulich attach to the 1893 Report of the Committee of Ten?

20. (a) What problem became evident in the 1918 Report on the Cardinal Principles of Secondary Education?

    (b) How was the goal set for high schools to be achieved at that time?

21. During the nineteenth century, who were the four great men Ulich credits with providing American education with its philosophical and methodical principles?

22. According to Ulich, what five factors are combined in John Dewey's thinking?

23. What does Ulich say is the curse of American education?

24. Why does Ulich believe young American college students are not given more freedom in their studies?

25. What five contemporary needs does Ulich identify for our American schools?

PAUL WOODRING, A Short History of Teacher Education in the United States

26. Describe briefly the nineteenth-century normal schools and teacher institutes Woodring describes in his short history of teacher education.

27. Woodring's thesis is that requirements for teacher education have changed, and he predicts a clearly perceivable direction which he believes will improve it.
    (a) What is his prediction?

    (b) What two major trends, as Woodring sees it, appeared in teacher education in the nineteenth century?

28. During the present century, teacher education has made great strides forward, according to the author. State the most outstanding ones.

29. In Woodring's words, what was the normal school at its worst? At its best?

30. How is the present amount of uniformity in teacher education courses accounted for by Woodring?

31. What is nearly always included in the required teacher education program?

32. Outline Woodring's concept of the program for a Master of Arts degree in teaching.

33. Outline the widespread agreement existing today regarding what should be included in teacher education programs.

FOR FURTHER READING

Bailyn, Bernard, *Education in the Forming of American Society* (Chapel Hill: University of North Carolina Press, 1960).
   Presents the author's ideas on how education affects culture and dominating institutions together with how the beliefs of a culture affect education.

Butts, R. Freeman, "Search for Tomorrow," *NEA Journal,* March 1960, pp. 33–48.
   An excellent outline of the story of American education. The author, a noted historian, traces education over the years as it has attempted to meet the needs of a growing American society. One of the questions he asks is: "What kind of education will best develop the free citizen and the free person?" The discussion offers answers to this and other questions arising from colonial to modern times.

Butts, R. Freeman, and Lawrence A. Cremin, *A History of Education in American Culture* (New York: Holt, Rinehart and Winston, 1953).
   A detailed treatment of the history of American education. The authors show the close relationship between society, schools, and other educational agencies and its significance in the development of our educational programs.

Conant, James B., "The Relevance of Jefferson's Ideas Today," *Thomas Jefferson and the Development of American Public Education* (Berkeley: University of California Press, 1962).
   Traces Jefferson's ideas and his work in establishing free education beyond the elementary school and points out the relevance of those ideas today. The principle of universal education advocated by Jefferson and our present belief in the need for colleges and universities are offered as evidence that Jefferson's proposals have been incorporated into the pattern of our educational structure.

Tyack, David B., ed., *Turning Points in American Educational History* (Waltham, Mass.: Blaisdell, 1967).
   A broad range of events marking the end of old eras and the various beginnings of new eras are discussed. The views of the various contributors regarding some of the reasons why certain events affected education provide provocative reading.

Philosophy

4
Philosophy of Education

F. BRUCE ROSEN

Three basic problems in educational philosophy are identified, and a number of specific reasons for studying the different philosophies are presented in this brief introduction to the study of philosophy. Professor Rosen refers to philosophy as a measuring stick for current educational practices and in this sense shows his driving interest in applying philosophy to the overall educational process. This selection is presented to inspire and encourage study in philosophy and to show that applications are meaningful personally to you as a future teacher.

Philosophy

1. Definition of Philosophy

When we speak of *Philosophy* we use a term which may be viewed in two senses. The first of these is that of the word itself which literally means "love of wisdom." But to love wisdom does not necessarily make one a philosopher. Today, we think of philosophy in a more limited sense as man's attempt to give meaning to his existence through the continued search for a comprehensive and consistent answer to basic problems. It is this second sense of the word which makes the philosopher an active person; one who seeks answers, rather than one who simply sits around engaging in idle and frivolous speculation. Today, most philosophers are actively concerned with life. They seek answers to basic problems. Thus we find that philosophers are *doing* as well as *thinking,* and it is their thinking which guides their doing. What they do is rooted in the search for answers to certain types of problems and the tentative answers they have formulated.

SOURCE: F. Bruce Rosen, *Philosophic Systems and Education* (Columbus, Ohio: Charles E. Merrill Co., 1968), chap. 2. Reprinted by permission of the publisher.

After serving on the faculty of Auburn University for more than three years, F. Bruce Rosen became Southern Director of Education for the Anti-Defamation League. He has contributed much to the field of education through extensive research and publications in the field of philosophy.

2. Some Basic Problems

When we speak of problems in the philosophical sense, we usually refer to three broad categories: problems of being, problems of knowing, and problems of value. The first of these is known by the technical name of *ontology,* the second is called *epistemology,* and the last is usually referred to as *axiology.* Each of these categories has several technical subheadings, but for our present purposes these are not important. Each of the above categories represents a type of question, but they are not in and of themselves questions. Some of the questions which one might ask that would fall into one or more of these categories are:

Who am I?
What am I?
Why am I here?
What do we mean by here?
What is real?
What is good?
What is beautiful?
What can we know?
How can we come to know?

As these and other similar questions are explored and answered in such a way as to build a logical and consistent system, a philosophy is built. Within the system we build or accept, we find the logical answer to the questions of a day to day nature.

Should I pay my income tax?
Is it wrong to burn my draft card?
What should my behavior be with members of the opposite sex?
As a teacher should I use corporal punishment?
What limits, if any, should be imposed on academic freedom?
Is it more important to study the classics or to emphasize the sciences?

Obviously at one time or another we will all stray from our pattern. There is no perfect philosophical system which will answer all of our questions all of the time. The important point is that we will generally operate in a manner which is consistent and compatible with our basic beliefs—our philosophy.

Philosophy and the Culture

1. Definition of Culture

There are a great many different definitions of the word *culture.* One of the foremost scholars in the field of cultural anthropology, Bronislaw Malinowski, has referred to culture as "the fullest context of all human activities." [1] The word *culture* in its broadest sense should not be confused with *culture* defined as those special trappings which set apart one social class from another. For the anthropologist or sociologist culture consists of the material and non-material products of human endeavor; it is our total man-made environment. Clyde Kluckhohn describes it as follows:

By "culture" anthropology means the total life way of a people, the social legacy the individual acquires from his group. Or culture can be regarded as that part of the environment that is the creation of man.[2]

This is a much broader category than most of us realize at first. It not only includes the "things" of life, but the "ways" of life as well. It includes our laws, our values which determine so many of our laws, our books, our eating habits, our foods, our art works, our furniture, and to a great degree, our likes and dislikes. Members of a culture are bound by it to a degree far greater than they imagine. They behave in culturally sanctioned or approved ways because they are unable to imagine any others. They behave as they do because a culture is a complex intertwining of groups and subgroups which determines patterns of action for members of the group.

2. Philosophy as a Part of Our Culture

As was stated, philosophy and philosophizing are both the love of wisdom and the search for it. Since the existing wisdom is a part of our culture, and since the means of searching for wisdom are culturally determined, it will be seen that there exists a close relationship between the culture and philosophy. Philosophy is a man-made system of thought which is shaped by the culture. But philosophy is more than this. It must also be the cutting edge of progress; the blade against which a culture tries itself. Philosophy is both the shaped and the shaper. If a culture does not move ahead, if it does not change, it must soon grow static and eventually die. But a culture can change only to the degree that people in it bring about change. This is, in part, the function of the philosopher. It is the *active* role of philosophy and for many the role of the philosopher as a change-agent is his most important function.

Philosophy of Education

1. Definition of Philosophy of Education

It is unlikely that there has ever been or ever will be a pure philosophy of education. In large measure the way we think and feel about educational matters is determined by the way we think and feel about other things.

[1] Bronislaw Malinowski, *Sex, Culture, and Myth* (New York: Harcourt, Brace & World, Inc., 1962), p. 196.
[2] Clyde Kluckhohn, *Mirror for Man* (New York: Premier Books, 1959), p. 20.

If we are opposed to a large federal government it is likely that we will support a state or even a local control of schools. If, on the other hand, we feel that the federal government should play an increasing welfare role in our society we would probably support greater involvement of the federal government in education.

How we feel about corporal punishment will probably find its roots in our conception of the nature of man; our curriculum will be a function of epistemological considerations, and our axiology will determine to some degree the role of the school in the shaping of the community.

If one is consistent, we can say that one's position on medical care for the aged is probably related to one's position on the role of the federal government in education. Thus, a philosophy of education simply becomes a part of our broader philosophy. Educational philosophizing then is part of total philosophizing, but if we are to give it an educational emphasis we might say that we are concerned with developing a logical and consistent framework through which the educative process may be fruitfully viewed.

a. Educational philosophizing concerns itself with many of the same questions as "pure" philosophy. Even where the questions are not the same they are often no more than variants. For example, while the "pure" philosopher may ask, "How does a person come to know something?" the educational philosopher may go one step further and ask, "What are the specific classroom conditions under which a person is most likely to learn?"

b. Philosophies of education provide a more particularized frame of reference through which to view the educational process. There is no question that education can be viewed through the general philosophical system one adopts, but if one is particularly concerned with education it is necessary and appropriate to emphasize certain questions and certain aspects within the broader philosophical position in order to particularize it for educational thought.

Why Study the Various Philosophies of Education

1. Limited Number of Problems

There are really very few new problems in education. As the unknown cynic of Ecclesiastes wrote:

> What has been is what will be,
>   and what has been done is what will be done;
>   and there is nothing new under the sun.
> Is there a thing of which it is said,
>   "See, this is new"?
> It has been already,
>   in the ages before us.[3]

[3] Eccles. 1:9–10.

Many problems which seem new to us today have their origins in antiquity and only seem new to us because we have not focused on them for a very long time. Other problems which have been with us for generations are, at times, seen out of perspective because we forget their historical antecedents. The problem of truancy and school dropouts has, in recent years, appeared to be one of our most baffling; yet it is the very same problem that bothered an unknown scribe in Sumer some 3,500 to 4,000 years ago. Even then school did not appeal to many young men and the advice of the father has not changed much in the ensuing centuries:

> You who wander about in the public square, would you achieve success? Then seek out the first generations. Go to school, it will be of benefit to you. My son, seek out the first generations, inquire of them.
>
> Perverse one over whom I stand watch—I would not be a man did I not stand watch over my son—I spoke to my kin, compared its men, but found none like you among them. . . . Because my heart had been sated with weariness of you, I kept away from you and heeded not your fears and grumblings. Because of your clamorings, yes, because of your clamorings—I was angry with you—yes, I was angry with you. Because you do not look to your humanity, my heart was carried off as if by an evil wind. Your grumblings have put an end to me, you have brought me to the point of death.[4]

In more current language we hear the father remonstrating with his son, "What do you want to be for the rest of your life, a bum?" "Why can't you be a good kid like your cousin?" And, finally, the anguished cry which has followed the disobedient child down through the ages, "You and your complaining will be the death of me."

In the *Republic* Plato raises the question of what type of education is most appropriate for those who will be the leaders or guardians of the state. The whole question of education for good citizenship is debated at great length in the *Republic,* and while most of us would find ourselves in disagreement with the system of education advocated by Plato, we would all admit that the question of an appropriate education for citizenship is still a perplexing problem and one which has been of concern to leaders of our country from colonial days to the present.

One of the major functions of philosophy of education is the clarification of problems. The philosopher of education must help to define and redefine the problem under consideration until it has been stripped down to its bare essentials.

2. Wide Variety of Solutions

One of the most immediate values in the study of a variety of philosophies of education is that it allows one to see a number of different and alternative

---

[4] Quoted in Samuel Noah Kramer, *History Begins at Sumer* (New York: Doubleday & Company, Inc., Anchor Books, 1959), p. 14.

solutions to a single problem. Each of the solutions is part of a broader framework of educational thought which in turn is part of a philosophical system. Thus, each solution is part of a consistent viewpoint. This is not to suggest that any alternative solution is necessarily correct, or for that matter, that it is incorrect. Any, all, or none of the solutions may work; any, all, or none of the solutions may be correct. Each point of view provides us with a different measuring stick for current educational practices.

3. Clarify Our Own Thinking

A study of the various philosophies of education allows us to clarify our own thinking and beliefs about education. By studying the best thought on education over the centuries, we can find both approaches to problems and solutions to problems that have vexed us. The study of the history of educational thought also permits us to see where our own beliefs are incompatible and where they are internally inconsistent or in need of modification.

4. Develop a Point of View

It is true that there are many solutions to individual problems, but to simply select at random or on the basis of the first solution to come to hand is to be eclectic. No really adequate philosophy of education can be built like a patchwork quilt without end. We cannot simply keep adding pieces because they may be needed, or they may fit, or they look pretty.

Eclecticism is a real and present danger for one who does not know enough about the basic assumptions of educational thought. It is only through the study of educational philosophy that the individual can build his own point of view or philosophical system through which the total educational program may be fruitfully viewed, and within which he may make intelligent decisions and help bring about modifications in the existing educational structure.

5

The Goals of Education

PAUL WOODRING

We present here a philosophical preference for greater emphasis on liberal education rather than on training for vocational competence. Woodring states that clear goals for education must rest on an answer to the question "What changes [do] we expect to take place in the individual as a result of his education?" He distinguishes between responsibilities assumed by any one social institution and those assumed by and belonging to the parents. He also discusses comprehensive lists of goals for education, each in its historical context.

WHEN a foreign educator visits American schools he is impressed by the amount of activity going on in them. He sees children and adolescents working in classrooms, shops, laboratories, and libraries, playing in bands and orchestras, and exercising in gymnasiums. He sees drum majorettes expertly twirling batons and cheerleaders jumping about frenetically in front of packed bleachers. And he is told that all this is part of our educational program.

But if he asks, "Just what is the purpose of all this activity? What do you hope to accomplish by it?" he gets a vague answer from the students and a not very clear one from teachers and administrators. From the educators he may hear something about "the whole child" or "the well-rounded man" and perhaps something about "adjustment" and the importance of "getting along with people." He discovers that some of the high-school students are preparing for college while others are working to "develop a marketable skill." From the teachers of academic subjects he may hear some mention of the importance of "transmitting our cultural heritage" and of "critical thinking." But he finds little agreement on the goals of education and not much clarity of thought regarding them.

SOURCE: Paul Woodring, *Introduction to American Education* (New York: Harcourt Brace Jovanovich, Inc., 1965), pp. 38–52. Copyright © 1965 by Harcourt Brace Jovanovich, Inc. Reprinted by permission of the publisher.

For biographical data on Paul Woodring, see Selection 3.

Some Conflicting Views

There is no lack of strongly held opinions on what the goals of education ought to be—almost everyone, whether he is a parent, teacher, philosopher, or pupil, has an opinion. But, in a pluralistic society, opinions differ so widely that it is difficult to reach a consensus on which a stable policy can be based.

Amateurs who set out to state the goals of education often find themselves making a list of subjects—history, science, literature, grammar, and the three R's. Professionals sometimes make the same mistake. But the subjects of instruction are not goals. They are means toward ends. And we cannot make wise decisions about the means until we know what the ends are to be. We are more likely to achieve clear thinking about goals if, instead of asking what subjects should be studied, we ask what changes we expect to take place in the individual as a result of his education.

Many American parents see education as an opportunity for their children "to get ahead in the world"—to find more congenial and profitable employment, to rise in social position, and to live better. They are impressed by the frequently cited evidence that high-school graduates make more money than dropouts, while college graduates make still more. They are understandably prone to judge the school's program by what it does for their own children rather than by what it does for the nation or the culture.

Educators, throughout history, have accepted responsibility for promoting the child's mental development and increasing his range of knowledge. But the great majority of schools have also accepted moral training and character-building as educational goals. Since ancient times, many schools have also assumed responsibility for the development of health and vigor through sports.

Traditionally the activities promoted by schools have been divided into two parts: the curriculum, which is designed to achieve those goals considered essential, and extracurricular activities, which usually are elective because they are rated as less important.

During the first half of the twentieth century a strong case was made for eliminating the distinction and for making all parts of the school program a part of the curriculum. This reflected a change in goals. The schools had accepted many new responsibilities, and educators had grown reluctant to say which were more important than the others because they had accepted responsibility for the development of the "whole child." They cited psychological evidence that all aspects of a child's development—physical, mental, moral, emotional, and social—are interrelated and that each influences all the others.

An uncritical acceptance of the "whole child" concept led many teachers to believe that they must accept as much responsibility for the child's social life and recreation, and for his physical and mental health, as for his intellectual development. This does not logically follow.

The fact that a child develops as a whole does not mean that the school, or any other one institution, must accept the full responsibility. It is true that when the child comes to school he brings with him his hopes, fears, and aspirations as well as his physical and emotional adjustments and maladjustments. The teacher must be sensitive to these because they may interfere with the child's capacity for learning. The school, as an institution, may properly accept some degree of responsibility for the child's health and recreation if the parents and the community so desire. If it is a boarding school, it must accept a very large share of the responsibility.

But the American public school is a day school which the child attends for only a part of each day and for only about half the days of the year. The whole child comes to school, but in the middle of the afternoon the whole child goes to his home where he spends many more hours than he does at school. Obviously, his parents must accept the major responsibility for many aspects of his development.

During the 1950s many parents joined with critics who were protesting that many schools had accepted so many different responsibilities that the energies of teachers were being diverted from the traditional responsibility for academic learning and intellectual development. A good many teachers and educational leaders were ready to agree that a clearer distinction should be made between the responsibilities of teachers and those of parents. Although schools still continue to accept a wide range of responsibilities, the current trend is toward a reestablishment of priorities and a greater emphasis on academic learning.

During the 1940s one group of educators had taken the position that the child's adjustment to his physical and social environment should be the major goal of education. This view, too, came under sharp attack in the 1950s. It was pointed out that social adjustment is too easily confused with conformity, that adjustment to the world of today is poor preparation for living in the world of tomorrow, and that the educated man should be prepared to change and improve the world rather than to adapt himself to it uncritically.

In recent years Admiral Hyman Rickover has become the spokesman for a group of Americans who believe we must shift the emphasis from personal to national goals. Alarmed by the threat of atomic annihilation, they see national survival as an end—perhaps *the* end—of education. They contend that unless we survive as a free nation all other goals are futile. They hold that only an improved educational system, specifically designed to recognize and nourish scientific and technological talent and leadership, can save us. This concern was reflected in the National Defense Education Act of 1958, which provided for better selection of talent and improved instruction in mathematics, science, and foreign languages but gave no assistance whatever to the other liberal studies.

Many historians and classicists, as well as some educational philosophers, are convinced that even national survival is too limited a goal. Those who take the long view are convinced that the proper goal of education is cultural continuity. They contend that a knowledge of the history, literature, philosophy, art, and science of the past is the best possible preparation for the future, because it enables the child to participate fully in his culture, to build upon the past, and to avoid the mistakes of his ancestors. Of all the views of education this is the most stable and persistent.

Schools that have tried to work toward all these goals at once have found it difficult, both because time and facilities are limited and because the goals are not entirely compatible. Until priorities are established, teachers do not know where to place the major emphasis, and school administrators have no logical basis for rejecting the demands of those who ask the schools to add endlessly to their already vast range of activities. The effort to do everything that anyone wants done is one of the major problems besetting American schools today. If we are unclear about our objectives, we are likely to try to do too many things and to run the risk of doing nothing well.

Obviously the schools within our complex system may properly have a wide variety of goals that differ from institution to institution. The goals of an elementary school are somewhat different from those of a secondary school or a college. The goals of American education as a whole must be much broader and more comprehensive than those of any one school or type of school. Yet it seems clear that there should be some unity of purpose and some agreement on priorities in the elementary and secondary schools that children are required to attend.

The Responsibility for Policy-Making

The adjectives "parochial," "independent," and "public" indicate the kinds of control under which schools operate as well as the sources of their support. The policy of a parochial school is controlled by a religious group, and its goals must be consistent with those of the group. The goals of an independent school are usually set by the founder, though they may be greatly altered over the years by governing boards responsive to the pressures of alumni, parents, and potential donors.

The enormously complex forces that mold policy in a public school are often not apparent to an outsider. In a strictly legal sense, each state has control over the public schools within its boundaries. Some state legislatures are much more prone to exercise this authority than others, but the legislatures of all states have at some time passed compulsory-attendance laws and laws setting standards for teacher certification. Some have gone much further. A state legislature may even prescribe the curriculum if it wishes to do so. Several state legislatures, at the urging of special-interest groups, have passed laws requiring specified amounts of instruction in certain subjects. Educators, almost unanimously, oppose such curriculum-making by legislatures, because the construction of a sound curriculum requires greater professional knowledge and more time than a legislature can give it.

Within the limits imposed by state law, local school boards (which in most cases are elected by the people) have authority over the schools. Some boards choose to exercise much broader authority than others. In the larger cities the boards, traditionally, have concentrated their attention on problems of school finance and building construction and have delegated to superintendents the problems of selecting teachers and planning the curriculum. School boards in smaller towns often are less willing to delegate full responsibility to their superintendents. Some have been prone to take an active part in administrative decisions that would in a larger city be left to superintendents and principals.

But the full and truthful answer to the question "Who makes school policy?" is not revealed by a description of the legal structure. School laws are rarely written by members of the state legislature. More often they are drawn up by state school boards, teachers' organizations, taxpayers' organizations, or some other group and then passed by the legislature after a hearing. The individuals and groups that appear in these legislative hearings play a large role in making school policy.

Every school board responds to some extent to pressures from citizens' groups, patriotic and religious organizations, minority groups, organized labor, business and industrial organizations, professional groups, and the local and national press, radio, and television. There is nothing reprehensible about this—this is the way democracy works—but the fact that schools are vulnerable to so many conflicting influences makes it difficult for them to establish consistent policies based on preestablished goals.

Over the years, a few respected educators who have commanded large audiences—Horace Mann, John Dewey, and James Conant, for example—have played a role in determining policy by influencing the thinking of parents and teachers. On the local level, many lesser educational leaders have played a part through the force of their personalities and the clarity of their ideas. Both those who are critical of the schools and those who propose innovations also influence school policy.

There are counterpressures that make for some degree of stability. Regional accrediting agencies, though they have no legal authority, tend to stabilize the policies of high schools, since few school boards or superintendents will risk having their schools removed from the "accredited" lists. Colleges, by means of their entrance requirements, exert a great deal of control over the high-school curriculum, particularly in those communities from which many graduates seek admission to colleges with rigorous entrance standards. Tradition alone is a powerful stabilizing influence. Often it makes for too much rigidity and resistance to change. The fact that certain subjects have long been taught at certain levels and in certain ways is accepted by many people, including parents, administrators, teachers, and students, as sufficient reason for continuing to teach them that way.

It is not surprising that a school board, faced with all these countervailing forces, finds it difficult to establish school policy. And, if the board passes the responsibility on to professional educators, the educators find decision-making no less difficult.

Decisions about goals cannot be made by asking all the people in a community to decide. If all citizens were asked to indicate their choices of goals, the list would be riddled with inconsistencies. If all were asked, "Do you want the schools to give more attention to the three R's in the elementary school and to the academic subjects in high school?" it seems likely that the majority would answer yes. But if the same citizens were asked, "Should the schools give more attention to driver education, health, and vocational training?" there is little doubt that many again would say yes, ignoring the fact that more attention to these things would mean less emphasis on the academic skills.

Because the public schools belong to the people, the philosophy that governs them must be consistent with the will of the people. Though decisions about goals cannot be made by the total electorate, whoever makes them must do so in the public interest. And the public interest, in the words of Walter Lippmann, "may be presumed to be what men would choose if they saw clearly, thought rationally, acted disinterestedly and benevolently."

The philosophy that governs the public schools must reflect the concept of the good life held by the majority of our people. Because ours is a pluralistic nation, it must allow for diversity; because we live in an evolving culture, it must provide for change. Yet our educational philosophy cannot merely reflect the shifting whims of an uncertain people; it must have deep roots and possess the stability provided by those roots.

Comprehensive Lists of Goals

Local school boards, because of their vulnerability to local pressures, need the guidance and support of those who are in a position to take a broader and more long-range view and who have taken the time to inquire deeply into educational problems. In an effort to assist local boards in formulating policy, numerous professional and lay groups have drawn up lists of goals considered appropriate for the public schools. Some of these statements have been much more useful than others.

The most comprehensive list was that prepared in 1938 by the Educational Policies Commission—a distinguished body of men and women who, at that time, were among the leaders of American education. Stated in terms of the characteristics that an educated person should possess, the list was made up of forty-three items that included everything from the ability to read, to good judgment in spending money, good health, and eagerness to be "a participant and spectator in many sports and other pastimes.[1]

Though it was widely quoted, because of the great prestige of the Educational Policies Commission, this list did not prove to be very useful either to school boards or teachers. It seemed to justify as an *educational* objective everything that even the most visionary person could suggest as an appropriate school activity. It opened the door to all kinds of pressures on the schools to accept ever-increasing responsibilities. There was something here for everyone, no matter what his view of education might be. It is possible that the American people would accept such a list as a statement of the good society, but it is most unlikely that they would agree that everything on the list ought to be a responsibility of the school.

Since the Second World War, laymen have shown increasing interest in educational problems and have joined with educators in their efforts to restate and clarify educational objectives. One result of this interest was the White House Conference on Education of 1955, which included 1,800 delegates from all parts of the nation. The report of this conference includes the following statement of the schools' responsibilities:

It is the consensus of these groups that the schools should continue to develop:
1. The fundamental skills of communication—reading, writing, spelling, as well as other elements of effective oral and written expression; the arithmetical and mathematical skills, including problem solving. . . .
2. Appreciation of our democratic heritage.
3. Civic rights and responsibilities and knowledge of American institutions.
4. Respect and appreciation for human values and for the beliefs of others.
5. Ability to think and evaluate constructively and creatively.
6. Effective work habits and self-discipline.
7. Social competency as a contributing member of his family and community.
8. Ethical behavior based on a sense of moral and spiritual values.
9. Intellectual curiosity and eagerness for life-long learning.
10. Esthetic appreciation and self-expression in the arts.
11. Physical and mental health.
12. Wise use of time, including constructive leisure pursuits.

[1] *The Purposes of Education in American Democracy* (Educational Policies Commission, Washington, D.C., 1938), pp. 50, 72, 90, 108.

13. Understanding of the physical world and man's relation to it as represented through basic knowledge of the sciences.

14. Awareness of our relationship with the world community.

It is significant of the changes in emphasis that occurred between 1938 and 1955 that the White House Conference list (which is much shorter than the earlier one) omits such goals as "efficiency in buying," "consumer protection," and "courtesy," which were stressed in 1938. And we are no longer told that every educated person must be a participant in "many sports and pastimes."

But the White House Conference Report still has serious limitations that reduce its usefulness to teachers and school boards. It fails to discriminate between such primary goals as the ability to think and to communicate through the written word, and secondary goals, such as health, for which another profession bears the major responsibility.

The White House Conference stressed the need for priorities: "We recommend that school authorities emphasize the importance of priorities in education. . . . It is essential that schools pursue a policy of giving children first things first." But the list of goals did not indicate clearly what those priorities should be.

A third statement of goals appears in the report of the NEA's "Project on Instruction." In 1959 the National Education Association inaugurated a massive project and instructed its director and staff to "make thoughtful and creative recommendations to serve as a guide to the profession and the public in their combined efforts to study and improve the quality of the instructional program in the schools."

The overview volume of the report, published in 1963, takes a further step toward the establishment of priorities for the schools:

Priorities for the schools are the teaching of skills in reading, composition, listening, speaking (both native and foreign languages), and computation . . . ways of creative and disciplined thinking, including methods of inquiry and application of knowledge . . . competence in self-instruction and independent learning . . . fundamental understanding of the humanities and the arts, the social and natural sciences, and mathematics . . . appreciation of a discriminating taste in literature, music, and the visual arts . . . instruction in health and physical education.

Responsibilities best met by joint efforts of the school and other social agencies include: development of values and ideals . . . social and civic competence . . . vocational preparation.

The decision to include or exclude particular school subjects or outside-of-class activities should be based on: (1) the priorities assigned to the school and to other agencies; (2) data about learners and society, and developments in the academic disciplines; (3) the human and material resources available in the school and community.[2]

[2] *Deciding What to Teach*, NEA Project on Instruction (National Education Association, Washington, D.C., 1963).

The fact that this statement lists goals in the order of their priorities, and the fact that it distinguishes sharply between responsibilities specific to the schools and those properly shared with other social agencies make it more useful to teachers than were the earlier lists.

Vocational Competence
as an Educational Goal

In a broad sense, nearly all education is preparation for work. The child learning to read and write is taking the first step toward preparing himself for a wide range of vocations. A knowledge of mathematics, science, and English is essential preparation for many of the jobs available today.

Preparation for the professions has always been a major goal of universities. Some of the earliest institutions of higher learning were established to prepare boys for the priesthood, and many European universities have long been organized into faculties of medicine, law, theology, and philosophy.

Because the learned professions rest upon substantial bodies of scholarly knowledge, a university may prepare students for them without departing from its traditional academic and intellectual emphasis. But when a college or a high school undertakes to prepare students for one of the nonprofessional vocations—machine operation, auto-mechanics, carpentry, or beauty culture—it must introduce courses foreign to the traditions of secondary and higher education. The demand for such courses has led to widespread controversy between those who prefer to retain the academic and intellectual goals of education and those who wish to provide education of a more immediately practical nature.

This controversy has a long history, but the opposition of academic scholars has not prevented the establishment of vocational schools. Some of the early private academies offered vocational training, and some of the first public secondary schools were "manual training high schools." The Smith-Hughes Act of 1916 provided federal support for vocational training, and since that time most public high schools have offered courses in agriculture, home economics, and the skilled trades. Recently, numerous educators have insisted that every student should have an opportunity to develop a "marketable skill" before he graduates from high school.

Since the passage of the Land Grant College Act of 1862 many American colleges and universities have offered courses in agriculture and the mechanical arts as well as courses in business education. More recently, many junior colleges have offered a still wider variety of vocational courses.

This vocational emphasis has been vigorously criticized by educators who fear that it will weaken the academic program. No one denies the need for vocational skills, but there is serious disagreement about whether such skills should be acquired in high school and college, in the technical and trade schools that students enter after completing their academic education, or in industrial apprenticeship programs.

Critics of high-school vocational courses point out that the jobs which require technical training also require a firm grounding in the basic academic subjects. If this is not gained in high school it is not likely to be gained anywhere, because it is much easier for an adult to learn to operate a new machine on the job than it is for him to repair his deficiencies in mathematics, physics, or English after he leaves school. For students who do not go on to college, the high school is the last opportunity to study the academic subjects with the assistance of a teacher. If they spend their high-school years in vocational courses, their liberal education is neglected and its lack may later restrict both their vocational opportunities and their capacity to take full advantage of life in a civilized community.

It has also been pointed out that our technology is changing so rapidly that many students now in school will spend their adult lives in jobs that do not exist today, cannot yet be predicted, and consequently cannot be prepared for. Although it may be helpful for an adolescent to take an exploratory vocational course in high school, it is not appropriate for him to undertake extensive vocational training until he has made a firm vocational choice. It is a misuse of his time and of educational resources, for example, for a boy to devote a major portion of his high-school years to vocational agriculture if he later changes his mind and moves to a city to work in a factory or an office. Yet many farm boys have done exactly that.

Vocational training is sometimes proposed as an alternative for students who are unable to comprehend the academic subjects taught in high school. Some urban high schools now offer courses in preparation for the service professions that do not require a high level of academic aptitude. Most of the vocational courses commonly offered in high school, however, prepare students for the skilled trades, and vocational teachers vigorously oppose opening such courses to boys and girls of low intelligence. They point out that the skilled trades require a fair amount of general intelligence as well as a knowledge of mathematics and science. A carpenter must be able to compute the length of a rafter which is the hypotenuse of a right-angle triangle. An electrician must know the meaning of kilowatts, amperes, and ohms. The courses that prepare students for these trades are not for slow learners.

In spite of these criticisms, vocational courses are firmly established in high schools, and it seems probable that their number and variety will continue to expand. It is essential, however, that the vocational courses offered in high school be broad and general rather than narrow and specific, in order to prepare students for changes in the kinds of work available. The time devoted to vocational training should be limited to a small proportion of the total time in high school, so that students may have an opportunity to gain the liberating knowledge and understanding of man and his world which are essential to free men in a free nation.

Liberal Education

Liberal education is designed to develop human beings to their fullest capacity rather than to prepare them for trades or professions. Its aim is to teach each man to think for himself and to make wise independent decisions. It is called "liberal" because its purpose is to liberate men from the bonds of ignorance, prejudice, and provincialism.

This view of education appeared in Athens in the fifth and fourth centuries B.C. It has undergone many changes over the years and has taken many forms. At times it has almost been lost, but it has a vitality all its own which recurrently brings it to the fore. It is doubtful that a self-governing nation can maintain its free institutions without schools which are based on the liberal tradition.

In ancient Greece liberal education was considered appropriate only for citizens; and in Athens, where there were many slaves, only a minority of the people were eligible for such an education. But today, in the United States and in many other nations, all men and women are eligible for citizenship. Consequently, the liberal view of education now is appropriate for all.

Although the American liberal-arts college takes its name from the liberal view of education, such education is not to be identified with any single kind of college or, indeed, even with higher education. Much education that is truly liberal in nature is available in elementary and secondary schools and even in vocational schools, while some of the courses offered by liberal-arts colleges are not liberal in the classic sense but are closely related to the vocational goals of education. It is in the better liberal-arts colleges, however, that the liberal view of education finds its foremost defenders.

One of the clearest and most comprehensive of recent statements of the meaning of liberal education is found in a report of the School and College Study of General Education, which synthesizes the views of representatives of three universities (Harvard, Yale, and Princeton), and three independent secondary schools (Andover, Exeter, and Lawrenceville). The fact that this statement is found in a report on "general education" suggests that general education, in its best form, is not greatly different from liberal education in its best form:

The liberally educated man is articulate, both in speech and writing. He has a feel for language, a respect for clarity and directness of expression, and a knowledge of some language other than his own. He is at home in the world of quantity, number, and measurement. He thinks rationally, logically, objectively, and knows the difference between fact and opinion. When the occasion demands, however, his thought is imaginative and creative rather than logical. He is perceptive, sensitive to form, and affected by beauty. His mind is flexible and adaptable, curious and independent. He knows a good deal about the world of nature and the world of man, about the culture of which he is a part, but he is never merely "well-informed." He can use what he knows, with judgment and discrimination. He thinks of his business or profession, his family life, and his avocations as parts of a larger whole, parts of a purpose which he has made his own. Whether making a professional or a personal decision, he acts with maturity, balance, and perspective, which come ultimately from his knowledge of other persons, other problems, other times and places. He has convictions, which are reasoned, although he cannot always prove them. He is tolerant about the beliefs of others because he respects sincerity and is not afraid of ideas. He has values, and he can communicate them to others not only by word but by example. His personal standards are high; nothing short of excellence will satisfy him. But service to his society or to his God, not personal satisfaction alone, is the purpose of his excelling. Above all, the liberally educated man is never a type. He is always a unique person, vivid in his distinction from other similarly educated persons, while sharing with them the traits we have mentioned.

This statement is notable in several respects. Despite its breadth and comprehensiveness it makes no mention of training for specific vocations. It says nothing at all about social adjustment or conformity; on the contrary, it calls attention to the uniqueness of each educated individual. It emphasizes broad knowledge and understanding rather than rote learning and memorization. It emphasizes the importance of clarity of expression and stresses values.

Liberal education, thus defined, is a sound, indeed an essential, goal for all schools. It should be initiated in the elementary school, continued in the high school, and brought to a higher level in college. It can be combined with other goals but it cannot safely be neglected.

6

Aims of Education

ALFRED NORTH WHITEHEAD

The aims that should govern education as Whitehead perceives them reflect the influence of the British organization of curriculum, which requires the study in depth of a few broad subjects. Whitehead endorses eliminating "inert ideas" and seeking to produce men of culture and expert knowledge. You may notice that Whitehead's discussion of education is in sharp contrast to the discussion of educational goals by Woodring in the previous selection. Both authors, however, share a deep concern and recognize the need for giving serious considerations to the purposes of education. It is essential that you analyze Whitehead's views of knowledge and learning as you seek to understand such concepts as "inert ideas" and his "seamless coat of learning."

CULTURE is activity of thought, and receptiveness to beauty and humane feeling. Scraps of information have nothing to do with it. A merely well-informed man is the most useless bore on God's earth. What we should aim at producing is men who possess both culture and expert knowledge in some special direction. Their expert knowledge will give them the ground to start from, and their culture will lead them as deep as philosophy and as high as art. We have to remember that the valuable intellectual development is self-development, and that it mostly takes place between the ages of sixteen and thirty. As to training, the most important part is given by mothers before the age of twelve. A saying due to Archbishop Temple illustrates my meaning. Surprise was expressed at the success in after-life of a man, who as a boy at Rugby had been somewhat undistinguished. He answered, "It is not what they are at eighteen, it is what they become afterwards that matters."

In training a child to activity of thought, above all things we must beware of what I will call "inert ideas"—that is to say, ideas that are merely re-

SOURCE: Alfred North Whitehead, *The Aims of Education* (New York: The Macmillan Company, 1929), pp. 1–14. Copyright 1929 by the Macmillan Company, renewed 1957 by Evelyn Whitehead. Reprinted by permission of the publisher.

The late Alfred North Whitehead received his university education in England and taught there for many years. Coming to the United States in 1924, he taught philosophy at Harvard University for twelve years, after which time he retired to an emeritus professorship. He distinguished himself in his early years as a logician and mathematician, co-authoring, with Bertrand Russell, *Principia Mathematica*. He was also internationally known for his writings in philosophy and education.

ceived into the mind without being utilised, or tested, or thrown into fresh combinations.

In the history of education, the most striking phenomenon is that schools of learning, which at one epoch are alive with a ferment of genius, in a succeeding generation exhibit merely pedantry and routine. The reason is, that they are overladen with inert ideas. Education with inert ideas is not only useless: it is, above all things, harmful—*Corruptio optimi, pessima.* Except at rare intervals of intellectual ferment, education in the past has been radically infected with inert ideas. That is the reason why uneducated clever women, who have seen much of the world, are in middle life so much the most cultured part of the community. They have been saved from this horrible burden of inert ideas. Every intellectual revolution which has ever stirred humanity into greatness has been a passionate protest against inert ideas. Then, alas, with pathetic ignorance of human psychology, it has proceeded by some educational scheme to bind humanity afresh with inert ideas of its own fashioning.

Let us now ask how in our system of education we are to guard against this mental dryrot. We enunciate two educational commandments, "Do not teach too many subjects," and again, "What you teach, teach thoroughly."

The result of teaching small parts of a large number of subjects is the passive reception of disconnected ideas, not illumined with any spark of vitality. Let the main ideas which are introduced into a child's education be few and important, and let them be thrown into every combination possible. The child should make them his own, and should understand their application here and now in the circumstances of his actual life. From the very beginning of his education, the child should experience the joy of discovery. The discovery which he has to make, is that general ideas give an understanding of that stream of events which pours through his life, which is his life. By understanding I mean more than a mere logical analysis, though that is included. I mean "understanding" in the sense in which it is used in the French proverb, "To understand all, is to forgive all." Pedants sneer at an education which is useful. But if education is not useful, what is it? Is it a talent, to be hidden away in a napkin? Of course, education should be useful, whatever your aim in life. It was useful to Saint Augustine and it was useful to Napoleon. It is useful, because understanding is useful.

I pass lightly over that understanding which should be given by the literary side of education. Nor do I wish to be supposed to pronounce on the relative merits of a classical or a modern curriculum. I would only remark that the understanding which we want is an understanding of an insistent present. The only use of a knowledge of the past is to equip us for the present. No more deadly harm can be done to young minds than by depreciation of the present. The present contains all that there is. It is holy ground; for it is the past, and it is the future. At the same time it must be observed that an age is no less past if it existed two hundred years ago than if it existed two thousand years ago. Do not be deceived by the pedantry of dates. The ages of Shakespeare and Molière are no less past than are the ages of Sophocles and of Virgil. The communion of saints is a great and inspiring assemblage, but it has only one possible hall of meeting, and that is, the present; and the mere lapse of time through which any particular group of saints must travel to reach that meeting-place, makes very little difference.

Passing now to the scientific and logical side of education, we remember that here also ideas which are not utilised are positively harmful. By utilising an idea, I mean relating it to that stream, compounded of sense perceptions, feelings, hopes, desires, and of mental activities adjusting thought to thought, which forms our life. I can imagine a set of beings which might fortify their souls by passively reviewing disconnected ideas. Humanity is not built that way—except perhaps some editors of newspapers.

In scientific training, the first thing to do with an idea is to prove it. But allow me for one moment to extend the meaning of "prove"; I mean—to prove its worth. Now an idea is not worth much unless the propositions in which it is embodied are true. Accordingly an essential part of the proof of an idea is the proof, either by experiment or by logic, of the truth of the propositions. But it is not essential that this proof of the truth should constitute the first introduction to the idea. After all, its assertion by the authority of respectable teachers is sufficient evidence to begin with. In our first contact with a set of propositions, we commence by appreciating their importance. That is what we all do in after-life. We do not attempt, in the strict sense, to prove or to disprove anything, unless its importance makes it worthy of that honour. These two processes of proof, in the narrow sense, and of appreciation, do not require a rigid separation in time. Both can be proceeded with nearly concurrently. But in so far as either process must have the priority, it should be that of appreciation by use.

Furthermore, we should not endeavour to use propositions in isolation. Emphatically I do not mean, a neat little set of experiments to illustrate Proposition I and then the proof of Proposition I, a neat little set of experiments to illustrate Proposition II and then the proof of Proposition II, and so on to the end of the book. Nothing could be more boring. Interrelated truths are utilised *en bloc,* and the various propositions are employed in any order, and with any reiteration. Choose some important applications of your theoretical subject; and study them concurrently with the systematic theoretical exposition. Keep the theoretical exposition short and simple, but let it be strict and rigid so far as it goes. It should not be too long for it to be easily known with thoroughness and accuracy. The consequences of a plethora of half-digested theoretical knowledge are deplorable. Also the theory should not be muddled up with the practice. The child should have no doubt when it is proving and when it is utilising. My point is that what is proved should be utilised, and that what is utilised should—so far as is practicable—be proved. I am far from asserting that proof and utilisation are the same thing.

At this point of my discourse, I can most directly carry forward my argument in the outward form of a digression. We are only just realising that the art and science of education require a genius and a study of their own; and that this genius and this science are more than a bare knowledge of some branch of science or of literature. This truth was partially perceived in the past generation; and headmasters, somewhat crudely, were apt to supersede learning in their colleagues by requiring left-hand bowling and a taste for football. But culture is more than cricket, and more than football, and more than extent of knowledge.

Education is the acquisition of the art of the utilisation of knowledge. This is an art very difficult to impart. Whenever a text-book is written of real educational worth, you may be quite certain that some reviewer will say that it will be difficult to teach from it. Of course it will be difficult to teach from it. If it were easy, the book ought to be burned; for it cannot be educational. In education, as elsewhere, the broad primrose path leads to a nasty place. This evil path is represented by a book or a set of lectures which will practically enable the student to learn by heart all the questions likely to be asked at the next external examination. And I may say in passing that no educational system is possible unless every question directly asked of a pupil at any examination is either framed or modified by the actual teacher of that pupil in that subject. The external assessor may report on the curriculum or on the performance of the pupils, but never should be allowed to ask the pupil a question which has not been strictly supervised by the actual teacher, or at least inspired by a long conference with him. There are a few exceptions to this rule, but they are exceptions, and could easily be allowed for under the general rule.

We now return to my previous point, that theoretical ideas should always find important applications within the pupil's curriculum. This is not an easy doctrine to apply, but a very hard one. It contains within itself the problem of keeping knowledge alive, of preventing it from becoming inert, which is the central problem of all education.

The best procedure will depend on several factors, none of which can be neglected, namely, the genius of the teacher, the intellectual type of the pupils, their prospects in life, the opportunities offered by the immediate surroundings of the school, and allied factors of this sort. It is for this reason that the uniform external examination is so deadly. We do not denounce it because we are cranks, and like denouncing established things. We are not so childish. Also, of course, such examinations have their use in testing slackness. Our reason of dislike is very definite and very practical. It kills the best part of culture. When you analyse in the light of experience the central task of education, you find that its successful accomplishment depends on a delicate adjustment of many variable factors. The reason is that we are dealing with human minds, and not with dead matter. The evocation of curiosity, of judgment, of the power of mastering a complicated tangle of circumstances, the use of theory in giving foresight in special cases—all these powers are not to be imparted by a set rule embodied in one schedule of examination subjects.

I appeal to you, as practical teachers. With good discipline, it is always possible to pump into the minds of a class a certain quantity of inert knowledge. You take a text-book and make them learn it. So far, so good. The child then knows how to solve a quadratic equation. But what is the point of teaching a child to solve a quadratic equation? There is a traditional answer to this question. It runs thus: The mind is an instrument, you first sharpen it, and then use it; the acquisition of the power of solving a quadratic equation is part of the process of sharpening the mind. Now there is just enough truth in this answer to have made it live through the ages. But for all its half-truth, it embodies a radical error which bids fair to stifle the genius of the modern world. I do not know who was first responsible for this analogy of the mind to a dead instrument. For aught I know, it may have been one of the seven wise men of Greece, or a committee of the whole lot of them. Whoever was the originator, there can be no doubt of the authority which it has acquired by the continuous approval bestowed upon it by eminent persons. But whatever its weight of authority, whatever the high approval which it can quote, I have no hesitation in denouncing it as one of the most fatal, erroneous, and dangerous conceptions ever introduced into the theory of education. The mind is never passive; it is a perpetual activity, delicate, receptive, responsive to stimulus. You cannot postpone its life until you have sharpened it. Whatever interest attaches to your subject-matter must be evoked here and now; whatever powers you are strengthening in the pupil, must be exercised here and now; whatever possibilities of mental life your teaching should impart, must be exhibited here and now. That is the golden rule of education, and a very difficult rule to follow.

The difficulty is just this: the apprehension of general ideas, intellectual habits of mind, and pleasurable interest in mental achievement can be evoked by no form of words, however accurately adjusted. All practical teachers know that education is a patient process of the mastery of details, minute by minute, hour by hour, day by day. There is no royal road to learning through an airy path of brilliant generalisations. There is a proverb about the difficulty of seeing the wood because of the trees. That difficulty is exactly the point which I am enforcing. The problem of education is to make the pupil see the wood by means of the trees.

The solution which I am urging, is to eradicate the fatal disconnection of subjects which kills the vitality of our modern curriculum. There is only one subject-matter for education, and that is Life in all its manifestations. Instead of this single unity, we offer children—Algebra, from which nothing follows; Geometry, from which nothing follows; Science, from which nothing follows; History, from which nothing follows; a Couple of Languages, never mastered; and lastly, most dreary of all, Literature, represented by plays of Shake-speare, with philological notes and short analyses of plot and character to be in substance committed to memory. Can such a list be said to represent Life, as it is known in the midst of the living of it? The best that can be said of it is, that it is a rapid table of contents which a deity might run over in his mind while he was thinking of creating a world, and has not yet determined how to put it together.

Let us now return to quadratic equations. We still have on hand the un-answered question. Why should children be taught their solution? Unless qua-dratic equations fit into a connected curriculum, of course there is no reason to teach anything about them. Furthermore, extensive as should be the place of mathematics in a complete culture, I am a little doubtful whether for many types of boys algebraic solutions of quadratic equations do not lie on the spe-cialist side of mathematics. I may here remind you that as yet I have not said anything of the psychology or the content of the specialism, which is so nec-essary a part of an ideal education. But all that is an evasion of our real question, and I merely state it in order to avoid being misunderstood in my answer.

Quadratic equations are part of algebra, and algebra is the intellectual in-strument which has been created for rendering clear the quantitative aspects of the world. There is no getting out of it. Through and through the world is infected with quantity. To talk sense, is to talk in quantities. It is no use say-ing that the nation is large,—How large? It is no use saying that radium is scarce,—How scarce? You cannot evade quantity. You may fly to poetry and to music, and quantity and number will face you in your rhythms and your octaves. Elegant intellects which despise the theory of quantity, are but half developed. They are more to be pitied than blamed. The scraps of gibberish, which in their school-days were taught to them in the name of algebra, de-serve some contempt.

This question of the degeneration of algebra into gibberish, both in word and in fact, affords a pathetic instance of the uselessness of reforming educa-tional schedules without a clear conception of the attributes which you wish to evoke in the living minds of the children. A few years ago there was an outcry that school algebra was in need of reform, but there was a general agreement that graphs would put everything right. So all sorts of things were extruded, and graphs were introduced. So far as I can see, with no sort of idea behind them, but just graphs. Now every examination paper has one or two questions on graphs. Personally I am an enthusiastic adherent of graphs. But I wonder whether as yet we have gained very much. You cannot put life into any schedule of general education unless you succeed in exhibiting its relation to some essential characteristic of all intelligent or emotional perception. It is a hard saying, but it is true; and I do not see how to make it any easier. In making these little formal alterations you are beaten by the very nature of things. You are pitted against too skilful an adversary, who will see to it that the pea is always under the other thimble.

Reformation must begin at the other end. First, you must make up your mind as to those quantitative aspects of the world which are simple enough to be introduced into general education; then a schedule of algebra should be framed which will about find its exemplification in these applications. We need not fear for our pet graphs, they will be there in plenty when we once begin to treat algebra as a serious means of studying the world. Some of the simplest applications will be found in the quantities which occur in the simplest study of society. The curves of history are more vivid and more informing than the dry catalogues of names and dates which comprise the greater part of that arid school study. What purpose is effected by a catalogue of undistinguished kings and queens? Tom, Dick, or Harry, they are all dead. General resurrections are failures, and are better postponed. The quantitative flux of the forces of modern society is capable of very simple exhibition. Meanwhile, the idea of the variable, of the function, of rate of change, of equations and their solution, of elimination, are being studied as an abstract science for their own sake. Not, of course, in the pompous phrases with which I am alluding to them here, but with that iteration of simple special cases proper to teaching.

If this course be followed, the route from Chaucer to the Black Death, from the Black Death to modern Labour troubles, will connect the tales of the mediaeval pilgrims with the abstract science of algebra, both yielding diverse aspects of that single theme, Life. I know what most of you are thinking at this point. It is that the exact course which I have sketched out is not the particular one which you would have chosen, or even see how to work. I quite agree. I am not claiming that I could do it myself. But your objection is the precise reason why a common external examination system is fatal to education. The process of exhibiting the applications of knowledge must, for its success, essentially depend on the character of the pupils and the genius of the teacher. Of course I have left out the easiest applications with which most of us are more at home. I mean the quantitative sides of sciences, such as mechanics and physics.

Again, in the same connection we plot the statistics of social phenomena against the time. We then eliminate the time between suitable pairs. We can speculate how far we have exhibited a real causal connection, or how far a mere temporal coincidence. We notice that we might have plotted against the time one set of statistics for one country and another set for another country, and thus, with suitable choice of subjects, have obtained graphs which certainly exhibited mere coincidence. Also other graphs exhibit obvious causal connections. We wonder how to discriminate. And so are drawn on as far as we will.

But in considering this description, I must beg you to remember what I have been insisting on above. In the first place, one train of thought will not suit all groups of children. For example, I should expect that artisan children will want something more concrete and, in a sense, swifter than I have set down here. Perhaps I am wrong, but that is what I should guess. In the second place, I am not contemplating one beautiful lecture stimulating, once and for all, an admiring class. That is not the way in which education proceeds. No; all the time the pupils are hard at work solving examples, drawing graphs, and making experiments, until they have a thorough hold on the whole subject. I am describing the interspersed explanations, the directions which should be given to their thoughts. The pupils have got to be made to feel that they are studying something, and are not merely executing intellectual minuets.

Finally, if you are teaching pupils for some general examination, the problem of sound teaching is greatly complicated. Have you ever noticed the zig-zag moulding round a Norman arch? The ancient work is beautiful, the modern work is hideous. The reason is, that the modern work is done to exact measure, the ancient work is varied according to the idiosyncrasy of the workman. Here it is crowded, and there it is expanded. Now the essence of getting pupils through examinations is to give equal weight to all parts of the schedule. But mankind is naturally specialist. One man sees a whole subject, where another can find only a few detached examples. I know that it seems contradictory to allow for specialism in a curriculum especially designed for a broad culture. Without contradictions the world would be simpler, and perhaps duller. But I am certain that in education wherever you exclude specialism you destroy life.

We now come to the other great branch of a general mathematical education, namely Geometry. The same principles apply. The theoretical part should be clear-cut, rigid, short, and important. Every proposition not absolutely necessary to exhibit the main connection of ideas should be cut out, but the great fundamental ideas should be all there. No omission of concepts, such as those of Similarity and Proportion. We must remember that, owing to the aid rendered by the visual presence of a figure, Geometry is a field of unequalled excellence for the exercise of the deductive faculties of reasoning. Then, of course, there follows Geometrical Drawing, with its training for the hand and eye.

But, like Algebra, Geometry and Geometrical Drawing must be extended beyond the mere circle of geometrical ideas. In an industrial neighbourhood, machinery and workshop practice form the appropriate extension. For example, in the London Polytechnics this has been achieved with conspicuous success. For many secondary schools I suggest that surveying and maps are the natural applications. In particular, plane-table surveying should lead pupils to a vivid apprehension of the immediate application of geometric truths. Simple drawing apparatus, a surveyor's chain, and a surveyor's compass, should enable the pupils to rise from the survey and mensuration of a field to the construction of the map of a small district. The best education is to be found in gaining the utmost information from the simplest apparatus. The provision of elaborate instruments is greatly to be deprecated. To have constructed the map of a small district, to have considered its roads, its contours, its geology, its climate, its relation to other districts, the effects on the status of its inhabitants, will teach more history and geography than any knowledge of Perkin Warbeck or of Behren's Straits. I mean not a nebulous lecture on the subject, but a serious investigation in which the real facts are definitely ascertained by the aid of accurate theoretical knowledge. A typical mathematical problem should be: Survey such and such a field, draw a plan of it to such and such a scale, and find the area. It would be quite a good procedure to impart the necessary geometrical propositions without their proofs. Then, concurrently in the same term, the proofs of the propositions would be learnt while the survey was being made.

Fortunately, the specialist side of education presents an easier problem than does the provision of a general culture. For this there are many reasons. One is that many of the principles of procedure to be observed are the same in both cases, and it is unnecessary to recapitulate. Another reason is that specialist training takes place—or should take place—at a more advanced stage of the pupil's course, and thus there is easier material to work upon. But undoubtedly the chief reason is that the specialist study is normally a study of peculiar interest to the student. He is studying it because, for some reason, he wants to know it. This makes all the difference. The general culture is designed to foster an activity of mind; the specialist course utilises this activity. But it does not do to lay too much stress on these neat antitheses. As we have already seen, in the general course foci of special interest will arise; and similarly in the special study, the external connections of the subject drag thought outwards.

Again, there is not one course of study which merely gives general culture, and another which gives special knowledge. The subjects pursued for the sake of a general education are special subjects specially studied; and, on the other hand, one of the ways of encouraging general mental activity is to foster a special devotion. You may not divide the seamless coat of learning. What education has to impart is an intimate sense for the power of ideas, for the beauty of ideas, and for the structure of ideas, together with a particular body of knowledge which has peculiar reference to the life of the being possessing it.

The appreciation of the structure of ideas is that side of a cultured mind which can only grow under the influence of a special study. I mean that eye for the whole chess-board, for the bearing of one set of ideas on another. Nothing but a special study can give any appreciation for the exact formulation of general ideas, for their relations when formulated, for their service in the comprehension of life. A mind so disciplined should be both more abstract and more concrete. It has been trained in the comprehension of abstract thought and in the analysis of facts.

Finally, there should grow the most austere of all mental qualities; I mean the sense for style. It is an aesthetic sense, based on admiration for the direct attainment of a foreseen end, simply and without waste. Style in art, style in literature, style in science, style in logic, style in practical execution have fundamentally the same aesthetic qualities, namely, attainment and restraint. The love of a subject in itself and for itself, where it is not the sleepy pleasure of pacing a mental quarter-deck, is the love of style as manifested in that study.

Here we are brought back to the position from which we started, the utility of education. Style, in its finest sense, is the last acquirement of the educated mind; it is also the most useful. It pervades the whole being. The administrator with a sense for style hates waste; the engineer with a sense for style economises his material; the artisan with a sense for style prefers good work. Style is the ultimate morality of mind.

But above style, and above knowledge, there is something, a vague shape like fate above the Greek gods. That something is Power. Style is the fashioning of power, the restraining of power. But, after all, the power of attainment of the desired end is fundamental. The first thing is to get there. Do not bother about your style, but solve your problem, justify the ways of God to man, administer your province, or do whatever else is set before you.

Where, then, does style help? In this, with style the end is attained without side issues, without raising undesirable inflammations. With style you attain your end and nothing but your end. With style the effect of your activity is calculable, and foresight is the last gift of gods to men. With style your power is increased, for your mind is not distracted with irrelevancies, and you are more likely to attain your object. Now style is the exclusive privilege of the expert. Whoever heard of the style of an amateur painter, of the style of an amateur poet? Style is always the product of specialist study, the peculiar contribution of specialism to culture.

English education in its present phase suffers from a lack of definite aim, and from an external machinery which kills its vitality. Hitherto in this address I have been considering the aims which should govern education. In this respect England halts between two opinions. It has not decided whether to produce amateurs or experts. The profound change in the world which the nineteenth century has produced is that the growth of knowledge has given foresight. The amateur is essentially a man with appreciation and with immense versatility in mastering a given routine. But he lacks the foresight which comes from special knowledge. The object of this address is to suggest how to produce the expert without loss of the essential virtues of the amateur. The machinery of our secondary education is rigid where it should be yielding, and lax where it should be rigid. Every school is bound on pain of extinction to train its boys for a small set of definite examinations. No headmaster has a free hand to develop his general education or his specialist studies in accordance with the opportunities of his school, which are created by its staff, its environment, its class of boys, and its endowments. I suggest that no system of external tests which aims primarily at examining individual scholars can result in anything but educational waste.

Primarily it is the schools and not the scholars which should be inspected. Each school should grant its own leaving certificates, based on its own curriculum. The standards of these schools should be sampled and corrected. But the first requisite for educational reform is the school as a unit, with its approved curriculum based on its own needs, and evolved by its own staff. If we fail to secure that, we simply fall from one formalism into another, from one dung-hill of inert ideas into another.

In stating that the school is the true educational unit in any national system for the safeguarding of efficiency, I have conceived the alternative system as being the external examination of the individual scholar. But every Scylla is faced by its Charybdis—or in more homely language, there is a ditch on both sides of the road. It will be equally fatal to education if we fall into the hands of a supervising department which is under the impression that it can divide all schools into two or three rigid categories, each type being forced to adopt a rigid curriculum. When I say that the school is the educational unit, I mean exactly what I say, no larger unit, no smaller unit. Each school must have the claim to be considered in relation to its special circumstances. The classifying of schools for some purposes is necessary. But no absolutely rigid curriculum, not modified by its own staff, should be permissible. Exactly the same principles apply, with the proper modifications, to universities and to technical colleges.

When one considers in its length and in its breadth the importance of this question of the education of a nation's young, the broken lives, the defeated hopes, the national failures, which result from the frivolous inertia with which it is treated, it is difficult to restrain within oneself a savage rage. In the conditions of modern life the rule is absolute, the race which does not value trained intelligence is doomed. Not all your heroism, not all your social charm, not all your wit, not all your victories on land or at sea, can move back the finger of fate. To-day we maintain ourselves. To-morrow science will have moved forward yet one more step, and there will be no appeal from the judgment which will then be pronounced on the uneducated.

We can be content with no less than the old summary of educational ideal which has been current at any time from the dawn of our civilisation. The essence of education is that it be religious.

Pray, what is religious education?

A religious education is an education which inculcates duty and reverence. Duty arises from our potential control over the course of events. Where attainable knowledge could have changed the issue ignorance has the guilt of vice. And the foundation of reverence is this perception, that the present holds within itself the complete sum of existence, backwards and forwards, that whole amplitude of time, which is eternity.

7

John Dewey's Challenge to Education

OSCAR HANDLIN

Two selections on John Dewey bring the philosophical readings to an end. Here, Oscar Handlin treats his subject largely as an academic question, while in the following selection, William Kilpatrick presents his personal observations and evaluations of Dewey. Handlin contends that Dewey was striving to reconstruct education on a sound basis, and it is quite probable that Handlin's own interest in social history stimulated a keen awareness of Dewey's contribution to education. Dewey regarded as a serious deficiency in American education the inability of Americans, in general, to adjust their conceptions of education

SOURCE: Oscar Handlin, *John Dewey's Challenge to Education* (New York: Harper & Row, 1959), pp. 39–49. Copyright © 1959 by Harper & Row. Reprinted by permission of the publisher.

Oscar Handlin has been professor of American history at Harvard University since 1954, and editor of the Library of American Biography. Among his best-known books are *The American People in the Twentieth Century, Adventure in Freedom,* and *Race and Nationality in American Life.* In 1952 he received the Pulitzer Prize for *The Uprooted,* a study of the social and personal problems of American immigrants.

to the changing world about them. The irritation felt by Dewey in respect to the divorce of the school from its culture was largely responsible for his achievement of narrowing the gap between the classroom and the world outside it. As you read the challenge that Dewey presented to American education, you should raise questions with regard to current educational assumptions and present-day school programs.

IT WAS the achievement of John Dewey to have couched his criticism of the divorce between experience and education in more meaningful terms. His practical contact with the problems of the schools of the 1880's and 1890's stimulated his philosophical inquiries into the nature of knowledge; and his understanding of the learning process supplied a theoretical basis to his views on proper pedagogy. The development of his ideas was thus meaningfully related to the context of the times in which he lived.

When Dewey came as instructor to the University of Michigan in 1884, he brought with him intellectual attitudes shaped by two forces. His early upbringing in Vermont had been permissive to the point of chaos; the most valuable lessons he had learned had been outside the classroom and independently carried forth. His own training had thus been almost casual and had certainly been free of the rigidity to be imposed on American schools after 1870. Recollections of his experience as a student no doubt influenced his later critical view of what education was becoming in the last quarter of the nineteenth century.

His philosophical background also raised questions with regard to current assumptions. From his graduate work under George S. Morris at Johns Hopkins he carried away a commitment to Hegelian idealism, which nurtured his hostility to dualisms of every sort and left him dubious as to the validity of all such dichotomies as those between education or culture and society or life.[1]

But at Michigan, Dewey's formal philosophical views and his personal memories were challenged by the necessities of instruction and by his immersion in the life of a community. To make his ideas comprehensible to the young men and women in his classrooms was but a fraction of his task. In addition, he had to be aware of the relationship of his work to the world about him; and as a member of the faculty of a state university, he also had to concern himself with the problems of the public school system related to it. President Angell always regarded it as one of the chief duties of the university "to keep in close touch with the state system of public education." That preoccupation was reflected in Dewey's proposal to publish a general

[1] Sidney Hook, *John Dewey, an Intellectual Portrait* (New York, 1939), p. 13; Jerome Nathanson, *John Dewey* (New York, 1951), pp. 10 ff.; Max Eastman, *Heroes I Have Known* (New York, 1942), pp. 278 ff.

"Thought News"; and it emerged also in his earliest books, the core of which was analysis of the ways of knowing. The title of the volume in which he collaborated in 1889 was significant: *Applied Psychology: An Introduction to the Principles and Practices of Education.*[2]

His marriage in 1886 and the move to Chicago in 1894 added to the weight of the practical considerations in the development of his thought. The intellectual associations at the exciting new university were undoubtedly stimulating; but the exposure to the immediate problems of teaching in a great and expanding metropolis were fully as much so. Experiments in new education were already in progress in Chicago; and the Deweys at the Experimental School undoubtedly profited from them. But it is, in any case, clear that the main outlines of their work were set up on a pragmatic rather than a theoretical basis. That is, Dewey began to treat the problems of education not from an abstract, previously defined position of what ought ideally to be, but rather from a concrete estimate of deficiencies that actually existed.[3]

The systematic exploration of these problems did not follow until later. The first extensive exposition of Dewey's position came in the lectures collected as *The School and Society* (1899), a work which was still largely critical and negative. A fuller analysis appeared seventeen years later in *Democracy and Education*. But the general propositions enunciated in that work rested upon a very careful case by case study of particular experiments in the new education. Dewey's general conclusions were thus the products of more than twenty years of experience. His ideas were not formulated in the abstract but through the encounter with the conditions of learning in the United States in the closing decades of the nineteenth century.

The necessity for grappling with a development that had divorced the school and its culture from society and its life was an irritant that compelled Dewey to define his ideas on education. Those ideas were integrally related to his comprehensive conceptions of the character of knowledge, the mind, human nature, the experimental process, and the values of democracy. As he clarified his thoughts on education he also refined his views on these more general philosophical issues.[4]

But his conceptions also had a pragmatic attractiveness that converted many Americans who did not accept or were unfamiliar with the wider impli-

[2] Willinda Savage, "John Dewey and 'Thought News,' " Claude Eggertsen, ed., *Studies in the History of Higher Education in Michigan* (Ann Arbor, 1950), pp. 12 ff.; A. S. Whitney, *History of the Professional Training of Teachers at the University of Michigan* (Ann Arbor, 1931), pp. 34, 35; Max Eastman, *op. cit.*, pp. 291, 292.

[3] P. A. Schilpp, ed., *The Philosophy of John Dewey* (New York, 1951), p. 452; Katherine Mayhew, *The Dewey School* (New York, 1936).

[4] See, in general, G. R. Geiger, *John Dewey in Perspective* (New York, 1958); Morton White, *Social Thought in America* (Boston, 1957), pp. 94 ff.; P. A. Schilpp, *op. cit.*, pp. 419 ff.

cations of his philosophy. His ideas were persuasive because they revealed the evident weaknesses of the schools as they were.

What Was Wrong with American Education

The realm of the classroom in the 1890's was totally set off from the experience of the child who inhabited it. The teachers' lessons encrusted by habit, the seats arranged in formal rows, and the rigid etiquette of behavior all emphasized the difference between school and life. Hence learning consisted of the tedious memorization of data without a meaning immediately clear to the pupil.

Dewey, whose own education as a boy was free of all such rigidity, objected strenuously that these conditions stifled the learning process, for they prevented the student from relating his formal studies to his own development as a whole person.

The educator therefore had to narrow the distance between the classroom and the world outside it. Society was changing rapidly under the impact of urbanization and industrialization, and not always for the better. But the teacher ought not therefore pretend that his pupils still walked along the lanes of an eighteenth-century village back to a rustic farmhouse. He had to take account of the city streets and of the American home as it actually was.[5]

The educator could end the school's isolation by pulling it into a closer relationship with the family and the community. Awareness of the homes, the neighborhood environment, and the business and professional life about it would enable the school to function more effectively and also to widen its influence. By recognizing the unity of the child's experience, it could communicate more directly with him and at the same time break down the pernicious "division into cultured people and workers." It would then cease to be alien and hostile in the eyes of its students and become instead a natural part of their habitat within which they sought satisfaction of their own needs.[6]

In such schools, the "subject matter in history and science and art" could be so presented that it would have "a positive value and a real significance in the child's own life." What was taught would justify itself because it answered questions the student himself asked. He would not be forced to study the map to learn what the world was like; but exploring the world about him, would come to wonder how it looked on the map. History and literature would cease to be the elegant furnishings of an abstract culture; the pupil would be drawn to them out of his own desire to know himself and his ori-

[5] John Dewey, *The School and Society* (Chicago, 1899), pp. 18–22.
[6] John Dewey, *op. cit.*, pp. 38, 82 ff.

gins. Mathematics would no longer be a burdensome exercise in mental discipline but would be sought as a practical way of managing quantities.[7]

Instruction, under such conditions, could be carried forward as a succession of direct experiences on the child's part. From Rousseau, Dewey had learned that education was not something to be forced upon youth. It involved rather a process of growth antedating the pupil's admission to the school and extending beyond his departure from it. In teaching it was essential always to take account of the conditions of learning, to impart the ability to read, to write, and to use figures intelligently in terms that were themselves meaningful and real. That meant at the lower grades an emphasis on activities over abstractions, not as ends in themselves but as means of evoking stimulating questions.[8]

Learning would then become incidental to the process of dealing with authentic situations. Children who played at making things readily learned to weave, but in doing so began to wonder how cotton and wool came to be formed into their own garments. Those who had practice in electing a class president found it natural to inquire how the city elected a mayor.

The school was thus not simply to pander to a child's liking for interesting activities. It was to select those which led him on to a widening of significant achievements. Knowledge of geography, government, history, and arithmetic was acquired through the continual reconstruction of the student's own experiences. As he absorbed the significance of what he did, he was able to direct his attention to ever broader and more meaningful subjects. Furthermore, interest in the achievement of a practical end could steadily be transformed into interest in the process, that is into "thinking things out" intellectually or theoretically. The whole of education could thus be conceived as the process of learning to think through the solution of real problems.[9]

A school firmly oriented in the world of its pupils could dispense with discipline through the external force of keeping order. Children whose interest was actively engaged in their studies did not need policing. They could be permitted more than the usual amount of freedom, not for the purpose of relaxing real discipline, but to make possible the assumption of larger and less artificial responsibilities, the performance of which would evoke order from within.[10]

The establishment of voluntary patterns of obedience not only facilitated the teacher's task; it also emphasized that which was most important in

[7] John Dewey, op. cit., p. 113.

[8] E. C. Moore, "John Dewey's Contributions to Educational Theory," John Dewey, the Man and His Philosophy (Cambridge, 1930), p. 23.

[9] G. R. Geiger, op. cit., pp. 197–198; Sidney Hook, op. cit., pp. 177 ff.

[10] John Dewey, op. cit., pp. 124, 125; John Dewey, Democracy and Education (New York, 1916), p. 138.

education—its moral purpose. "All the aims and manners which are desirable in education are themselves moral. Discipline, natural development, culture, social efficiency, are moral traits—marks of a person who is a worthy member of that society which it is the business of education to further." Education was not simply a preparation for what would later be useful. It was more, "getting from the present the degree and kind of growth there is in it." From the very start therefore the child would become acquainted with, and through his life learn ever better, the relationship of knowledge to conduct. That was the most worthy function of his schooling.[11]

The Relevance of Dewey's Critique

Dewey's central conceptions of education are thus directly related to criticisms of the system that had developed in the United States between the time when he had ended his own schooling in Vermont and the time when he moved to Chicago. The conditions that evoked his revolt have changed radically since 1894; yet his comments have by no means lost their timeliness.

In some sixty years since the experimental school in Chicago opened its doors, John Dewey's ideas have had a profound effect upon American education. Despite the occasional errors in their application to practice and despite the distortions by uncritical enthusiasts, the schools have profited immensely from his influence.

There have been failings, but due largely through a disregard of the spirit of Dewey's intentions. In the hands of mediocre or incompetent teachers, new techniques have sometimes become ends in themselves. Dewey valued the experiment and the laboratory as means through which the pupil could learn by discovery. But when instruction is so routinized that the student knows from the manual what he will find before he puts his eye to the lens, the microscope has added nothing to his education. There is no point to substituting modern for ancient languages if dull teachers make one as dead as the other.

The danger of the abuse of techniques as ends in themselves has certainly been heightened by the tendency in many states to emphasize method over content in the preparation of the teacher. Yet Dewey always insisted that method could not be divorced from content. The subject matter and the means of communicating it were inextricably bound together; and a successful performance depended on the mastery of both. It is ironic now to find Dewey often blamed in retrospect for the proliferation of empty courses in "education" and for the "certification racket" that makes completion of a for-

---

[11] John Dewey, *Democracy and Education*, pp. 362, 417; John Dewey, *School and Society*, pp. 124, 125; John Dewey, *Reconstruction in Philosophy* (New York, 1920), pp. 183–185.

mal quota of methods courses the prerequisite to teacher licensing. "Consider the training schools of teachers," he wrote in 1899. "These occupy at present a somewhat anomolous position for thus they are isolated from the higher subject matter of scholarship, since, upon the whole, their object has been to train persons *how* to teach, rather than *what* to teach." [12]

Much of Dewey's writing was addressed to the problems of the elementary school, which in his day were most pressing. But neither at that nor at any other level did he regard familiarity with techniques as an alternative to command of the substance of subject matter. The two were inseparable at any level, for each acquired meaning from its relationship to the other.

Insofar as they are focused upon these abuses the complaints of the critics of Deweyism have a measure of validity. But the accusation that progressive education has kept Johnny from learning how to read or how to use a slide rule is unfounded and dangerous. It tends also to obscure the genuine improvements that have emanated from his influence.

In 1928, in an article on Soviet education, John Dewey pointed to the significance of the Russian achievement—far earlier than his detractors of thirty years later. But he did not then take, nor would he now have taken, technological proficiency or advances in rocketry as a test of the excellence of an educational system. He was certainly not impressed in the 1930's by the accomplishments of the Nazis in the same fields. Nor would he have overlooked in any comparison the counter-balancing achievements of our own educational system in medicine, in the peaceful branches of science, and in the humanities. [13]

The crucial test, rather, was the extent to which education served as a vital instrument teaching the individual to behave in the world about him. In his own society, Dewey warned that "academic and scholastic, instead of being titles of honor are becoming terms of reproach." He took that as a measure of the isolation of the schools and the negligence of the culture; and he feared that without an immediate reform schools would become empty and ineffective and the culture would be weakened from within. That accounted for the urgency with which he wrote. [14]

Dewey did not intend that his criticisms should become the creed of a sect or party; and he was uncomfortable when the label "Progressive" was attached to his ideas. He directed his revolt not against tradition but against a rather recent development—the gap created by the inability of Americans to adjust their conceptions of education and culture to the terms of the changing

[12] John Dewey, *School and Society*, p. 80.
[13] John Dewey, "Impressions of Soviet Russia IV: What Are the Russian Schools Doing?; V: New Schools for a New Era," *New Republic*, LVII (1928), pp. 64–67, 91–94; P. A. Schilpp, *op. cit.*, p. 471.
[14] John Dewey, *School and Society*, p. 36.

world about them. Unwilling to limit the scope of either education or culture by the lines of an artificial definition, he insisted upon broadening both by re-establishing their relationship to life.[15]

Late in life, reflecting upon the developments of a half-century, he made this clear, when he defined the new education as hostility to "imposition from above," to "learning from texts and teacher," to "acquisition of isolated skills and techniques by drill" to "preparation for a more or less remote future" and to "static aims and materials." Against those aspects of the school of the late nineteenth century he had called for the "expression and cultivation of individuality," for "learning through experience," and for "acquaintance with an ever-changing world." [16]

That much can be ascribed to the reaction against the trends of the 1880's and 1890's. But Dewey had no intention of proceeding entirely upon a basis of rejection. "When external authority is rejected," he pointed out in another connection, "it does not follow that all authority should be rejected, but rather that there is need to search for a more effective source of authority." In his times, the disjunction between the school and society had enshrined external and arbitrary authority in American education. His revolt, which is comprehensible in terms of his times, aimed to end that disjunction and sweep away that authority as a step in the reconstruction of education on a sounder basis.

[15] R. F. Butts and L. A. Cremin, *op. cit.,* pp. 343 ff., 384; L. A. Cremin, "Revolution in American Secondary Education," *Teachers College Record,* LVI (1955), pp. 301 ff.
[16] John Dewey, *Experience and Education* (New York, 1938), p. 56.

8

Personal Reminiscences on Dewey and My Judgment of His Present Influence

WILLIAM H. KILPATRICK

The following selection presents some personal observations and evaluations of John Dewey as a leading figure in philosophy and the philosophy of education. Kilpatrick attempts to place Dewey in his proper perspective among the other great men of the field. As a former student and colleague of Dewey, Kilpatrick is uniquely qualified to write about the study and work by Dewey which brought about his philosophical convictions and resulted in the great impact he had on American education. Of particular interest to future teachers will be the origin of Dewey's own philosophy of life and its relation to his philosophy of education, in which the psychology of William James played a major role.

MY FIRST personal contact with Professor Dewey was in an 1898 summer course in education at the University of Chicago. However, I got little from the course; I was not ready for its thinking and I was not accustomed to Dewey's method of teaching. His practice, as I later learned, was to come to the class with a problem on his mind and sit before the class thinking out loud as he sought to bring creative thinking to bear on his problem.

A monograph by Dewey, "Interest as Related to Will," which I studied two years later under Charles DeGarmo, did have a deep and lasting effect on me and on my thinking. In it Dewey was analyzing a controversy as to the relative educative effect of "interest" and "effort" upon a pupil. The "interest" proponents had perverted the Herbartian doctrine of "interest" into a superficial "sugar-coating" device of "making things interesting"; the "effort" side, led by William T. Harris, charged that such "sugar-coating" would spoil

SOURCE: *School and Society,* October 10, 1959, pp. 374–375. Reprinted by permission of the publisher.

The author (1871–1965) began his teaching career at Mercer University, later serving there as acting president. He was dedicated to public service, serving as chairman of the American Youth for World Youth from 1946 to 1951 and as chairman of the Bureau of Intercultural Education from 1940 to 1951, and participated in numerous other national and international activities. In 1953, he won the Brandeis Award for Humanity Service.

children and was wrong anyway. What was needed was the building of character, and effort was essential to accomplishing this. To secure effort they proposed to coerce children into effort, by threats and punishment when necessary.

Dewey said, in effect, you are both wrong; by sugar-coating you cannot make things effectively interesting: and coerced effort—forcing children to go through motions without putting themselves into what they do—will fail to build character. Especially you have misunderstood the inherent relation between interest and effort; typically, personally felt interest is the first stage of an on-going experience in which correlative personal effort is the effecting stage. Thus, proper interest and proper effort cannot be opposed: they are, in essence, correlative, the one leading to and demanding the other.

At that time, I was a college professor of mathematics, but for several years I had been indulging in education as a side interest. This Cornell experience of Dewey, with its new insight into the educative process as character-building, persuaded me to give up mathematics and center my interest henceforth on education as my life-work. For various good reasons I could not act on my change of interest until 1907, when I received a scholarship to Teachers College, Columbia. Prof. Dewey was then teaching philosophy at Columbia; and for the next three years I took all his courses, having decided meanwhile to major in philosophy of education.

I entered upon my 1907 work with Prof. Dewey thinking that in philosophy he still was a neo-Hegelian. For a time, Dewey—along with many others—had followed this neo-Hegelian line; and I, too, after working in philosophy at Johns Hopkins in 1895–96, had accepted it as my personal outlook. But now I found that Dewey, stressing the conceptions of process, the continuity of nature, and the method of inductive science, had built an entirely new philosophy, later called Experimentalism. As I worked with him during three constructive years, I gave up neo-Hegelianism and accepted instead the new viewpoint, thereby gaining a fresh and invigorating outlook in life and thought.

From that time until Prof. Dewey's death in 1952, I had great satisfaction in the many contacts with him. Dewey read and approved the manuscript of my 1912 book, "The Montessori System Examined." When he himself had finished seven chapters of "Democracy and Education," he turned these over to me for criticism and to suggest other topics for completing the book. I was then teaching a course in Principles of Education; so I made a list of philosophic problems that troubled me in this course and turned them over to Dewey. At first he rejected my list, but later he redefined a number of the problems and these now appear as chapters in the completed book.

Another instance of personal experience with Dewey came after he had retired from Columbia and I meanwhile had accumulated considerable experience in teaching philosophy of education. He was offered a post as visiting professor in philosophy of education. Though his reputation as a creative thinker in both philosophy and philosophy of education was unsurpassed, he felt unsure as to certain practical details of the new post and accordingly came to me for advice. That I was glad to help needs no words here.

As to the origin of Dewey's educational ideas, some thought he had derived these from Rousseau and Froebel. I once asked him about this and he told me explicitly that he had not read either one until after he had formed his educational outlook. He did say in another connection, that he had got help in his educational thinking from Francis W. Parker, who was active in education in Chicago when Dewey came to the University of Chicago. As to the origin of Dewey's philosophy of life (and, consquently, of education), he himself makes it clear that he got his psychology from William James. This means, as Dewey later brought out, that he and James were both deeply indebted to Darwin's "Origin of Species." It seems probable that from this source Dewey derived the conceptions of process, continuity of nature, and the method of inductive science referred to earlier. It also seems that certain important elements in Dewey's outlook—his belief in equality—came from the creative frontier background which he shared in his Vermont family in common with so many other Americans.

As to Dewey's comparative place in the history of philosophy, I place him next to Plato and Aristotle. As to his place in the history of philosophy of education, he is, as I see it, the greatest the world has yet beheld. As to his current influence in education, I place him in company with William James, Francis W. Parker, and Edward L. Thorndike—those who most efficiently have helped to shape our existent American educational thinking.

EVALUATION

F. BRUCE ROSEN, **Philosophy of Education**

1. (a) In what two ways does Rosen view "philosophy"?

   (b) How is the word "philosophy" used today?

   (c) How does the philosopher of today reflect the contemporary use of the term?

   (d) Of what direct value is this kind of philosophy to education?

2. Explain how Rosen regards philosophy to be both the shape and the shaper of our culture, and what happens when it does not fulfill this function.

3. Name the three broad categories into which philosophy is divided and briefly tell with what each deals.

4. (a) Give the definition of the word "culture" as Malinowski, a cultural anthropologist, states it.

   (b) What does Rosen give as the meaning of culture in its broadest sense?

   (c) Why does he believe people in a culture behave as they do?

5. Does Rosen view philosophy of education as a distinct philosophical area of study? Briefly tell what his views are.

6. What four major reasons does Rosen give for requiring a student to study various philosophies?

PAUL WOODRING, **The Goals of Education**

7. (a) How does Woodring think the educational scene appears to a visitor in the United States?

   (b) How is the view explained to the visitor?

8. (a) The "whole child" concept of learning is a trend severely criticized by Woodring. What does he point out as being basically illogical in this concept?

   (b) What is the reason the author believes that parents must accept the major responsibility?

118

9. (a) What three terms does the author use to describe the kinds of controls under which schools operate?

(b) What reasons does the author offer to support his position that decisions about educational goals cannot be made by asking all of the people in the community?

(c) Since the public school system in America belongs to the people, how does this affect decisions on its philosophy?

10. Numerous comprehensive lists of educational goals have been prepared throughout the history of America. Woodring favors the 1963 statement giving an overview of a 1959 NEA report, largely because of the priorities it recognizes. Why does he say this statement is more useful to teachers than some other statements?

11. Woodring concludes his selection with somewhat detailed discussions on vocational and liberal education. What does he say on the following questions?
    (a) What is education in a broad sense?

(b) What two illustrations are given?

(c) What justification is given for universities offering programs which have traditional academic and intellectual emphasis?

(d) What has led to the long-standing controversy over nonprofessional emphasis in high school and universities?

(e) What is basically essential regarding vocational courses?

(f) What is the aim of liberal education?

(g) Why is it called "liberal"?

(h) Where are the foremost defenders of liberal education?

(i) What does the statement in a report of the School and College Study of General Education emphasize?

(j) Where does liberal education belong?

ALFRED NORTH WHITEHEAD, **Aims of Education**

12. Explain (1) Whitehead's main purpose of education, (2) his concept of "inert ideas," (3) his two educational commandments, and (4) his view of the ultimate aim of education.

13. What does Whitehead mean when he says "We should make the pupil see the woods by means of the trees?"

14. (a) What was the only remark Whitehead made on the meaning of "understanding" on the literary side of education?

    (b) What does he see as the only use of a knowledge of the past?

    (c) On the scientific and logical sides of education, what ideas does Whitehead see as positively harmful?

    (d) What does he mean by this?

15. (a) In scientific training what is the first thing one does with an idea?

    (b) What does Whitehead say we are only just now realizing about the art and science of education?

    (c) How does he define education at this point in his writing?

    (d) Where should theoretical ideas find important applications?

    (e) Upon what factors will the best procedure depend?

16. Whitehead discusses the utility of education in considering the aims which should govern education. He states that knowledge, style, and power are acquisitions of the educated mind.
    (a) What does Whitehead mean by "power"?

    (b) How does he define "style"?

    (c) In its finest sense, how does he describe style?

    (d) How does style affect your activity?

    (e) Why does the author regard style as valuable?

17. (a) What two major faults does Whitehead find with English education?

    (b) What is his position with respect to a system of external tests which aims primarily at examining individual scholars?

    (c) What alternative system has he conceived?

18. (a) What does Whitehead give as an absolute rule in the education of any nation?

    (b) How does he see the role of science in the future?

    (c) What, in the final analysis, is the essence of education?

    (d) What is religious education?

OSCAR HANDLIN, **John Dewey's Challenge to Education**

19. Oscar Handlin's interest in social history piqued his keen awareness of the contribution John Dewey made to education. On what basis does Handlin believe Dewey's ideas were meaningful to the times in which Dewey lived?

20. What accounts for Dewey's questioning of all dichotomies between education (or culture) and society (or life)?

21. How were Dewey's formal philosophical views challenged at the University of Michigan, when he taught there?

22. How did Dewey's move from a theoretical to a pragmatic basis affect his treatment of educational problems?

23. Dewey's achievement of bringing together experience and education through a pragmatic approach is the outcome of his irritation with the divorce of the school from its culture. To what conceptions of Dewey's are these ideas integrally related?

24. List some of the major points made by Dewey in regard to what is wrong with American education.

25. (a) What does Handlin give as the ultimate aim of Dewey's revolt against the disjunction between the school and society?

26. (a) In Dewey's new definition of education, which clearly reflects his unwillingness to limit the scope of either education or culture, what specifically is he rejecting?

    (b) What goals is he willing to accept in contrast to the above nineteenth-century aspects?

WILLIAM H. KILPATRICK, **Personal Reminiscences on Dewey and My Judgment of His Present Influence**

27. (a) William Kilpatrick, who later in life became an outstanding educator in his own right, learned little from his first course under Dewey. How does he explain this?

    (b) What was Dewey's usual teaching method and what was its aim?

28. What are the major points discussed by Kilpatrick in his reminiscences on Dewey?

29. (a) What monograph by Dewey had a deep and lasting effect on Kilpatrick?

    (b) What controversial issue does it discuss?

    (c) State the position held by each proponent in the controversy.

    (d) Briefly state what Dewey says on the issue.

30. (a) Briefly trace Dewey's experiences in relation to his philosophy.

    (b) What did his new philosophy stress?

31. In what four ways does the author reveal that he worked professionally with Dewey?

32. (a) What does Dewey say is an origin of his educational thinking?

    (b) Who influenced his own philosophy of life?

33. (a) What does this reveal about both Dewey and William James?

    (b) What three aspects basic to Dewey's educational philosophy could also have come from this same source?

34. In what way does Kilpatrick think the creative frontier of Dewey's life might have affected his beliefs?

35. Where does Kilpatrick envision Dewey's place in the history of (a) philosophy and (b) philosophy of education?

36. Where does the author place Dewey in relation to his current influence in education?

FOR FURTHER READING

Arnstine, Donald, *Philosophy of Education* (New York: Harper & Row, 1967).
An analysis of various theories of learning and teaching, which delves into options of their philosophical assumptions and their social consequences.

Frasier, James E., "Philosophical Foundations of American Education," *An Introduction to the Study of Education,* 3d ed. (New York: Harper & Row, 1965).
Describes the need for the student to be developing a clear-cut philosophy of his own as he prepares to teach. The importance of this need is based on the fact that a teacher takes his philosophy with him when he enters the classroom, that is, it is reflected in the way he thinks about the problems of education and the teaching profession.

Kneller, George, "Contemporary Educational Theories," *Foundations of Education,* 2d ed. (New York: John Wiley & Sons, 1967).
A philosophical discussion of educational theories examining two central meanings of theory and exploring theories that lead to programs of reform. The author regards education as a highly practical field and traces the problems of education to roots in philosophy. He also admonishes any educator who does not use philosophy, stating that he is inevitably superficial.

Stinnett, T. M., "The Current Status of the Teaching Profession," *The Profession of Teaching* (Washington, D.C.: The Center for Applied Research in Education, 1962).
Stinnett gives the reader a picture of teaching as a profession as it is today, critically evaluating the current status of the profession.

Ulich, Robert, *Philosophy of Education* (New York: American Book Company, 1961).
Deeply held convictions on philosophical issues and aspects of education are reflected in this volume. As Ulich states in his preface, "every prospective teacher (and indeed, every intelligent citizen in a democracy) should, sooner or later, think about" these things.

Psychology

9

Psychology and the Teaching Art

WILLIAM JAMES

America's foremost psychologist at the end of the nineteenth century, and often recognized by many as the father of pragmatism, William James, in his Talks to Teachers *(1879), made one of the earliest efforts to apply the principles of psychology to education. He describes psychology as a means for teachers to experiment, to clarify their knowledge of the subject being taught, and to better understand the pupils they are teaching. The selection that follows is an excellent introduction to the study of psychology and its significance for education.*

IN THE GENERAL ACTIVITY and uprising of ideal interests which every one with an eye for fact can discern all about us in American life, there is perhaps no more promising feature than the fermentation which for a dozen years or more has been going on among the teachers. In whatever sphere of education their functions may lie, there is to be seen among them a really inspiring amount of searching of the heart about the highest concerns of their profession. The renovation of nations begins always at the top, among the reflective members of the State, and spreads slowly outward and downward. The teachers of this country, one may say, have its future in their hands. The earnestness which they at present show in striving to enlighten and strengthen themselves is an index of the nation's probabilities of advance in all ideal directions. The outward organization of education which we have in our United States is perhaps, on the whole, the best organization that exists in

SOURCE: William James, *Talks to Teachers* (New York: W. W. Norton Company, 1958), pp. 21–27. Reprinted by permission of the publisher.

It is often said of William James (1842–1910) that his greatest contribution to psychology was the research he directed that helped establish the discipline as an independent science. His brother, Henry, became equally famous as a novelist, and it has been observed that William wrote psychology like a novelist while Henry wrote novels like a psychologist. Among his major works are *The Principles of Psychology, The Varieties of Religious Experience,* and *Pragmatism.*

any country. The State school systems give a diversity and flexibility, an opportunity for experiment and keenness of competition, nowhere else to be found on such an important scale. The independence of so many of the colleges and universities; the give and take of students and instructors between them all; their emulation, and their happy organic relations to the lower schools; the traditions of instruction in them, evolved from the older American recitation-method (and so avoiding on the one hand the pure lecture-system prevalent in Germany and Scotland, which considers too little the individual student, and yet not involving the sacrifice of the instructor to the individual student, which the English tutorial system would seem too often to entail),—all these things (to say nothing of that coeducation of the sexes in whose benefits so many of us heartily believe), all these things, I say, are most happy features of our scholastic life, and from them the most sanguine auguries may be drawn.

Having so favorable an organization, all we need is to impregnate it with geniuses, to get superior men and women working more and more abundantly in it and for it and at it, and in a generation or two America may well lead the education of the world. I must say that I look forward with no little confidence to the day when that shall be an accomplished fact.

No one has profited more by the fermentation of which I speak, in pedagogical circles, than we psychologists. The desire of the schoolteachers for a completer professional training, and their aspiration toward the 'professional' spirit in their work, have led them more and more to turn to us for light on fundamental principles. And in these few hours which we are to spend together you look to me, I am sure, for information concerning the mind's operations, which may enable you to labor more easily and effectively in the several schoolrooms over which you preside.

Far be it from me to disclaim for psychology all title to such hopes. Psychology ought certainly to give the teacher radical help. And yet I confess that, acquainted as I am with the height of some of your expectations, I feel a little anxious lest, at the end of these simple talks of mine, not a few of you may experience some disappointment at the net results. In other words, I am not sure that you may not be indulging fancies that are just a shade exaggerated. That would not be altogether astonishing, for we have been having something like a 'boom' in psychology in this country. Laboratories and professorships have been founded, and reviews established. The air has been full of rumors. The editors of educational journals and the arrangers of conventions have had to show themselves enterprising and on a level with the novelties of the day. Some of the professors have not been unwilling to co-operate, and I am not sure even that the publishers have been entirely inert. 'The new psychology' has thus become a term to conjure up portentous ideas withal; and you teachers, docile and receptive and aspiring as many of you are, have been plunged in an atmosphere of vague talk about our science, which to a great extent has been more mystifying than enlightening. Altogether it does seem as if there were a certain fatality of mystification laid upon the teachers of our day. The matter of their profession, compact enough in itself, has to be frothed up for them in journals and institutes, till its outlines often threaten to be lost in a kind of vast uncertainty. Where the disciples are not independent and critical-minded enough (and I think that, if you teachers in the earlier grades have any defect—the slightest touch of a defect in the world—it is that you are a mite too docile), we are pretty sure to miss accuracy and balance and measure in those who get a license to lay down the law to them from above.

As regards this subject of psychology, now, I wish at the very threshold to do what I can to dispel the mystification. So I say at once that in my humble opinion there *is* no 'new psychology' worthy of the name. There is nothing but the old psychology which began in Locke's time, plus a little physiology of the brain and senses and theory of evolution, and a few refinements of introspective detail, for the most part without adaptation to the teacher's use. It is only the fundamental conceptions of psychology which are of real value to the teacher; and they, apart from the aforesaid theory of evolution, are very far from being new.—I trust that you will see better what I mean by this at the end of all these talks.

I say moreover that you make a great, a very great mistake, if you think that psychology, being the science of the mind's laws, is something from which you can deduce definite programmes and schemes and methods of instruction for immediate schoolroom use. Psychology is a science, and teaching is an art; and sciences never generate arts directly out of themselves. An intermediary inventive mind must make the application, by using its originality.

The science of logic never made a man reason rightly, and the science of ethics (if there be such a thing) never made a man behave rightly. The most such sciences can do is to help us to catch ourselves up and check ourselves, if we start to reason or to behave wrongly; and to criticise ourselves more articulately after we have made mistakes. A science only lays down lines within which the rules of the art must fall, laws which the follower of the art must not transgress; but what particular thing he shall positively do within those lines is left exclusively to his own genius. One genius will do his work well and succeed in one way, while another succeeds as well quite differently; yet neither will transgress the lines.

The art of teaching grew up in the schoolroom, out of inventiveness and sympathetic concrete observation. Even where (as in the case of Herbart) the advancer of the art was also a psychologist, the pedagogics and the psychology ran side by side, and the former was not derived in any sense from the latter. The two were congruent, but neither was subordinate. And so everywhere the teaching must *agree* with the psychology, but need not necessarily be the only kind of teaching that would so agree; for many diverse methods of teaching may equally well agree with psychological laws.

To know psychology, therefore, is absolutely no guarantee that we shall be good teachers. To advance to that result, we must have an additional endowment altogether, a happy tact and ingenuity to tell us what definite things to say and do when the pupil is before us. That ingenuity in meeting and pursuing the pupil, that tact for the concrete situation, though they are the alpha and omega of the teacher's art, are things to which psychology cannot help us in the least.

The science of psychology, and whatever science of general pedagogics may be based on it, are in fact much like the science of war. Nothing is simpler or more definite than the principles of either. In war, all you have to do is to work your enemy into a position from which the natural obstacles prevent him from escaping if he tries to; then to fall on him in numbers superior to his own, at a moment when you have led him to think you far away; and so, with a minimum of exposure of your own troops, to hack his force to pieces, and take the remainder prisoners. Just so, in teaching, you must simply work your pupil into such a state of interest in what you are going to teach him that every other object of attention is banished from his mind; then reveal it to him so impressively that he will remember the occasion to his dying day; and finally fill him with devouring curiosity to know what the next steps in connection with the subject are. The principles being so plain, there would be nothing but victories for the masters of the science, either on the battlefield or in the schoolroom, if they did not both have to make their application to an incalculable quantity in the shape of the mind of their opponent. The mind of your own enemy, the pupil, is working away from you as keenly and eagerly as is the mind of the commander on the other side from the scientific general. Just what the respective enemies want and think, and what they know and do not know, are as hard things for the teacher as for the general to find out. Divination and perception, not psychological pedagogics or theoretic strategy, are the only helpers here.

But, if the use of psychological principles thus be negative rather than positive, it does not follow that it may not be a great use, all the same. It certainly narrows the path for experiments and trials. We know in advance, if we are psychologists, that certain methods will be wrong, so our psychology saves us from mistakes. It makes us, moreover, more clear as to what we are about. We gain confidence in respect to any method which we are using as soon as we believe that it has theory as well as practice at its back. Most of all, it fructifies our independence, and it reanimates our interest, to see our subject at two different angles,—to get a stereoscopic view, so to speak, of the youthful organism who is our enemy, and, while handling him with all our concrete tact and divination, to be able, at the same time, to represent to ourselves the curious inner elements of his mental machine. Such a complete knowledge as this of the pupil, at once intuitive and analytic, is surely the knowledge at which every teacher ought to aim.

Fortunately for you teachers, the elements of the mental machine can be clearly apprehended, and their workings easily grasped. And, as the most general elements and workings are just those parts of psychology which the teacher finds most directly useful, it follows that the amount of this science which is necessary to all teachers need not be very great. Those who find themselves loving the subject may go as far as they please, and become possibly none the worse teachers for the fact, even though in some of them one might apprehend a little loss of balance from the tendency observable in all of us to overemphasize certain special parts of a subject when we are studying it intensely and abstractly. But for the great majority of you a general view is enough, provided it be a true one; and such a general view, one may say, might almost be written on the palm of one's hand.

Least of all need you, merely *as teachers,* deem it part of your duty to become contributors to psychological science or to make psychological observations in a methodical or responsible manner. I fear that some of the enthusiasts for child-study have thrown a certain burden on you in this way. By all means let child-study go on,—it is refreshing all our sense of the child's life. There are teachers who take a spontaneous delight in filling syllabuses, inscribing observations, compiling statistics, and computing the per cent. Child-study will certainly enrich their lives. And, if its results, as treated statistically, would seem on the whole to have but trifling value, yet the anecdotes and observations of which it in part consists do certainly acquaint us more intimately with our pupils. Our eyes and ears grow quickened to discern in the child before us processes similar to those we have read of as noted in the children,—processes of which we might otherwise have remained inobservant. But, for Heaven's sake, let the rank and file of teachers be passive readers if they so prefer, and feel free not to contribute to the accumulation. Let not the prosectuion of it be preached as an imperative duty or imposed by regulation on those to whom it proves an exterminating bore, or who in any way whatever miss in themselves the appropriate vocation for it. I cannot too strongly agree with my colleague, Professor Münsterberg, when he says that the teacher's attitude toward the child, being concrete and ethical, is positively opposed to the psychological observer's, which is abstract and analytic. Although some of us may conjoin the attitudes successfully, in most of us they must conflict.

The worst thing that can happen to a good teacher is to get a bad conscience about her profession because she feels herself hopeless as a psychologist. Our teachers are overworked already. Every one who adds a jot or tittle of unnecessary weight to their burden is a foe of education. A bad conscience increases the weight of every other burden; yet I know that child-study, and other pieces of psychology as well, have been productive of bad conscience in many a really innocent pedagogic breast. I should indeed be glad if this passing word from me might tend to dispel such a bad conscience, if any of you have it; for it is certainly one of those fruits of more or less systematic mystification of which I have already complained. The best teacher may be the poorest contributor of child-study material, and the best contributor may be the poorest teacher. No fact is more palpable than this.

So much for what seems the most reasonable general attitude of the teacher toward the subject which is to occupy our attention.

10
Piaget and His Methods and Overview of Piaget's Theory

JOHN L. PHILLIPS, JR.

More than twenty years ago, Jean Piaget was convinced of the validity of his theories but, for academic reasons, psychologists in America generally did not accept them. Piaget's basic idea, which underlies his theoretical structures, deals with "structure" as the systematic properties of an event and "function" as biologically inherited modes of interacting with the environment. These elements and their interrelatedness enter into Piaget's explanation of a child's cognitive developments. Methods of teaching based on some of his theories have only begun to be applied recently in some of our schools. Evidence of general acceptance is beginning to appear among leading psychologists in the field of educational psychology. Hence, this selection—an overview of some of the

SOURCE: John L. Phillips, Jr., *The Origins of Intellect: Piaget's Theory* (San Francisco, Calif.: W. H. Freeman and Company, 1969), pp. 3–11. Copyright © 1969 by W. H. Freeman and Company. Reprinted by permission of the publisher.

The author is an educational psychologist who has devoted almost twenty years of his professional life to students at Boise Junior College in Utah, where he is presently professor of psychology and chairman of the Department of Psychology. He is also an active member of numerous local, state, and national committees on education and psychology, and is a frequent contributor to professional publications, among them the *Journal of Educational Psychology* and the *Journal of Counseling Psychology*.

*theories and methods attributed to Piaget—has become required reading for
the modern teacher.*

JEAN PIAGET is a Swiss psychologist who was trained in zoology and
whose major interests are essentially philosophical. He and his associates
have been publishing their findings on the development of cognitive processes
in children since 1927, and have accumulated the largest store of factual and
theoretical observations extant today.

Piaget is often criticized because his method of investigation, though somewhat modified in recent years, is still largely clinical. He observes the child's
surroundings and his behavior, formulates a hypothesis concerning the structure that underlies and includes them both, and then tests that hypothesis by
altering the surroundings slightly—by rearranging the materials, by posing
the problem in a different way, or even by overtly suggesting to the subject a
response different from the one predicted by the theory.

An example of the method is the investigation of the preoperational child's
conception of velocity. The child observes the movement of an object through
points *A, B, C,* and *D.* He reports that the object passed through point *D*
"after" point *A* and that it took "more time" to get from *A* to *C* than from
A to *B.* From this it might reasonably be inferred that the child's conception
of temporal succession and duration is the same as that of an adult. But the
investigation doesn't stop there. The subject is then presented with the simul-
taneous movements of *two* objects. The investigator systematically varies the
actual distance through which each of the objects move, their time in transit,
and their initial and terminal positions relative to one another. When that is
done, the child no longer responds as an adult would in similar circumstances. For example, if two objects move simultaneously—i.e., if they start
simultaneously and stop simultaneously—but at different velocities, the child
will deny their simultaneity of movement. To him, each moving object has a
different "time," and one that is a function of the *spatial* features of the display.

The systematic manipulation of variables illustrated by that example is certainly in the tradition of classical experimental science. The example, however, is drawn from one of the more rigorous of the studies done by Piaget
and his colleagues. Their investigations often begin with naturalistic observations and continue as an interaction between the child and the "experimenter"
—an interaction in which each varies his behavior in response to that of the
other.

Another example may serve to illustrate the point: it is an "experiment"
designed to reveal the child's conception of number. The child is presented
with an assemblage of coins and a large number of flowers; he is asked to tell

how many flowers he can purchase with the coins if the price of each flower is one coin. Here is a transcript of one such encounter:

Gui (four years, four months) put 5 flowers opposite 6 pennies, then made a one-for-one exchange of 6 pennies for 6 flowers (taking the extra flower from the reserve supply). The pennies were in a row and the flowers bunched together: "What have we done?—*We've exchanged them.*—Then is there the same number of flowers and pennies? —*No.*—Are there more on one side?—*Yes.*—Where?—*There* (pennies). (The exchange was again made, but this time the pennies were put in a pile and the flowers in a row.) Is there the same number of flowers and pennies?—*No.*—Where are there more?—*Here* (flowers).—And here (pennies)? —*Less.*[1]

This shifting of experimental procedures to fit the responses of a particular subject makes replication difficult, and the results may be especially susceptible to the "experimenter effect." [2] The reader who feels impelled to criticize Piaget's method is in good company. But before becoming too enthusiastic a critic, he should be sure to note the deliberate effort that is made to give the child opportunities for responses that would *not* fit the theory. He should also keep in mind Piaget's epistomological position that knowledge is action.[3] The subject is continually acting. His actions are structured, and they are also to some extent autonomous. The investigator must therefore continually change his line of attack if he is to follow those actions and to discern their underlying structure.

Relation to Other Theories

The early work of Piaget's Geneva group was given considerable attention in the scholarly press, but because psychology, especially in the United States, was at that time dominated by associationistic theories of learning and by content-oriented psychometrics, their work generated little interest.

[1] Jean Piaget and Alina Szeminska, *The Child's Conception of Number*, translated by C. Gattegno and F. M. Hodgson, New York: Humanities Press, 1952. (Original French edition, 1941.)

[2] Sometimes called the "Rosenthal effect," after R. Rosenthal, who in several recent studies has demonstrated that even in apparently objective experimental situations, the experimenter can influence the subject's behavior in a number of subtle and unacknowledged ways (facial expression, tone of voice, etc.). Even rat subjects perform better for experimenters who expect them to do so, presumably because of differences in handling by different experimenters (R. Rosenthal and K. L. Fade, "The Effect of Experimenter Bias on the Performance of the Albino Rat," *Behavioral Science*, 1963, pp. 183–189, and R. Rosenthal and R. Lawson, "A Longitudinal Study of Experimenter Bias on the Operant Learning of Laboratory Rats," *Journal of Psychiatric Research*, 1964). An interesting study of the experimenter effect in humans is R. Rosenthal and L. Jacobson, *Pygmalion in the Classroom*, 1968.

[3] "Action" need not necessarily be motor.

The current explosion of interest in Piaget's work is an expression of the same concern that produced Hebb's neurological theory and the various contemporary models of the brain as an information-processing system. That concern was probably occasioned not so much by a sudden increase in dissatisfaction with existing theories as by the advances that have taken place recently in neurophysiology and computer engineering.

In any case, Piaget's observations and formulations are today a definite focus of theoretical and professional interest in psychology. The theory is cognitive rather than associationistic,[4] it is concerned primarily with structure rather than content—with *how* the mind works rather than with *what* it does. It is concerned more with understanding than with prediction and control of behavior.

These remarks can of course only be made by way of emphasis, for we can never know the *how* except through the *what;* we can only infer central processes from the behaviors that they organize. An affirmation of one kind of analysis does not necessarily imply a negation of the other. There are conflicts between them, but often the dissonance is more apparent than real, and a careful reading of both kinds of analysis often reveals a harmony that could not be seen at first glance. Hebb's work especially has shown us the way here, and his *magnum opus* [5] is highly recommended to the serious student of psychological theory.

Before turning to the first of Piaget's periods of development, let us take a quick overview of the theory. . . .

Overview of Piaget's Theory

Structure and Function

The basic underlying idea is that *functions* remain invariant but that *structures* change systematically as the child develops. This change in structures is development.

Another term found often in Piaget's writing is *content,* by which he means observable stimuli and responses. We may talk in abstract terms about "function" and "structure," but as soon as we cite an actual example, we must deal also with content.

[4] A cognitive theory is concerned especially with central organizing processes in higher animals, and it recognizes a partial autonomy of these processes, such that the animal becomes an actor upon, rather than simply a reactor to its environment. Actually, the opposite of all this, the so-called associationist doctrine, is to some extent a straw man; for excepting B. F. Skinner, who abjures all theories, there is probably no prominent psychologist today who does not explicitly recognize the importance of mediating processes. But there is a difference in emphasis, and like most straw men this one serves the purpose of accentuating that difference.

[5] D. O. Hebb, *The Organization of Behavior,* New York: John Wiley & Sons, Inc., 1949.

Such an example might be: "A baby looks at a rattle and picks it up." The structure of this event includes the means (looking, reaching, grasping) and the end (stimulation from the object in hand). Each of these is related to the other, and it is this relatedness that Piaget calls "structure." [6] The function of the baby's act is *adaptation*—i.e., the reception and registration of inputs, and the accommodation of each element to the others. "Content" refers to the patterns of input and output.

The term "structure" refers to the systemic properties of an event; it encompasses all aspects of an act, both internal and external. "Function," however, refers to biologically inherited modes of interacting with the environment—modes that are characteristic of such integrations in all biological systems. With reference to intelligence, this inherited "functional nucleus" imposes "certain necessary and irreducible conditions" [7] on structures. There are two basic functions: *organization* and *adaptation*. Every act is organized, and the dynamic aspect of organization is adaptation.

Discontinuities in structure continually arise out of the continuous action of invariant functions. Throughout the developmental period, functions are permanent. But structures are transitory; if they weren't, there would be no development.

Assimilation. If we think of the human brain as a machine for processing information, we must realize not only that it is an exceedingly complex machine, but also that its internal structure is continually changing. We are reminded of Hebb's notion that the precise pattern of cortical activity initiated by an incoming stimulus is a function not only of the pattern of that stimulus, but also of what is already going on in the brain. This is close to what Piaget means by assimilation.

Assimilation occurs whenever an organism utilizes something from its environment and incorporates it. A biological example would be the ingestion of food. The food is changed in the process, and so is the organism. Psychological processes are similar in that the pattern in the stimulation is changed and, again, so is the organism.

In introductory psychology courses it is demonstrated that even the perception of an object is not a faithful reproduction of a stimulus pattern. For example, our perception of objects remains the same even though changes in distance, angle of view, and amount of light produce rather striking differences in the size, shape, brightness, and hue of the image that is actually projected onto the retina. (This is, of course, the phenomenon known as "object constancy.") Beyond that, objects are invested with meaning—i.e., they are categorized in terms of such dimensions as familiarity, threat, and beauty. In sum, the input is changed to fit the existing "mediating" processes. The or-

[6] Each by itself has its own structure, too. See also footnote 9.

[7] Piaget, *The Origins of Intelligence in Children,* translated by Margaret Cook, New York: International Universities Press, 1952, p. 3. (Original French edition, 1936.)

ganism is always active, and its cognitions—even perceptions of its immediate surroundings—are as much a function of this activity as they are of the physical properties of the environment.

Accommodation. But at the same time that the input is being changed by the mediating processes, the mediating processes are being changed by the input. Object constancy, which was just used to illustrate the former, can also be used to illustrate the latter. Each "correction" that is applied by the brain to a retinal image had to be learned—i.e., the mediating processes that act upon the input have themselves been shaped by that input.

Take size constancy, for example. Think of the thousands upon thousands of times that the size of an image on your own retina has covaried with distance from you to the object. Other inputs, such as proprioceptive ones that arise as you have approached the object, and the temporal relations among these, all have contributed to the changing of patterns of mediation.[8] The mechanism by which these changes occur Piaget calls accommodation.

Functional Invariants: Assimilation and Accommodation. Accommodation and assimilation are called "functional invariants" because they are characteristic of all biological systems, regardless of the varying contents of these systems. They are not, however, always in balance, one with the other.

Temporary imbalances occur when a child is imitating (accommodation over assimilation) and when he is playing (assimilation over accommodation). Behavior is most adaptive when accommodation and assimilation are in balance, but such a balance is always temporary, because the process of adaptation reveals imperfections in the system. (See the section below on *Equilibration.*)

Schemata. As I mentioned previously, cognitive development consists of a succession of changes, and the changes are structural.

The structural units in Piaget's system are called *schemata,* which is the plural of *schema.* Schemata are roughly equivalent to the "mediating processes" of Hebb and others.[9] They form a kind of framework onto which incoming sensory data can fit—indeed must fit; but it is a framework that is continually changing its shape, the better to assimilate those data.

Figure 1 summarizes some of these relationships.

---

[8] There is recent evidence that some of this organization is innate (T. G. R. Bower, "The Visual World of Infants," *Scientific American,* vol. 215, no. 6 [December 1966], pp. 80–92, and "Phenomenal Identity and Form Perception in an Infant," *Journal of Perception and Psychophysics,* 1967, pp. 74–76).

[9] Actually, Piaget's schemata include also the stimulus that triggers the mediating processes and the overt behavior that presumably is organized by them. Moreover, this whole process can involve interactions among schemata; i.e., they can assimilate each other. Schema, then, is the generic unit of structure. The earliest schemata are relatively simple, but with continued functioning, it becomes increasingly appropriate to consider such synonyms as "strategies," "plans," "transformation rules," "expectancies," etc.

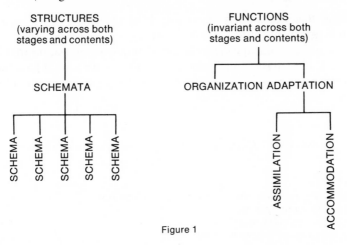

Figure 1

Equilibration. One concept that is *not* represented by the diagram is that of *equilibration.* The word will not be used again in this book, but the idea to which it refers should be kept constantly in mind while studying Piaget's theory in subsequent chapters, for it was the inspiration for the theory in the first place and remains its overarching principle.

The idea is that structures continually move toward a state of equilibrium, and when a state of relative equilibrium has been attained, the structure is sharper, more clearly delineated, than it had been previously. But that very sharpness points up inconsistencies and gaps in the structure that had never been salient before. Each equilibrium state therefore carries with it the seeds of its own destruction, for the child's activities are thenceforth directed toward reducing those inconsistencies and closing those gaps.

The process by which structures change from one state to another is called *equilibration,* and the result of that process is a state of *equilibrium.* Equilibrium is always dynamic and is never absolute, but the achievement of a relatively equilibrated system of actions is the expected conclusion of each of the several units of development listed in Table I.

Developmental Units

Piaget conceives intellectual development as a continual process of organization and reorganization of structure, each new organization integrating the previous one into itself. Although this process is continuous, its results are discontinuous; they are qualitatively different from time to time. Because of that, Piaget has chosen to break the total course of development into units called *periods, subperiods,* and *stages.* Note carefully, however, that each of these cross sections of development is described in terms of the *best* the child can do at that time. Many previously learned behaviors will occur even though he is capable of new and better ones.

Let us now examine the theory in detail, following the outline that appears in Table I; then, having analyzed each unit in its turn, we'll look back and see whether it is possible to discern the unifying threads that run through all of them.

TABLE I.   *Units in the Development of Intelligence*
According to Piaget

Sensorimotor Period—six stages

Exercising the ready-made sensorimotor schemata	0–1 mo.[10]
Primary circular reactions	1–4 mo.
Secondary circular reactions	4–8 mo.
Coordination of secondary schemata	8–12 mo.
Tertiary circular reactions	12–18 mo.
Invention of new means through mental combinations	18–24 mo.

Concrete Operations Period [11]

Preoperational subperiod	2–7 yr.
Concrete operations subperiod [12]	7–11 yr.

Formal Operations Period   11–15 yr.

[10] All age ranges are approximations. In children of any age range one can usually find manifestations of more than one stage or period. The important point is that the same *sequence* of development occurs in every child.

[11] Because Piaget and his co-workers have not been consistent in their indexing, the reader may encounter slightly different classifications in other readings, especially in discussions of middle childhood. More refined classifications have been devised, notably some that include stages within subperiods, but those will not be used here.

[12] Because it might seem confusing to use the same words in a generic category and in one of its subcategories, I suggest that the reader look upon the former as a unit that includes preparation for concrete operations, and the latter as a subunit that includes only the culmination of that development.

11
The Act of Discovery

JEROME BRUNER

Bruner, like Piaget, has conducted studies of cognitive growth extensively, but he differs from Piaget in his theories on the subject. Bruner discusses the act of discovery as an interesting dimension of the organizing processes in learning. Comparison of these two great educators and their contributions to education provides a rich background of information on the subject.

THE immediate occasion for my concern with discovery is the work of the various new curriculum projects that have grown up in America during the last few years. Whether one speaks to mathematicians or physicists or historians, one encounters repeatedly an expression of faith in the powerful effects that come from permitting the student to put things together for himself, to be his own discoverer.

First, I should be clear about what the act of discovery entails. It is rarely, on the frontier of knowledge or elsewhere, that new facts are "discovered" in the sense of being encountered, as Newton suggested, in the form of islands of truth in an uncharted sea of ignorance. Of if they appear to be discovered in this way, it is almost always thanks to some happy hypothesis about where to navigate. Discovery, like surprise, favors the well-prepared mind. In playing bridge, one is surprised by a hand with no honors in it and also by one that is all in one suit. Yet all particular hands in bridge are equiprobable: to be surprised one must know something about the laws of probability. So too in discovery. The history of science is studded with examples of men "finding out" something and not knowing it. I shall operate on the assumption that discovery, whether by a schoolboy going it on his own or by a scientist culti-

SOURCE: Jerome Bruner, *On Knowing: Essays for the Left Hand* (Cambridge, Mass.: Harvard University Press, 1962), pp. 83–87. Copyright © 1962 by the President and Fellows of Harvard College. Reprinted by permission of the publisher.

Dr. Bruner, professor of psychology at Harvard University and head of its Center for Cognitive Studies, has written extensively on the nature of educational and cognitive processes, and has made outstanding contributions to the subjects of thinking, cognition, and other related areas in psychology. He is frequently said to be the most challenging writer of the twentieth century in the field of education. Among his many writings, his best-known book is *Toward a Theory of Instruction* (1966), and his most recent *The Relevance of Education* (1971). Bruner has conducted research that suggests marked and exciting changes in the teacher's role and reflects, in part, the effects of a multimedia instructional emphasis.

vating the growing edge of his field, is in its essence a matter of rearranging or transforming evidence in such a way that one is enabled to go beyond the evidence so reassembled to new insights. It may well be that an additional fact or shred of evidence makes this larger transformation possible. But it is often not even dependent on new information.

Very generally, and at the risk of oversimplification, it is useful to distinguish two kinds of teaching: that which takes place in the *expository mode* and that in the *hypothetical mode*. In the former, the decisions concerning the mode and pace and style of exposition are principally determined by the teacher as expositor; the student is the listener. The speaker has a quite different set of decisions to make: he has a wide choice of alternatives; he is anticipating paragraph content while the listener is still intent on the words; he is manipulating the content of the material by various transformations while the listener is quite unaware of these internal options. But in the hypothetical mode the teacher and the student are in a more cooperative position with respect to what in linguistics would be called "speaker's decisions." The student is not a bench-bound listener, but is taking a part in the formulation and at times may play the principal role in it. He will be aware of alternatives and may even have an "as if" attitude toward these, and he may evaluate information as it comes. One cannot describe the process in either mode with great precision of detail, but I think it is largely the hypothetical mode which characterizes the teaching that encourages discovery.

Intellectual Potency

I should like to consider the differences among students in a highly constrained psychological experiment involving a two-choice machine.[1] In order to win chips, they must depress a key either on the right or the left side of the apparatus. A pattern of payoff is designed so that, say, they will be paid off on the right side 70 per cent of the time, on the left 30 per cent, but this detail is not important. What is important is that the payoff sequence is arranged at random, that there is no pattern. There is a marked contrast in the behavior of subjects who think that there is some pattern to be found in the sequence—who think that regularities are discoverable—and the performance of subjects who think that things are happening quite by chance. The first group adopts what is called an "event-matching" strategy in which the number of responses given to each side is roughly commensurate to the proportion of times that it pays off: in the present case, 70 on the right to 30 on the left. The group that believes there is no pattern very soon settles for a

[1] J. S. Bruner, J. J. Goodnow, and G. A. Austin. *A Study of Thinking*. New York: John Wiley, 1956.

much more primitive strategy allocating *all* responses to the side that has the greater payoff. A little arithmetic will show that the lazy all-and-none strategy pays off more if the environment is truly random: they win 70 per cent of the time. The event-matching subjects win about 70 per cent on the 70 per cent payoff side (or 49 per cent of the time there) and 30 per cent of the time on the side that pays off 30 per cent of the time (another 9 per cent for a total take-home wage of 58 per cent in return for their labors of decision).

But the world is not always or not even frequently random, and if one analyzes carefully what the event matchers are doing, one sees that they are trying out hypotheses one after the other, all of them containing a term that leads to a distribution of bets on the two sides with a frequency to match the actual occurrence of events. If it should turn out that there is a pattern to be discovered, their payoff could become 100 per cent. The other group would go on at the middling rate of 70 per cent.

What has this to do with the subject at hand? For the person to search out and find regularities and relationshps in his environment, he must either come armed with an expectancy that there will be something to find or be aroused to such an expectancy so that he may devise ways of searching and finding. One of the chief enemies of search is the assumption that there is nothing one can find in the environment by way of regularity or relationship. In the experiment just cited, subjects often fall into one or two habitual attitudes: either that there is nothing to be found or that a pattern can be discovered by looking. There is an important sequel in behavior to the two attitudes.

The Sequel

We have conducted a series of experimental studies on a group of some seventy school children over a four-year period.[2] The studies have led us to distinguish an interesting dimension of cognitive activity that can be described as ranging from *episodic empiricism* at one end to *cumulative constructionism* at the other. The two attitudes in the above experiments on choice illustrate the extremes of the dimension. One of the experiments employs the game of Twenty Questions. A child—in this case he is between ten and twelve—is told that a car has gone off the road and hit a tree. He is to ask questions that can be answered by "yes" or "no" to discover the cause of the accident. After he completes the problem, the same task is given him, though this time he is told that the accident has a different cause. In all, the procedure is repeated four times. Children enjoy playing the game. They also differ quite markedly in the approach or strategy they bring to the task. In

[2] J. S. Bruner and Others. *The Processes of Cognitive Development* (in preparation).

the first place, we can distinguish clearly between the two types of questions asked: one is intended to locate constraints in the problem, constraints that will eventually give shape to an hypothesis; the other is the hypothesis as question. It is the difference between, "Was there anything wrong with the driver?" and "Was the driver rushing to the doctor's office for an appointment and the car got out of control?" There are children who precede hypotheses with efforts to locate constraint and there are those who are "potshotters," who string out hypotheses noncumulatively one after the other. A second element of strategy lies in the connectivity of information gathering: the extent to which questions asked utilize or ignore or violate information previously obtained. The questions asked by children tend to be organized in cycles, each cycle usually given over to the pursuit of some particular notion. Both within cycles and between cycles one can discern marked differences in the connectivity of the children's performances. Needless to say, children who employ constraint location as a technique preliminary to the formulation of hypotheses tend to be far more organized in their harvesting of information. Persistence is another feature of strategy, a characteristic compounded of what appear to be two factors: sheer doggedness and a persistence that stems from the sequential organization that a child brings to the task. Doggedness is probably just animal spirits or the need to achieve. Organized persistence is a maneuver for protecting the fragile cognitive apparatus from overload. The child who has flooded himself with disorganized information from unconnected hypotheses will become discouraged and confused sooner than the child who has shown a certain cunning in his strategy of getting information —a child who senses that the value of information is not simply in getting it but in being able to carry it. The persistence of the organized child stems from his knowledge of how to organize questions in cycles and how to summarize things to himself.

Episodic empiricism is illustrated by information gathering that is unbound by prior constraints, that is deficient in organizational persistence. The opposite extreme, what we have called cumulative construction, is characterized by sensitivity to constraint, by connective maneuvers, and by organized persistence. Brute persistence seems to be one of those gifts from the gods that make people more exaggeratedly what they are.

. . . There is a word more to say about the ways in which the problem solver may transform information he has dealt with actively. The point arises from the pragmatic question: what does it take to get information processed into a form best designed to fit some future use? An experiment by R. B. Zajonc in 1957 suggests an answer.[3] He gave groups of students information of a controlled kind, some groups being told that they were to transmit the in-

[3] R. B. Zajonc. Personal communication (1957).

formation later on, others that they were merely to keep it in mind. In general, he found more differentiation of the information intended for transmittal than of information received passively. An active attitude leads to a transformation related to a task to be performed. There is a risk, to be sure, in the possible overspecialization of information processing. It can lead to such a high degree of specific organization that information is lost for general use, although this can be guarded against.

Let me convert the foregoing into an hypothesis. Emphasis on discovery in learning has precisely the effect on the learner of leading him to be a constructionist, to organize what he is encountering in a manner not only designed to discover regularity and relatedness, but also to avoid the kind of information drift that fails to keep account of the uses to which information might have to be put. Emphasis on discovery, indeed, helps the child to learn the varieties of problem solving, of transforming information for better use, helps him to learn how to go about the very task of learning. So goes the hypothesis; it is still in need of testing. But it is an hypothesis of such important human implications that we cannot afford not to test it—and the testing will have to be in the schools.

12

Teaching: An Emerging Behavioral Science

HENRY S. PENNYPACKER

Psychological applications to the task of teaching might well be one of the benchmarks in educational history. Many scholars in education and related fields have attempted to delineate teaching in precise terminology. Henry Pennypacker has done so, starting with the premise that to educate means to modify behavior. From there he spells out how this can be done. The following selection gives the reader a glimpse of what might become the instructional design of schools in the future.

SOURCE: This selection was written especially for this book.

The author is presently teaching at the University of Florida, where he was previously chairman of the Department of Psychology. He resigned the chairmanship to allow more time for research and improvement of instruction, his real interests. He continually participates in research studies and experimentation in schools and colleges throughout the United States.

THE DICTIONARY defines the verb *to teach* as follows: "To impart knowledge by lessons; give instruction to; guide by percept or example; instruct; as, to *teach* a class." Armed only with that definition, a visitor from another planet would be hard put to differentiate instances of teaching from all of the other activities he would observe the denizens of this planet engaged in. The reason for this difficulty, of course, is obvious; the dictionary defines teaching in terms of what it purports to accomplish but provides no clue either as to how it is to be accomplished or how one might measure the extent to which it has been accomplished. Certainly, then, if our celestial visitor were to pursue his inquiry into the phenomena of teaching he would need to look beyond the contents of his pocket earth dictionary, which had thoughtfully been provided him before he left his home planet. Hopefully, it would occur to him to turn to psychology for help in answering his questions. In particular, he might observe some of the teachers of psychology who are in the process of applying the discoveries and principles of their science to the task of instructing the untutored in the subject matter of that discipline.

How does a psychologist define teaching? B. F. Skinner, a very prominent psychologist who had devoted a major portion of his life to unraveling the complex phenomena of teaching, defines teaching as "arranging environmental contingencies so that learning can occur." This definition extends the dictionary definition by one important step. It tells us that teaching involves direct action upon the environment of another person (whom we may call a learner) so as to produce something called learning. Teaching, thus defined, is therefore an indirect process as far as the learner is concerned. The teacher acts upon the environment which, in turn, acts upon the learner so as to produce something called learning. But what is learning and how are we to know when that has occurred?

It is generally agreed among psychologists that learning is not directly observable but rather, is to be inferred from observable changes in behavior. This fits with our everyday usage of the term learning. When we say that a child has learned to walk we are summarizing something like the following set of behavioral observations: on a given day, we observe that the child retains an upright posture while placing one foot in front of the other without support from stationary objects and that this behavior was not observed to occur on the previous day. A parent would summarize this event excitedly by saying "Sammy learned to walk today."

Following Skinner's definition of teaching, a parent might be said to be teaching Sammy to walk if he or she arranges Sammy's environment in such a way that walking is maximally likely to occur and be followed by pleasurable rather than painful consequences for Sammy. This might be accomplished by placing pillows around the floor for Sammy to fall on without hurting himself, by holding his hands and gradually releasing them while staying close to catch him should he begin to fall, and so on. In any case, if we wish to document the occurrence of learning, and hence teaching, we must define and measure behavioral events and observe their change over time. Thus, a contemporary psychological definition of teaching would be "arranging environmental contingencies so as to generate orderly and measurable changes in behavior from which learning may be inferred."

The critical feature of the foregoing definition of teaching is the necessity of behavioral measurement. We may say that we have taught a person something when, as a direct result of our action upon his environment, he is now doing something that he was not previously doing. In order to make such a statement, one must first measure the behavior before any environmental operations are performed. One may then introduce an environmental change, such as a lecture, textbook, or course, and again measure the behavior; if a change has occurred, and similar changes are not observed to occur in the case of people who have not had their environment similarly changed, we may infer that learning has taken place. Regardless of what we infer, however, we will *know* that a change in behavior has occurred and that its occurrence is a result of a change made in the environment.

The function of the teacher, then, may now be specified in terms of two essential characteristics: (a) to specify in advance and devise ways of measuring changes in the behavior of people called students or learners, and (b) to modify the environments of those students in ways maximally likely to ensure the occurrence of the desired behavioral changes. Let us now consider how the teacher might proceed to carry out this function.

His first task is to specify in recordable terms the behavioral objectives of the course. What is the student expected to be able to *do* after taking the course? "The student should read grade-level material at a rate of X words per minute with no more than Y errors per minute"; "the student will respond correctly to problems on the math fact sheet at a rate greater than or equal to X problems per minute"; and "the student should be able to write an essay about the cultural habits of the Eskimos in which correct statements occur at a rate of X per minute and the rate of errors or irrelevancies does not exceed Y per minute" over examples of behavioral objectives that have been specified by teachers in terms of our most sensitive behavioral measure—rate.

The teacher's next task is to obtain an initial measure of his behavior, or some closely related behavior in case the target behavior does not yet exist, from each of his students.

With the ultimate behavioral objective in mind, he should then plan a course for each student that will enable each to attain the desired behavioral objective within some specified period of time. This process is not unlike planning a trip with the aid of a map or chart; one sits down, identifies the starting point and ending point, and then traces the route in between, frequently noting landmarks or checkpoints that he will encounter along the way if he remains on the desired route or path.

With the planning finished and, ideally, the goal agreed upon by both teacher and student, the teacher and student set out together along the desired course, the student behaving as he will in response to particular features of his environment designed and introduced by the teacher. Just as travelers check their progress against a map or chart, frequent assessment of where the student is with respect to his planned progress through the course is essential if one is to avoid getting irretrievably lost. Navigators of ships and airplanes make daily or hourly calculations of their positions with respect to the planned path of their voyage. Prudent cross-country travelers by car pay almost continuous attention to such things as highway signs and names of towns as they follow road maps. The frequency of such checking ensures that if the traveler gets off course, he can get back on again quickly.

In the case of academic courses it has been found that frequent, even daily samples of the student's performance are of inestimable value in ensuring that the student's behavior is changing in the desired direction. Further, just as navigators and travelers make use of maps and charts in maintaining their position along a desired path, so has it been found to be of great assistance to both student and teacher if a daily performance chart of progress through the course is maintained for each individual student. By keeping a daily performance chart, both student and teacher are able to verify that the behavior is changing in the direction of the desired objective or, in the event that it is not, appropriate changes in the student's environment can be made before an undesirable deviation becomes so large as to be essentially irreversible in the time alloted for the course and the student is forced to withdraw or receive a failing grade. Thus, a good teacher may be viewed as a sort of a behavior manager who manipulates those features of the student's environment that are at his disposal and continuously evaluates the effect of such manipulations upon the behavior of his students, always striving to keep the behavior moving in a direction compatible with the objectives of the course.

Exactly how does a teacher alter the environment of a student? In order to properly answer this question we must first recognize that with respect to a particular measured bit of student performance, say an assignment or a quiz, we may identify three major classes of environmental events: those that occur before the performance, those that occur during it, and those that occur after it. For convenience, let us call those environmental events that precede a particular student performance *antecedents,* those that occur at the time of the student performance *concurrents,* and those that follow the student performance *subsequents.* Among the antecedent events that are frequently manipulated in most courses we can include lectures, textbooks, films, tape recordings, programmed workbooks, and demonstrations.

Little systematic attention has been paid to concurrent events, but the list of them would include such things as the temperature and humidity of the room in which the student is performing, the number of other people and the noise level in that room, and the internal environment of the student himself, that is, whether he is hungry, sleepy, excited, or stoned.

The third class of environmental events, which we call subsequents, includes scores, changes in light displays or printed symbols on a teaching machine or computer, words of praise or blame by the instructor, changes in the appearance of the performance chart, and usually, with eventual finality, a letter grade.

It is unfortunate but true that most research on teaching has been limited to manipulation of various antecedent events. As a result, we have an abundance of highly specialized and expensive curricular materials, computers, audiovisual systems, and the like. Largely as a result of our failure to keep pace with these developments with the development of sensitive and efficient procedures for making and charting frequent measurements of student performance, we have relatively little detailed information of the specific effects of these various curricular devices on individual student performance. In recent years, however, a few psychologists, notably Lindsley, Ferster, Keller, McMichael and Correy, Sheppard and MacDermot, and Johnston and Pennypacker have begun doing systematic research on teaching, including the teaching of psychology at the college level. In order to do such research, these psychologists have been forced to develop more sensitive methods of measurement of student performance and, in so doing, have provided us with ways of assessing the effects of any and all environmental changes on student behavior. In particular, these investigators have generally found that subsequent events— those events that occur immediately after student's performance—must be managed with great care because they have a powerful effect on the student's subsequent behavior. For example, Keller has found that praise by a peer following a short interview on a particular portion of the subject matter, where the interview was conducted by the peer, is a very effective way to develop accurate verbal behavior in college students. The same technique has been used to advantage with fifth graders by Ehrhardt. Similarly, Johnston and Pennypacker have shown that permitting the student to update a daily chart of his performance and display that chart in a semipublic place ensures high rates and percentages of correct question answering. It must be remembered, though, that research on teaching incorporating direct and nearly continuous measurement of individual student behavior is an area of educational research that has only been entered in the last two or three years, so relatively little is known with this level of precision and a great deal of exciting work remains to be done.

One thing has become reasonably clear in the course of this and related research. The role of the lecture in the teaching enterprise has been poorly understood and greatly exaggerated. As a means of transmitting information, the lecture became outmoded with the invention of the printing press. Now, with the addition of audio and video tapes that can be stopped and replayed over and over again it is a trifle barbaric to continue to expect students to assimilate large amounts of information on line, as they must if they are to obtain it from a lecturer.

What then is the appropriate role of the lecture? Although practically no research has been addressed directly to this question, we may strongly suspect that the lecture and lecturing will eventually be defined as the primary environmental variables through which one alters student motivation. "Turning the student on" is probably the best phrase we use today to describe this role. In this context, the lecture can be of extraordinary value if an environment is provided almost immediately after the lecture in which the student may engage in behavior appropriate to the objectives of the course. Most everyone will agree that the "turned on" feeling that comes with a particularly stimulating movie, concert, or lecture is relatively short lived, lasting only a few hours or at most a day or two. If the student has no opportunity to engage in course-related behavior soon after a stimulating lecture, the motivational effect of the lecture will not be discernible in terms of a change in his course-related behavior, but may have enhancing effects on a variety of unrelated behaviors such as bull sessions, extracurricular activities, or even demonstrations.

The development of precise methods of recording and indirectly changing student performance permits, for the first time, direct evaluation of teaching. Just as an effective airline navigator is one who nearly always guides the pilot along the correct course and rarely, if ever, gets lost, so the effective teacher becomes a person who guides each and every one of his students along the desired course of behavior change and rarely, if ever, allows one to get lost or fail. If teachers routinely assign the grade of A to those students who have achieved or exceeded the behavioral objectives of the course, and if we agree to define teaching in terms of the complex series of actions upon the student's environment that maintain his progress on the desired course, then evaluation of teaching is reduced to merely determining the percentage of students who objectively earn the grade of A. When this practice becomes commonplace, teaching will be recognized as a profession deserving of the label and members of the profession will be judged according to their relative frequency of success in achieving their stated objective, just as physicians, lawyers, architects, and members of other professions are presently judged. The coming of that day can only be awaited with eagerness and enthusiasm by students and teachers alike.

EVALUATION

WILLIAM JAMES, **Psychology and the Teaching Art**

1. (a) What does James observe as a promising feature in nineteenth-century American education?

   (b) List six or seven of the happiest features of American scholastic life during that period, as James sees them.

2. James states that no one profits more from the fermentation among teachers than do psychologists.
   (a) What does he say as having been the desire and the aspiration of these teachers?

   (b) What has this led to?

   (c) Identify the purpose for teachers that James believes knowledge concerning the mind's operation might serve?

3. (a) What aspects of psychology did James regard as being valuable to teachers?

   (b) How does James compare psychology and teaching?

   (c) What is essential if teaching is to benefit from psychology?

4. What three steps for teaching does James identify in the application of principles from the science of war?

5. What gives psychologists confidence in respect to methods they use?

6. (a) How much study of psychology do most teachers need?

   (b) What weakness appears when teachers go too intensely into the study of psychology?

   (c) Of what value is child psychology to teachers?

7. (a) What does James feel is the worst thing that can happen to a teacher in regard to a knowledge of psychology?

   (b) Why?

JOHN L. PHILLIPS, **Piaget and His Methods and Overview of Piaget's Theory**

8. (a) What has been a frequent criticism of Jean Piaget as a psychologist?

   (b) Explain his method briefly.

9. (a) What is Piaget's special area of child study?

   (b) What is his epistomological position in his experimental procedures?

   (c) Before joining with the critics of Piaget, what does the author recommend we do?

10. (a) What is the focus today of Piaget's observations and formulations?

    (b) Since Piaget's theory is cognitive rather than associationistic, with what is it concerned?

11. (a) What is the basic underlying idea of Piaget's theory?

    (b) Give the author's explanations of the terms "structure" and "function."

    (c) Name the two basic "functions."

12. (a) When does "assimilation" occur in the cognitive process? What is given as a biological example?

    (b) How are psychological processes similar?

    (c) How does the mediating process exist?

13. What does Piaget mean by "accommodation"?

14. (a) Why are accommodation and assimilation called "functional invariants"?

    (b) When do temporary imbalances between these invariants occur?

    (c) Why is a balance always temporary?

15. (a) What are the structural units in Piaget's system called?

    (b) What are these roughly equivalent to?

    (c) How do they operate?

16. What is meant by "equilibration"?

17. (a) Name the units into which Piaget has broken down the total course of development.

    (b) Give his reason for doing so.

JEROME BRUNER, **The Act of Discovery**

18. What is Bruner's thesis in "The Act of Discovery"?

19. Give the author's hypothesis on the act of discovery and its effect on the learner.

20. What causes Bruner concern about discovery?

21. In essence, briefly state what Bruner says is involved in discovery.

22. (a) What types of teaching does Bruner describe?

    (b) How does Bruner distinguish between these two types?

23. (a) In the experiment reported by Bruner, which studied the differences among students in a psychological experiment, into what two habitual attitudes do the students often fall?

    (b) Does the payoff sequence in winning chips follow a planned pattern?

    (c) Describe the general behavior toward winning found in each group of students.

24. How is this significant to a study of the act of discovery?

25. Define and give examples of "episodic empiricism" and "cumulative constructionism" as dimensions of cognitive activity.

HENRY S. PENNYPACKER, **Teaching: An Emerging Behavioral Science**

26. (a) What weakness in the dictionary definition of the word "teaching" does Pennypacker point out?

    (b) To learn what "teaching" means, where would Pennypacker have us turn?

27. (a) How does psychologist B. F. Skinner define "teaching"?

    (b) How does Skinner's definition extend that of the dictionary?

28. What roles are played by (1) the teacher and (2) the learner in Penny-packer's methods?

29. (a) What two events must take place according to Pennypacker if we are to "document" the occurrence of learning?

    (b) Can learning actually be observed?

30. (a) State Pennypacker's definition of teaching.

    (b) The necessity of behavioral measurement is regarded as the critical feature in the definition of teaching given by Pennypacker. Outline briefly the function of the teacher and the three specific tasks in performing his function.

31. (a) Once the planning has been completed, what is considered essential to continued progress toward the objectives?

    (b) Why is this an advantage?

32. Give Pennypacker's description of a good teacher.

33. Identify three major classes of environmental events which alter a student's environment.

34. Give examples of each of these events.

35. Pennypacker contends that the role of the lecture in teaching has been poorly understood and greatly exaggerated. What does he say is the appropriate role of the lecture and the reinforcement of its values?

36. (a) How does the author believe we can achieve direct evaluation of teaching?

    (b) How does he say that evaluation may be reduced to determining percentage of students who objectively earn the grade of A?

    (c) How does he predict that this practice will affect teaching professionally?

FOR FURTHER READING

Bigge, Morris L., and Maurice P. Hunt, "What Is Teaching?" *Psychological Foundations of Education*, 2d ed. (New York: Harper & Row, 1968).
   The authors provide a detailed treatment of teaching as the application of psychology to human development and learning, as well as a summary of a number of historically prominent theories regarding man's psychological nature. Answers to such questions as the following are given: "If students learn, has teaching occurred?" "How may college students best study children?"

Bower, Eli M., and William G. Hollister, eds., *Behavioral Science Frontiers in Education* (New York: John Wiley and Sons, 1967).
   A scholarly discussion of significant and recent ideas in educational theory. The selections in this book of readings reflect a deep insight of the ego process involved in education and will open new frontiers of study for you in your role as a teacher.

Bruner, Jerome, "Needed: A Theory of Instruction," *Educational Leadership* (Association for Supervision and Curriculum Development, 1963).
   A comprehensive discussion on the author's belief that psychology and the field of curriculum design have and continue to suffer jointly from the lack of a theory of instruction. His notion has fascinated and challenged many fine teachers as they work toward establishing teaching as a recognized profession.

Keniston, Kenneth, *The Uncommitted: Alienated Youth in American Society* (New York: Harcourt Brace Jovanovich, 1968).
   You may or may not agree with many of the explanations found here for the so-called generation gap. Whether or not you agree, you will undoubtedly enjoy the author's discussion of cultural roots.

Trow, William Clark, *Teacher and Technology* (New York: Meredith Publishing Company, 1963).
   An authoritative treatment on the utilization of technology for improving learning and teaching in our search for excellence in education. The author shows that the new technology is a natural outgrowth of the old and familiar. His thoughts call for our careful study and certainly warrant it.

Sociology

13

Free Public Schools — A Way to National Unity

HENRY STEELE COMMAGER

A sociological approach to education in a free society follows. Commager iden-tifies four specific tasks that were imposed on the schools throughout the history of establishing the present system. He states that these tasks have been com-pleted and then summarizes what he declares as the remarkable achievement of the American public schools up to the present time.

NO OTHER PEOPLE ever demanded so much of schools and of education as have the American. None other was ever so well served by its schools and its educators.

From the very beginning of our national existence, education has had very special tasks to perform in America. Democracy could not work without an enlightened electorate. The States and sections could not achieve unity with-out a sentiment of nationalism. The nation could not absorb tens of millions of immigrants from all parts of the globe without rapid and effective Ameri-canization. Economic and social distinctions and privileges, severe enough to corrode democracy itself, had to be overcome. To schools went the momen-tous responsibility of inculcating democracy, nationalism, and equalitarian-ism.

The passion for education goes back to the beginnings of the Massachu-

SOURCE: Henry Steele Commager, *Living Ideas in America* (New York: Harper & Row, 1951), pp. 546–548. Copyright © 1951, 1964 by Henry Steele Commager. Re-printed by permission of the publisher.

Currently professor of history at Amherst College, where he has taught since 1956, Henry Steele Commager has had more than thrty years of teaching experience. During his career he has been an extraordinarily prolific editor and writer in American history: *The Growth of the American Republic, Documents in American History, America: The Story of a Free People,* and *Search for a Usable Past* are just a few of the more than two dozen volumes he has edited or written.

setts Bay Colony; the Law of 1647, for all its inadequacy, set up the first even partially successful system of public education anywhere in the world. Only three universities in Britain antedate those of America, and by the time of independence America boasted more colleges than did the mother country, while the State Universities of the early national period represented something new under the sun.

From the first, then, education was the American religion. It was—and is —in education that we put our faith; it is our schools and colleges that are the peculiar objects of public largess and private benefaction; even in architecture we proclaim our devotion, building schools like cathedrals.

Has this faith been justified? A case might be made out for justification on purely scholarly grounds, for after all the highest of our schools of higher learning are as high as any in the world. But this is a somewhat narrow test. Let us look rather to the specific historical tasks which were imposed upon our schools and which they have fulfilled. The first and most urgent task was to provide an enlightened citizenry in order that self-government might work. It is well to remember that democracy, which we take for granted, was an experiment—and largely an American experiment. It could not succeed with a people either corrupt or uninformed. People everywhere—as Jefferson and the spokesmen of the Age of Reason believed—were naturally good, but they were not naturally enlightened. To enlighten the people was the first duty of a democracy, and an enlightened people, in turn, saw to it that "schools and the means of education" were forever encouraged.

The second great task imposed upon education and on the schools was the creation of national unity. In 1789 no one could take for granted that the new nation, spread as it was over a continental domain, would hold together. Yet Americans did manage to create unity out of diversity. Powerful material forces sped this achievement: the westward movement, canals and railroads, a liberal land policy, immigration, and so forth. No less important were intellectual and emotional factors—what Lincoln called those "mystic chords of memory stretching from every battlefield and patriot grave to every living heart and hearthstone." These—the contributions of poets and novelists, naturalists and explorers, orators and painters—were transmitted to each generation anew through the schools.

The third task imposed on schools was that which we call Americanization. Each decade after 1840 saw from two to eight million immigrants pour into America. No other people had ever absorbed such large and varied racial stocks so rapidly or so successfully. It was the public school which proved itself the most efficacious of all agencies of Americanization— Americanization not only of the children but, through them, of the parents as well.

A fourth major service that the schools have rendered democracy is that of overcoming divisive forces in society and advancing understanding and equality. The most heterogeneous of modern societies—heterogeneous in race, language, color, religion, background—America might well have been a prey to ruinous class and religious divisions. The divisive forces did not, however, prevail, and one reason that they did not prevail is that the public school overcame them. In the classroom the nation's children learned and lived equality. On the playground and the athletic field the same code obtained, with rewards and applause going to achievements to which all could aspire equally, without regard to name, race, or wealth. . . .

14
Toward a Nationwide Educational Policy

JAMES B. CONANT

A different view of American education than Commager's is presented by Conant. The proposals discussed deserve your thoughtful study, for they direct our nation toward a commitment to definitive and commendable principles in educational policy. Conant's proposal for a coordinated effort originating from a compact between the separate states is not simple. Its complexity is obvious, but it is quite conceivable that his proposal could serve as the framework for implementing and sustaining "education for excellence" in the United States.

AS WE HAVE SEEN, educational policy in the United States has been determined in the past by the more or less haphazard interaction of (1) the leaders of public school teachers, administrators and professors of education, (2)

SOURCE: James Bryant Conant, *Shaping Educational Policy* (New York: McGraw-Hill Book Company, 1964), pp. 109–110, 121–124, and 128–134. Reprinted by permission of the publisher.

James Bryant Conant is a scholar and writer in the fields of chemistry, history, and education, and is widely regarded as an educational reformer. As a graduate and later president of Harvard University, he commands a respect accorded few public figures in education. Three of his books—*The American High School Today, Slums and Suburbs,* and *The Education of American Teachers*—are ranked high among the significant educational works of recent years. Although his critical analysis of the American high school and teacher education, with special attention to certification policies and practices, was a dispassionate and documentary survey of American education, it provoked a great deal of resentment and criticism among so-called professional educators.

state educational authorities, (3) a multitude of state colleges and universities, (4) private colleges and universities, and (5) the variety of agencies of the Federal government, through which vast sums of money have flowed to individual institutions and the states.

It is my thesis that such a jumble of influential private and public bodies does not correspond to the needs of the nation in the 1960s. Some degree of order needs to be brought out of this chaos, primarily for the benefit of the on-coming generations, but also, to achieve a more effective use of public and private moneys.

At the high school level and below, policy should not be determined solely by either "public school people" or state officials, but wise decisions cannot be made if either is excluded. At the level beyond the high school, plans cannot be made by the state alone, nor by private institutions alone, nor by Washington alone. But no nationwide policy can be successfully formulated if any one of the three is excluded. A single state, as the California action shows, can develop a master plan for higher education; any single state can, as New York has shown, keep its schools well up-to-date with the educational revolution. Congress can help meet the problems presented by the revolution by grants for specific purposes and a handsome assist to institutions of higher education. But all this does not add up to a nationwide educational policy, let alone a national educational policy which would be the equivalent of the national policy in Great Britain [1] or France.

The fact is, of course, that without a drastic Constitutional amendment nobody is in a position to establish an educational policy in the United States. It is my contention that some form of cooperative exploration of educational problems between the states and the Federal government is imperative. We cannot have a national educational policy, but we might be able to evolve a *nationwide policy.*

. . . . .

In general I am convinced that educational systems cannot be exported or imported either as a whole or in part. Nevertheless I cannot help raising the question whether we do not need in the United States to create some sort of organization which will have the confidence of the state governments on the one hand, and on the other can bring to a focus a discussion of the important topics in education. Indeed I would hope there would be eventually not only a discussion but interstate cooperation.

An initial step along such a road was taken in 1949 with the establishment by sixteen states of the Southern Regional Education Board. Later (in 1953)

---

[1] The report of the committee appointed by the prime minister under the chairmanship of Lord Robbins "to review the pattern of full-time higher education" is an excellent example of long range flexible planning. The report was published late in 1963 and has received wide support.

came the formation of the Western Interstate Commission for Higher Education (thirteen states) and still later the New England Board of Higher Education (six states). Two of these regional boards or commissions are based on formal interstate compacts approved by Congress. Originally it was planned to have the Southern Regional Board also based on an interstate compact approved by Congress, but the idea was abandoned and its status is now that of an interstate agreement. All three agencies now embrace thirty-five states, leaving only twelve Midwestern states, in addition to New York, New Jersey, and Pennsylvania, outside any regional compact. A resolution urging the exploration of proposals for an interstate compact was adopted in 1954 by the Midwestern Regional Conference of the Council of State Governments. But in 1955 the committee reported against the proposal. Three years later eleven of the leading universities in the same area (including two private universities) formed the private voluntary organization known as the Committee on Institutional Cooperation. The chief purpose of this committee is to "improve the educational and public services offered by its member institutions while minimizing the cost of these services by fostering cooperation in instruction and research, particularly at the graduate level."

Clearly, both organizations created by agreement only and by interstate compact have a wider aim than can be possible for the association of a small group of universities. Indeed, one of the prime motives for the formation of these regional interstate planning commissions was the idea of improving and increasing educational opportunities for all the youth in the states involved. This it is hoped will be accomplished by the establishment of coordinated educational programs. As one person has well said, "We believed that we could better meet some of the problems in higher education by cooperation between the states rather than by competition."

The boards created by these interstate compacts are in theory at least regional planning agencies for higher education. None, I believe, has any authority or control over state activities or other educational institutions. However, by gathering facts and figures and identifying problems, the members of the staff can acquaint educators, legislators, and the public with the problems the region faces; expert consultants can recommend solutions. What has been achieved has been through persuasion, since no authority by coercion is even implied in the arrangement.

An example provided by the New England Board is typical of the good that may be accomplished in this manner. Facts made available to a university president in one state made it possible for him to withstand local pressures to establish a new program in a specialized area. He could point out that a similar program in the university in another state was already well developed and available. The objective is to prevent (by persuasion) a proliferation of programs and curricula when the needs of the region do not require them. The New England Board endeavors to bring into conferences legislative leaders as well as governors, budget officers, and educators to discuss programs throughout the area.

The work of these interstate boards is clearly only in its first stages, but the results, at least in some cases, show much promise. At the post-high-school level, where state differences are so great, at least some coordination of the diverse interests in a region may be possible. It is interesting to note that in all these interstate activities the emphasis is on education beyond the high school—indeed in most instances exclusively in this area. The reasons are evident. The forces I have already referred to have produced a considerable degree of uniformity in the schools. Out of this uniformity within each state has come a belief that the financing of the schools, in contrast to the state colleges and universities, was largely a matter of teachers' salaries. And the teachers' organizations have operated to reinforce this idea. The consequence has been that at least until recently there has appeared to be no reason for any official arrangement for the exchange of information about school problems and school finances among the states.

The states that have entered into these interstate compacts have certainly taken important steps in the direction of a rational approach to our educational problems. But one is still bound to ask: Are these regional pacts enough? They are excellent in principle and could be most effective in operation, but why only regional agreements? Why not a new venture in cooperative federalism? Why not a compact among *all* the states?

To be quite specific, let me be bold and make a suggestion for a possible way by which the road to the development of a nationwide educational policy might be opened up. *Let the fifty states, or at least fifteen to twenty of the more populous states, enter into a compact for the creation of an "Interstate Commission for Planning a Nationwide Educational Policy."* The compact would have to be drawn up by the states and approved by Congress. The document would provide for the membership of the commission and provide the guidelines for its operation. Each state would be represented, though a group of less populous states might decide to be represented by one person. Each state would be ready to listen to any conclusions of the commission but, of course, would not be bound to follow its recommendations.

Since such an interstate commission would be concerned with the drawing up of plans, *not* with administration, I see no constitutional or legal reason against a state legislature authorizing one or more persons to participate in it. Nor do I see any obstacles to a legislature expressing its willingness to examine any reports coming from such a group. The matter of finances might raise issues. It might be difficult to get any considerable number of state legislatures to appropriate the money; but I hope not, for if it were proposed that the Congress of the United States do so, certainly the cry of states' rights might be raised. Yet I would hope the commission would invite the chief United States school officer, the Commissioner of Education, as well as other Federal officials to attend each conference.

. . . . . .

I must admit that the record of national committees on education, however authorized and however appointed, is not such as to lead one to be optimistic about the results to be accomplished by still another committee. Yet the creation of a national commission which would be an interstate educational planning commission whose existence was the result of a compact between the states would be something quite new. It differs from schemes for appointing a Presidential or Congressional advisory commission in several respects. In the first place, because the commission would be an interstate commission, the reports of the working parties would be automatically concerned with state-by-state variations and would recognize the realities of the conditions in each state. In the second place, the recommendations would be directed to the state legislatures or state boards of education and would be considered by the state authorities because each state had been involved in the creation of the undertaking. In the third place, the magnitude and detailed nature of the financial demands required would be spelled out in such a way that Congress (through its own committees) and the Office of Education (through its own staff) could explore the significance of each item in terms of the function of the Federal governmental agencies.

Each working party would have to start with certain premises agreed upon by the commission. Within the framework thus established, the working party would be required first to make an exhaustive factual study of the structure state by state, second to come up with specific recommendations to the state authorities (the chief state school officer, the state school board, or the legislature). There might well be dissenting opinions on many points. The right to public dissent would be inherent in accepting an appointment on the working party. The more controversial the area, the more necessary would be such a provision.

Admittedly, in setting up any working party, the most difficult task for the interstate commission would be an agreement on what I have called the framework. And to let a working party loose in any controversial area without some guidelines would be to insure catastrophic failure at the onset. Certain premises could be agreed on without much difficulty. These would constitute part of the framework for all of the working parties. In my opinion, these premises might be formulated somewhat as follows:

1. It is assumed that our present form of government should be perpetuated; to that end all future citizens of the nation should receive an education that will prepare them to function as responsible members of a free society,

as intelligent voters and, if appointed or elected to public office, as honest reliable servants of the nation, state, or locality.

2. It is assumed that each state is committed to the proposition of providing free schooling to all the children in the state through twelve grades. (Though the Federal government has no power to proclaim the doctrine of free schools, practically the action of all the states during the last 100 years enables the interstate commission to declare that providing free public schooling is a nationwide policy of the United States.)

3. It is assumed that in every state the parents have a right to send their children to private schools, colleges, and universities instead of to the publicly supported institutions. This assumption follows from the interpretation of the Federal Constitution by the Supreme Court on more than one occasion.

4. It is assumed that each state *desires* to have all normal children in the state attend school at least five hours a day, 150 days a year, at least until they reach the age of 18, but that the states differ and will continue to differ in regard to the laws requiring school attendance and the way special provisions are provided for physically and mentally handicapped children.

5. It is assumed that each state accepts the responsibility of providing for the education of at least some of its youth beyond high school; the organization and financing of such education, however, differs and will continue to differ state by state; in each state opportunities for education beyond high school now include at least one university chartered by the state and largely supported by public funds; the continuation of such universities as centers of research, advanced study, and above all, fearless free inquiry is essential to the welfare of the state and the nation.

6. It is assumed that the education provided in high school and beyond by public institutions is designed to develop the potentialities of all the youth to fit them for employment in a highly industrialized society.

7. The financing of education, including research and scholarly work in the universities, is a concern of private universities, the states, and the Federal government.

The declaration of some such set of premises by an interstate commission would be the first step in shaping a nationwide educational policy. If each state legislature would pass a resolution accepting such a declaration, we should for the first time as a nation be officially committed to certain basic principles of educational policy. We now assume these principles to be valid, but in fact they have never been promulgated by representative assemblies and could not be promulgated by the Congress.

After formulating the premises of American education (the framework, as I have called it), the commission would determine what subjects to explore and name the working parties. Then many months later the commission would reconvene to receive the reports of the working parties, discuss them, and pass them on with comment to the legislatures of all the states represented. The working committees should be what the name implies. Their composition should be such as to represent diverse views of experts, and unanimous reports would *not* be expected. The layman's criticism would best come, I should think, from the interstate planning commission, which I envisage as being made up of distinguished citizens of each state who are *not* educators (the sort of person one finds on boards of trustees of our most famous universities). An alternate scheme in which the working parties contained laymen as well as educators need not be excluded.

However the working parties are composed, they should proceed to explore in depth the differences state by state and put these differences at the center of the debate when it came to making recommendations. If this were done, it would be almost certain that there would be different recommendations for different states, though one would hope not fifty in each case! How many working parties should be set up is a question. The topics which might be considered could be as many as twenty-five or thirty. But the scheme should not be endangered by an excessive burden of work. Merely as illustration, therefore, I suggest at the outset, working parties devoted to the following seven areas, without implying priorities:

1. Education in grades 13 and 14 (junior colleges) and the relation of this education to (a) professional training in a university and (b) the need for technicians. I have heard more than once that, as a nation, we are in short supply of the kind of person who is trained in some European countries in a course that is more practical and less scientific than the usual four-year engineering course in the United States. This working party would, of course, consider the supply and demand of technical personnel, and would have to be in close contact with the second and third parties on the list.

2. Education for employment immediately on leaving high school, including vocational courses in high school and post-high school.

3. Science and engineering, including an inquiry into supply and demand of those prepared for research and development and the facilities available for training such personnel.

4. The education of the Negro.

5. The education of members of the medical profession.

6. Uniformity of standards for degrees beyond the master's degree.

7. The promotion of research and scholarly endeavors in *all* fields in our institutions of higher education.

I hardly need point out that problems of finance would be encountered by all the working parties. One would also meet the problem of Federal aid to private colleges and universities already alluded to [in Chapter 3] and the present concentration of Federal funds for research in a relatively few centers. There are those who might consider the financial implications of the conclusions of the working parties and of the commission as a whole the most significant part of the undertaking. To quote once again from the OECD [2] report:

> The task of financing the expansion of higher education is formidable. It is unlikely to be solved by recourse to private sources; the poorer states will look increasingly for general fiscal aid to the federal government and pressure is likely to mount for general aid to higher education. . . . If, as we think, the question of research support should in principle be separated from the question of aid to teaching in higher education, then those programs which are designed to spread the net for talent and to help the poorer states would be seen more clearly as contributing towards the building of a strong popular and national system of national education.

To which one can agree but point out that since the creation and location of new centers for higher education is a state affair, any approach to the questions raised by the OECD examiners must be *in part* on a state-by-state basis.

There is a vast complex of interconnected questions to be answered before one can make a start at developing a rational *nationwide* educational policy. In raising and answering the questions, university faculties, administrators, state and Federal officials must be concerned. In the last analysis in many instances vital decisions must be made by the duly elected legislative bodies. Therefore in the early stages of the inquiry representatives of the lay public must play an active part, for what is needed is something far removed from institutional bargaining. What is needed is a national inquiry initiated by the elected representatives of the people in fifty states.

The OECD examiners may or may not be right when they conclude "that the federal government ought to become a major source [of funds] by *direct contribution to the teaching functions of higher education.*" But I for one agree with the reply of one member of the American delegation who answered an examiner's question about the extent to which the Federal government can stimulate or initiate statewide planning. The Under-Secretary of the U.S. Department of Health, Education and Welfare, Mr. Nestingern said "that the momentum for developments of this kind must be generated at the state level with the cooperation of local communities. Under the American system this cannot be done by the Federal government, which is not in a po-

[2] The Organization for Economic Cooperation and Development is composed of the following member countries: Austria, Belgium, Canada, Denmark, France, the Federal Republic of Germany, Greece, Iceland, Ireland, Italy, Luxemburg, the Netherlands, Norway, Portugal, Spain, Sweden, Switzerland, Turkey, the United Kingdom, and the United States. This organization undertook a review of national policies for science and education to assist member countries in reassessing their programs.

sition to initiate state planning." And he added that the Office of Education could encourage planning and help in the development of state plans.

To generate momentum at the state level requires that each state put its educational planning machinery in good order. To this end, I conclude this book by appealing to all citizens concerned with education to make their voices heard at the state capitals. To the end that more order be introduced into the present national picture, I appeal to members of state legislatures and of the Congress to examine the need for some sort of interstate cooperation. Anyone who examines the facts I have presented in the preceding pages will be convinced, I feel sure, of the need of more detailed state-by-state study of American education. For only by such a study, looking forward to prompt action, can we arrive at a *nationwide policy* adequate to meet the challenges of the new and awesome age in which we live.

EVALUATION

HENRY STEELE COMMAGER, **Free Public Schools—A Way to National Unity**

1. What is the thesis of Commager's "Free Public Schools—A Way to National Unity"?

2. What special tasks does Commager say are the responsibility of American education in regard to the Americanization of the tens of millions of immigrants to the United States?

3. According to Commager, what are the four major tasks that education has had to perform in the United States?

4. What does the author believe prevents divisive forces from prevailing in the public schools?

5. How does Commager believe Americanization was achieved?

6. Who does Commager say is attacking the schools of America?

7. List ten reasons Commager gives for the continuous pressure and attack on American schools.

JAMES B. CONANT, **Toward a Nationwide Educational Policy**

8. Conant names five contributors to the shaping of educational policy in the United States. Name them and tell what Conant considers to be their ability to meet the needs of our nation in the 1970's.

9. (a) At high school levels and below, who does Conant say should make educational decisions?

   (b) At levels above high school, who should?

10. What is the major difference between a nationwide educational policy as proposed here and a national policy?

11. Conant states that "without a drastic constitutional amendment nobody is in a position to establish an educational policy in the United States." Why does he believe this?

12. What does Conant suggest in regard to the establishment of an educational policy?

13. List some early steps along the road to interstate cooperation.

14. What promise for improving education does Conant see in the work of the interstate boards up to the 1960's?

15. (a) What would Conant have the fifty states do about a nationwide educational policy?

    (b) How would it be initiated?

    (c) How would the various states have representation?

    (d) To what degree would the members of this commission be bound to its findings?

16. Make a diagram showing the structure, composition, and functions of the proposed interstate commission.

17. List in outline form the set of premises Conant suggests for setting up the working parties of the interstate educational planning commission.

18. What are the seven areas to which the working parties should devote themselves at the outset?

19. Summarize Conant's final suggestions for establishing a nationwide planning commission.

FOR FURTHER READING

Adler, Mortimer J., "Labor, Leisure, and Liberal Education," *Journal of General Education,* October 1951, pp. 33–45.
    A fine discussion of how Adler views liberal education in an industrial democracy such as ours. He distinguishes between labor and leisure, purporting that liberal education is to be understood in terms of leisure. He describes education as a practical activity and implies a need for a reappraisal of one's cultural perspective.

Bendiner, Robert, *The Politics of Schools: A Crisis in Self-Government* (New York: Harper & Row, 1969).
    Decentralization and local control of schools are thoroughly studied and well analyzed. Bendiner draws somewhat startling conclusions, which should prompt you to probe your own thoughts on the subject.

Dewey, John, *Democracy and Education* (New York: Macmillan, 1961).
    The date of this publication might mislead you, for this is one of the modern classics. You will find this a most stimulating book from the beginning to the end, but if time does not permit you to enjoy it now, select one or two selections fully and study them well.

Pestalozzi, Johann H., "Education for the Different Classes," *Prologue to Teaching,* ed. M. B. Smiley and J. S. Diekhoff (New York: Oxford University Press, 1959).
    Pestalozzi spent the greater part of his later years in theoretical and practical exposition of elementary education. Here he gives his definition of elementary training in which he takes the position that it demands harmony with conditions and circumstances unique to different social ranks. The definition is not at all dated, and is applicable to our considerations of the culturally disadvantaged people in the United States today.

Reissman, Frank, *Strategies Against Poverty* (New York: Random House, 1969).
    Many common misconceptions about social classes, especially the culturally deprived, are vividly described. The author tells about strategies against poverty that he believes will work, since there is greater understanding of the true problem.

Salisbury, Robert H., "Schools and Politics in the Big City," *Harvard Educational Review,* XXXVII (Summer 1967), 408–424.
    An excellent analysis of education as a critical issue in the urban society of American political institutions. The original version of this paper was delivered as the Alfred Dexter Simpson Memorial Lecture at Harvard University, November 12, 1965. The author's concluding statement suggests that more local

political leadership in education and coordination of the schools with other portions of the community will improve conditions.

Veblin, Thorstein, *The Theory of the Leisure Class* (New York: Macmillan, 1898).

Ideas come from and are discussed by great men. The ideas presented here at the turn of the century are as timely today as they were then. They also reflect the thoughts that emanate only from great thinkers.

Anthropology

15
Education in a Transforming Culture

GEORGE D. SPINDLER

Describing how traditional and emergent cultural values affect education, Spindler explains, in this selection, why he believes that the greatest effect on education is a result of a radical shift in these values. He then analyzes the all-too-frequent attacks on education that have marked the past ten years in this country. His views on the participation of educators in knifing attacks on each other may be somewhat discouraging to potential teachers, but they will provide you with a perspective that should make you both better informed citizens and more responsible teachers.

THE American public school system, and the professional educators who operate it, have been subjected to increasingly strident attacks from both the lay (non-educationist) public, and from within the ranks. My premise is that these attacks can best be understood as symptoms of an American culture that is undergoing transformation—a transformation that produces serious conflict. I shall discuss this transformation as a problem in culture change that directly affects all of education, and everyone identified with it.

The notion of social and cultural change is used persuasively, if carelessly, by too many writers to explain too much. Generalized allusions to technological change, cultural lag, the atomic age, and mass society, are more suggestive than clarifying. We must strike to the core of the change. And my argument is that this core can best be conceived as a radical shift in values.

SOURCE: *Harvard Educational Review,* Vol. 25 (Summer 1955), pp. 145–156. Copyright © 1955 by the President and Fellows of Harvard College. Reprinted by permission of the publisher.

George D. Spindler is professor of anthropology at Stanford University. Perhaps he has made his most significant contribution to education through his writings, which analyze the condition of American education from an anthropological point of view, as is suggested by the titles of such of his works as *Education and Anthropology, Culture and Education,* and *Culture in Process.*

167

The anthropologist, and I speak as one but not for all, sees culture as a goal-oriented system. These goals are expressed, patterned, lived out by people in their behaviors and aspirations in the form of values—objects or possessions, conditions or existence, personality or characterological features, and states of mind, that are conceived as desirable, and act as motivating determinants of behaviors. It is the shifts in what I believe are the core values in American culture, and the effect of these shifts on education today, that I wish to discuss. I will present these shifts in values as the conditions of life to which education and educators, whether progressives, experimentalists, conservatives, or in-betweens, must adapt—and to which they are adapting, albeit confusedly. My emphasis within the value framework will be upon shifts in the conception of the desirable character type, since education can never be freed from the obligation to support, if not produce, the kind of personality, or social character deemed desirable in society.

But first I must specify what sources are to be used as the factual baseline for generalization, even though there is no avoiding the necessity of going beyond these facts in the discussion to follow. There is a body of literature on American culture, as a culture, and the changes within it. I have drawn most heavily from the anthropologists, like Margaret Mead, Clyde and Florence Kluckhohn, Gregory Bateson, Lloyd Warner, and Geoffrey Gorer, and a few sociologists, like David Riesman. Their writings range from the highly intuitive to the relatively observation-based. Though there is consensus, and a surprising degree of it, on the part of these students of American culture, little they say can be or is intended by them to be taken as proven.

These writings are useful, but most emphasize static patterning in values more than change in values. To extend my factual baseline I have been collecting relevant data from college students for the past four years. The sample consists of several hundred students, ranging in age from 19 to 57 years, mainly graduates in professional education courses, and representing socio-economic strata describable as lower-middle to upper-middle class. The sample is as representative of this professional group and these economic strata as any regionally biased sample can be. I have used two simple value-projective techniques. The aim has been to find out what features of social character (the term I will use to designate those personality elements that are most relevant to social action) the students in the sample hold as being valuable and that presumably determine much of their behavior in classrooms. The first of these techniques is a series of 24 open-ended statements, such as "The individual is————," "Intellectuals should————," "All men are born———." The second of these techniques is to require each student to write one brief paragraph describing his (or her) conception of the "Ideal American Boy."

The various qualifications, problems, and discrepancies in analysis appearing in the treatment of the results cannot be discussed here. Let it suffice to say that I have subjected the responses of the students in the sample to a straight-forward content analysis—counting numbers of responses that fall into certain categories appearing from the data themselves.[1] Perhaps some examples will illustrate both the techniques and the kinds of materials from which I am going to draw in the rest of this article.

From the open-ended sentence value-projective technique, results like these have been obtained: "All men are born————," "equal" (70% of all responses), "wolves," "stupid," "dopes," "hot-blooded" (a miscellaneous negative category of 28%—provided mainly by females in the sample); "Artists are————," "queer," "perverted," "nuts," "effeminate" (a negative-hostile category of 38% of all responses), "different," "people," "few" (a neutral category of 35%), "creative," "smart," "original," "interesting" (a positive category of 25%); "Intellectuals should————," "be more sociable," "be more practical," "get down to earth" (a mildly derogative category of 36%), "keep it under cover," "drop dead," "shut up" (an openly hostile category 20%), "apply their intellect," "study," "create," "think" (a neutral to positive category of 40%); Nudity is————, "vulgar," "obscene," "profane," "repulsive" (a negative-moralistic category of 43%), "pleasant," "self-expressive," "beautiful," "healthy" (an enthusiastic-positive category of 20%), "depends on how interpreted," "alright in some places," "depends on who is looking" (a relativistic category of 30%).[2]

The values are self-evident, and do not call for discussion, as such, for the moment. What is more important is that this fairly homogeneous sample of students provides a wide range of response to each of these statements, excepting for the purposefully stereotyped "All men are born————." And not only is there a wide range of response evidenced, but many of the categories of response to a single statement can be considered as contradictions with respect to each other. This suggests that although there are clear modalities of values in this sample, there are also differences between people and groups of people in respect to what they believe is good.

The material gathered together as results from the "Ideal American Boy" technique are even more suggestive. A sentence-content analysis procedure reveals that the desirable features of character are ranked in the following order, from highest number of mentions, to lowest number: He should be *sociable,* like people, and get along well with them; he must be *popular,* be

---

[1] The analysis is still in process and will be subject to modifications in procedure. The statements in this article are based on a preliminary analysis of 328 individual protocols.

[2] Where percentages do not total 100 it is because various miscellanea are omitted.

liked by others; he is to be *well-rounded,* he can do many things quite well, but is not an expert at anything in particular; he should be *athletic* (but not a star), and *healthy* (no qualifications); he should be *ambitious* to succeed, and have clear goals, but these must be acceptable within limited norms; he must be *considerate of others,* ever-sensitive to their feelings about him and about events; he should be a *clean-cut Christian,* moral and respectful of God and parents; he should be *patriotic;* and he should demonstrate *average academic ability,* and *average intellectual capacity.*

These are the characteristics of the ideal American boy seen as most important by the students in the sample. Leadership, independence, high intelligence, high academic ability, individuality, are mentioned relatively infrequently (in about 20% of the descriptive paragraphs). But individuals do vary in the pattern of characteristics that are combined in the paragraph. Some emphasize the high achievement and individualized characteristics just mentioned. Some include elements from the modal list and combine them with these latter items. But the majority emphasize the sociable, well-rounded, average characteristics ranked above.

The implications seem clear. The keynote to the character type regarded as most desirable, and therefore constituting a complex of values, is *balance, outward-orientedness, sociability,* and *conformity* for the sake of harmony. Individuality and creativity, or even mere originality, are not stressed in this conception of values. Introspective behavior is devaluated (even intellectuals are suspicioned by many). Deviancy, it seems, is to be tolerated only within the narrow limits of sociability, of general outwardness, of conformity for harmony ("Artists are perverts"). The All-American boy is altogether average.

The materials just cited not only serve to illustrate the technique, but more important for present purposes, indicate rather clearly the fabric of the value pattern that I believe to be emerging as the dominant core of the social character values in American culture (providing one can assume, as I am here, that the middle-class culture is the core of our way of life—the pattern of norms against which lower- and upper-class cultures are seen as deviations). From this point on, I shall use the implications of this data, along with the content of anthropological and sociological writings on American culture, without further reference to the factual baseline itself. The purpose is to sketch in bold strokes the major dimensions of culture change in our American society and relate them in explanatory style to the contretemps of modern public education and educators.

In doing this, I cannot indicate all of the logical and analytic steps between data and generalization, since this is not a research report. The statements I will make now about American values, their shift, and the effect on education, are based upon the varying responses of different age groups in the sample, upon person-to-person variation in responses, and upon variations in response and particularly contradictions of response within single individual protocols (the total set of responses for a single individual).

On the basis of these kinds of data, and in the light of the perceptive works of the fore-mentioned writers on American Culture, I believe it is clear that a major shift in American values has, and is taking place.[3] I find it convenient to label this shift as being from *traditional* to *emergent*. The values thus dichotomized are listed under their respective headings below, with explanatory statements in parentheses.

Traditional Values	*Emergent Values*
Puritan morality (Respectability, thrift, self-denial, sexual constraint; a puritan is someone who can have anything he wants, as long as he doesn't enjoy it!)	*Sociability* (As described above. One should like people and get along well with them. Suspicion of solitary activities is characteristic.)
Work-Success ethic (Successful people worked hard to become so. Anyone can get to the top if he tries hard enough. So people who are not successful are lazy, or stupid, or both. People must work desperately and continuously to convince themselves of their worth.)	*Relativistic moral attitude* (Absolutes in right and wrong are questionable. Morality is what the group thinks is right. Shame, rather than guilt-oriented personality is appropriate.)
Individualism (The individual is sacred, and always more important than the group. In one extreme form, the value sanctions egocentricity, expediency, and disregard for other people's rights. In its healthier form the value sanctions independence and originality.)	*Consideration for others* (Everything one does should be done with regard for others and their feelings. The individual has a built-in radar that alerts him to others' feelings. Tolerance for the other person's point of view and behaviors is regarded as desirable, so long as the harmony of the group is not disrupted.)
Achievement orientation (Success is a constant goal. There is no resting on past glories. If one makes $9,000 this year he must make $10,000 next year. Coupled with the work-success ethic, this value keeps people moving, and tense.)	

---

[3] I have been particularly influenced by the writings of David Riesman and particularly his *The Lonely Crowd*, now available in a Doubleday Anchor Book edition, 1953, (with Nathan Glazer and Reuel Denny).

Traditional Values	*Emergent Values*
Future-time orientation (The future, not the past, or even the present, is most important. There is a "pot of gold at the end of the rainbow." Time is valuable, and cannot be wasted. Present needs must be denied for satisfactions to be gained in the future.)	*Hedonistic, present-time orientation* (No one can tell what the future will hold, therefore one should enjoy the present—but within the limits of the well-rounded, balanced personality and group.)
	Conformity to the group (Implied in the other emergent values. Everything is relative to the group. Group harmony is the ultimate goal. Leadership consists of group-machinery lubrication.)

I believe American Culture is undergoing a transformation, and a rapid one producing many disjunctions and conflicts, from the traditional to the emergent value systems outlined above. It is probable that both value systems have been present and operating in American Culture for some time, perhaps since the birth of the nation. But recently, and under the impetus of World Wars, atomic insecurities, and a past history of "boom and bust," the heretofore latent tendencies in the emergent direction have gathered strength and appear to be on the way towards becoming the dominant value system of American Culture.

Like all major shifts in culture, this one has consequences for people. Culturally transitional populations, as anthropologists know from their studies of acculturating Indian tribes, Hindu villages, and Samoan communities (among others), are characterized by conflict, and in most severe form—demoralization and disorganization. Institutions and people are in a state of flux. Contradictory views of life are held by different groups and persons within the society. Hostilities are displaced, attacks are made on one group by another. And this applies as well to the condition of American Culture—the context of American education.

The traditionalist views the emergentist as "socialistic," "communistic," "spineless and weak-headed," or downright "immoral." The emergentist regards the traditionalist as "hidebound," "reactionary," "selfish," or "neurotically compulsive." Most of what representatives of either viewpoint do may be regarded as insidious and destructive from the point of view of the other. The conflict goes beyond groups or institutions, because individuals in our transitional society are likely to hold elements of both value systems concomitantly. This is characteristic, as a matter of fact, of most students included in the sample described previously. There are few "pure" types. The social character of most is split, calling for different responses in different situations, and with respect to different symbols. So an ingredient of personal confusion is added that intensifies social and institutional conflict.

I hypothesize that the attacks upon education, which were our starting point, and the confusion and failure of nerve characterizing educators today, can be seen in clear and helpful perspective in the light of the conflict of traditional and emergent values that has been described. It is the heart of the matter. The task then becomes one of placing groups, institutions, and persons on a continuum of transformation from the one value system to the other. Without prior explanation, I should like to provide a simple diagram that will aid at least the visual-minded to comprehension of what is meant. With this accomplished I will provide the rationale for such placement and discuss the implications of it in greater detail.

The diagram is meant to convey the information that different groups operating in the context of relations between school and community, educator and public, occupy different positions on the value continuum, with varying degrees and mixtures of traditional and emergent orientations. It should be understood that the placements indicate hypothecated tendencies, that no one group representing any particular institution ever consists of "pure" value types, but that there is probably a modal tendency for the groups indicated to place on the transformation, or continuum line, in the way expressed in the diagram.

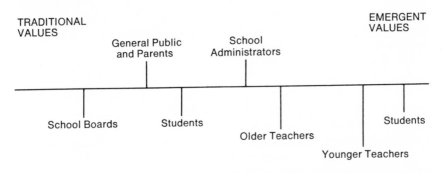

The rationale for the placement of the various groups on the value continuum is fairly complex, but let me try to explain some salient points. School boards are placed nearest the *traditional* end of the continuum because such boards are usually composed of persons representing the power, *status-quo,* elements of the community, and of persons in the higher age ranges. They are therefore people who have a stake in keeping things as they are, who gained their successes within the framework of the traditional value system and consequently believe it to be good, and who, by virtue of their age, grew up and acquired their value sets during a period of time when American Culture was presumably more tradition-oriented than it is today.

The general public and parent group, of course, contains many elements of varying value predilection. It is therefore unrealistic to place this public at any particular point in the value continuum. But I hypothesize that the public *tends* to be more conservative in its social philosophy than the professional education set. The placement to the left of center of the continuum ("left" being "right" in the usual sense) takes on further validity if it is seen as a placement of that part of the public that is most vocal in its criticism of educators and education—since most of the criticisms made appear to spring out of value conflicts between traditionalist and emergentist positions. Parents complain that their children are not being taught the "three R's" (even when they are), that educators want to "socialize" the competitive system by eliminating report cards, that children are not taught the meaning of hard work. These all sound, irrespective of the question of their justification or lack of it, like traditionalist responses to change in an "emergent" direction.

Students are placed at two points on the transformation line because it is clear that those coming from traditionalist family environments will tend to hold traditionalistic values, but hold them less securely than will their parents (if our hypothesis for over-all change is valid), while other students who come from emergent-oriented families will tend to place even further, as a function of their age and peer groups, towards the emergent end of the line than their parents would. This is only partially true, indeed, for such a rationale does not account for the fact that offspring in revolt (and many American children from 6 to 16 are in a state of revolt against parental dictums) may go to extremes in either direction.

School administrators, older, and younger teachers, place at varying points on the emergent half of the transformation line. I have placed them there because I believe that the professional education culture (every institution has its own way of life, in this sense) that they have acquired in the schools and colleges of education has a clear bias towards an emergent-oriented ethos. Many of my educationist colleagues will reject this interpretation, and indeed, such interpretations are always guilty of over-generalization. Others of my colleagues will welcome such a characterization, but still question its validity. My case must rest on the basis of contemporary educational philosophy, theory, and practice. The emphasis is on the "social adjustment" of the individual, upon his role as a member of the group and community. Most of the values listed under the *emergent* heading are explicitly stated in educational literature as goals. Some of them, such as conformity to the group, are implicit. This value, in particular, grows out of the others, is more or less unintended, and constitutes a *covert* or *latent* value, by definition. This is, admittedly, a little like accusing a man of hating his mother, but not knowing it, and such accusations are usually rejected, or rationalized out of existence. But I believe that it is literally impossible to hold the other values in this system and avoid placing a strong emphasis on group harmony, and group control of the individual. My data, at least, gathered largely from graduate students in professional education courses, indicate that this is the case.

But educators and schools do not all come off the same shelf in the supermarket. Older teachers will tend, I hypothesize, to hold relatively traditionalist views by virtue of their age, and time of their childhood training (when they acquired their basic values)—a period in American culture when the traditionalist values were relatively more certain and supported than they are at present. Younger teachers were not only children and acquired their personal culture during a relatively more emergent-oriented period of American history, but they have been (I hypothesize) exposed to a professional education culture that has become rapidly more emergent-oriented in its value position. They are therefore placed near the extreme of the transformation line in the emergent direction.

School administrators come from a different shelf in the same section of the supermarket. They, to be sure, range in age from young to old, come from different family backgrounds, and have been exposed in varying degrees to the professional education culture. But sociological and anthropological studies of the influence of status and role on behavior and perception indicate that these factors tend to over-ride others, and produce certain uniformities of outlook. The school administrator's role is a precarious one—as any school principal or superintendent knows. He faces towards several different audiences, each with different sets of demands—school boards, parents, power groups, teachers, and students—as well as other administrators. He has to play his role appropriately in the light of all these demands. The fact that many cannot, accounts for the increasingly short tenure of personages like school superintendents. But to the extent that he plays *across the board* he will place somewhere towards the center of the line of transformation. Furthermore, his dependence upon the school board, and the power groups in the community, in many cases will tend to make his outlook relatively more conservative, and probably more traditionalistic, than that of his teachers—at least the younger ones. There are many exceptions, of course. I am only claiming *tendencies.*

My thesis, I hope, is clear by now. I am attempting to explain, or help explain, the increasingly bitter and strident attacks on schools and educators, and the conflict and confusion within the ranks. I have claimed that this situation can better be understood as a series of complex but very real conflicts in core values. And I have tried to show the direction of the values shift in American culture and place the various actors in the drama upon a transformation line within this shift.

In this perspective, many conflicts between parents and teachers, school boards and educators, parents and children, and between the various personages and groups within the school system (teachers against teachers, administrators against teachers, and so on) can be understood as conflicts that grow out of sharp differences in values that mirror social and cultural transformation of tremendous scope—and for which none of the actors in the situation can be held personally accountable. This is the real, and perhaps only contribution of this analysis. If these conflicts can be seen as emerging out of great sociocultural shifts—out of a veritable transformation of a way of life—they will lose some of their sting. To understand, the psychiatrist says, is to forgive.

But now, though it seems indeed improper at this point, permit me to add another complication to an already complicated picture. I have tried to make it clear that not only are there variations in values held by groups and different parts of the social body and school institutions, but that there are also various values, some of them contradictory, held by single individuals as diverse streams of influence in their own systems. This is always true in rapid culture-change situations, as the anthropologist and philosopher know.

This means that the situation is not only confused by groups battling each other, but that individuals are fighting themselves. This has certain predictable results, if the anthropological studies of personal adaptation to culture change have any validity. And I believe that those results can be detected in the behaviors of most, if not all, of the actors in the scene. Let me try to clarify this.

I will deal only with teachers, as one of the most important sets of actors on this particular stage. I hypothesize that the child training of most of the people who become teachers has been more tradition than emergent value-oriented. They are drawn largely from middle- to lower-middle social class groups in American society, and this segment of the class structure is the stronghold of the work-success ethic and moral respectability values in our culture (even in a culture that is shifting away from these values). Furthermore, it seems probable that a selective process is operating to draw a relatively puritanistic element into the public school teaching as an occupation. Self-denial, altruism, a moralistic self-concept, seem to be functional prerequisites for the historically-derived role of school teacher in American society (I might have said "school marm").

If this can be granted, then only one other ingredient needs to be added to explain several persistent types of personal adaptation to value conflicts observable among school teachers. That ingredient is one already spelled out— the relatively heavy emphasis, within the professional education culture, on the emergent-oriented value system. Teachers-to-be acquire their personal culture in a more tradition-oriented familiar environment, but they encounter a new kind of culture when in training to become school teachers—in the teacher-training institutions. There is, in this experience, what the anthropologist would call a discontinuity in the *enculturation* of the individual.[4] This is a particular kind of culture-conflict situation that anthropologists have recently begun to study, but mostly in non-western societies undergoing rapid change towards a western way of life.

On the basis of observations of a fair sample of teachers in coastal communities and in the middle west, I hypothesize that three types of adaptation to this personal culture-conflict situation and experience are characteristic.

Ambivalent: This type is characterized by contradictory and vacillating behavior, particularly with respect to the exercise of discipline and authority. The type tends to be *laissez-faire* in some classroom situations, and authoritarian in others, depending upon which behavior is called into being as a defense against threat of loss of control.

Compensatory: This type is characterized by one of two modes of behavior. The teacher overcompensates consistently either in the direction of the emergent or the tradition-centered values. In the first mode he (or she) tends to become a member of a *group-thinkism* cult—a perversion of progressive educational philosophy in action. The total stress is placed on social adjustment. Individuality is not sanctioned to any significant degree. Conformity to the group becomes the key to success. The type, in its extreme form, is a caricature of the better features of the emergent-centered values set. The second type compensates for internal culture-conflict in the opposite direction, and becomes an outright authoritarian. Tight dominance is maintained over children. All relationships with them are formalized and rigid. No deviation is allowed, so curiously enough, there is a convergence in the end-results of both types. This type is a caricature of the better features of the tradition-centered values set.

Adapted: This type can be either traditional or emergent value oriented. But the compensatory and ambivalent mechanisms operating in the first two types are much less intense, or absent. The teacher of this type has come to terms with the value conflict situation and experience, and has chosen (consciously or unconsciously) to act within the framework of one or the other value set. There is consequently a consistency of behavior, and the mode of classroom management and teacher-student relationship is not a caricature of either value system.

No one is in a position to say which of these types is represented in greatest numbers among American public school teachers today, and there are few "pure" types. Certainly there are many traditional and emergent-oriented teachers who have adapted successfully to the personal culture-conflict situa-

---

[4] *Enculturation* is a new, but useful term being used by social scientists. It stands for the process through which the individual acquires the culture of his group or society.

tion and discontinuity of enculturative experience described. But equally certainly there are many school teachers who fall more clearly into one or the other typologies. It would be asking too much to suppose that a cultural values-conflict situation as intense as the one transforming American culture could be handled without strain by the key agent of the culture-transmission process—the school teacher. But again, to understand is to forgive.

In any event, it seems clear that if conditions are even partially of the nature described, the group culture-conflict situation resulting in attacks by representatives of those groups upon each other is intensified and at the same time confused by the personal culture-conflict problem. Both processes must be seen, and understood, as resultants of a larger culture-transformation process.

In conclusion to this by-far unfinished analysis (the next 20 years may tell the more complete story), let me make it clear that I am not castigating either the emergentists, or the traditionalists. Value systems must always be functional in terms of the demands of the social and economic structure of a people. The traditional mode has much that is good about it. There is a staunchness, and a virility in it that many of us may view with considerable nostalgia in some future time. But rugged individualism (in its expedient, ego-centered form), and rigid moralism (with its capacity for displaced hate) become nonfunctional in a society where people are rubbing shoulders in polyglot masses, and playing with a technology that may destroy, or save, with a pushing of buttons. The emergentist position seems to be growing in strength. Social adaptability, relativistic outlooks, sensitivity to the needs and opinions of others, and of the group, seem functional in this new age. But perhaps we need, as people, educators, anthropologists, and parents, to examine our premises more closely. The emergentist can become a group conformist—an average man proud of his well-rounded averageness—without really meaning to at all.

And lastly I would like to reiterate the basic theme of this article. Conflicts between groups centering on issues of educational relevance, and confusions within the rank and file of educators, can be understood best, I believe, in the perspective of the transformation of American culture that proceeds without regard for personal fortune or institutional survival. This transformation, it is true, can be guided and shaped to a considerable degree by the human actors on the scene. But they cannot guide and shape their destiny within this transformation if their energies are expended in knifing attacks on each other in such a central arena as education, or if their energies are dissipated in personal confusions. I am arguing, therefore, for the functional utility of understanding, and of insight into the all-encompassing transformation of American culture and its educational-social resultants.

16
A Redefinition of Education

MARGARET MEAD

A strong belief that schools must pace their program offerings to the rapidly changing world in which we live has led Margaret Mead to propose a restructuring of the educational system. In redefining education, Professor Mead places greater emphasis on the individual (child or adult) and his personal educational needs. Discussing our present conception of what the educational institution is, she goes on to explain that in the future, education must consist of "lateral," as well as "vertical," transmission of knowledge. In this light, she describes the teacher as any informed person who shares his knowledge with the uninformed. As a matter of fact, this description of a teacher may be said to be a reasonably accurate one today: in all walks of life, one finds the young teaching the old and vice versa.

WHEN WE LOOK realistically at today's world and become aware of what the actual problems of learning are, our conception of education changes radically. Although the educational system remains basically unchanged, we are no longer dealing primarily with the vertical transmission of the tried and true by the old, mature, and experienced teacher to the young, immature, and inexperienced pupil in the classroom.

This was the system of education developed in a stable, slowly changing culture. By itself, vertical transmission of knowledge no longer adequately serves the purposes of education in a world of rapid change.

What is needed and what we are already moving toward is the inclusion of another whole dimension of learning: the lateral transmission, to every sentient member of society, of what has just been discovered, invented, created, manufactured, or marketed.

This need for lateral transmission exists no less in the classroom and laboratory than it does on the assembly line with its working force of experienced

SOURCE: *NEA Journal,* October 1959, pp. 15–17. Reprinted by permission of the author and publisher.

One of the outstanding anthropologists of this century, Margaret Mead is famous for her studies of the native cultures of Samoa and New Guinea. She has often turned her attention to the problems of education and culture, and has led the way for increased contributions by anthropologists to education. Currently associated with the American Museum of Natural History, she is the author, among other works, of *The School in American Culture, Cultural Patterns and Technical Change,* and *Childhood in Contemporary Culture.*

179

and raw workmen. The man who teaches another individual the new mathematics or the use of a newly invented tool is not sharing knowledge he acquired years ago. He learned what was new yesterday, and his pupil must learn it today.

The whole teaching-and-learning continuum, once tied in an orderly and productive way to the passing of generations and the growth of the child into a man, has exploded in our faces. Yet even as we try to catch hold of and patch up the pieces, we fail to recognize what has happened.

We have moved into a period in which the break with the past provides an opportunity for creating a new framework for activity in almost every field— but in each field the fact that there has been a break must be rediscovered. In education there has been up to now no real recognition of the extent to which our present system is outmoded.

Historians point sagely to the last two educational crises—the first of which ended with the establishment of the universal elementary school and the second with the establishment of the universal high school—and with remarkable logic and lack of imagination they predict that the present crisis will follow the same pattern.

According to such predictions, the crisis will last until 1970, when it will end with the establishment of universal college education, accessible in principle to all young Americans.

Implicit in this prediction is a series of other dubious assumptions, such as these:

1. Our educational system has fallen behind in something and should therefore arrange to catch up.
2. Our difficulties are due to the "bulge," the host of babies that tricked the statisticians.
3. The pendulum is swinging back to sense—to discipline and dunce caps, switches, and multiplication tables.

But in the midst of the incessant discussion and the search for scapegoats to take the blame for what everyone admits is a parlous state, extraordinarily little attention is being paid to basic issues. Everyone simply wants more of what we already have: more children in more schools for more hours studying more of something.

Likewise, scant attention is paid to the fact that two great new educational agencies, the armed services and industry, have entered the field, and there is little awareness of the ways in which operations in these institutions are altering traditional education.

But most important, the pattern itself is hardly questioned, for we think we know what education is and what a good education ought to be. However deficient we may be as a people, as taxpayers, or as educators, we may be actualizing our ideals.

An occasional iconoclast can ask: "Wouldn't it be fine if we could scrap our whole school system and start anew?" But he gets no hearing because everyone knows that what he is saying is nonsense. Wishful dreams of starting anew are obviously impractical, but this does not mean that someone should not ask these crucial questions:

Is our present historic idea of education suitable for people in the mid-twentieth century, who have a life expectancy of 70 years, and who live in a world of automation and global communication, ready to begin space exploration and aware of the possibility of bringing about the suicide of the entire human species?

Is it not possible that the problem of the educational system's obsolescence goes beyond such issues as methods of teaching reading or physics, or the most desirable age for leaving school, or the payment of teachers, or the length of summer holidays, or the number of years best devoted to college?

Is not the break between past and present—and so the whole problem of outdating in our educational system—related to a change in the rate of change? For change has become so rapid that adjustment cannot be left to the next generation. Adults must—not once, but continually—take in, adjust to, use, and make innovations in a steady stream of discovery and new conditions.

Is it not possible that an educational system that was designed to teach what was known to little children and to a selected few young men may not fit a world in which the most important factors in everyone's life are those things that are not yet, but soon will be known?

Is it not equally possible that our present definition of a pupil or a student is out of date when we define the learner as a child (or at best an immature person) who is entitled to moral protection and subsistence in a dependency position and who is denied the moral autonomy that is accorded to an adult?

Looking at our educational system today, we can see that in various ways it combines these different functions:

1. The protection of the child against exploitation and the protection of society against precocity and inexperience
2. The maintenance of learners in a state of moral and economic dependency
3. Giving to all children the special, wider education once reserved for those of privileged groups, in an attempt to form the citizen of a democracy as once the son of a noble house was formed
4. The teaching of complex and specialized skills which, under our complex system of division of labor, is too difficult and time-consuming for each set of parents to master or to hand on to their own children
5. The transmission of something which the parents' generation does not know (in the case of immigrants with varied cultural and linguistic backgrounds) to children whom the authorities or the parents wish to have educated.

To these multiple functions of an educational system, which in a slowly changing society were variously performed, we have added slowly and reluctantly a quite new function: education for rapid and self-conscious adaptation to a changing world.

That we have as yet failed to recognize the new character of change is apparent in a thousand ways. Despite the fact that a subject taught to college freshmen may have altered basically by the time the same students are seniors, it is still said that colleges are able to give students "a good education" —finished, wrapped, sealed with a degree.

Upon getting a bachelor's degree, a student can decide to "go on" to a higher degree because he has not as yet "completed" his education, that is, the lump of the known which he has decided to bite off. But a student who has once let a year go by after he is "out of school" does not "go on," but rather "goes back" to school.

And as we treat education as the right of a minor who has not yet completed high school, just so we equate marriage and parenthood with getting a diploma; both indicate that one's education is "finished."

Consistent with our conception of what a student is, our educational institutions are places where we keep "children" for a shorter or longer period. The length of time depends in part on their intelligence and motivation and in part on their parents' incomes and the immediately recognized national needs for particular skills or types of training.

Once they have left, we regard them as in some sense finished, neither capable of nor in need of further "education," for we still believe that education should come all in one piece, or rather, in a series of connected pieces, each presented as a whole at the elementary, secondary, and the college level. All other behaviors are aberrant.

So we speak of "interrupted" education—that is, education which has been broken into by sickness, delinquency, or military service—and we attempt to find means of repairing this interruption. Indeed, the whole GI bill, which in a magnificent way gave millions of young men a chance for a different kind of education than they would otherwise have got, was conceived of primarily as a means of compensating young men for an unsought but unavoidable interruption.

Thus we avoid facing the most vivid truth of the new age: No one will live all his life in the world into which he was born, and no one will die in the world in which he worked in his maturity.

For those who work on the growing edge of science, technology, or the arts, contemporary life changes at even shorter intervals. Often, only a few months may elapse before something which previously was easily taken for granted must be unlearned or transformed to fit the new state of knowledge or practice.

In today's world, no one can "complete an education." The students we need are not just children who are learning to read and write, plus older students, conceived of as minors, who are either "going on" with or "going back" to specialized education. Rather, we need children and adolescents and young and mature and "senior" adults, each of whom is learning at the appropriate pace and with all the special advantages and disadvantages of experience peculiar to his own age.

Each and every one of these is a learner, not only of the old and tried—the alphabet or multiplication tables or Latin declensions or French irregular verbs or the binomial theorem—but of new, hardly tried theories and methods: pattern analysis, general system theory, space lattices, cybernetics, and so on.

Learning of this kind must go on, not only at special times and in special places, but all through production and consumption—from the technician who must handle a new machine to the factory supervisor who must introduce its use, the union representative who must interpret it to the men, the foreman who must keep the men working, the salesman who must service a new device or find markets for it, the housewife who must understand how to care for a new material, the mother who must answer the questions of a four-year-old child.

In this world, the age of the teacher is no longer necessarily relevant. For instance, children teach grandparents how to manage TV, young expediters come into the factory along with the new equipment, and young men invent automatic programing for computers over which their seniors struggle.

This, then, is what we call the lateral transmission of knowledge. It is not an outpouring of knowledge from the "wise old teacher" into the minds of young pupils, as in vertical transmission. Rather, it is sharing of knowledge by the informed with the uninformed, whatever their ages. The primary prerequisite for the learner is the desire to know.

To facilitate this lateral transmission of knowledge, we need to redefine what we mean by primary and secondary education. We need to stop thinking that free and, when necessary, subsidized education is appropriate only when it is preliminary to an individual's work experience.

Instead of adding more and more years of compulsory education (which would further confuse the meaning of education and the purpose of schools), we need to separate primary and secondary education in an entirely new way:

By primary education we would mean the stage of education in which all children are taught what they need to know in order to be fully human in the world in which they are growing up—including the basic skills of reading and writing and a basic knowledge of numbers, money, geography, transportation and communication, the law, and the nations of the world.

By secondary education we would mean an education that is based on primary education, and that can be obtained in any amount and at any period during the individual's whole lifetime.

After agreeing upon this redefinition, we could begin to deal effectively with the vast new demands that are being made on us. The high schools would be relieved of the nonlearners. (It would be essential, of course, that industry, government, or some other social group accept the responsibility of employing or otherwise occupying these persons.)

But more important, men and women, instead of preparing for a single career to which—for lack of any alternative—they must stick during their entire active lives, would realize that they might learn something else. Women, after their children became older, could be educated for particular new tasks, instead of facing the rejection that today is related to fear about the difficulty of acquiring new learning in middle age.

Whatever their age, those obtaining a secondary education at any level (high school, college, or beyond) would be in school because they wanted to learn and wanted to be there at that time.

In an educational system of this kind, we could give primary education and protection to children as well as protection and sensitive supervision to adolescents. We could back up to the hilt the potentiality of every human being —of whatever age—to learn at any level.

The right to obtain secondary education when and where the individual could use it would include not only the right of access to existing conventional types of schools but also the right of access to types of work training not yet or only now being developed—new kinds of apprenticeship and also new kinds of work teams.

In thinking about an effective educational system, we should recognize that the adolescent's need and right to work is as great as (perhaps greater than) his immediate need and right to study. And we must recognize that the adult's need and right to study more is as great as (perhaps greater than) his need and right to hold the same job until he is 65.

We cannot accomplish the essential educational task merely by keeping children and young adults—whom we treat like children—in school longer. We can do it by creating an educational system in which all individuals will be assured of the secondary and higher education they want and can use any time throughout their entire lives.

EVALUATION

GEORGE D. SPINDLER, **Education in a Transforming Culture**

1. How does Spindler explain the "increasingly strident attacks" on the American public school system?

2. What does Spindler regard as the core of this conflict?

3. (a) From what point of view does the author choose to discuss these attacks?

   (b) What is his emphasis within this framework?

4. (a) List the five traditional and five emergent values Spindler perceives as reflecting cultural value shifts in American society.

   (b) Give explanatory statements of the values you have identified in this cultural shift.

5. (a) What does Spindler say is the effect of this shift in cultural values upon education?

   (b) Sketch the diagram showing the author's values continuum and place the seven different groups he has identified in their respective positions on this continuum.

6. (a) What does Spindler say about the rationale for placement of these various groups on the continuum?

   (b) Briefly state Spindler's rationale for his placement of each group.

7. Identify three functional prerequisites which Spindler sees as accounting for the tradition value-oriented "school marm."

8. (a) What are the three types of adaptation to the personal culture-conflict situation and experience viewed by the author as being characteristic of many teachers today?

   (b) Briefly define each of these.

9. What is the basic theme of Spindler's selection?

MARGARET MEAD, **A Redefinition of Education**

10. (a) Describe how education conceived the transmission of knowledge in a stable, slowly changing culture, according to Mead.

    (b) What approach does Mead advocate for coping most effectively with today's world of rapid change?

    (c) Does she recommend total rejection of the old method? Briefly explain.

11. According to Mead, with what are people concerning themselves, instead of the basic issues?

12. List five traditional functions of the educational system.

13. What new function does Mead add to the above to meet today's educational needs?

14. (a) What does the author say is the most vivid truth of the new age?

    (b) What is the outcome of this, if we are to accept it as the truth?

15. (a) In the lateral transmission of knowledge, what is it that occurs between all persons regardless of age?

    (b) What does Mead say is needed in order to facilitate lateral transmission?

16. (a) Identify the two major divisions into which Mead would restructure education.

    (b) In terms of content, how has Mead dichotomized these levels of education?

17. How is motivation inherent in the philosophy of the restructured education scheme Mead proposes?

18. What is Mead's final word of advice for accomplishing the essential educational tasks?

FOR FURTHER READING

Kluckhohn, Clyde, "Queer Customs," *Mirror for Man* (New York: McGraw-Hill, 1949).
  A fun kind of reading in which the attitude of the author is that cultures are like "Topsy," they just grow. His writing reflects this with more than a trace of good humor. Kluckhohn calls for recognition and tolerance of cultural differences among the people of the world and suggests that an understanding of our own culture and that of others is fundamental to changing this narrow contemporary world.

Mead, Margaret, "Our Educational Emphases in Primitive Perspective," *Teaching: Essays and Readings,* ed. K. Yamanoto (Boston, Mass.: Houghton Mifflin, 1969).
  A discussion of education in its cultural context, as a cultural process. The author equates the newborn child in a modern city and the savage infant born into some primitive South Sea tribe. She says that "both have everything to learn." This is a selection that can help you to find a new meaning to the old word "teaching."

PART TWO

Education
as an Academic Field

Every subject has a structure, a rightness,
a beauty. It is this structure that provides
the underlying simplicity of things, and it
is by learning its nature that we come to
appreciate the intrinsic meaning of a subject.

JEROME S. BRUNER
"Structure in Learning,"
NEA Journal,
March 1963, p. 26.

Education has many applications, one of which is teaching. Historically speaking, education has had practically no problem receiving recognition as a unique academic field. However, pedagogy, the science of teaching, has met many obstacles that have prevented its admission to the professional arena of science. The group of selections you will now read deal with the academic field in all its major aspects. The first four selections reflect the approach taken by educators of the field through the years. These are followed by an overview of American education as it is organized and financed. The last six selections report on some interesting innovative practices that appear to be changing the responsibilities and roles of school administrators, teachers, and other school personnel.

In "Lectures to School-Masters on Teaching" (Selection 17), Samuel R. Hall gives the qualifications he believed should be required for teaching. The emphasis he places on personal attributes in contrast to literary competencies is not at all surprising when one considers that he was writing in the early nineteenth century, a time not far removed from the puritan period in American history.

In the next two selections, John S. Brubacher (Selection 18) and Harry S. Broudy (Selection 19) discuss teaching with quite a different emphasis than did Hall. Their focus is upon the teaching process and its procedures as the teacher's personal characteristics seem to fade into the background. Students will find an open door here to discussions on the finer points of the teaching process. They may agree or disagree with the analogy drawn by Brubacher between teaching and the techniques of fine art instruction, but his description of a good teacher is an invitation to evaluate teachers by application of this analogy. Broudy also regards teaching as an art, but this point of view tempts him to relegate all but the so-called art of teaching to mechanical instructional devices. He is severely critical of teachers and predicts that computer-based instruction in our schools will eliminate many of them.

In "Accountability for Student Learning" (Selection 20), Erwin Harlacher and Eleanor Roberts inform us that the new instructional concept of guaranteed learning can be traced to the attention currently being given to "accountability" in education. They are critical of teaching-centered classrooms and advocate that learning-centered classrooms should replace them. Their prediction is that this change would result in a marked increase in the number of students who will learn what is being taught. The authors identify three areas in which major changes must occur within instructional programs if instruction is to be improved and if student learning is to be increased. Students will see a relationship between some production techniques in the business world and the instructional techniques recommended here. This selection brings us center stage in the twentieth century's demands for accountability in education.

The organization and financing of American education is the next topic considered. The overview of education in the United States which John Paxton presents (Selection 21) has been carefully written so that a visitor to this country could be intelligently informed on the subject. To provide an understanding of the structure of education in the United States, Cann (Selection 22) delineates the organization of education on the national, state, and local levels. The charts accompanying both of these selections will serve as a basis for further study and as a guideline for understanding more complex administrative structures.

A selection on school finance (Selection 23), taken from a statement published by the National Education Association, concludes this group of readings. Perhaps one of the most relevant parts of this selection for prospective teachers will be the identification of basic responsibilities placed upon the teaching profession in the area of school financing.

Innovations in education are changing educational practices. In "An Educational System Analyzed" (Selection 24) Burton G. Andreas states that an individual's education is comprised of social and psychological processes and his formal education is a subsystem of his on-going development. Andreas's analysis of education includes six specific steps that he claims will lead to individualized development. His explanation appears somewhat oversimplified when we consider the maturation-learning psychology upon which his theory is based.

Next (Selection 25), Harold S. Davis describes very precisely why team teaching is desirable and how to organize an effective team teaching program. After a student follows each step Davis outlines, and certainly after he has had some experience in this way of organizing team teaching, it is quite probable that he will dispute the description of team teaching Andreas presents in the previous selection. Davis does not draw any parallel or appear to differentiate between "team teaching" and "teaching teams" and, in fact, the description of his technique seems to indicate that such an analogy would be of doubtful validity. Andreas's and Davis's views deserve a careful comparison.

One other innovation now being implemented in many schools in the United States is differentiated staffing. A statement by the United States Commissioner of Education (Selection 26) discusses a basis for introducing this innovation. Students will recognize some similarities here between the Lancastrian system of instruction practiced at the turn of the present century and differentiated staffing practices. Also implied, although not declared here, is the prospect of a definitive hierarchy of jobs within a school system and subsequently a scale of pay matching each level of task and responsibility. This hierarchy is unequivocally declared as part of differentiated staffing in "Towards a Differentiated Teaching Staff" (Selection 27), in which John M. Rand and Fenwick English openly challenge traditional salary scales in American schools. They advocate the change and present the Temple City plan as a model for rewarding teachers who assume greater responsibilities in the instructional program. Both selections on differentiated staffing will help you to anticipate some of the changes when you enter the teaching profession in the present decade.

"The Phantom Nongraded School" (Selection 28) by William P. McLoughlin criticizes those educators who claim to have nongraded schools when in fact they do not. McLoughlin raises a number of points worth your thoughtful consideration, for there are school administrators and teachers who too frequently claim to be innovators who actually are not. Here it is well to remember that "saying it is so does not make it so."

The next selection, "Opportunities for Enterprise in Education" (Selection 29) by Donald D. Durrell, has been chosen to show you that there *are* opportunities for an enterprising person in education. Durrell's prognosis for teacher education holds special significance for those already in the teaching profession as well as others preparing to enter the field. His concept of cooperative competitive education is somewhat novel, as are his ten predictions for education. His ideas will appeal to the imagination of creative individuals even though they may not agree with them. Again, this is a reading that probes into the unknown with a certain element of audacious courage.

From the earliest teachers' institutes to current elaborate teacher preparation programs, teacher education has included, in varying degrees, both the study of recognized disciplines and pedagogy. Pedagogy has never received recognition as a science, for various reasons. One reason without a doubt has been the failure to identify precise pedagogical principles and to support these principles with adequate empirical data. When the science of teaching is admitted to the professional arena of the sciences, then perhaps teaching will move toward recognition as a profession. As a future teacher, an awareness of these facts will help make your study of the readings in this part of the book more meaningful to you.

The Past and the Present

17

Lectures to School-Masters on Teaching

SAMUEL R. HALL

Following is one of the earliest lectures to teachers given by Samuel Hall. In it he addresses himself to "school-masters," since women teachers were accepted only at the "dame school" level in early American education. Considering the requirements for teachers as Hall believed they should be, it is interesting to notice that many of these reflect qualifications expected of teachers today. He appears to give more attention to the personal qualifications of a teacher than to academic requirements for teaching. However, Hall does state that a "defect" in a teacher's knowledge unequivocally infers a "defect" in his teaching, and he places the responsibility for laying the foundation of an education directly upon the teacher.

1. HAVING ADVERTED in the preceding Lecture, to certain existing evils, unfriendly to the character and usefulness of common schools, I shall, in this, call your attention to *the requisite qualifications of an instructer.* This subject is of high importance. All who possess the requisite *literary* attainments, are not qualified to assume the direction of a school. Many entirely fail of usefulness, though possessed of highly cultivated minds. Other things are required in the character of a good school-master. Among these, *common sense* is the first. This is a qualification exceedingly important, as in teaching school one has constant occasion for its exercise. Many, by no means deficient in intel-

SOURCE: Gerald Lee Gutek, *An Historical Introduction to American Education* (New York: Thomas Y. Crowell Co., 1970), pp. 163–166. Reprinted by permission of the publisher.

The author (1795–1877) founded the first private normal school for teachers in 1823 at Concord, New Hampshire. He was a graduate of one of the early academies, the Kimball Union Academy, and then devoted the remainder of his life to teaching. The first textbook written for teachers in American schools was Hall's *Lectures on School-keeping* (1829), in which he revealed the serious lack in teachers who were "keeping" schools then.

lect, are not persons of *common* sense. I mean by the term, that faculty by which things are seen as they are. It implies judgment and discrimination, and a proper sense of propriety in regard to the common affairs of life. It leads us to form judicious plans of action, and to be governed by our circumstances, in the way which men in general will approve. It is the exercise of reason, uninfluenced by passion or prejudice. It is in man nearly what instinct is in brutes. Very different from genius or talent, as they are commonly defined, it is better than either. Never blazing forth with the splendor of noon, but it shines with a constant and useful light.

2. *Uniformity of temper* is another important trait in the character of an instructer. Where this is wanting, it is hardly possible to govern or to teach with success. He, whose temper is constantly varying, can never be uniform in his estimation of things around him. Objects change in their appearance as his passions change. What appears right in any given hour may seem wrong in the next. What appears desirable to-day, may be beheld with aversion to-morrow. An uneven temper, in any situation of life, subjects one to many inconveniences. But when placed in a situation where his every action is observed and where his authority, must be in constant exercise, the man who labors under this malady is especially unfortunate. It is impossible for him to gain and preserve respect among his pupils. No one who comes under the rule of a person of uneven temper, can know what to expect or how to act.

3. A capacity to *understand and discriminate character,* is highly important to him who engages in teaching. The dispositions of children are so various, the treatment and government of parents so dissimilar, that the most diversified modes of governing and teaching need to be employed. The instructor who is not able to discriminate, but considers all alike, and treats all alike, does injury to many. The least expression of disapprobation to one, is often more than the severest reproof to another; a word of encouragement will be sufficient to excite attention in some, while others will require to be urged, by every motive that can be placed before them. All the varying shades of disposition and capacity should be quickly learned by the instructer, that he may benefit all and do injustice to none. Without this, well meant efforts may prove hurtful, because ill-directed, and the desired object may be defeated, by the very means used to obtain it.

4. Teachers should possess much *decision of character.* In every situation of life this trait is important, but in none more so, than in that of which I am treating. The little world, by which he is surrounded, is a miniature of the older community. Children have their aversions and partialities, their hopes and fears, their plans, schemes, propensities and desires. These are often in collision with each other and not unfrequently in collision with the laws of the school, and in opposition to the best interest of themselves. Amidst all these, the instructer should be able to pursue a uniform course. He ought not

to be easily swayed from what he considers right. If easily led from his purpose, or induced to vary from established rules, his school must become a scene of disorder. Without decision, the teacher loses the confidence and respect of his pupils. I would not say, that, if, convinced of having committed an error, or of having given a wrong judgment, you should persist in the wrong. But I would say, it should be known as one of your first principles in school-keeping, that what is required must be complied with in every case, unless cause can be shown why the rule ought, in a given instance, to be dispensed with. There should *then* be a frank and easy compliance with the reasonable wish of the scholar. In a word, without decision of purpose in a teacher, his scholars can never be brought under that kind of discipline, which is requisite for his own ease and convenience, or for the improvement in knowledge, of those placed under him.

5. A school-master ought to be *affectionate*. The human heart is so constituted, that it cannot resist the influence of kindness. When affectionate intercourse is the offspring of those kind feelings which arise from true benevolence, it will have an influence on all around. It leads to ease in behavior, and genuine politeness of manners. It is especially desirable in those who are surrounded by the young. Affectionate parents usually see their children exhibit similar feelings. Instructers who cultivate affection, will generally excite the same in their scholars. No object is more important than to gain the love and good will of those we are to teach. In no way is this more easily accomplished than by a kind interest manifested in their welfare; an interest which is exhibited by actions as well as words. This cannot fail of being attended with desirable results.

6. A just *moral discernment,* is of pre-eminent importance in the character of an instructer. Unless governed by a consideration of his moral obligation, he is but poorly qualified to discharge the duties which devolve upon him. He is himself a moral agent, and accountable to himself, to his employers, to his country and to his God, for the faithful discharge of duty. If he have no moral sensibility, no fear of disobeying the laws of God, no regard for the institutions of our holy religion, how can he be expected to lead his pupils in the way that they should go? The cultivation of virtuous propensities is more important to children than even their intellectual culture. The *virtuous* man, though illiterate, will be happy, while the learned, if *vicious,* must be miserable in proportion to his attainments. The remark of the ancient philosopher, that 'boys ought to be taught that which they will most need to practise when they come to be men,' is most true. To cultivate virtuous habits, and awaken virtuous principles;—to excite a sense of duty to God and of dependence on Him, should be the first objects of the teacher. If he permits his scholars to indulge in vicious habits—if he regard nothing as sin, but that which is a transgression of the laws of the school, if he suffer lying, profaneness, or other crimes, to pass unnoticed and unpunished, he is doing an injury for

which he can in no way make amends. An instructer without moral feeling, not only brings ruin to the children placed under his care, but does injury to their parents, to the neighborhood, to the town and, doubtless, to other generations. The moral character of instructers should be considered a subject of very high importance; and let every one, who knows himself to be immoral, renounce at once the thought of such an employment, while he continues to disregard the laws of God, and the happiness of his fellow men. Genuine piety is highly desirable in every one entrusted with the care and instruction of the young; but morality, at least should be *required,* in every candidate for that important trust.

7. Passing over many topics connected with those already mentioned, I shall now remark on the necessary literary qualifications of a school-master. It will at once be apparent that no one is qualified for this business, who has not a thorough knowledge of the branches required to be taught in common schools. These are Reading, Spelling, Writing, Grammar, Arithmetic, Geography, and in some states the History of the United States. All these branches are necessary, to enable individuals to perform the common business and common duties of life. The four first are requisite in writing a letter on business or to a friend. The fifth is required in the business transactions of every day. The two last are necessary to enable every one to understand what he reads in the common newspapers, or in almost every book which comes within his reach. Of each of these branches, the instructer should certainly have a thorough knowledge; for he ought to have a full knowledge of what he is to teach. As he is to lay the *foundation* of an education, he should be well acquainted with the first principles of science. Of the letters of the alphabet such disposition is made, as to produce an immense number of words, to each of which a distinct meaning is given. 'The nature and power of letters, and just method of spelling words,' should be very distinctly understood. If there be defect in *knowledge* here, there must be a defect in teaching. A man cannot be expected to teach that which he does not know himself. Among all the defects I have witnessed in the literary qualification of instructers, the most common, by far the most common, have been here. Among a great number, both of males and females, I have found *very few* who possessed the requisite knowledge of the nature and power of letters, and rules of spelling. The defect originates in the fact, that these subjects are neglected after childhood, and much that is learned then is subsequently forgotten. Teachers, afterwards, especially of academies, presume that these subjects are familiar, and seldom make the inquiry of scholars, whether they have sufficient knowledge on these points. As a considerable part of every school is composed of those who are learning to spell and read, much importance is attached to the requisite qualifications of the teacher, to lay a proper foundation for subsequent attainments.

18

Teaching as a Fine Art

JOHN S. BRUBACHER

The next two selections in this study of education as an academic field look closely at teaching as an art. It has often been debated whether teaching is an art or science. Brubacher reflects on the nineteenth-century controversy over whether teaching was an art or a science, but his discussion is restricted in that he chooses to regard it solely as an art and even more precisely as a fine art. His basic criterion for measuring the effectiveness of teaching is the quality of subjectivity in a teaching situation.

Constantly seeking a perfection of technique which yields clarity and unity together with an ever increasing joy in his art is the deepest satisfaction of life, according to this author.

IN THE nineteenth century there was a great controversy over whether teaching was a science or an art. Prior to that time teaching, it was generally agreed, was an art. After that time, teaching steadily advanced toward the coveted status of a science. My present plea is that you prospective teachers regard it, not only as an art and a science, but as a fine art as well.

Perhaps you are somewhat surprised to hear teaching classified as a fine art. Conventionally the fine arts have been restricted to such arts as music, painting, and dancing. But it seems to me unfair, even undemocratic, to limit the fine arts to such a limited number of media. Not every one has talent in music, painting, and dancing. Therefore, if other media are not admitted, many will be deprived of the great joy and satisfaction which comes from producing a fine art. I want to propose that all the arts—the industrial, domestic, and agricultural arts as well as those of music, painting, and dancing —be considered capable of treatment as fine arts.

The mechanic who keeps working at a motor till it hums smoothly without a skip or a knock gets a satisfaction in his work which is not to be compared unfavorably with that of the musician who works to perfect an arpeggio. The wife who bakes a pie with flaky crust and sweet flavored contents can take a

SOURCE: *School of Education Bulletin,* the University of Michigan, Vol. 16, No. 8 (May 1941), pp. 115–119. Reprinted by permission of the publisher.

The author has taught at Dartmouth College, Columbia University, the University of Michigan, and also spent a year at the American University in Beirut, Lebanon, as professor of the history and philosophy of education. His major contributions are his publications in history, philosophy, and the legal aspects of education.

pride in her product which should not suffer in comparison to that of the artist who models in clay. And who is to say that the farmer who turns a neat furrow does not know the satisfaction of ploughing as a fine art?

Obviously, the determination of whether teaching is a fine art does not and should not depend upon the medium through which it expresses itself. The character of teaching as a fine art rather lies in a different direction, in the way in which it treats its medium. Let us first look for this character in the etymology of the phrase "fine art." The word "art" stems from the Latin *ars* (*artis*) which points to the agency of man in trying to do or make something, in contriving to adapt the means at hand to the purposes or ends which he has in mind. The corresponding Greek word is $\tau\epsilon\chi\nu\dot{\eta}$ from which we derive our English "technique."

The word "fine" takes its genesis in the Latin word *finis* meaning finish or end. This genesis has a double significance for our purposes. On the one hand fine art means "finished" art. Finished art not only indicates art that has been completed but art that has been so thoroughly well done that little or nothing remains to do to it. If not perfect, it at least has been perfected. On the other hand, fine art may mean that an art or technique is pursued not merely as a means to an end but as an "end" in itself. Technique, like the play, is the thing.

So described, can teaching be a fine art? An art or technique it certainly is. And the only thing which stands in the way of its being a fine art is the fact that we as teachers don't keep working at it day in and day out to perfect it at every point. Let me commend such an objective to you as you begin your careers as teachers.

But how will you know whether your teaching is approaching the stage of fine art? Naturally you must have some criteria by which to judge your work and by which to guide your further efforts. I suggest that the criteria of the fine art of teaching are the same as the criteria of any other fine art. These criteria have three dimensions: intensity, clarity, and unity.

Let us take the first criterion, intensity. Teaching becomes a fine art to the extent that it results in an intensification of interest or heightened appreciation by both pupil *and* teacher in the work at hand. Unless there is this deepening of feeling, teaching, no matter how good, is but craftmanship. Teaching as a fine art, therefore, is something more than just "good" or "effective" teaching. The good Herbartian teacher might be measured by his command of the "five steps." The effective project teacher might be measured by his understanding of the project technique. But the artistic teacher is judged by the degree to which his teaching, no matter what technique he employs, gives more intense emotional satisfaction from the activity learned.

Perhaps the point may be illustrated by the experience of a school superintendent who promoted a promising young teacher over the head of a much older member of the staff. The latter naturally protested and inquired whether his twenty years experience did not count at all. To this complaint the superintendent replied, "I beg your pardon. You have not had twenty years experience, but only one, which you have repeated nineteen times!"

Or take the designer of women's hats. Suppose he succeeds in creating one with graceful lines and a pleasing combination of colors. And then suppose that, delighted with his success, he manufactures a hundred or more such hats. To be sure, the first of these hats was a work of fine art, but how about the succeeding ones? Was each of these a work of fine art too? Hardly. Each was like the preceding. There was no new increment of emotional feeling each time the hat was duplicated.

If teaching seems to become monotonous, if the succession of classes becomes "humdrum," it is a sure sign that the teaching is failing of the standard of fine art. To use the same lesson plan, to repeat the same method, to cling to the same curriculum year after year is fatal to artistic teaching. To be sure, the teacher, like the actor, must constantly keep studying his lines. This is not to keep from forgetting them but to search them for some new addition of feeling. Not every audience laughs or cries at the same point or in response to the same gesture or tone of voice. The good actor must be alive to these differences. And so must the teacher be alert to individual differences in his classes. Only by seizing on the different and novel will he make his teaching a creative experience, a fine art.

Now let us take the second criterion of fine art, clarity. Teaching becomes a fine art in proportion as it leads to the clarification of meaning, to heightened discrimination. Fine discrimination makes the teacher sensitive to the fine points of his techniques. Here the word "fine" emphasizes very small or subtle phases of his art. Take tight-rope walking, for instance. The beginner makes gross adjustments in order to balance himself. He lurches to the right and then lurches to the left. The expert, however, maintains his balance by movements that are almost imperceptible for their fineness. Yet it is these little movements which, when added all together, make up the artistic performance.

It is no different in teaching. The teacher who attends a good teachers college or a good school of education will soon learn to make the major adjustments. But the fine adjustments—these come only by persistent attention to detail over the years. Such persistent attention to detail is undoubtedly arduous. Yet the true artist finds genuine joy in the mastery of detail, however arduous the process. If he does not, if the mastery of each new detail does not bring an intensification of interest, then, as already seen, he must be on guard lest his teaching fall away from the high standard of fine art.

One of the finest examples I know of a teacher's command of detail occurred in my college class on theme writing. There we had to write a daily theme about a page in length. On a single page we had to catch and portray some amusing incident, some color we had seen, some feeling we had experienced. And we had to write it so well that the reader vicariously derived the same reaction to it we ourselves had had. To show us the "fine" points of writing one day the instructor read us a theme of his own composition. In it he took us up to the top floor of the freshman dormitory where he leaned out of the window watching a hurdy-gurdy grinder down below. Some of the freshmen were heating pennies and throwing them down. How funny it seemed to see the surprise of the hurdy-gurdy grinder when he suddenly had to drop his prize. The next moment our instructor told the same story to us from the hurdy-gurdy grinder's point of view. Our faces sobered at once when we thought of adding cruelty to the already great burden of making so meager and precarious a living. To be able to cause amusement and disgust on the same facts in a few minutes time, I say, required command of the finest and subtlest detail of teaching.

Clarity demands not only fine discrimination but also communication. If the teacher achieves clarity of understanding through teaching but the pupil does not, then we have gained only half a loaf of the fine art of teaching. In other words, the fine art of teaching is peculiarly a social art. Clarity must be communicated or teaching fails of being a fine art. The composers of modern music and the painters of modern art often seem to ignore their public and still maintain the fineness of their art. But again let me say, the teacher simply cannot do this; he must communicate his meaning or surrender his claim to being an artist.

Finally, let us consider the third criterion, unity. Teaching approaches a fine art when it results in enabling both pupil and teacher to comprehend the unity of the whole process. There are various patterns which this unity might take. I have space to mention but one, the unity which results where the teaching procedure selected is seen as peculiarly appropriate to the end in view. Perhaps no finer example of such unity of means to end in teaching is on record than is to be found in the life of that master teacher, Jesus.

When the people wanted to stone the woman taken in adultery, did Jesus read them a lecture on morality? No. He simply said, "Let him who is without sin cast the first stone." Again, when his interrogators sought to trap him on the question of paying tribute to Caesar, did Jesus read them a lecture on political economy? Did he give them a lecture on the relations of church and state? Not at all. He merely asked them to show him a coin. Seeing the head of Caesar thereon, he merely said, "Render unto Caesar the things that are Caesar's and unto God the things that are God's." These instructions are amazingly to the point. They comprehend much, yet bring it all to a focus on a single unitary point.

We started by noting that the nineteenth century witnessed a controversy over whether teaching could be a science as well as an art. Let no one think that teaching can be made the arena for a current dispute between the interests of science and the interests of fine art. Some have tried to contend that the educational scientist is oriented outward toward the solution of a problem while the educational artist is oriented inward to giving expression to a feeling or mood. I submit that there should be nothing ineffable or inscrutable about the fine art of teaching. The interests of science and art are not opposed but mutually dependent. If the teacher is to intensify feeling, communicate clarity, and achieve unity, he must have a scientific knowledge of the psychology of the learning process. Only so will he be able to gain his ends with the sureness and dependability that is characteristic of artistic teaching.

Pragmatism, which many think is a philosophy of science, is not opposed to fine art either. Yet many have interpreted Dewey to mean that the teacher need teach no more thoroughly than to enable the child to "get by." In handwriting, for example, it is supposed to be enough if the child is taught a legibility that will "get by" for purposes of communication. The development of a beautiful or a "fine" hand is seldom attempted. A careful rereading of Dewey should prove that there is nothing in his philosophy of education which opposes the consummatory pleasure to be taken in the perfection of a technique on its own account. On the contrary, he actually recommends it!

So, I commend to you the earnest pursuit of teaching careers in which you will constantly seek that perfection of technique which yields clarity and unity together with an ever increasing joy in your art. Indeed, the man who has not learned to get this satisfaction from his chosen work—whether doctor, lawyer, merchant, or what have you—has been deprived of one of the deepest satisfactions which life yields.

19
Mirabile Dictu

HARRY S. BROUDY

In this selection, Broudy is critical of teachers and their frequent failure to let themselves "intrude into the learning process" when they teach subjects rather than pupils. This accounts for his observation that teaching machines may well

SOURCE: Harry S. Broudy, *Paradox and Promise in Life and Education* (Englewood Cliffs, N.J.: Prentice-Hall, Inc., 1961), pp. 74–85. Reprinted by permission of the author.

Presently professor of psychology and education at the University of Illinois, Harry S. Broudy is the author of *Building a Philosophy of Education* and *Democracy and Excellence in American Secondary Education*.

take over much of the future instruction in the schools. A comparison of Broudy and Brubacher shows that Brubacher focuses on the art of teaching and its perfection, while Broudy places greater emphasis on the teacher's personal influence on children. Both authors allude to specific factors they regard as being characteristic of teaching as an art. At the same time, neither author identifies any means of measuring the techniques, skill, or procedures inherent in the teaching task. You should be aware of this, for specific factors for study and evaluation of teaching are available.

ABOUT MIRACLES modern men are prone to overhasty generalization. Either they regard miracles as the irresponsible intervention into the affairs of men by supernatural powers and therefore to be summarily dismissed as superstition, or they go to the other extreme and marvel at the wonders wrought by scientists and accord them the reverence ordinarily reserved for the Divine.

A more modest attitude would define miracles as events for which no cause can be assigned, at least not at the moment when it is being sought. This attitude, I submit, restores to the miracle a useful status in daily life where events whose causes we cannot ascertain and which have an impact upon our lives that is peculiarly fortunate or unfortunate occur frequently. After an airplane disaster reporters ferret out the names of persons who had scheduled passage on the ill-fated craft but who failed to board the flight for one reason or another. One had forgotten something in the checkroom and returned to retrieve it. Another was not aboard because he had one too many cocktails, and still another decided at the very last moment to return to his wife instead of seeking a new life elsewhere. These escapes are properly regarded as miraculous, because their cause is mysterious or hidden from us, and also in that they intersect our life plans as if they were designed to fit in positively or negatively with them.

The miraculous, in the sense I am proposing to use it, is a blend of ignorance and chance that is far more potent in the conduct of life than knowledge and design.

Civilization and education, it ought to be noted, are consistently on the side of knowledge and purpose and against ignorance and chance. This is as it should be, save for the circumstance that increasing knowledge and purposeful action does not necessarily decrease the volume of life controlled by ignorance and chance. The reason is simple: every deliberately instituted act —driving to the shopping center to buy groceries, for example—sets up chains of events other than and in addition to those that result in buying the groceries. For example, one waves to the postman on the way, or one inadvertently fails to return the greeting of a diffident student. These events in turn set up their own chains of events that in turn intersect with other chains. Theoretically one could calculate all of these adventitious results before undertaking an action, and perhaps with pocket electronic computers we shall one day be aware of all the consequences of our own acts. Shall we also be aware of all the consequences of all the acts of everyone else? Can we look forward to becoming computers orbiting about the Computer of Computers?

The schools, being on the side of knowledge and foresight, are naturally not the best place for human beings to learn to cope with the miraculous. Or to be more precise, the school is not a good place to learn how to adjust one's life to the miraculous, for, strictly speaking, one can do little with the miraculous but adjust to it. And yet the school perhaps misses a good bet in not paying more attention to those adventitious events that have changed the course of history. For these are the really interesting items and not the logically obvious ones. They transform the causal chain into a drama.

In general, schoolmen interpret the miraculous as a Divine intervention into terrestrial affairs and consequently are reluctant to give it room in school affairs. Not being sufficiently respectful of ignorance and chance, they seek causes for everything and infer them long before the data warrant their doing so. So while denying the miraculous, they often strive for goals that it is impossible for them to achieve in their current state of knowledge or control. In other words, they strive for the impossible precisely because they deny the reality of honest-to-goodness, everyday miracles. Among these miracles are the influences of a teacher on a particular pupil at a particular point in his developmental history.

Every man when in a suitable anecdotal mood can relate an incident that inspired him to unusual effort. For one man it was a hero in life or in literature; for another it was a woman; occasionally a parent or a teacher was the trigger that released enormous energy in behalf of some cause or other. Sometimes, however, it was not a person as such who effected the change, but rather an event or a situation.

Quite frequently, one might suppose, these dramatic motivations occur in school. A schoolman, one might also suppose, would almost sell his soul to find the secret springs that give these motivating events and persons their power. This secret would indeed be the pedagogue's philosopher's stone. Its touch would transform a reluctant schoolboy into an inspired learner and, correlatively, transform teaching from drudgery to a kind of inspirational magic.

Psychology, especially educational psychology, disdaining all mystical nonsense, has offered us a number of formulae in terms of which the pedagogue can so program his instruction that the hidden springs of motives will be released—not mysteriously but by design. To this end, lists of motives, instincts, interests, drives, and needs have been prepared. They show, for example, that at such-and-such an age, the boy will naturally love to play war games and the girl with dolls.

These developmental schedules are not without their use. They prevent the beginning teacher from becoming ridiculous in that they indicate the "normal" incitements to adequate school behavior. They help in choosing literature for children, as well as toys and games, appropriate to their needs, interests, etc. They are reliable because they represent interests that children have actually displayed and not the observers' ideas about what the children ought to be interested in. Finally, a child whose tastes in these matters is noticeably deviant can be cut out of the herd, so to speak, for special study. Nevertheless, these interest schedules do not tell us about the more dramatic transformations of a child's life in which the whole aspirational schema is radically changed.

Of less use to the pedagogue are the more general theories of human motivation. For example, it is now customary to invoke the principle of security as a means of diagnosing children's difficulties in school. Unfortunately, feelings of insecurity can be used to explain equally well such diverse behaviors as extraordinary scholastic achievement, scholastic failure, undue devotion to one's parents, and abnormal hostility toward one's home.

Will a teacher who makes a child secure inspire him to a significant change in his motivational pattern? Or will a teacher who destroys a child's security inspire him to unusual achievement? That depends, one is told, on the nature of the child and presumably on the nature of the teacher also. So there seems to be no easy substitute for studying the child, the teacher, and, one might add, all other relevant circumstances in their particulars. But is it the duty or is it within the competence of the teacher to undertake such clinical study?

Those who argue that teaching is an art rather than a science probably have in mind this difficulty of predicting pupil behavior from general principles. The artist is never sure ahead of time just what impression his work will make—even on himself. He is guided more by what the work already done requires than by the prescription of a set of rules. Teachers work on a similar basis. One tries a posture, approach, or gambit and a sense of rapport ensues that seems to call for this question or that remark. Did it come off? Who knows? Many years later one may find out that for a certain student it did, but more often it turns out to have been one of those ineffectual tries that sank into pallid oblivion.

Schoolrooms go on from day to day not by dramatic successes but by routine. These are the standard tasks and expectations that provide momentum to sustain the engine between piston strokes of inspiration and insight. Nor are the lives of pupils a succession of red-letter days. One of the more damaging misconceptions of prospective teachers is that they must have exciting lessons every day. Both the Progressives and the Idealists foster such an illusion, for both are given to enthusiasm and find it hard to pace themselves through the less exciting intervals of life.

It is perhaps a truism that a reliable combination of routine and variation makes life interesting and therefore endurable. But it is less obvious that teaching, when one becomes sufficiently self-conscious about the surprises latent in even its most routine moments, has a more intense fascination, an almost frightening fascination, than most occupations. For in no calling are the results of what one does so pregnant with possibilities for the pupil and yet so unpredictable—unpredictable as to the person they will affect, when the effect will take place, and what it will be.

There come to mind two examples of influence on young pupils that may make some of these abstract remarks more concrete.

The first is that of Katie. This lady was an eighth-grade teacher in a fairly large school. The other eighth grade was under the governance of a Miss Belinda. Both women were past middle age. Katie was known as a tough teacher and her colleague was known as a gentle, lovable teacher who was "as easy as pie."

As the end of the seventh-grade year approached, pupils began to wonder to which of the eighth grades they would be assigned. Nobody knew the principle of selection, and in those days parents would have been backward about trying to influence the authorities in such affairs. In any event, the pupils believed that some impersonal fate allotted them to the lioness or to the lamb.

With the girls the hope was pretty generally in favor of the lamb. Not only would there be a less threatening atmosphere so far as studies were concerned, but romance would not be so rudely suppressed as it would be by Katie's rough tongue. The girls knew, however, that some of them would land in the lair of the lioness, and for them the last day of school was a day of doom. As each girl learned her fate, dejection or elation was spelled out eloquently on her face.

Among the boys the sentiments were less uniform. Some, like the girls, dreaded a hard taskmaster, especially if their scholastic caliber was not high. The more gentle temperaments dreaded the austerity for which Katie's room was noted, but other boys looked forward to Katie's eighth grade as a trial of their manhood, both of mind and soul: of mind, because a good report card from Katie was about as clear a sign of scholastic distinction as the town could provide; of soul, because to take the tongue lashings, the whippings, and the other cruel and unusual punishments for which Katie was notorious was something like surviving basic training with the United States Marines. For young men of this mettle the great fear was that they would *not* land in Katie's room. Certain it was that there were only two kinds of men: those who had gone through Katie's room and those who had not.

One entered her classroom in September with teeth clenched waiting for the blow. The long assignments came as predicted. The sharp rebukes for mistakes were duly delivered; there were some sharp hand rappings. But one waited all year for Katie to throw her famed dictionary at the class tough; one waited in vain for the cruel and unusual punishments.

It is hard to say whether the boys were more relieved or disappointed. It would not do, of course, to reveal the true state of affairs to outsiders. On the other hand, the more daring lads who were tempted into overconfidence by the unexpected mildness of Katie's demeanor were set upon so firmly and so promptly that her reputation remained secure. The truth of the matter was, of course, that the alleged horrible goings-on in Katie's room had been invented by generations of schoolboys as a tribute to their own imagined toughness, and each tale expanded with every repetition. Thus it was that when men who had been Katie's pupils asked each other whether they remembered the time when Katie had whipped every boy in the room, or when one boy had been forced to read out loud for two hours at a stretch, nobody could recall the incidents, but they were ready to believe that they had occurred. Indeed, with the years Katie's opportunities for sadism were radically reduced by the fact that her authority was less and less frequently challenged.

Pupils learned a great deal in that one year and some for the first time discovered how much work they could do and how satisfying scholastic achievement could be. It was an exciting year not because they learned exciting things but because they were living, they thought, dangerously. So great was her reputation that such activities as part singing, drawing, and reading aloud from Webster's orations (with expression) were transformed from sissy stuff to more or less manly exercises.

Many teachers tried to build a similar reputation and most of them failed miserably. Perhaps because they did not have her gray hair, her black neckband, and pince-nez. Perhaps they lacked her inward self-assurance. Above all, they probably lacked her authenticity, for Katie never tried to build a tradition. She was herself and the tradition grew about her as naturally as did the grayness of her hair. For all one knows, many a boy or girl was thoroughly miserable in her classes and was too frightened to learn much of anything; but this possibility (or actuality) somehow never became part of the tradition.

In modern parlance Katie's room exemplified a fairly pure form of what the late Kurt Lewin called an authoritarian school atmosphere. The teacher made all the assignments without consulting the pupils. She issued commands and made demands; disobedience was immediately and not gently punished. There was a minimum of interaction among the pupils; whispering, when she chose to be aware of it, was a major offense; passing notes was a pastime so dangerous that only the toughest pupils ever engaged in it. As for her method of teaching, perfect reproduction of a model response was all she knew.

Whether it was arithmetic or part singing, spelling or declamation, everything had to be done just as she wanted it done. She had only a blackboard, some maps, and the textbook as teaching tools. She was, in short, an exemplar of every sin in the pedagogical decalogue.

And yet, in another sense, she was an exemplar of nothing because she created a unique sort of authoritarian atmosphere in which the hardy ambitious pupil could test himself by a criterion that his peers accepted. It was also a haven for the compliant, docile child, who became more so during his year with Katie. It was an exciting authoritarianism, a rigidity with a difference, with almost a hint of the splendor that military rigor sometimes acquires. She was not fussy or nagging; she was neither conspicuously kind nor unkind.

The point of all this is that Katie and her methods could not be reduced to a formula which could then be judged pedagogically good or bad, any more than a particular painting can be judged good or bad simply because it was done in the Romantic style. For some pupils it worked wonders; for others it was disastrous. What schools in her day lacked was the ability to make a good guess as to which pupils needed Katie and which should be steered away from her, and one is far from sure that schools have made any considerable progress in matching pupil-styles and teacher-styles.

The second example is furnished by an incident that occurred in the seventh grade to a young chap who had come to this country when he was seven or eight years of age. By then he had been thoroughly acclimated and had settled down to an uneventful passage from grade to grade. His marks were neither poor nor good. His parents accepted his achievements as about suitable to his talents. It was a nice adjustment all around. Then one day the children were asked to write a theme or composition about some event in their lives that they thought was interesting and significant. Everyone chewed pencils thoughtfully and there accrued the usual bag of themes about a visit to one's aunt in Cleveland, the dog who was nearly run over by a trolley car, the new bicycle, how to make an electric bell, a birthday party. The papers were collected by the teacher and life went on as usual.

Perhaps a week or even two weeks later the principal, a youngish dark man by the name of Halloran, entered the room, held a whispered conversation with the teacher and began to read a composition.

It was a limping tale about a sea voyage on a passenger liner. In those days, near the end of World War I, there were still many immigrant children in school, and it was not at all surprising that some of them would remember the trip across the ocean either as a traumatic or nostalgic episode in their lives. With some sense of drama, Principal Halloran delayed announcing the authorship until the end of the reading. The revelation caught everyone, including the author, by surprise. The author, of course, knew it was his composition but he was no less puzzled than his classmates at the distinction bestowed upon his literary effort. For one thing, his immigrantish oddness had long since worn away and he was thoroughly Americanized in speech, dress, and all the minor vices. For another, his accomplishments in school were so indifferent that this honor seemed thoroughly out of character.

From that day on, however, he regarded himself as a writer and began to take on the behaviors of a student as well. At the Memorial Day exercises he was selected to render the Gettysburg address and thereafter each teacher referred to him as the boy "who could write."

In high school his compositions became concoctions of bombast and undue solemnity, but he was named editor of his school paper, and in college at least one of his English professors encouraged him to write. One of his efforts achieved the distinction of being rejected by the late Henry Mencken with the notation "has some promise." He was salutatorian of his class in high school, valedictorian of his class in college, and voted the man most likely to succeed (at what was not specified).

He did not fulfill the prophecy, at least not in the field of literature. He did not return to class reunions often enough to enable his classmates to make a proper appraisal of his accomplishments. Nevertheless, the episode on the afternoon the principal read his little composition about a sea voyage was as critical a point in his life as the discovery that she is beautiful is to an adolescent girl.

As for Principal Halloran, he left the school system at the end of the year and was never heard from again. Not that he disappeared or took up a life of crime, but for the seventh graders he ceased to exist when he left the school system. One cannot be sure that the results of his gesture were ever made known to him; one hopes they were. Being the person he was, he no doubt repeated this gesture many times in his school career, and one is tempted to capitalize on the episode described here by urging teachers to read the compositions of indifferent pupils aloud or persuading the principal to do so. But who would be willing to predict the results of such readings?

Indeed, the lessons of Principal Halloran and Katie may be quite different from what at first glance they seem to be. It is not that they furnish paradigms of teaching or that they exemplify any profound teaching principles. Rather, they exemplify the frightening fact that in the act of teaching we create situations and stimuli whose consequences are beyond calculation, even if it occurred to us to calculate them.

When such small behaviors produce such great results, who is to blame a teacher for trembling with anxiety at the close of each day? What remark, what gesture, what grimace, what quip, what praise, what reproof produced what effects on which pupils? And what effects will tomorrow and the day after that engender?

The engineer responsible for the structural integrity of a huge span, the surgeon whose every movement is significant, the general with thousands of lives at his command are familiar symbols of vast responsibility. We wonder at times how these men bear up under it. Yet a teacher—not a mighty person on any scale—daily radiates influences on many many children. The engineer has control over what is being built; the surgeon sees the effect of his movements; the general, one hopes, takes only well-calculated risks. The teacher, however, is often playing blind man's buff, not knowing whom he touches and how the touch is received. Responsibility in such a situation takes on a tinge of desperation.

Mercifully not many teachers are like Socrates, who could never forget the gravity of the teaching relation, who so carefully desisted from letting himself intrude into the learning process. He was the midwife merely helping the pupil bring his own conceptions to birth. But it was an impossible role. His pupils could not help learning Socrates as well as themselves. Perhaps it is wrong to say that we teach subjects, and it is difficult to understand what is meant by saying that we teach pupils, but the teacher never fails to teach himself to the pupil.

That is why teaching machines may well take over the bulk of instruction in the years to come. Even the best of human teachers is not an efficient teaching machine. All that a human teacher can add to the mechanics of instruction is himself, his peculiar organization of experience, which, fortunately or not, is induplicable. His thoughts are not merely true or false; they are profound or shallow, significant or trivial, interesting or boring. Most important of all, he is a source of praise and reproof.

It is also fortunate that, by and large, school teachers do not reflect on the peculiar responsibilities they bear and, aside from an occasional shudder, they manage to ignore the effects of themselves on their pupils. Only in this way can they concentrate on the routine of instruction and school keeping.

Perhaps responsibility, like our clothes, when continually worn loses its weight. Men's work would cease altogether if their gaze were forever inward, brooding on the possible consequences of their acts. Blessed are the routines that make so many actions so automatic that they no longer need thought and reflection. Like other professionals, the professional teacher becomes aware of responsibility only in critical situations.

Certainly it would be an unsubtle teacher who would wear his care upon his sleeve and allow his pupils to sense his anxiety. Sören Kierkegaard, the Danish theologian, never tired of asking about the mien proper for a genuine Christian. If a true Christian were to avoid pride, over-confidence with respect to salvation, false humility, the escape mechanism of monasticism, smugness, meddlesomeness in the name of neighborly love, and a half hundred other demeanors incompatible with the Christian spirit, just how should he behave?

Kierkegaard's answer was long, dialectical, and overly subtle, but roughly stated it came to suggesting a kind of disguise, an outward mien that belied the inward questioning, anxiety, and concern. And perhaps something like this is the unhappy answer for the genuine teacher as well.

It means that teachers cannot hover like mother hens over their little charges, nor does it mean a prying concern for the home life and private concerns of the pupil. It does not mean a sentimental "love of children" or being a pal to teen-age boys. To none of these roles is the teacher uniquely essential. Yet when we ask for something positive, there is no one image to recommend, just as there is no one image appropriate to the genuine Christian spirit.

About all one can say is that the teacher, first of all, must be himself, and, second, that he be concerned about the pupil, but in a peculiar way. He is himself *for* the pupil, while his concern for the pupil is disguised behind a concern for a subject of instruction. Thus it looks as if Teacher X is teaching arithmetic, but his concern, as Rousseau pointed out, is what is happening to the pupil when he has an arithmetical insight. In exemplifying a genuine human perspective of life, the teacher must seem to be wholly unconscious of being an example.

Perhaps this is a roundabout way of stressing the inward dimension of life whenever the transaction is between persons rather than between persons and things, which is sometimes called "subjectivity." It is that reflexive power by which the person's experience is split into a content and an awareness of that content. The content can be classified and described; it is what we have in common with our fellow men; it is what psychology and sociology can study. With the awareness of the content, matters stand otherwise. Because the individual's experience is growing from moment to moment, how he receives each new moment is a unique creative occasion in history. However intelligible it is after the individual has acted and added an item to the content of his experience, at the moment of receiving the future into the present he is in spiritual solitude. Hence many of his acts are miraculous in the sense of the word that has been described.

It is almost impossible for one individual to express his subjectivity directly, his peculiar way of receiving the world. If he tries to say it in ordinary language, his words become universals and they describe not him alone but the experience of mankind in general, for they describe what is common, not what is individual. As we try to communicate our attitude toward the world we are beset by doubts and hesitations. Are we being unduly modest? Or falsely so? Are we seeking sympathy? Are we trying to save our ego at the expense of others? In short, are we telling the truth about ourselves?

At such times a poem, a song, a picture may express better what it is we feel than words, and ocasionally, if we are fortunate, we can act out what we feel; we exhibit ourselves instead of describing ourselves. Such manifestations have a strange power over the beholder. What I mean here is akin to the effect upon us of the complete authenticity of a child absorbed in some act, or an adult in that rare moment when he has forgotten that he might be observed.

At other times we resort to indirect communication in the form of irony, the parable, the comic, the paradox, the dialectical. In these forms of speech things are suspended between opposites, between the literal and the figurative, the particular and the general, the comic and the tragic, the sublime and the ridiculous. Such a communication communicates nothing in the strict sense of the word, for it is logically a kind of nonsense. Yet it arouses in the hearer the emotional state the communicant wishes him to have.

Perhaps the teacher also communicates indirectly; perhaps this indirectness is what mocks every attempt to formalize a Katie's or a Halloran's influence into a method. Perhaps behind their objective, almost impersonal approach to the classroom there was an intense inwardness, a profound concern with what might happen to each pupil at every moment. Children, one is almost forced to conclude, can sense this inner reality behind the disguise of externals. How else are we to explain why they forgive an adult long before the adult can forgive himself for the acts of anger and cruelty he perpetrates upon them? What teacher has not had the eerie feeling that pupils are penetrating his outer words and gestures and reading off the real meaning behind them?

The sense of the miraculous, the sense of the infinite volume of life's possibilities is essential to the depth dimension of personality. Life achieves a stereoscopic effect by combining views from various perspectives into a set of deeds and demeanors we call a personality. It would be strange if straightforward analysis of overt behavior succeeded in trapping all the contrasts and nuances that give depth to the teacher and the teaching act. Perhaps that is why millions of dollars spent on isolating the traits of the successful teacher have turned up all sorts of interesting and valuable information about all sorts of things—indeed about everything except the object of the search itself.

20

Accountability for Student Learning

ERWIN L. HARLACHER AND
ELEANOR ROBERTS

The changing needs of the present age are demanding that educational institutions develop behavioral objectives by which professional accountability of their instructional program may be given. This might well be the dawning of a new age in education, for if education is to become a profession and accountable for its performance it must establish and be prepared to enforce acceptable standards.

This attention to accountability, measurable in large part through student achievement, might be a factor indicative of a swing in the educational pendulum from emphasis on teaching as an art to teaching as a science. As Harlacher and Roberts draw the currently popular parallel between education and corporations "with their technological know-how," it should not be difficult to visualize the application of a taxonomy of behavioral objectives and to anticipate great public support to those who challenge the effectiveness of the traditional concept of schooling. The present emphasis, most certainly, is now on measurement of the effectiveness of instruction by a teacher.

EVER SINCE the Texarkana experiment in "guaranteed learning" made its appearance on the national education scene in April of 1969, boards of education and college boards of trustees have been wondering about the accountability of their institutions for the learning that does (or does not) take

SOURCE: *Junior College Journal,* Vol. 41, No. 6 (March 1971), pp. 27–30. Reprinted by permission of the authors and publisher.

Erwin L. Harlacher is the first president of Brookdale Community College in New Jersey. Before entering administration full time in 1960 at Foothill College in California, he served as chairman of journalism at various colleges. In 1965, Dr. Harlacher joined the staff of Oakland Community College in Michigan as vice-president and moved to his present position in 1968. He has published often throughout his professional career and is a frequent contributor to a number of education periodicals.

Eleanor Roberts is assistant director of developmental research and evaluation at Brookdale Community College. During the ten years she was an editor with the University of California Press, her area of specialization became educational research, and in this work she participated in some thirty school district surveys in California and Nevada. In addition to her research reporting, she is a successful playwright and fiction writer, having earned, among other recognition, the Mark Twain award for contributions to children's literature with her *Once Upon a Summertime.*

place there. Certainly, there is no question that simply to make programs of learning available and, by sometimes heavy-handed and didactic methods, to cram as many facts into young heads as possible (the tell 'em-and-test 'em system) does not vindicate an educational institution's attrition and failure rates. Neither does such a procedure advance the presumable cause of education; namely, to produce a maximum number of self-confident, self-reliant, self-motivating, and self-fulfilling citizens for active participation in the mainstream of American life.

The old notion that only the so-called "best brains" are worthy of development because only these can effectively be used in the economy has long since become obsolete. Similarly, the idea that a majority of students represent pint-sized containers into which it is impossible to pour quart-sized content has been proved erroneous, both empirically and through careful research. Classroom activities have, nevertheless, remained teacher and teaching centered (rather than learner and learning centered), with the teacher sitting or standing before his students presenting them with facts, much as he did in the Middle Ages. The result has been that too many educators have succumbed to the illusion that only a small percentage of students have the capacity to learn what is being taught.

In some respects, this may be true; for "what is being taught" is not necessarily synonymous with "what is being learned." As a profession, we have talked for years about individual differences among learners, without having done much about trying to understand the relationship of those differences to strategies that promote learning. We have come now to that point in time when it is necessary to realize, along with Benjamin Bloom, that:

> . . . highly developed nations must seek to find ways to increase the proportion of the age group that can successfully complete both secondary and higher education. The problem is no longer one of finding the few who can succeed. The basic problem is to determine how the largest proportion of the age group can learn effectively those skills and subject matter regarded as essential for their own development in a complex society.[1]

Bloom is convinced that "fully 90 per cent of all students can master learning tasks." But, he cautions:

> If the schools are to provide successful and satisfying learning experiences for . . . [this] 90 per cent . . . major changes must take place in the attitudes of students, teachers, and administrators; changes must also take place in teaching strategies and in the role of evaluation.[2]

The implications here seem clear. Behaviors change only when a realistic set of goals and subgoals has been formulated for the institution as a whole,

---

[1] [2] Bloom, Benjamin S. "Learning for Mastery." *UCLA Evaluative Comment,* May 1968, p. 2.

and when practical objectives for implementing these goals at the classroom level have been posed and tested to determine their relevance. But, in all cases, each individual involved in the total process must be accountable for the satisfactory performance of his role in the overall scheme.

Brookdale's Philosophical Platform

At Brookdale, before the college opened in September 1969, the board of trustees adopted a philosophical platform covering broadly the philosophy and objectives of the institution. But more specific guidelines were needed if the college was to fulfill its mission of "bringing higher educational opportunities within geographic and financial research of all citizens" in its host community, the entire county of Monmouth in New Jersey. Thus, during the ensuing summer, Brookdale administrators conducted a two-day workshop on institutional goals and performance objectives. Working from the philosophical platform, the group developed a more precise mission statement, institutional goals and subgoals, and tentative activities for implementation.

Declaring that the college would fulfill its mission as effectively and/or economically as would a traditional educational institution, the mission statement further avowed that accomplishment would come about through achievement of ten specific institutional goals:

1. Institute the concept of accountability by defining outcomes, differentiating processes, and evaluating results for all undertakings
2. Prepare students for entry into and appreciation of actual careers
3. Provide educational opportunities that facilitate human development
4. Facilitate the development of the broadly educated person
5. Develop an instructional program that accommodates individual differences in learning rates, aptitudes, prior knowledge, etc.
6. Engender in each student a concern for excellence and a desire for continuous learning
7. Develop an institution whose total environment is dedicated to learning and is open to those who desire to learn
8. Utilize the total community as a laboratory for learning
9. Contribute to the educational, economic, social, and cultural development of the host community
10. Provide for continuous institutional evaluation.

Most of the few cautious excursions into the realm of accountability that have been taken in recent months have occurred at the classroom level. Certainly, the classroom is where accountability should begin for, as John Roueche remarked at a recent conference on improvement of teaching, "It's the teacher, not the student, who should be held accountable for the student's failure to learn." But does this concept go far enough? Should not administrators, too, be held accountable for student achievement of predetermined learning objectives? Not to do so is rather like holding the bookkeeper in a corporation's business office accountable for his president's embezzlement of funds, while the president himself skips off to South America with the loot. Accountability should be demanded not at one level but at all institutional levels, especially in the college—the demand originating with the board of trustees as a board policy. The Brookdale board of trustees recently approved the following policy on accountability:

Consonant with its philosophy to provide equal opportunity for all citizens to gain post high school educational experiences that will prepare them for meaningful participation in the social and economic life of the contemporary world, Brookdale Community College subscribes to the concept that accountability for student learning is an accepted responsibility of the entire college community.

Therefore, the President shall implement a process of periodic evaluation of the instructional program, and shall report his findings to the board of trustees on an annual basis, to include:

1. The success of students in attaining learning objectives, including student attrition rates
2. The success of students in occupations entered into upon leaving the college, including employer's perceptions of the efficacy of the college's career programs
3. The success of students who transfer to other institutions
4. The extent to which the college programs are fulfilling the stated overall philosophy and objectives of the college
5. The responsiveness of the college programs to a student's initial and/or changed career aspirations.

Corporate Organization

Going back to the corporation for an analogy, it seems obvious that corporate organization differs very little from the organization of a college. There is (1) a board of directors, which is responsible to the stockholders; there are (2) the executive officers, who are responsible to the board; (3) division managers and department heads who are responsible to one or more of the executive officers; and (4) under each of these, the "performers"—those whose expertise in executing specialized segments of the total endeavor helps to move the enterprise toward achieving its goals. These performers, in our analogy, may be equated with teachers. The executive officers compare with administrators, and the board of directors with the college board of trustees.

Corporate quotas (goals in our terminology) for any given period are not self-producing. They are developed by management after careful consideration of the corporation's past performance, its current operational design, its future potential—and accountability for the achievement of the overall goals rests with the executive officers.

Carrying the analogy a little further, the corporation recognizes that all stockholders have the right to a guaranteed share in the overall profits, proportional to the amount of their investment. Similarly, the college must recognize that students—the stockholders in the educational enterprise—are entitled to fair returns for their investment of time, effort, and ability in the learning process.

Many educators have been accustomed to think of ability in terms of aptitude for particular kinds of learning, so that John Carroll's assertion that "aptitude is *the amount of time* required by the learners to attain mastery of a learning task" [3] seems somewhat startling. Yet, in point of fact, it is merely a restatement of the principle on which self-paced learning is based. And several recent studies [4] have verified that although most students eventually reach mastery on each learning task, some achieve it much sooner than others. Thus, it becomes the responsibility of the teacher to discover, on an individual basis, the amount of time each student requires to master the learning experiences provided in any set of objectives governing the units of knowledge to be acquired in a given course of study, and to provide more effective learning conditions for those who need more time.

Developing Learning Objectives

It would appear obvious, then, that insofar as the instructional program is concerned, the development of learning objectives is the first step in the total process of accountability. Such objectives represent a unit of production and make it possible to verify whether the production occurred or not. But, although it is easy enough to recommend the development of learning objectives and perhaps to enumerate the steps in the process, it is *not* an easy matter to get viable objectives.[5] This means that learning objectives require periodic "internal audit" to determine how well they are guiding the student

[3] Carroll, John A. "A Model of School Learning," *Teachers College Record,* 1963. pp. 723–33.

[4] Atkinson, R. C. *Computerized Instruction and the Learning Process.* Report No. 122, Stanford, California: Institute for Mathematical Studies in the Social Sciences, 1967. Glaser, R. "Adapting the Elementary School Curriculum to Individual Performance." *Proceedings* of the 1967 Invitational Conference on Testing Programs. Princeton, New Jersey: Educational Testing Service, 1968.

[5] Mager, Robert F. *Preparing Instructional Objectives.* Palo Alto, California: Fearon Publishers, 1962. Also Johnson, Stuart R. and Johnson, Rita B. *Developing Individualized Instructional Material.* Palo Alto, California: Westinghouse Learning Press, 1970.

toward salient activities and changed behaviors. Thus, in the process of accountability, evaluation becomes a highly important factor.

Accountability cannot be limited to teachers, however. Each administrative unit must develop performance objectives and evaluative techniques by which to ensure accountability in the noninstructional activities. To this end, it is recommended that program planning procedures be instituted. In essence, each activity (office, department, etc.) of the institution is assigned a set of functional responsibilities, in addition to the institutional goals which have priorly been evolved. Each administrator takes these two documents—the goals and functional tasks—and plans a set of programs within his functional area that serve to accomplish some aspects of the institutional goals. These programs then provide a basis upon which to assign accountability in the noninstructional areas. Coupled with this program planning is a costing process that leads into program planning budgeting, and this brings to full cycle the concept of management by objectives for the total institution.

The Texarkana Experiment

In the Texarkana experiment, which has been variously evaluated during the time it has been in existence, it was decided to bring in "big business" to execute a plan which could have been implemented by those in charge of the school system, had management by objectives been operative. Weaknesses in the educational program might early have been discovered and corrected instead of being allowed to accumulate. Ongoing evaluation of each learning objective and each performance objective would have welded the entire organization into a cohesive whole, accountable for the individual mastery of specific learning tasks by the children in the system.

Actually, under conditions of the experiment, there is little accountability involved, except in terms of monetary bonuses or penalties accruing from the firm's success or nonsuccess in producing student learning that is "guaranteed." But for how long? The editor of *Phi Delta Kappan* raised that very question in the June 1970 issue:

One of our early disappointments in Texarkana was the discovery that the schools' contract with Dorset [Educational Systems, who are conducting the experiment] does not include a clause, discussed at the negotiations stage, which would have provided penalties should initial gains disappear after six months. Thus temporary spurts so familiar to educational researchers . . . may fade away without anybody noticing.[6]

[6] Elam, Stanley. "The Age of Accountability Dawns in Texarkana." *Phi Delta Kappan*, LI, June 1970, p. 509.

On the positive side, Texarkana may be just the right catalyst to stimulate constructive action on the part of educators—self-preserving, if you will, but certainly long overdue. Is there any reason why educators can't develop and put into action the same kind of technological know-how of which industry boasts? Is there any reason why schools of education cannot develop courses of study that will fit generations of educators to meet the challenges of current educational needs? It is one thing to make an administrator accountable if he has the modern tools with which to work; it is quite another to hold him accountable if he's using a hand plow to do a job that requires a bulldozer.

Accountability: A Privilege

That accountability should be built into every college program there is little doubt. But accountability must be regarded a privilege—not a burden, nor a checkrein on teachers and administrators alike. Rather, it should be considered a kind of self-scoring quiz that will reveal how far-fetched our institutional goals are—or how realistic; how nebulous our learning objectives are—or how well structured; how successful our programs are in motivating students to remain in college—or in suggesting that they might as well drop out.

But accountability for the programs offered and the results produced cannot be based on an M & M reward system. When colleges set up goals and objectives, they don't require monetary or stock issue incentives. Their goals and objectives merely describe the purpose for which they are in business. And, as in any profitable business, they must be accountable for the quality of their end product. What kind of human being will a student be when, after two years, he walks again through the open door into the world of work or advanced study?

It is the responsibility of the community college to offer as many educational opportunities to as many citizens of its community as they may find useful. It is its equal responsibility to see that the maximum number of students who enter its doors—90 per cent of them, if Professor Bloom's projection is accurate—leave again with learnings mastered and a clear knowledge of how to apply those learnings to life in the real world. The excellent institution is not the one that flunks out 60 per cent of its students. The excellent institution—the accountable institution—is the one that can declare, "When students finish their studies here, 90 per cent of them can do these things."

If educators undertake to provide "guaranteed accountability" (not guaranteed performance, for there are too many ways of covering up mistakes in this area), they will be forced to acquire and execute the technological know-how of which private industry now appears to be the sole source. This is the only course open to them if they are to preserve the enormous gains education has made over its long history and, at the same time, apply the technology that can facilitate accomplishment of their goals. In such circumstances, faith in the community college's seriousness of purpose and determination to fulfill its mission within its community will be revitalized, and those who are involved in the teaching-learning process will acquire new vigor.

An educational credo for the nation's community colleges might well include the following nine articles of belief:

1. We believe that both administrators and teachers ought to be accountable for student failures

2. We believe that an individual educational plan or prescription ought to be developed for each student, utilizing a wide variety of learning experiences

3. We believe that an educational institution ought to be judged on the basis of what it does for and with students and not on the basis of their opening handicaps

4. We believe in learning for mastery by all students—not just a chosen few

5. We believe that the instructional program ought to accommodate individual differences in learning rates, aptitudes, and prior knowledge, for a college exists, not to measure the extent of its students' failures, but to evaluate the depth of their successes

6. We believe that the individualization of instruction requires the provision of optional paths to learning, and the utilization of a highly diversified teaching/learning team composed of full-time teachers, part-time teachers, media specialists, counselors, paraprofessionals, peer tutors, and community volunteers

7. We believe that education must be learner and learning centered, measured by performance criteria—not teacher and teaching centered

8. We believe that teachers ought to be managers of the learning process—change agents, guides, mentors, questioners—not feeders of information

9. And we believe that each learner ought to be able to start where he is and become all that he is capable of becoming.

EVALUATION

SAMUEL R. HALL, **Lectures to School-Masters on Teaching**

1. (a) In "Lectures to School-Masters on Teaching," Hall identifies seven requisite qualifications of an instructor. Name the seven and briefly give Hall's major reasons for each.

   (b) In what ways will the teacher's ineffectiveness be expressed if these seven qualifications are not present?

2. (a) Give Hall's two statements defining "common sense."

   (b) What three factors does he imply in his definition?

   (c) What does he believe is the outcome of a teacher's use of common sense?

3. (a) What ultimate goal need a school teacher have in all his teaching, according to Hall?

   (b) State the reason he gives for supporting this goal.

JOHN S. BRUBACHER, **Teaching as a Fine Art**

4. Brubacher describes teaching as a "fine art." How does he rationalize teaching as being both an art and a science?

5. Identify and define the three characteristics of a good teacher which Brubacher discusses.

6. In Brubacher's words, what does he believe to be one of the deepest satisfactions of life? Indicate your agreement or disagreement with his final comment.

HARRY S. BROUDY, **Mirabile Dictu**

7. Many students regard Broudy as being exceptionally critical of education. What is your reaction?

8. (a) Do you think his ideas about computer instruction are reasonable and have a degree of feasibility?

(b) Give the reason for your answer.

(c) If you believe his ideas about computer instruction have any credibility, indicate the learning levels for its use.

9. (a) What role in education would Broudy have the human teacher play?

(b) On the basis of your answer to the above question, would you say Broudy advocates eliminating the human teacher? Give your reasoning.

ERWIN L. HARLACHER and ELEANOR ROBERTS, **Accountability for Student Learning**

10. What do Harlacher and Roberts imply as a source of the present emphasis given to "accountability" for learning?

11. Do the authors place the responsibility for failure rates in schools upon didactic methods?

12. To what do the authors attribute the illusion held by many educators that only a small percentage of students have the capacity to learn what is being taught?

13. What is their alternative?

14. Do you agree with Bloom's statement that "fully 90 per cent of all students can master learning tasks"?

15. In what two areas have the authors contended that major changes must take place if Bloom is to be proven right?

16. What relationship do the authors see between behavior changes and the goals or objectives for learning?

17. (a) Harlacher and Roberts made a sharply critical observation of the Texarkana experiment. What is the observation?

(b) How do they believe that individual mastery of specific learning tasks by children can be accounted for in the school system?

(c) How parallel are accountability for student learning and contract performance in the Texarkana experiment?

(d) What do the authors suggest as being of positive value to education in this experiment?

18. According to Harlacher and Roberts, what goals and objectives do colleges describe for themselves?

19. What do the authors view as a major responsibility of a community college?

FOR FURTHER READING

Dewey, John, "Plan of Organization of the University Primary School," *John Dewey as Educator,* ed. A. G. Wirth (New York: John Wiley & Sons, 1966).
A reading that will help you to make another comparison of the past and the present. Dewey's University Primary School was established in order to put his theories into practice, and his plan is presented succinctly in this detailed discussion.

Lessinger, Leon, "The Movement for Accountability," *Every Kid a Winner: Accountability in Education* (Palo Alto, Calif.: Science Research Associates, College Division, 1970).
An appropriate companion piece to the selection "Accountability for Student Learning" and an excellent probing into the significance of the present-day emphasis on educational accountability.

Leuder, Edward, "The McLuhan Thesis: Its Limits and Its Appeals," *English Journal,* Vol. 57, No. 4, April 1968.
An unusual thesis well presented. McLuhan's observations on modern mass media are supported by his own utilization of computer tape recorders and other innovative technological devices.

Mann, Horace, "The Business of the Schoolroom Is the Interest of Society," *Prologue to Teaching,* ed. M. B. Smiley and J. S. Diekhoff (New York: Oxford University Press, 1959).
Mann's views on this subject may be somewhat amazing but cannot be said to be illogical. His contributions to the improvement of education affected education during his lifetime and ever since then.

The Organization
and Financing
of American Education

21
Education in the United States
of America
JOHN PAXTON

The following is a concise description of education in the United States, to-gether with statistics on both public and nonpublic schools. While the data presented may not initially appeal to the average student, it should interest him to know that Paxton writes on this topic annually for The Statesman's Yearbook *and attempts to present education in the United States so that readers from other countries may have an accurate overview of educational affairs here.*

Education

UNDER the system of government in the United States of America, elementary and secondary education is committed in the main to the several states. Each of the 50 states has a system of free public schools, established by law, with courses covering 12 years. There are 3 structural patterns in common use: the 8–4 plan, meaning 8 elementary grades followed by 4 high school grades; the 6–3–3 plan, or 6 elementary grades followed by a 3-year junior high school and a 3-year senior high school; and the 6–6 plan, 6 elementary

SOURCE: John Paxton, ed., *The Statesman's Yearbook*, 1970–1971 (New York: St. Martin's, 1970), pp. 539–541. Reprinted by permission of the author and St. Martin's Press, Inc., The Macmillan Company of Canada, and Macmillan London and Basingbroke.

The author is editor of *The Statesman's Yearbook* and has also authored a number of books in the fields of trade and marketing. Prior to his association with the *Yearbook,* he served as head of a college economics department for eleven years.

225

grades followed by a 6-year high school. All plans lead to high-school graduation, usually at age 17 or 18. Vocational education is an integral part of secondary education. In addition, all but 5 states have kindergartens and some states have 2-year junior colleges as part of the free public school system. Each state has delegated a large degree of control of the educational programme to local school districts (numbering 20,440), each with a board of education (usually 3 to 9 members) elected locally and serving mostly without pay. The school policies of the local districts must be in accord with the laws and the regulations of their state Departments of Education. Almost every state has compulsory school attendance laws; in 37 states and the District of Columbia children are required to attend school until the age of 16 years; in 7 states until 17 and in 4 states until 18.

The Census Bureau estimates that in April 1960 only 3,055,000 or 2.4 percent of the 126m. persons who were 14 years of age or older were unable to read and write; in 1930 the percentage was 4.8. In 1940 a new category was established—the 'functionally illiterate', meaning those who had completed fewer than 5 years of elementary schooling; for persons 25 years of age or over this percentage was 5.9 in March 1968 (for the non-white population alone it was 17.3 percent); it was 1.1 for white and 2.6 percent for non-whites in the 25–29-year-old group. The Bureau reported that in March 1968 the median years of school completed by all persons 25 years old and over was 12.1, and that 10.5 percent had completed 4 or more years of college. For the 25–29-year-old group, the median school years completed was 12.5 and 14.7 percent had completed 4 or more years of college.

In the autumn of 1968, 6,928,000 students (4.1m. men and 2,809,000 women) were enrolled in 2,483 colleges and universities; 1.63m. were first-time students. Total enrolment represents a number equal to 30 per 100 persons between the ages of 18 and 24.

Public elementary and secondary school revenue is supplied from county and other local sources (53 percent in 1965–66), state sources (39.1 percent) and federal sources (7.9 percent). The tendency is for the counties and local units to contribute less and for the state and federal sources to contribute more. In 1965–66 the amount, including interest, expended on public elementary and secondary schools was $21,845m., representing an annual cost per pupil of $558. In addition, $3,755m., or $96 per pupil, was expended for capital outlay. Estimated expenditures for private elementary and secondary schools in 1965–66 were $3,700m. In 1966–67 the 2,400 universities and colleges expended $14,302m., of which $8,361m. was spent by institutions under public control. Federal funds for higher education amounted to 25.5 percent of current income; educational and general income from state governments totalled 28.1 percent; students contributed in fees 24.9 percent, and all other sources 21.5 percent.

Vocational education below college grade, including the training of teachers to conduct such education, has been federally aided since 1938. During the school year 1967–68 enrolments in the vocational classes were: Agriculture, 851,158; distributive occupations, 574,785; health occupations, 140,-987; home economics, 2,283,338; trade and industry, 1,628,542; technical education, 269,832; office occupations, 1,735,997. Federal support funds were $262.6m.

Summary of statistics of schools (public and non-public), teachers and pupils in autumn 1968 (compiled by the United States Office of Education):

Schools by level	Number of schools	Teachers	Enrolment
Elementary schools:			
Public	73,216	1,079,000	27,418,000
Non-public	15,340 (a)	151,000	4,400,000
Secondary schools:			
Public	26,597	864,000	17,543,000
Non-public	4,606	84,000	1,400,000
Higher education:			
Public	1,011	335,000	4,892,000
Non-public	1,472	189,000	2,036.000
Total	122,242	2,702,000	57,689,000

(a) 1965–66.

Most of the non-public elementary and secondary schools are affiliated with religious denominations. Of the children attending non-public schools, 87 percent are enrolled in Roman Catholic schools, 8 percent in other church-related schools and 5 percent in schools which are not affiliated to a religious denomination.

During the school year 1967–68 high-school graduates numbered 2,702,000 (1,341,000 boys and 1,361,000 girls). Institutions of higher education conferred 666,710 bachelor's and first professional degrees for the academic year 1967–68, 390,507 to men and 276,203 to women; 176,749 master's degrees, 113,519 to men and 62,230 to women; and 23,089 doctorates, 20,183 to men and 2,906 to women.

Nearly 122,000 foreign citizens were on American college and university campuses during the academic year 1967–68; 110,300 were students, and 11,600 were scholars engaged in research or teaching. The percentages of students coming from various areas were: Far East, 34; Latin America, 20; Europe, 15; Near and Middle East, 12; North America, 11; Africa, 6;

Oceania, 2. There were 8 US institutions enrolling 1,500 or more, the greatest number, 6,002, being at the University of California (all campuses).

School enrolment, October 1968, embraced 74.9 percent of the 4.1m. who were 5 years old; 98.3 percent of the 4.2m. aged 6; 99.1 percent of the 28.9m. aged 7–13 years; 94.3 percent of the 15m. aged 14–17; 50.4 percent of the 6.6m. aged 18 and 19; 21.4 percent of the 14m. aged 20–24 years.

The US Office of Education estimates the total enrolment in the autumn of all the country's educational institutions (public and non-public) at 58.4m. (57.6m. in the autumn of 1968); this was 29 percent of the total population of the USA as of 1 September 1969.

Elementary: Public schools, 27.4m. (27.4m. in 1968); non-public schools, 4.3m. (4.4m.); total, 31.7m. (31.8m.).

Secondary: Public schools, 18.2m. (17.5m.); non-public, 1.4m. (1.4m.); total, 19.6m. (18.9m.).

Higher education: Universities, other 4-year colleges and 2-year institutions of higher education, 7.1m. (6.9m.).

The number of teachers in the public elementary and secondary schools in the autumn of 1969 is estimated at 2m. The average annual salary of the public school teachers was about $7,900 in 1968–69.

All states require at least a bachelor's degree, and 3 states require completion of 5 years of college work for secondary school teachers; 47 states require a bachelor's degree for elementary school teachers, and the other states at least 2 years of college work. Thirty states, the District of Columbia and Puerto Rico require that the applicant for a teaching certificate be a citizen of the United States or that he must have filed a declaration of intent. Twenty-five states, the District of Columbia and Puerto Rico require that the applicant subscribe to an oath of allegiance or loyalty to the United States and the state.

22

The Organization of Education in the United States

MARJORIE CANN

The structural organizations of education at the national, state, and local levels of administration have some commonality of responsibilities as well as a number of unique characteristics. The brief overview that follows will introduce you to the formal organization at these three levels. For a study in greater depth, you should seek reliable sources in your library, where more information is available, but this selection is a good start.

At the National Level

HISTORICALLY, the responsibility for education lies chiefly with each of the individual states in the nation since no constitutional provision was made at the national level for education. This lack of central national control has occasionally been the cause of what might be interpreted as overcompensation by some highly centralized state departments. This is seen in the resistance by strong state departments to advice and assistance from the federal government. Financial assistance, professional standardization for better prepared teachers, provisions for pupil transportation, building funds, and other types of support are needed in many states. As it has become clearer that assistance from the federal government is one source of help that many of the states now seek, the initial resistance has decreased. The fear that their control will be lost if their financial independence is removed has often been expressed by state representatives.

Despite resistance to federal intervention in education, the United States Office of Education (USOE) has evolved as a central educational office on the national level and its chief education officer, the United States Commissioner of Education, is playing an increasingly stronger leadership role in educa-

SOURCE: This selection was prepared especially for this book.

Head of the Department of Behavioral Sciences and associate professor of education and psychology at Pensacola Junior College since 1967, Dr. Cann has contributed a number of articles to professional journals as well as co-authoring *A Synthesis of Teaching Methods,* a textbook that has enjoyed international success. She began her teaching career in a small rural school and since then has taught in almost every type of public and private school in both Canada and the United States.

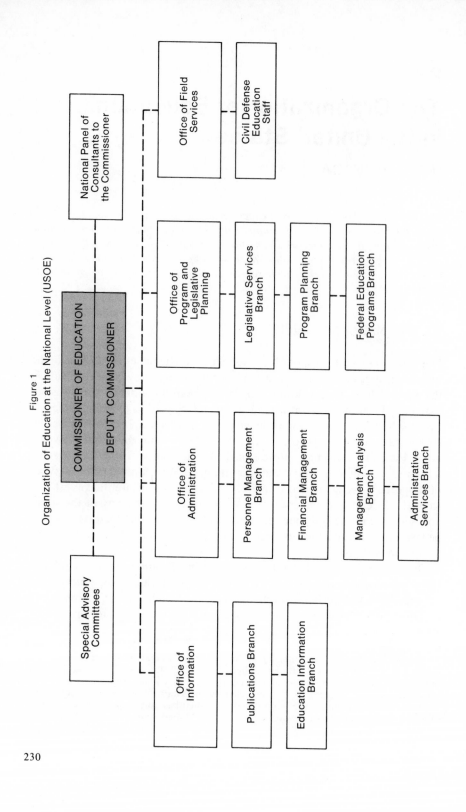

Figure 1
Organization of Education at the National Level (USOE)

tional matters. The USOE has functioned mainly as a high-level advisory group in research analysis and special projects. There is no valid evidence to support the fears of the states who are fighting to remain independent of a central educational agency. In the interim, decentralization of education at the state level has clearly become more effective in improving education and the implementation of educational policies at the local level. These two developments appear to be providing a counterbalance that will strengthen formally organized education in this country.

Education at the national level is shown in Figure 1. Further particulars on the functioning of each office at the various levels may be found in the annual reports of the United States Office of Education. The USOE is the federal government's agency for collecting data on education, disseminating it, and disbursing certain federal funds. Congress established it primarily to show the condition and progress of education and otherwise promote the cause of education. Resources of its specialists are made available to educational organizations through correspondence, conferences, and publications.

At the State Level

The state departments of education in all fifty states of this country hold the responsibility for establishing and maintaining public schools. A state department of education consists of a state board of education, the chief state school officer, and the staff of the state education agency.

Members of the state boards of education are elected in some states and appointed in others. They are either elected by popular vote or by the state legislature. If appointed, either the governor or the chief state school officer makes the appointment. They may also hold the position *ex officio*.

More than 40 percent of the fifty states elect the chief state school officer, who holds the title generally of state commissioner or state superintendent. He is appointed in the remaining states. Where he is appointed, the appointment is generally made by the state board of education. Only in exceptional cases does the governor make this appointment. The chief state officer has a staff appointed by himself or by the state board of education. These appointed officials are known as the state department of education and consist of professional, supervisory, clerical, and maintenance personnel.

Figure 2 is presented here to show the typical structure and organization of a state department of education.

At the Local Level

Local school boards of education operate within the framework of references laid down by the state departments of education. They work closely

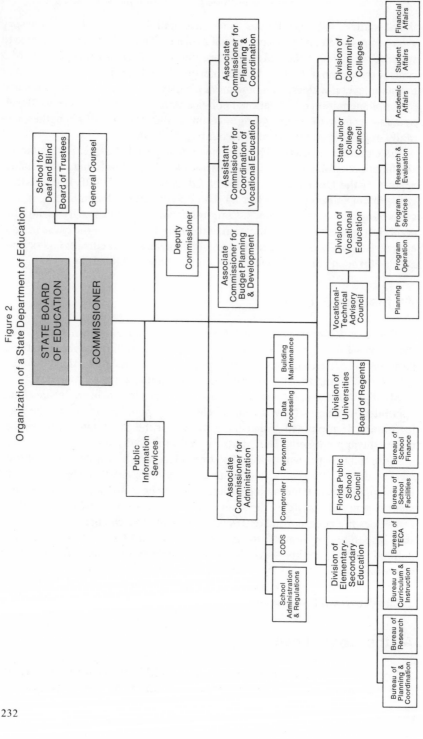

Figure 2
Organization of a State Department of Education

with the officials of their state department to interpret and carry out state educational policies, to formulate and determine local educational policies, and to supervise the operation of local educational institutions.

The chief education officer is either appointed or elected. His prime responsibility is to execute the policy of the local board. His deputy and the other officers are appointed. Administration and supervision in every phase of the educational process at the local level is the responsibility of the local chief officer. He also serves as chief professional administrator of the board of education.

In the past twenty-five years, education in many states of America has adopted the practice of consolidation. Consolidation combines small school districts into large units. It is believed that this results in better educational facilities and a more adequate supply of qualified teachers for the larger school districts.

Figure 3 illustrates one administrative organizational model of education at the local level.

As has been implied in this brief description of the organization of education at the national, state, and local levels, many variations are found throughout the country. Each structure was designed in the light of recognized needs and desired goals.

The Overall Design of Education in the United States

Education in the United States is divided into two major areas; elementary and secondary education or the public school system and higher education. The public school system generally follows one of three plans—the 8-4, the 6-3-3, or the 6-6. Each plan makes a distinction in their philosophy, specific objectives, emphasis, and curriculum. Each plan begins at the nursery school level and has a clear separation between what is called elementary or primary and secondary education. Variations are found within these separate levels especially in the intermediate years, which may be classed as junior high schools or middle schools and begin anywhere from the 6th year to the 8th year of schooling. Secondary education offers academic, vocational, or technical programs or all of these.

At the highest level of the American concept of a public school system has been created institutions of higher education. They offer college, university, and professional programs.

Higher education may begin with a two-year college program that terminates with an associate certificate. These two-year colleges offer three types of programs: the college preparatory program, vocational courses, or an extension of the high-school course.

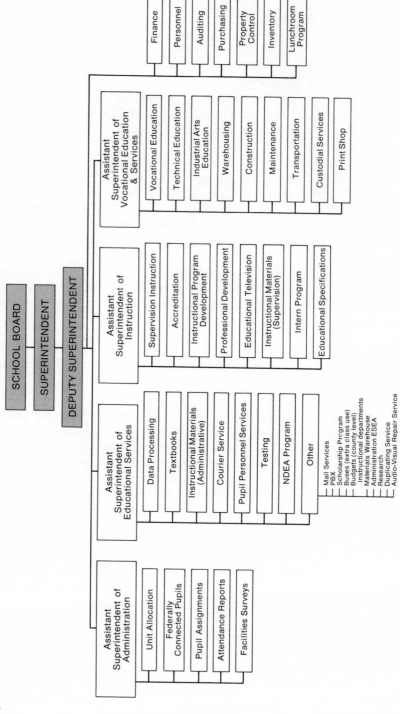

Figure 3 Organization of Education at the Local Level

234

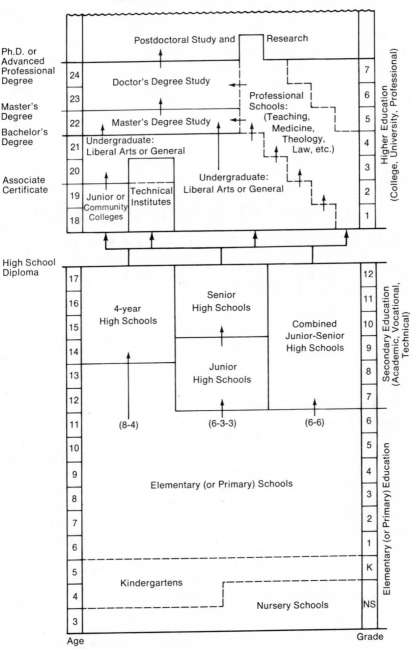

Figure 4
The Structure of Education in the United States*

Ph.D. or Advanced Professional Degree

Master's Degree

Bachelor's Degree

Associate Certificate

High School Diploma

Postdoctoral Study and Research

Doctor's Degree Study

Master's Degree Study

Undergraduate: Liberal Arts or General

Junior or Community Colleges   Technical Institutes

Undergraduate: Liberal Arts or General

Professional Schools: (Teaching, Medicine, Theology, Law, etc.)

Higher Education (College, University, Professional)

4-year High Schools

Senior High Schools

Junior High Schools

Combined Junior-Senior High Schools

(8-4)   (6-3-3)   (6-6)

Elementary (or Primary) Schools

Kindergartens

Nursery Schools

Secondary Education (Academic, Vocational, Technical)

Elementary (or Primary) Education

Age   Grade

*Source. U.S. Department of Health, Education, and Welfare, Office of Education.
Digest of Educational Statistics. 1965 edition. Bulletin 1965, No. 4. Washington, D. C.: Government Printing Office, 1965. p. xiv.

235

Higher education next moves into the four-year bachelor's degree program followed by the postgraduate program at the master's degree level and then the doctoral or advanced professional degree program. In education, a doctor of education degree (Ed.D.) may be taken in place of the traditional doctor of Philosophy degree (Ph.D.). Specific requirements vary within each graduate degree program just as they vary with the major and minor field requirements of the undergraduate degree programs.

23

The Support of American Schools: Ten Questions on School Finance

NATIONAL EDUCATION ASSOCIATION RESEARCH DIVISION

Presented here is a general statement on support of American schools. In its question and answer format lies the invitation to discussion of the important financial responsibilities of the American people.

1. *Why should public funds support education even though many parents can afford to pay for the education of their own children?*

Our society cannot function with an illiterate citizenry. Free public education has followed the extension of suffrage and the increasing needs of the economy and national security for highly skilled workers.

Education is necessary for the exercise of citizenship, for an individual to be an efficient producer and consumer in a free enterprise economic system, for individual self-realization, for the civilization of man, for healthful living, for cultural and scientific progress, for national defense, for self-discipline in the use of freedom. Our society depends on these qualities.

All society benefits when the individuals which comprise it are able to develop their talents and to use them constructively. This is the "social benefit" theory underlying public support of education.

SOURCE: *NEA Research Bulletin,* October 1965, pp. 86–89. Reprinted by permission of the publisher. This selection is the 1965 Report of the National Education Association Committee on School Finance.

The traditional legal justification of free schooling is not a citizen's right to an education, although few would deny this right today. It is the obligation imposed upon young citizens for the good of society. Young citizens are compelled to attend the public schools or to otherwise satisfy the states' minimum educational requirements with private schooling. Public funds have supported education beyond compulsory school-age limits because of the benefit all society gets from high levels of education.

While advantages accrue to the individual, the case for free public schools rests on the protection that the expenditure buys against an ignorant citizenry and the benefits the whole state gets from an educated citizenry.

2. *Who should determine how much money is spent on public education?*

The decisions on how much money will be spent on public education are reflected in the local school budget, but the total decision-making process involves all levels of government; all levels of the education profession speaking out on school needs; many individuals expressing opinions in financial elections and in the election of officials, in public hearings, and in contacts with public officials.

The federal government is an increasingly important source of school funds. Many aid programs stimulate matching state and local funds for specified programs. For example, the National Defense Education Act supplies funds to programs of special interest to national defense; and the availability of funds influences the decisions of state and local school governing bodies to direct more of their own funds to NDEA programs.

By determining the state aid for local school districts, the state legislature is important in setting the level of spending—the state can depress local support by permitting state funds to replace local funds, or it can stimulate local effort by providing financial incentives for local school districts to increase local efforts to support schools. In addition, many states restrict local taxing and borrowing powers. Unrealistic fiscal limits thwart local effort to support schools.

The local school authority is usually given the responsibility for the school budget. Most school systems start budgeting by determining how much was received and spent in the last fiscal period and how much will be available for next year. This retards the development of a quality school budget. Ideally a school board should decide what levels of education are needed irrespective of past offerings, and then determine the additional funds needed.

The professional staff has a primary responsibility for leadership in developing the school financial planning at all three governmental levels: federal, state, and local. And associations at all three levels—the National Education Association, the state education associations, and the local education associations—are actively working with citizens groups and public officials to present the financial needs of public education and to influence decisions on school support.

3. *How should the three levels of government share the cost of public education?*

All levels of government should share in financing the public schools. Today the federal government is almost as close to the people as the county courthouse in years gone by.

There are unique advantages to each tax system as a revenue agent for school support. The federal tax system, with heavy reliance on the progressive income tax, is the most responsive to economic growth, and is the least affected by fears of interstate and local competition for industry. State sales and excise taxes are a major source of state revenue for schools. In addition, state income taxes, severance taxes, and licenses and fees are also available for school support. Local revenues for schools, mainly property taxes, provide the means for local school authorities to support the type and quality of education the community wants and can afford. Local support, interest, and control of education are important in achieving quality.

Ways must be determined whereby the revenue of the federal and state governments can be brought into the local schools without destroying the advantages of local control. Much progress has been made in the techniques of combining state and local funds, but much needs to be done on the federal-state-local fiscal partnership.

4. *Is education an investment which pays dividends to society and to the individual?*

Money spent on education results in both consumption of goods and services and in the development of increased productive capacity of tomorrow's adults. Money spent on education has aspects of both consumption and production goods. It creates human wants and produces higher earning power. Hence it is an investment both in future consumption and in future earnings.

Investments in education pay tremendous returns in economic, social, and scientific progress both to individuals and to society.

Education is such a good investment that we should be putting a lot more money into it at all levels, nursery school through higher education and adult education both in general education and in training and retraining the experienced labor force.

5. *What is a state foundation program?*

The system by which the state takes into account local tax revenues for schools and apportions its grants-in-aid to the various districts is usually called the foundation program. State aid is apportioned to local school districts as general purpose and special purpose grants. General purpose grants are distributed without specification as to their use in financing the local program. Special purpose grants are designated only for the program or programs specified, such as driver education or libraries.

The foundation program describes the minimum program guaranteed in every district from local and state funds. The law usually sets a dollar amount per classroom, per pupil, or per teaching unit.

The minimum program can actually set the maximum provided throughout the state if state revenues are allowed to replace local effort. However, the foundation program can be designed to stimulate local effort. A few states have a program whereby additional state funds are granted to match additional local effort above the minimum program.

6. *Should we have equalization of tax resources and educational opportunity?*

All children should have equal educational opportunities regardless of where they might live in the state or the United States or how much taxable wealth exists in the districts which provide their schooling. Our human resources can be fully developed only when each child has the educational services he needs. Therefore, broad-based support should supplement local funds. State funds should be apportioned to local school districts to equalize the differences among the school districts in taxable wealth. Federal funds should equalize differences in the states' ability. Equalization has two dimensions: providing equal opportunities to the pupils and making more nearly equal the financial resources available to support the local school program.

7. *Why are school costs rising?*

Increasing *enrollments* are one factor in the increase in the total costs for schools. In addition, enrollments are increasing fastest at the secondary level where costs are highest. *Inflation* is another factor. The most important factor in cost increase in many school systems is *expansion of the school program* upward, downward, and outward to comprise a comprehensive system of education from nursery school through the fourteenth year for all youth, with emphasis on providing for individual differences.

8. *Does a higher level of school expenditure insure better quality of education?*

It is foolish to argue that a high expenditure insures quality education. Many conditions are associated with quality: good school organization, good administration, well-qualified teachers, good supporting staff, and high degree of interest in schools.

One research undertaking, Project TALENT, tested about one-half million high-school students in a sample of 19,000 high schools across the country in spring 1960. The school background factors that correlated best with test scores were starting salaries of teachers and average per-pupil expenditure. Almost all studies of cost-quality have concluded that a high educational expenditure is not the only ingredient of quality but it is a necessary one.

9. *Are school taxes too high?*

Many persons never relate their tax bill to the value of services received from government. To them, any tax is too high.

Over-reliance on one tax, the local property tax or a single state tax, for school support is conducive to attitudes that school taxes are too high. This is why the efforts of professional associations are directed to broadening the tax base for schools: at the local level to secure equalized property tax assessments, at the state level to secure both sales and income taxes for state school appropriations, and at the federal level to secure an increased share of broad-based federal revenues.

We have underinvested in education. High dropout rates and the young adults in the population who lack basic skills needed for employment are evidence of this underinvestment. We are at a high level of prosperity. We spent more in 1964 for all government services than in 1960, but we still spent more in the private sector of the economy than in the government sector. Despite a lower dollar gain, the government sector is advancing at a higher rate. Moreover, higher expenditures are needed for education to increase prosperity in the private sector.

10. *Why does the professional association work for increased taxes for schools?*

Professional associations are dedicated to advancing the welfare of pupils, teachers, and public education. This directs the efforts of the associations toward improvement of school organization, administration, curriculum and methods of teaching, preparation, recruitment, and retention of teachers and other school personnel, and toward an increase in the funds to pay for good schools.

No group has yet emerged to relieve the teaching profession of being the chief proponent of improvements in the school program and in the resources of schools to finance the salaries, materials, equipment, and buildings of a good school program. This role is uniquely lodged in the teaching profession.

EVALUATION

JOHN PAXTON, **Education in the United States of America**

1. (a) Prepare a diagram showing the three structural patterns in common use in the American system of free public schools as Paxton describes them in the opening paragraph of his selection.

   (b) Where does vocational education enter into these patterns?

   (c) Are kindergartens and two-year junior colleges within these public school structures?

2. The broad purposes of education in the United States aim to develop the individual and to achieve the maximum welfare of society through the cooperative efforts of individuals and groups.
   (a) By 1960, had the percentage of "functionally illiterate" shown that these purposes had been achieved?

   (b) Support your answer to (a) with specific data from the Paxton article.

3. (a) What was the estimated total enrollment of all educational institutions in the United States in 1968?

   (b) What was this figure for 1969?

   (c) What percentage of the 1969 total population was this?

   (d) Make a simple column tabulation of the figures given for (1) elementary, (2) secondary, and (3) higher education by the United States Office of Education as of September 1969.

   (e) What were the estimated number of teachers and the average salary of teachers in the public elementary and secondary schools in the fall of 1969?

MARJORIE CANN, **The Organization of Education in the United States**

5. (a) In "The Organization of Education in the United States," where does the author say responsibility for education has been placed historically?

   (b) How did this happen?

6. (a) According to Cann, what has this lack of control on the national level occasionally caused?

(b) How can this be seen?

(c) What does the author believe is an underlying cause?

6. What does the author say regarding the relationships between the national, state, and local departments of education in more recent years?

7. (a) What does Cann give as the functions of the USOE?

(b) List the four major offices of the USOE at the national level as given in the schema of the organization of education.

8. (a) Name the major offices shown in the schema for the organization of a state department of education.

(b) How is the chief office filled?

(c) What four broad categories of personnel are employed in a state department of education?

9. (a) What authority establishes the framework of references within which local school boards operate?

(b) What are three major functions of the local board?

(c) Make a listing of the facts presented here about the school superintendent.

(d) Explain what is meant by consolidation of schools and why it has been introduced in many areas.

(e) List the four major divisions found within the educational structure at the local level.

10. Since the federal government has shown tangible evidence of an interest in stimulating education through financial appropriation of funds and endowments, may we continue to hold to the position on support of public education found in the NEA statement on funding education?

11. Indicate whether or not you agree with the views expressed on revenue sources at the three levels of government in sharing the cost of public education, and present any other views you hold on this question.

N.E.A. RESEARCH DIVISION, **The Support of American Schools**

12. Compare the information given in "The Support of American Schools" on a state foundation program with your own state foundation program.

Conclude your comparison with a brief statement of your own opinion of the merits of each.

13. (a) What basic responsibility is placed on the teaching profession in "The Support of American Schools"?

   (b) How does this correlate with the various local and state departments' areas of responsibilities?

   (c) Make notes on differences and similarities as you understand them and prepare them for a class discussion.

FOR FURTHER READING

Morse, Arthur D., "Freeing the Teacher for Teaching," *Schools of Tomorrow, Today* (New York: Doubleday and Company, 1960).

An unusually detailed report of the exciting Bay City, Michigan, experiment with teacher aides. Although it occurred almost twenty years ago, the experiment remains a landmark for the introduction into education in the late sixties and seventies of the paraprofessional school staff member.

Innovations in Education

24
An Educational System Analyzed

BURTON G. ANDREAS

The opportunities for innovation in American education are greater today than ever before in the nation's history. Just as the industrial revolution of the nineteenth century affected instructional school programs and facilities, so are technological advances affecting science and industry. One outcome has been an attempt to apply to education what is referred to as the "systems approach." A systems approach to education may be described as the mobilization of science and technology to attack problems of administration and instruction in an objective, logical, and philosophical way. It starts by a definition of objectives with a description of the optimum design of required personnel, media, devices, and facilities. Andreas analyzes some of the changes that are already occurring. You, as a future teacher, will be able to catch the excitement of these changes and understand some of their significance as you study this and the other selections in this section.

THERE IS no "process of education"—no unitary phenomenon—despite the singular phrasing employed by Professor Bruner and others. Instead, numerous social and psychological processes constitute an individual's education. The student's formal schooling does not proceed in isolation. It is a part, a subsystem, of his ongoing development. His biologically based maturation and extra-school learning are important contributors to personal intellectual growth. These two processes naturally result in important individual differences requiring consideration of individuality in designing instruction.

SOURCE: Burton G. Andreas, *Psychological Science and the Educational Enterprise* (New York: John Wiley & Sons, 1968), pp. 19–36. Reprinted by permission of the publisher.

The author, a well-known American psychologist, is presently on the faculty of the University of Rochester. In addition to his major work, *Experimental Psychology,* his major contributions in his field have been in behavior theory, perceptual motor performance, and applied psychology.

Individual Development

To emphasize the triadic nature of individual development, I have given its complex components approximately equal representation in Figure 1. Closely related to a person's formal education are his endowments derived from biological maturation and his attainments in extra-school learning. The purposeful designing of the instructional subsystem must begin with attention to these natural and social contributors to individuality. Each child is unique in the maturational unfolding of his hereditary endowment and unique in the pattern of his home experience. Both of these forces are powerful determinants of his nature as he enters school for the first time, whatever his age. These two components of development are also continuing concomitants of education as well as its antecedents.

Individual Differences

Biological maturation cannot be modified by ordinary means. Heredity determines the sex of the child, greatly influences sensory acuities, contributes to motor capabilities, sets a general timetable for emerging capacities, and may even delimit the speed and power of mental operations. In bygone days psychologists indulged themselves in arguing the relative contributions of heredity and environment to intelligence. Today we better appreciate the complex interaction of these two components of individual development. The environment, especially the home experiences of preschool years, provides—or

Figure 1
Schematic Representation of the Triadic Nature of Individual Development

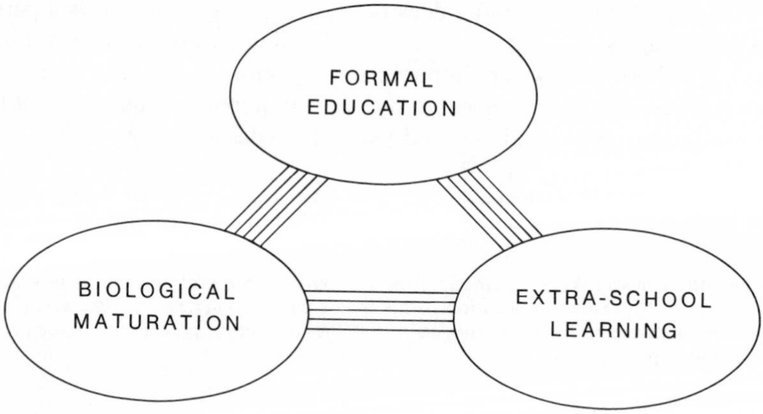

precludes—opportunity for varied learning which actually shapes the infant intellect. Thirty children arrive at the school door with 30 unique personalities. This great variance among learners is a chief obstacle to swift, smooth pedagogical progress.

Sex differences in maturation, with young boys lagging behind girls in cognitive development, are a fundamental problem for early elementary education. Whether its source be purely genetic or partly cultural, the real handicap with which boys face the important task of learning to read is one that deserves attention. Special language training or other preparatory instruction may be needed to get first-grade boys ready to tackle reading. It has even been proposed to write separate reading texts for boys and girls in the early grades. Alternatively, we might wait for maturational development to ready boys for their task, or we might provide individualized instruction that promotes progress in the individual child, boy or girl, each pupil working at his own level and pace. The problem, however it will be solved, illustrates the intimate relationship between the youngster's development and his requirements in formal education.

Specific sources of learned individual differences among primary grade pupils are not hard to locate. Although it may indeed be difficult to measure the effects of varied experiences, we may consider a few aspects of preschool life and home environment that offer promise or problems for formal schooling:

1. Early experience with adults and other children, especially in the realms of language and attitudes toward education.
2. Efforts by parents to teach specific knowledge and skills thought to be beneficial for school.
3. Nursery school or similar experience, as in the Head Start program.
4. Interaction with toys, games, and other artifacts and activities, including television.

Such extra-school learning as these represent may not only affect the realm of cognition or knowledge but may also shape attitudes and motives in most important ways for the young scholar's success or failure.

Critics of education often ignore individual differences in sounding a call for easy improvement. But sounder appraisals give our problem due recognition. A section of *Schools for the Sixties* is titled, "The Stubborn Fact of Individual Differences." It begins by stating that "human variability is real, inevitable, ineradicable, desirable, and indeed, essential" (p. 75). My editing of this statement would delete the word "ineradicable" as too strong, too pessimistic in tone. Differences from person to person will never be completely eliminated, of course, but they are significantly reducible; that is, the child who lags most may be given substantial help in catching up with his peers and with his personal potential.

First graders, we are told in *Schools,* vary in mental age from four years to eight, an IQ range from roughly 70 to 135. A similar picture is portrayed by school achievement measures, with the variance from the highest to the lowest achievers increasing as school years go on. "The spread between the quick and the slow increases with time," we are informed (p. 75). Perhaps a more revealing way to phrase this is to state that the range from top to bottom of the group increases with years of conventional classroom teaching, not merely with time. The teacher is not to blame here but rather the techniques of instruction and, more particularly, the system that sacrifices the slower student, letting him slip farther and farther behind. This might seem to be special pleading for the child at or near the mental retardation level. Actually, I intend the indictment of the system to be broader; while the slowest are slipping way below the majority of their peers in achievement, the greater number of "average" individuals are slipping below their own potential levels of accomplishment.

An Ideal Educational Design

The title of this chapter suggests a goal beyond reasonable reach. A thorough examination and description of education in all its complexity would take a dozen experts a decade to compile. If completed, the work would be a history, since the present shows so many signs of educational change. The much more modest effort undertaken here will sketch an ideal educational design. We shall point to recent trends directing our course in a systems approach to individualized process promotion.

If based on a maturation-learning psychology of individual development, an ideal educational enterprise might be schematized as in Figure 2. The scheme obviously takes the old notion of the educational ladder as its model. However, the rungs of this ladder are more analytically conceived than the grades of elementary and secondary school and the years of college and perhaps graduate school.

The elements of the static figure actually represent a sequence of measures to be undertaken in planning and accomplishing an ideal educational effort at any level of schooling:

1. Specifying objectives, a widely shared educational responsibility.
2. Recognizing biological maturation, extra-school learning, and the cultural ground as supporting the formal school effort.
3. Testing of aptitudes and achievements to guide the selection of a desirable unit of teaching for the individual.
4. Teaching appropriate content by the indicated techniques to accomplish a subgoal, a specified objective of the curriculum.
5. Testing for the attainment of the desired subgoal.
6. Later, final testing to assess the accomplishment of the student and the

Figure 2
Schematic Representation of an Educational System
Based on the Psychology of the Individual Learner

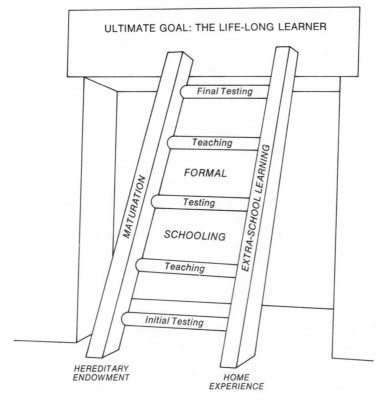

effectiveness of the educational effort in the light of the previously elucidated objectives.

Several aspects of an ideal educational effort deserve consideration of their systematic contribution.

Specified Objectives

A child's education begins before he is born, in the provisions that are made for it. Specified educational goals and plans for reaching them are fundamental problems in any society or community. On the matter of teaching aims, *Schools for the Sixties* declares, "It is necessary for the schools to choose relatively few important objectives, to work toward them consistently, and to review them periodically in the light of changing times" (p. 8). Noting the continuing decision-making that involves teachers, administrators, school board members, and legislators, the book goes on to claim general agreement on the broad aim of preparing young people to live in a changing society and to contribute constructively to it. A more specific set of objectives is for the student to "read, write, speak, compute, and think more effectively" (p. 30). This list of skills to be cultivated might be expanded to include the abilities to learn and to remember, although some would include these as aspects of thinking. Note the stress on promoting the acquisition of processes rather than the cramming of content into the brain. Learning facts can be endorsed, however, insofar as knowledge in the memory bank serves to undergird thought processes. Both what a student should know and what he should know how to do are valid objectives.

It is not my intent at this point to develop or promote an extended list of teaching aims. Such efforts are presented in scholarly works such as *Taxonomy of Educational Objectives* (Bloom, 1956; Krathwohl, Bloom, and Masia, 1964) as well as in public and private debates. I need only to endorse strongly the desirability of cooperative efforts to define objectives for individuals at different levels of education. Decisions on goals must necessarily precede planning for instructional content and methods, and testing. That is why they are so important. To teach without specified aims is to "define" objectives by default, with the risk that instructional outcomes will be found inadequate in any after-the-fact, after-the-forgetting assessment.

Goals must be made much more explicit than in their presentation in the "educationese" of Recommendation 19 of *Schools for the Sixties:* "The content of the curriculum should be organized in such ways that students may progress, from early to later school years, toward an increasing mature utilization and organization of their knowledge" (p. 58). The report's elaboration of this recommendation moves in the direction of specificity—but not very far. Education needs to emulate modern psychology in its widespread adoption of operational definitions. The outcomes of instruction must be stated in behavioral terms. What should the student be able to *do* after a semester of analytic geometry? after a semester of Spanish? after four weeks of instruction in reading? As Mager has cogently argued, specifying objectives is important not only for achievement testing but for designing the curriculum and techniques for its transmission. His book, *Preparing Instructional Objectives* (1962), offers great promise for improving education.

More arduous than merely stating terminal behaviors as instructional goals is the backward plotting of subgoals. As more and more elemental abilities are charted, a sequential course of behavioral modification is outlined. This mode of curriculum construction involves structural analysis of the subject matter, as Bruner (1960) has stressed, and the study of sequential transfer of skills, as emphasized in theory and empirical research by Gagné (1962).

Plotting Personal Progress

After a sequence of subgoals has been set forth, yielding a very detailed curriculum, progress may be charted on an individual basis. Instead of calculating where the average student should be after one semester of work, we can follow and guide each student at a pace appropriate for him. Instead of giving one boy a D for poor accomplishment, we give him an extra few days and specially designed instruction to help him attain more of the subgoals on his way toward mastery. This individualization for learning rate and method incorporates in education a realistic recognition of the fundamental fact about young learners—their individual differences.

Our ideal of tailoring our teaching to individual needs requires much more testing of the child than has been traditional. We shall need initial testing, intercurrent testing, and final testing. Due to the variance arising in preschool development, initial assessment of the young pupil's abilities and capacities must be an early step in his instructional program. The several tests to be administered will reveal what the child knows and what he can do—the raw materials for beginning his formal education. Deficiencies and strengths will be detected with diagnostic procedures more refined than those currently in use.

What abilities require appraisal as the young child begins his school life? Tests of vision and hearing must assure his readiness to profit from the guidance his teacher will offer. Simple observations and tests of manual dexterity, coordination, and perception will determine how he can profit from activities of the kindergarten and first grade. More specialized tests to be administered to the individual pupil will assess his verbal capacities in speaking and understanding. Language will be the vehicle of his instruction and of the very thinking processes that he will gradually acquire. One child's home environment will differ from another's in the models and practice opportunities provided for his acquisition of language fluency and comprehension. Particular difficulties may exist for the child from a home where English is not regularly spoken, but verbal problems will not be limited to such pupils.

The testing procedures required may be developed through extension and refinement of current psychological tests—verbal and picture vocabulary tests, assessment of memory for simple sentences, comprehension of directions given, and possibly some adaptations of word association and sentence completion techniques. This formidable battery of assessment procedures naturally will not all be administered in the first two weeks of school. During the early months, however, the teacher will want to establish a profile of each child's simple mental abilities. However rudimentary, these perceptual, motor, and verbal capacities are avenues to the developing mind. The pupil must hear the teacher's words, of course, but understanding them is crucial also.

To ignore the special needs of each child is to risk defects of early education that can create persistent difficulties in schooling. Insofar as all the tests required have not yet been developed and refined, I hope that psychologists will accept the challenge of aiding educators to devise them. The traditions of psychological testing, going back to Terman, Binet, and Galton, provide historical inspiration. The more modern proliferations of mental measurement, the work of many psychologists, offer promise of imaginative approaches. In a formal research effort psychological measurement experts might be guided by a model based on empirical research such as Guilford's structure of intellect (1959). They might also employ a similar configuration more closely related to school learning tasks, such as Jensen (1967, pp. 122–125) has suggested.

To learn to listen well, read well, speak well, and write well is to learn to think well. But there are additional thought processes whose promotion is also vital. Intelligent inquiry, inductive reasoning, insightful discovery, associative linking, memorizing, generalizing, deductive reasoning, creative thought—these are all important processes to be cultivated repeatedly in Bruner's spiral curriculum, and to be assessed frequently with intercurrent testing. This emphasis on testing for departures from the desired path of progress and then correcting for any deviation gives us a cybernetic curriculum. The teacher is the helmsman who steers the student back on course. To do this effectively, the steersman needs frequent readings of test instruments. If currently available tests and remedial instructional techniques are inadequate, then teachers and psychologists must develop some new ones.

Calling for initial assay of the cognitive side of development does not mean that other facets are to be neglected. A strong case can be made for considering social, emotional, and attitudinal aspects of children as extremely important to cultivate when school years begin. Attitudes are aptitudes. The young pupil who loves school will learn more easily. Motives and attitudes therefore also need early and continued assessment—another task requiring cooperation between teacher and psychologist.

Throughout a child's schooling, his individual instruction must be linked intimately with intercurrent testing. In what month of the school year do we do our most intensive testing? In September or May? Do we test to outline our opportunities or to find out our failings? The old system said teach, then test; the psychologist says test, then teach. Why the difference? Differing objectives in education may be the basis for the distinction in approach, exaggerated here for emphasis. The conventional curriculum stressed facts, figures, and formulas to be memorized. We taught them before we tested on them, of course. Psychology preaches process acquisition, the mastery of techniques of thought that lead to later learning. Diagnostic testing must delineate each learner's profile of thinking processes so that strengthening exercises may be prescribed for those that are weak. Admittedly, each learner needs a few facts. These, too, must be inventoried at intervals. But facts are mere food for thought, and thinking is a many-faceted thing.

Instructing the Individual

Teaching is a taxing, temper-testing task primarily because of the fundamental psychological fact of individual differences. Our pupils are all unique personalities, differing greatly in the abilities and capacities which they bring to our classroom. Often the critics of the schools overlook this impediment to easy educational accomplishment. But the obstacle of individual differences is also our opportunity. It provides us the chance to plan a personal path to attainment for each child after comparing his current capabilities with our curricular sequence of subgoals. Deficiencies in what has been learned can always, in principle, be remedied. Too often, in practice, they are not. This is not to ignore the valiant work done by remedial teachers; but much more of the work of all teachers needs to be of a healing sort. As Carroll has pointed out, "There is a very thin line between a teaching procedure as such, and a remedy, since all teaching can be called 'remedies for ignorance' " (1967, p. 43).

This view is exemplified in conference discussion by MacKinnon who says, in agreement with Provus,

". . . our greatest task in attempting to develop instructional media to encourage creativity is to develop media which will be used for those who are not of the highest intelligence. . . . If one has really already learned the techniques of reasoning and thinking, he doesn't need as much instruction as those who have not learned these techniques. . . ." (1966, pp. 194–195).

He later adds this emphasis: "Procedures and programs, I believe, must be tailor-made, if not for individual students, at least for different types of students" (1966, p. 197).

School experience and psychological experiments both strongly support the need to design teaching techniques that will cater to the capabilities of individual learners. After reviewing research on memorizing information, Melton uses the language of the theoretician to report to us from the psychology laboratories:

"If one accepts the notion that most memory is based upon such mediational recoding operations, and also the notion that stimuli differ in the ease of recodability, then it seems probable that the principal factors in verbal learning may be the availability and efficiency of such recoding (and decoding) operations that the subject performs on the sequence of events that is being experienced.

"The final step in the development of this thought is to assert that subjects differ in the speed and/or efficiency of recoding of input information, and there is ample evidence that this is the case" (1967, p. 248).

A translation to the school situation tells us that pupils differ in their ability to receive and retain the information we present because they differ in skill at recoding it for memory storage.

There follow two educational implications. We find, first, that we need to pace instruction differently for different students' absorption of the information. This has long been known, of course, and teachers have certainly tried to do this despite severe constraints of the classroom system. Today we may need to cast classroom constraint aside. We must cease talking to large groups of students and start instructing them as individuals. We may need to bring learners into direct contact with instructive sources—let them read for themselves, work out problems and exercises, listen to recorded lessons, and operate projectors for audiovisual aid with their learning. Second, we need to become alert to the possibility of actually training young children in potent processes of listening and encoding. This holds promise of lifetime learning gains for some who have not naturally, and would not normally, attain this type of mental proficiency, an aural parallel to the visual aspect of reading.

Since there are multiple learning processes and myriad individual differences, a very general principle of teaching calls for it to be varied. Even while we are working toward a theory of instruction that will permit us to specify a particular lesson for a particular learner at a certain locus in his progress through the curriculum, we must not overestimate our ability to do this now. By using a diversity of materials and methods, we may hope to accomplish by good fortune what we cannot yet do by good forecast. This does not mean we are to accept changes so often that we create curricular confusion. It is our challenge as teachers to bring a multimedium effort to bear on each learner's need to know while still maintaining his momentum toward mastery. In addition to increasing our chances for aiding our students, variety in our teaching may alleviate their boredom, or to put it more nicely, maintain their motivation. Let variety be the spice of learning.

Introducing new teaching methods or materials, Torrance (1966, pp. 164–165) has noted, often caused a different group of pupils to emerge as star performers in our classes. This is evidence that the earlier mode of instruction was not well-suited to those particular individuals. By innovating in the area of curricular materials and by offering wider latitude for learner activity, we allow more of our pupils to reach instructional goals by avenues for which they are best endowed by nature and past learning.

Verbal handicap may be a retardant to scholastic accomplishment in some children since so much of our conventional teaching is verbal in nature. As we seek to build verbal facility and comprehension in each student, we must also provide other avenues of impression upon his mind. Dynamic graphic or pictorial presentations should be particularly potent in the light of the numerous hours of TV watching which have attuned young viewers to the medium. This does not mean that teaching by television, per se, promises particular success. Educational television may evoke negative reactions if its content and continuity are inferior to the child's level of expectation. Commercial television has opened the audiovisual channel for reaching many young intellects expeditiously. It has also set a high technical standard to be matched.

One way to broaden the base of instruction is to let learners teach each other. A parallel to team-teaching may make learning teams out of small groups of students. Different items of information, or pointers to sources, may be distributed among a group. Each student brings his newly acquired knowledge to a group session for synthesis. Particular students may play a tutorial role quite naturally as such a cooperative learning venture proceeds. Individual motivation may be sustained by contagion from the group's manifest interest in solving the assigned instructional problem.

The small group format may yield dividends in process promotion as well as in gaining knowledge. Group members will have to acquire numerous skills of structuring problems, communicating questions, and synthesizing findings. Another benefit of team-learning may stem from its diversity and redundancy of interchange among the participants. As matters are examined from differing points of view, each learner may catch insight from one of the several ways that the material is structured. Quick learners may deepen their understanding by playing the teaching role. Slower learners may profit from the natural repetition of group discussion.

Torrance (1966, p. 149) has reminded us of Binet's observation of a half century ago. Noticing the varied learning modes of the preschool child—experimenting, playing games, singing, storytelling—Binet asked if these activities should not continue to be favored avenues of enlightenment when formal schooling begins. We do employ such forms of instruction in kindergarten and primary grades, of course, but perhaps we need to consider relying on them much more heavily for a greater portion of our curricular aims. Tuneful television commercials stick in our pupils' minds. Why shouldn't their lessons also have melodic motivation for memorization? If we modify our teaching in these directions, we will be working toward a naturalistic educational system.

An ideal approach to individualizing instruction is to make a choice among alternative teaching techniques or materials on the basis of aptitude information available for each learner. Suppose we discover that two instructional treatments interact with aptitude level. Treatment A, in a hypothetical example, might be preferable for teaching pupils of high measured aptitude, whereas Treatment B is more effective in promoting learning for those of lower ability level. If such an interaction is soundly established, then diagnostic aptitude testing becomes a useful guide in formulating instructional methods for our students. In presenting and evaluating this important possibility, Professor Cronbach offers three guidelines to the discovery and elucidation of interactions of test scores and teaching methods (1967).

First of all, Cronbach warns that general mental ability is not too promising in leading to useful selections of teaching methods. Students of higher mental age are likely to do better with almost any mode of instruction, he notes. In a few instances a well-sequenced programmed instruction unit has made poorer students equal to brighter ones in reaching the subgoal established, but this is not the strong interaction of method and mentality we would use most effectively. Most instances of programmed instruction do not serve to nullify ability differences. A more specific ability measure used in conjunction with achievement test results may be more useful in pointing to different teaching methods for pupils with differing score patterns. Cronbach's example of this, a study by G. L. Anderson, demonstrates the promise of fitting our instruction to the facts we find through testing.

Second, Cronbach suggests an alternative research strategy. Let psychologists have a hand in designing the instructional treatments, he says, after they have noted the psychological picture presented by test scores. Specialists in learning processes ought to be able to invent teaching modes and didactic materials that will work best for promoting learning in differing types of learners. I heartily agree that this is a worthy challenge for cooperative effort by psychologists, teachers, and subject-matter specialists. Even though a methods-by-mental-ability interaction is not attained as a boon for generally poor students, innovations may be devised that will benefit all students in a substantial way even though the brighter class members still gain most.

On the matter of selecting ways of teaching that attain a subgoal most expeditiously, Cronbach refers to a proposal by Gagné that signed numbers be taught by a choice of methods among spatial, verbal, or symbolic approaches. Although this tailoring of instruction would seem quite congruent with our emphasis on catering to individual differences, caution is indicated by Carroll (1967, p. 43). He warns that in selecting a particular approach we may enhance a student's ability to profit by that approach, but neglect the cultivation of other ideational channels. We would thus be attaining our immediate objective most efficaciously while overlooking needed progress toward a process-development goal. The consideration of aims required here serves to emphasize the importance of establishing numerous specific goals and working toward all of them quite consciously as we plan a course of instruction. Perhaps a resolution of the problem is first to use the approach to teaching that helps the student attain mastery of the new ideas most quickly. Then the alternative approaches could be interwoven as additional drill is provided. This might serve to develop those mental processes which had been shown weaker in testing by bringing them to bear on a topic newly mastered.

According to one's viewpoint, R. C. Anderson has pointed out (1967, pp. 81–87) that a high correlation between aptitude and achievement scores in an educational setting may be regarded as either desirable or undesirable. On the one hand, a high correlation suggests that teaching is enhancing natural ability, getting outstanding performance from the brighter students. In contrast, the relationship may signal that instruction is not appropriate for those of lesser initial abilities and therefore helps them less than is desirable. Anderson goes on to point out that a proper evaluation of an instructional method must pay attention to the overall level of proficiency attained by the student group as a whole. This emphasis on ultimate attainment is especially important since correlations of aptitudes and performance are often found to change with the acquisition of skill. Evidence on this point is offered in a chapter on motor learning by Fleishman (1967).

Fitting instructional procedures to the needs of particular individuals or groups of children is shown to be an appropriate approach by the successes attained in devising special teaching modes for retarded children. Although we cannot review a vast literature on this, we may cite some points made by Wischner (1967, p. 216). He reviews some of his basic studies of learning accomplished by retarded children. Two training techniques emerged as effective in different experiments. One study demonstrated the utility of spacing out the training sessions; these children are quite unable to learn certain tasks under concentrated practice conditions. The other finding demonstrated the utility of giving special attention to verbal labels in pretraining before administering a discrimination task. Although primarily relevant to special education efforts with children who have measurable handicaps of different sorts, this type of research result alerts us to the more general possibility of getting beneficial results for any instructional task by introducing certain variations in procedure. As teachers we need to stay very flexible in working to accomplish any educational objective. Informal research to discover more effective methods should certainly be undertaken. Careful checking will naturally be needed at a later point to be certain of the validity of any principle we generate in this way.

Final Testing

One other part of Figure 2 demands our attention. It is final testing at the end of each major segment of instruction—the course examination at the end of the unit, the semester, or the year. Most important, this terminal evaluation is considered an assessment of the instruction that has been given as well as of the students. This requirement recognizes our need to know how successful our teaching has been. We do need to know about the effectiveness of our work. Techniques and materials are proliferating prodigiously. Which are best? Some approaches must be more adequate than others for imparting the desired information and skills. Testing our pupils keeps them gaining their objectives. Testing ourselves keeps us improving. Surely quality control is as important for our product as for the pretty plastic purchase-play-and-throw-away items the manufacturer makes.

An Evolving Approach to the Ideal

An ideal educational design will give full attention to individual differences. It will define instructional objectives in specific behavioral terms. After testing has revealed each individual's need for instruction, particular units of work will be assigned. The teaching format, whether personal or programmed, will be selected on the basis of the pupil's learning style as revealed in his past performance data. Each child will move through the curriculum at his own rate, although this rate may be enhanced by upgrading motivation and goal attainment.

One approach to this ideal is found in Pittsburgh's Oakleaf Elementary School where a project entitled "Individually Prescribed Instruction" has been evolving since 1964. This educational effort is described quite fully by Lindvall and Bolvin (1967). The project, originated in the University of Pittsburgh's Learning Research and Development Center under the direction of Professor Glaser, has gained wide attention and has led to similar undertakings in other places. Now directed by Dr. Bolvin, the IPI project incorporates the individualized teaching after testing which ideally keeps each child at the growing edge of his potential for learning. In its broadest sense programmed instruction is embodied in this school's operation. In day-to-day activity, however, the children engage in many work-page exercises that are not strictly programmed in the narrow sense of the term. The authors make no claim that superior scholastic attainment results from Individually Prescribed Instruction; rather they suggest that the project demonstrates "an instructional technology which is possible of application to an almost unlimited variety of educational goals" (1957, p. 252).

The IPI system, wherever tried, can be no stronger than the second I, instruction. At Pittsburgh, and elsewhere, efforts are being made to improve the materials and methods by which the teaching is accomplished. In time, it is hoped, demonstrable gains in achievement levels will emerge from the system. Then empirical justification will have been joined to the logical rationale for individualizing instruction.

A systems approach to educational engineering represents a promising way to upgrade education. Instead of piecemeal tinkering with instructional elements, this strategy starts with thorough analysis of all components of an educational system with special attention to their interaction. The learner must be the key component in such an appraisal. Following analysis, the educational engineer will employ the assistance of numerous experts as he designs, develops, and tests a new system to attain educational goals. He will build on many basic principles of psychology and other disciplines. His efforts will necessarily be directed at components or subsystems at first; but ultimately educational engineering will be addressed to the complete designing of an educational system.

25
Organizing an Effective Team Teaching Program

HAROLD S. DAVIS

One of the changes already part of many school instructional designs is team teaching. Davis explains how to plan, execute, and evaluate team teaching on both elementary and secondary school levels. He deals with the actual implementation and evaluation of the results of team teaching and offers an answer to the question "Why team teach?" You, yourself, very likely will participate as one of a team of teachers someday and may come to regard it as a "venture in learning."

TEAM TEACHING is a phenomenon in American Education. It has undergone a steady, rapid growth. In fact, an NEA poll of 1400 elementary and secondary school principals showed the following growth in the use of teaching teams:

SOURCE: Harold Davis, *How to Organize an Effective Team Teaching Program* (Englewood Cliffs, N.J.: Prentice-Hall, Inc., 1966), pp. 11–14, 32–38, and 44–45. Copyright © 1966 by Prentice-Hall, Inc. Reprinted by permission of the publisher.

The author is chairman of the Department of Educational Administration and Supervision at Southern Connecticut State College. He has had more than twenty years of experience in education as both teacher and administrator and has won national recognition for his work as a consultant with more than one hundred school systems. In this capacity he has directed the implementation of new organizational designs for improving instruction, emphasizing staff utilization and team teaching. Formerly he was director of the Educational Research Council of America in Cleveland, Ohio.

	Elementary	Secondary
1955	5%	5%
1960	15	12
1965	30	31

What Is Team Teaching?

Although there are almost as many variations as there are teams, all team teaching is based on the premise that teachers can accomplish more working together than working alone. *Team teaching is any form of teaching in which two or more teachers regularly and purposefully share responsibility for the planning, presentation, and evaluation of lessons prepared for two or more classes of students.*

The key words in this definition are "regularly and purposefully share." Too many schools are prone to assemble children in the auditorium for a movie or lecture and then announce that they are engaged in team teaching. Some are under the mistaken impression that an exchange of classes constitutes team teaching. Others, at the elementary level confuse departmentalization with team teaching. Although such plans recognize the special abilities of teachers, none fit the definition. In such programs, teachers continue to work as independent agents. In contrast, team teaching assumes that the "whole" of the participants *working together* will make a greater contribution than the "sum" of the individuals working alone.

Team teaching is an organizational pattern, within which the school can greatly improve the quality of its instructional program. As will be evident from this booklet, the team composed of two or more teachers goes hand-in-hand with instructional improvement through (1) better utilization of staff, (2) greater flexibility in grouping, scheduling, and the use of space, (3) provision for large-group, small-group, and individual instruction, and (4) increased use of audiovisual aids.

As every observer of change in the nation's public schools knows, the basic concepts of team teaching are not entirely new. A few secondary schools involved in the Progressive Education Association's "Eight Year Study" experimented with organizational patterns similar to team teaching, and some elementary schools had used the principles of flexible grouping. Moreover, a number of universities had tapped the talents of outstanding professors for large-group instruction and had followed with small seminars for discussion. And, in preparation for World War II, the armed forces made tremendous use of audiovisual aids, including educational films and filmstrips, overhead projectors, and language laboratories.

These innovations did have some influence on the nation's elementary and secondary schools, but education was somewhat of a laggard when it came to introducing them on a widespread scale. Though an effective organizational pattern was badly needed to implement change, its evolution took a considerable period of time.

In 1956, NASSP, aided by the Ford Foundation and the Fund for the Advancement of Education, appointed its Staff Utilization Commission to discover, by study and experimentation, new and more effective means of staff utilization. Among the experiments, the one showing the most promise and given greatest attention was popularly called *team teaching*. By 1959, the Commission's capable administrator, J. Lloyd Trump, was able to state that the Commission had "stimulated sufficient momentum of interest among teachers and administrators" and that "continued support of experimentation by the Commission itself is no longer necessary." [1]

J. Lloyd Trump's prediction has been borne out by the facts. Team teaching is rapidly being introduced into the nation's schools. It is no longer experimental. It has been in use for years, and educators know that it works.

Types of Teams

Despite many variations, only two major types of teaching teams have evolved. We shall refer to them as *hierarchic* and *synergetic* teams.

Hierarchic Teams. We can liken the hierarchic team to a pyramid with the team leader at the apex, master teachers just below, and regular teachers at the base assisted by interns and aides. A major purpose of the hierarchy is to provide teachers with a means of professional advancement without having to leave the classroom. Well-known examples of this type of team are found in Lexington, Massachusetts; Pittsburgh, Pennsylvania; and in the Claremont program in southern California.

Although hierarchic teams offer many advantages, they embody some disadvantages. Many educators are inclined to feel that establishing levels tends to diminish the importance of the regular teacher's role, though supporters of the hierarchic arrangement claim that the teacher does not relinquish status in such a team.

Moreover, hierarchic teaching teams are not suited to the majority of our schools, for most superintendents and principals cannot replace present facilities or staff. They cannot expect foundation grants or help from universities, such as the schools mentioned above received, and they cannot afford to hire paraprofessional help. When looking for ways to improve instruction, they recognize that they must seek them within practical limits. Synergetic teams supply the answer.

---

[1] "Completing the Commission's Staff Utilization Studies," *Bulletin* of the NASSP, January 1960, p. 345.

Synergetic Teams. Synergetic teams are formed by two or more teachers willing to cooperate as professional equals. Such teams may be developed to work within conventional facilities and schedules. All it takes is *leadership, perseverance,* and *perspiration.*

On a synergetic team, the master teacher concept is repudiated and instructional leadership rotates according to need. For example, one member may assume the leadership for a single lesson or unit of work and relinquish it for the next. The stress is on working with, not for, colleagues.

Although synergetic teams sometimes select permanent leaders for administrative purposes, the "leader" generally does not receive extra pay or privileges for accepting the assignment. In some schools, department chairmen have become members of synergetic teams and wear two hats. Administratively, they carry the burden of extra duties, while instructionally, they function as regular members of teams and share leadership with teammates during various units of work.

Synergetic teams vary in their approach from limited cooperation to complete association. For this reason, these teams are sometimes referred to as cooperative or associative teams based upon the degree of partnership the participants achieve.

Implementing a Team Teaching Program

A successful team teaching program depends more on people than upon the purse, more on faculties than upon facilities. One may find dormant programs in schools "designed for team teaching" and dynamic programs in archaic buildings. Invariably, administrative leadership and careful planning are the keys to success. The principal who believes he can sit in his office and shuffle papers while teachers dream up new ideas, is suffering a delusion. As educational reports repeatedly state, *reform must be instituted by administrators.* Hammering home this point, a New York State report said: "Contrary to general opinion, teachers are not change agents for instructional innovations of major scope." Perhaps this explains why educational progress has been so slow. More principals should provide the necessary leadership.

Begin by Improving Faculty Meetings

As many administrators know, typical faculty meetings are frequently a waste of everyone's time. Teachers are often treated as functional illiterates. Rules and regulations that could be just as easily put into writing are read aloud. Precious hours are spent discussing "The Flower Fund" or other bits of equally unimportant administrivia.

If you are about to embark upon a truly innovative program, you must use such time for *dynamic* meetings. Encourage teachers to examine—and with an objective eye—the school's educational program. Make comparisons, not with what education is, but with what it ought to be. See that teachers explore, report on, and discuss new curricular ideas and teaching methods. When they become aware of weaknesses in the traditional program and recognize that you sincerely desire change, some will invariably volunteer to try a new approach. When this occurs, join them enthusiastically in cooperative, democratic planning.

Initiate Constructive Planning Sessions

Through active participation, you can help to build the harmonious interpersonal relationships so essential to the operation of a successful school. Be careful, however, to avoid dominating planning sessions. When the social climate is characterized by tension or submission, teachers are unlikely to have sufficient motivation to contribute constructively. On the other hand, in schools where administrators and teachers operate in partnership, the levels of instruction and morale are usually high.

Keep in mind that planning sessions are essential to success and that they must be regularly scheduled. Limited to his own ingenuity, a teacher often runs dry. Encouraged and stimulated by colleagues, he remains creative. As a wise father once said to his son, "If we each have a dollar bill and trade, we each still have one dollar. But if we each have an idea and trade, we each have two ideas."

Getting a Program Underway

An over-anxious administrator cannot launch a successful program through administrative fiat. Success comes about through changes in teachers' attitudes and through a growth in understanding, not through duress. When properly led, many teachers are willing to try team teaching; when pushed, most resist. Invariably, team teaching succeeds on a voluntary basis, but fails when imposed on unwilling or uncooperative teachers.

Conversely, an over-cautious administrator cannot develop a successful team if he insists on waiting for an abundance of funds or facilities. He should be willing to begin with as few as two team members in a single subject. If the first effort is carried out successfully by enthusiastic teachers, other courses and other teachers may be added in time.

EXAMPLES:

At Lutheran High School West, two teachers developed a synergetic team for the teaching of American history. During a single daily period, they met with 58 students in the school cafeteria. With the use of an overhead projector and portable screen, this room became a lecture hall. For discussion, pupils gathered around cafeteria tables in opposite corners of the room. Students engaged in independent study had ready access to an adjoining library. The cafeteria-library combination provided an excellent team teaching area and freed two critically needed classrooms. This initial project was closely watched from the time of its inception. Its success led to the formation of comparable teams in Lutheran High School East on the opposite side of Cleveland.

Using a similar approach, Freemont High School, Sunnyvale, California, began its project with two social studies teachers "teamed" in a course entitled "Senior Problems." From this inauspicious beginning in 1959, team teaching has spread throughout the building, a flexible schedule has been adopted, and the school is engaged in a program of total improvement.

Planning for Facilities and Equipment

Although some buildings severely handicap the development of teams, the imaginative principal will find new uses for old facilities. For example, if no specifically designed space is available for large-group instruction, have your teams use one of the following: auditorium, little theater, multi-purpose room, cafeteria, band room, choral room, study hall, or school lobby. When no suitable space is available, some schools have removed walls between rooms.

Fortunately, space and equipment for small-group discussion poses no problem. The only requirement is that students be able to engage in face-to-face discussion. Classrooms, library conference rooms, and cafeterias have all proven excellent. Although it is advantageous to work with only one small group at a time, many teachers have found that they can easily supervise two groups within the same or adjoining rooms. This, of course, depends upon the rapport established between teacher and pupils.

You may find space for independent study difficult to locate. Libraries in secondary schools are often inadequate and in elementary schools frequently nonexistent. In such schools, teams frequently improvise by using some classrooms for independent study while other classrooms are used for small-group discussion. By adding reference shelves, book trucks, tapes and records, earphones, filmstrip viewers, and other media, you can make such a plan feasible.

Also, when planning a team approach, see that your building is equipped with a thermographic or diazo copier for making transparencies and at least one overhead projector. This modern teaching tool has become indispensable for large-group instruction. Furthermore place the projector in the large-group area and leave it there. This is more advantageous than having teams check it in and out of an audiovisual room. When a projector is easily accessible, it is more likely to be used.

Using Old Facilities Successfully. In Mayfield, Ohio, a junior high principal is proving that a new program can be implemented in an old building. When his teachers were ready to start teaching in teams, a small gym, out of use for several years, was reopened and equipped with more than 100 folding chairs, an overhead projector, and screen for use with large groups. Tablet arm attachments were placed on the folding chairs so that students could take notes more conveniently.

The idea first began when his staff became aware of the Mayfield High School team teaching project, previously described. His teachers discussed the high school program in faculty meetings, and a number of interested teachers visited and observed the program in action. Although the high school teams were in the fields of English, history, and the humanities, four junior high science teachers were intrigued by the techniques. They felt the method could be adapted to teaching biology. The principal encouraged this interest and joined them in the planning. The schedule was reworked to organize four classes of 80 to 100 pupils.

Teachers developed a course outline, agreed upon responsibilities, and wrote tentative lesson plans for several units of work. They then discussed, revised, and prepared these plans in final form. As the semester progressed, they prepared new units of work in detail and tentatively planned subsequent units. This procedure allowed for change as experience was gained.

Lectures were prepared to include enrichment material as well as basic concepts. The lecturer also had the responsibility of providing pupils with seminar questions for discussion and with suggested assignments for independent study. Team members agreed that assignments need "to be stimulating, thought-provoking, and well planned. Busy work defeats our objectives and should never be included."

A weekly schedule was distributed to each student so he could plan in advance. Even the absentee was able to keep up with his work. The schedule included dates and times for lectures, seminars, independent study, laboratory work, and examinations. Seminars and independent study were normally scheduled at the same time for different groups. While three teachers observed small-group discussion, one teacher was in the library with the remaining students working individually with those who needed help.

Through careful planning, guidance, and supervision, the principal was able to insure the success of his first team. He made teachers feel comfortable about mistakes and gave team members a free hand to try new ideas as long as thought preceded effort.

Because the faculty was kept informed about this pilot project, interest generated among other members of the staff. Two English teachers combined classes for an experiment with communications techniques and were amazed to discover what pupils could accomplish when properly motivated. Two of their boys, while working on individualized projects, wrote a "History of Music." Using an organ to demonstrate beat, tempo, and style, they traced the development of classical, semiclassical, and popular music. Fascinated with the depth and quality of the performance, the teachers arranged for the entire school to hear the program. By means of music and commentary, these boys gave a new cultural insight to all of their schoolmates. The boys, previously considered "poor" students, indicated it was their most rewarding school experience.

As a result of this experiment, the teachers were encouraged to expand their efforts. They combined other classes for large-group instruction and made their first attempt at flexible grouping. By September 1965, these English teachers were able to inaugurate a team teaching program for all 10 of their classes.

Turning Liabilities into Assets. When the St. Edward High School in Lakewood, Ohio, was overcrowded, a number of faculty members agreed to try a form of team teaching. For example, two English and two history teachers fitted their four classes into one large and two small rooms. On one day, the two history classes were combined in the large room, while the two English classes met in the smaller rooms. The following day the procedure was reversed.

As an outgrowth of this initial effort, a major addition to the school plant was designed to include a materials preparation center, three amphitheater-type large-group instruction rooms, and an instructional materials center. The preparation center contains facilities for preparing audiovisual aids and houses a tape, film, and record library for teachers. The center also is wired for closed-circuit television broadcasting and includes a videotape recorder. Two of the large-group rooms seat 90 pupils and the third, 144. Since the rooms are fan-shaped, no student is seated more than 32 feet from the screen. The teacher can operate equipment by remote control, and has a choice of standard or rear view projection. The instructional materials center contains a library of books, films, and tapes; a team planning room; and study carrels for students. The addition is air-conditioned, and special areas are carpeted.

All of these facilities, designed to augment the team teaching program, permit experienced teachers to share their ability with a greater proportion of the student body. St. Edward is one of the few Catholic schools in America to have such an advanced educational plant; and, it all began when four classes had to be squeezed into three rooms.

Providing for Flexibility. Schools built today should be designed to provide for more efficient utilization—and for flexibility of space and equipment. In spite of great advances in school construction, many designers still cling to anachronistic ideas. For example, new schools are being built with stage facilities in the gym, which is in almost constant use during school hours and seldom available for plays, films or lectures. If it is used for PTA meetings or other assemblies in the evening, chairs must be hauled in and later removed. Gym floors are often ruined.

In the same building, one frequently finds a cafeteria standing empty a major portion of the day. With proper planning, this could have been designed as a cafetorium. In such a room, chairs and tables are already in position for meetings, and the space is available for large-group instruction or small-group discussion most of the day. In the John F. Kennedy High School at Wheaton, Maryland, operable walls are used to divide the space in a large cafeteria into two or more rooms. Kennedy High also has a divisible auditorium, similar to those at Norridge, Illinois, and at Boulder City, Nevada. Such divisible space provides for several large groups simultaneously.

Even in old buildings, flexibility may be obtained through remodeling. If a wall is removed between two rooms, each housing 30 pupils, the new space will easily accommodate 90 for large-group instruction. Similarly, a single classroom for 30, when divided into three small-group conference rooms, will hold 45 pupils. A library, equipped with study carrels, will certainly house the same number of students as comfortably as more conventional rooms.

We know children learn from teachers, by themselves, and from each other. In examining these three processes, many team teachers have found a basic way to plan lessons. They study the curriculum, develop objectives, determine essential ideas to be taught and then answer three questions:

1. What can students learn best from explanations by others?
2. What can students learn by interaction between themselves and their teachers?
3. What can students learn by themselves?

The answer to the first question suggests large-group instruction; to the second, small-group discussion; and to the third, independent study. If these three phases of the team teaching process are to be used effectively, the principal and his teachers must plan carefully.

In spite of evidence and experience to the contrary, too many teachers still insist that all teaching must be conducted in standard classrooms with equal size groups—and are apparently convinced that teaching cannot improve unless class size is reduced. Those teaching 40 pupils say 35 would be far better. Those with 35 insist 30 would be perfect. In more favored communities, those with 30 say they could really teach if only they had classes of 25. Through such empirical evidence, it seems that perfect class size is five less than whatever the teacher has now!

The conventional class of 30 pupils has proven to be the wrong size for most activities. It is inefficient for large-group instruction and ineffective for small-group discussion.

Within the team framework, flexibility is the keynote. Teachers vary the

size and structure of the group, the allocation of time, and the method of instruction to be used. When team teaching is properly conducted, it provides a
balanced program of (1) large-group instruction where material is visualized
rather than verbalized, (2) small-group discussion where ideas are expounded
and explored, and (3) independent study where the emphasis is on research
rather than rote.

Evaluating the Results of Team Teaching

Although team teaching is far beyond the experimental stage, and a multitude of administrators, teachers, pupils and parents proclaim its benefits, non-
subjective data are still scarce. In fact, those searching for an across-the-
board objective evaluation may be seeking the impossible. Many educators
engaged in team teaching feel that a person must be involved in the process
before he can give a valid opinion of its worth. They believe administrators
of team teaching programs are best qualified to measure improvements in use
of staff, facilities and equipment. They say team teachers are in the prime position to judge effective use of their time, energy and talent. And, they feel
pupils and parents are most competent to gauge interest in school and enthusiasm for learning.

Why Team Teach?

The three reasons given most often today for adopting team teaching are:

1. To improve staff utilization.
2. To improve use of facilities and equipment.
3. To improve instruction.

Improvements in staff utilization are readily apparent. Team teaching recognizes and encourages individual differences in teachers as well as in students. Flexibility and variation are emphasized. Repetition and duplication
are shunned. Savings in time and effort are reinvested in the individual child.
Extra effort is expended on planning and preparation. Talents are blended,
weaknesses are minimized. Teachers assume a variety of roles and teach in
their areas of interest and strength.

Common sense indicates a more economical use of public funds. When
centers are established for large-group instruction and independent study, a
limited amount of equipment serves a wide number of teachers and pupils.
Team teachers have discovered when they move out of their self-contained
rooms and share material as well as ideas, there are plenty of each to go
around.

The most important "subject" in any school is the child. This makes improvement of instruction a major goal. Although team teaching does not cure poor teachers, it does give them a chance to be observed, critiqued, and improved. Working alone, many teachers have retired not with 40 years of experience, but with one year of experience repeated 40 times. Working in teams, teachers have an opportunity for 40 years of professional growth.

Team teaching is a venture in learning. It is not for the teacher or principal who feels his educational goal has been reached; it is for the person who realizes he has just begun.

A sage once remarked: "There are three kinds of educators: those who make things happen, those who watch things happen and those who wonder what happened."

We need more of the first type!

26
Differentiated Staffing

UNITED STATES COMMISSIONER
OF EDUCATION

Differentiated staffing requires both specialization of the act of teaching and changes in the roles played by teachers. To introduce you to the implications inherent in differentiated staffing, two selections have been included. This first shows how development of four levels of teacher allocation and a diversity of specialized fields can be used to extend the talents of teachers to a higher degree. When and if such extensive reorganization of teaching is generally adopted, many changes will occur and these will be accompanied by subsequent modifications in the education of teachers.

THE DIVERSITY of demands upon schools and educators has grown to a point where an increase in the supply of qualified personnel by itself will not insure enough people to go around. A few schools are experimenting with the concept of differentiated staffing, one solution to the problem of how best to use the talents of our educators. It is based on carefully prepared definitions of the jobs educators perform, and goes beyond traditional staff allocations according to subject matter and grade level. For example, a differentiated

SOURCE: 1968 Report of the United States Commissioner of Education. Reprinted by permission of the Department of Health, Education, and Welfare, Office of Education.

staffing plan developed by Temple City, Calif., has created a logical hierarchy that includes not only teaching but instructional management, curriculum construction, and the application of research to the improvement of all systems.

Although, nationally, differentiated staffing is more concept than fact, the following four positions developed at Temple City suggest one way the plan might work:

1. The Associate Teacher is, typically, a beginning teacher, who spends most of his time in the classroom while simultaneously evaluating his performance in conferences with a supervisor.

2. The Staff Teacher, having had more experience, is assigned more difficult teaching responsibilities, including tutorial sessions and small group instruction, and additionally works on new curriculums and supervises their field testing.

3. The Senior Teacher, in addition to classroom teaching, consults with associate teachers, develops new teaching strategies, sets up inservice teacher training programs, and develops resource banks for new instructional units, including the use of media.

4. The Master Teacher has district-wide responsibilities in the application of research to curriculum design. At the same time he continues teaching in the classroom at least part of the time.

The aims of differentiated staffing can be realized through a number of different methods. Additional positions such as part-time tutors and aides on one hand and educational specialists on the other could be appended to either end of the hierarchy. Organization need not be hierarchial, but can be based on teams of peers. Whatever the method, however, the aim is to permit a variety of people to contribute. The housewife-teacher for instance, can make her services available on a schedule satisfactory to her, and without hindering the professional advancement of the career-minded teacher. Indeed, the career-minded teacher is stimulated by such a system, which provides not only a hierarchy of more challenging and more significant roles but also allows for promotion and advancement as a *teacher* instead of solely as an administrator or supervisor.

If such plans for differentiated staffing are to go beyond the experimental stage, however, we must recognize the relationship between the needs of the schools and of other institutions. Differentiated staffing presents a challenge to the present system of teacher education. It suggests, for one thing, that a college education might not be the only route to a teaching career; that a variety of systems, timetables, and entry points might be provided for teacher preparation; and that many in our population might contribute to, as well as benefit from, the education of young people. We will clearly need to develop new alliances, among community, school, and university, in order to develop and train educational personnel who can meet the challenges of such systems in the future.

27

Towards a Differentiated Teaching Staff

JOHN M. RAND AND FENWICK ENGLISH

This discussion of differentiated staffing also shows how attention is being given to increased specialization in education. The authors claim that since there now is extensive specialization within the profession, it is an appropriate time to modify instructional designs, and they present differentiated staffing as a most plausible approach to that end. However, both Rand and English, and the Commissioner of Education, agree that to do so will require "new alliances among community, school, and university."

THE ACUTE SHORTAGE of teachers and the growing movement toward teacher professionalization are placing unbearable strains upon the present organizational structure in education. The shortage is worst in the nation's largest metropolitan areas, where organizational structures are most rigid and inner-city children in greatest need of good education. In suburban districts there is growing constituent dissatisfaction. Taxpayers are balking at increasing education costs without some proof that the pudding will be better.

Rising militancy and mass "resignations" last fall are signs that teachers are dissatisfied with their roles as mere implementers of administrative decision. Their demands are certainly more inclusive than simply a raise in pay. Teachers are telling us something we should have known or predicted long ago. When a group of people increase their technical competence close to that of the top members of the hierarchy, lines of authority become blurred. The subordinate position begins to rest more upon arbitrary and traditional distinctions than upon competence to perform the job.

Teachers are demanding inclusion in the decision-making process in education. As Corwin says,[1] professionalism is associated positively with militancy. Rather than arouse hostility in administrators and lay boards, it should be welcomed as one sign that the teaching profession is coming of age.

[1] Ronald G. Corwin, "Militant Professionalism, Initiative and Compliance in Public Education," *Sociology of Education*, Vol. 38, pp. 310–31, Summer, 1965.

SOURCE: *Phi Delta Kappan*, Vol. 49, No. 5 (January 1968), pp. 264–268. Reprinted by permission of the authors and publisher.

At the time of publication of this selection, Mr. Rand was Superintendent of Schools and Mr. English was the Director of Differentiated Staffing in a project sponsored by the Unified School District of Temple City, California.

Increasing teacher specialization and competence mean that roles within the present educational structure are in the process of change. Teachers are recognizing that to break out of the ceilings imposed by the single salary schedule they must reexamine the assumptions which support it. The increasing need for high specialization and advanced training means that some teachers should be paid between $20,000 and $25,000 per year, as are specialists in other fields. So long as we have the single salary schedule, however, no one will get this amount. The money simply cannot be raised without a complete (and in the short run completely impossible) overhaul of tax structures, school financing, and public value systems.

Hence the dissolution of the single salary schedule is a must if the teaching profession is to advance. Teachers will generally admit that not all of them possess the same abilities or strengths. They reject the onus of "merit pay," however, as "unprofessional" or otherwise undesirable. Merit pay plans offer the advantage of dissolving the single salary schedule, but ordinarily make no distinction in job responsibilities of teachers. Added pay is for "merit," not for added responsibility. As long as teaching is considered an art, one man's "superior" teacher is another's "average" teacher. Judgment of teaching "excellence" must be based on careful research just beginning to emerge at some universities. We have a long way to go before we can specify on the basis of empirical evidence what teaching excellence consists of. Hence we do not have the foundation for merit pay.

The Temple City plan approaches the problem from a different perspective. Teachers are not treated the same. They may receive additional remuneration for increased professional responsibilities, which means change in their roles as teachers. These new responsibilities imply increased training and time on the job, and implicit in the concept of advancement is professional competence as a teacher, however it is measured. Teachers are not chosen to be paid more simply for continuing to perform their same functions; they are paid more for assuming increased responsibilities in the instructional program. They are selected on the basis of their experience and qualifications for the job by a professional panel and are retained only as they are able to perform adequately in their capacities. The Temple City Differentiated Staffing Plan, almost wholly designed by teachers, offers a way for teachers to receive remuneration of $20,000 per year by differentiating teaching roles and systematically enlarging their authority and decision-making powers to shape the instructional program.

The Temple City plan is not a brand new idea. Aspects of the plan have been espoused by Myron Lieberman,[2] J. Lloyd Trump,[3] and Robert Bush

[2] Myron Lieberman, *The Future of Public Education.* Chicago: University of Chicago Press, 1960.

[3] J. Lloyd Trump and Dorsey Baynham, *Guide to Better Schools.* Chicago: Rand McNally, 1961.

and Dwight Allen [4] at Stanford University. Allen was instrumental in developing the Temple City project, funded by the Charles F. Kettering Foundation of Denver, Colorado, for an 18-month study. The TEPS program of the NEA has also been active in proposing differentiated roles for professional personnel. The strength of the Temple City concept of differentiated staffing resides in a high degree of staff participation in its development. Indeed, the process of development is every bit as important as the product, i.e., an acceptable organizational design to implement the ideas of the professional staff.

The original model of differentiated staffing was developed by Allen and presented to the California State Board of Education in April of 1966 (see Figure 1). Later it was altered in the work done by Temple City teachers (see Figure 2). At the present, this model is undergoing further revision as a result of financial studies and further staff feedback. A brief sketch of the job descriptions follows.

Teaching Research Associate

The teaching research associate (TRA) is the "self-renewal" unit of the organization. His primary function is to introduce new concepts and ideas into the schools. He is well versed in research methodology and evaluation of instruction. The TRA may conduct field studies, but his major purpose is to translate research into instructional probes at the school level. The TRA functions in the present structure as a classroom teacher, as do all of the other personnel in the differentiated staffing plan, although in a limited capacity. In this way he does not lose sight of the receivers of his efforts. The TRA represents the apex of professional advancement for the aspiring teacher.

The teaching research associate meets all of Rogers' [5] criteria for initiating planned change in education. These are: (1) base the topics investigated on felt needs of practitioners; (2) create an educational structure to facilitate change; (3) raise the practitioners' ability to utilize the research results. Part of the TRA's responsibilities are implied in the third criterion mentioned by Rogers. Much of his liaison work with staff and current research will be to increase the sophistication level of teachers and help them use it in practice and evaluate its effectiveness.

---

[4] Dwight Allen and Robert Bush, *A New Design for High School Education*. New York: McGraw-Hill, 1964.

[5] Everett M. Rogers, "Developing a Strategy for Planned Change," paper presented at a Symposium on the Application of System Analysis and Management Techniques to Educational Planning in California, Orange, California, June, 1967.

Teaching Curriculum Associate

The teaching curriculum associate (TCA) also must possess knowledge of research methodology, except that his knowledge is more applicable to curriculum theory, construction, and evaluation. In addition, the TCA would be adept at modifying national curriculum studies to meet local needs and local teacher proclivities.

The TCA also works at raising the level of teacher specialization in specific subject areas. He is more of a communications specialist than the TRA. However, due to the overlap in some functions, and because it is difficult to separate research from curriculum and instructional improvement studies, these two functions will probably be combined into one position: the Teaching Research-Curriculum Associate.

The Senior Teacher

The senior teacher is primarily responsible for the application of curriculum and instructional innovations to the classroom. The senior teacher is an acknowledged master practitioner, a learning engineer, a skilled diagnostician of the learning process. He is the teacher's teacher.

The senior teacher as an instructional advisor heads a subject group and represents this area on the school academic senate. He shares with the school principal the selection, performance, and evaluation of his colleagues in that subject specialty. In a team teaching situation, the senior teacher would function as a team leader. At least one-half of this teacher's day would be with students.

The Staff Teacher

In a sense, all teachers in the differentiated staffing plan are staff teachers. A full-time staff teacher spends his school hours with students. He performs the same professional functions as most teachers in typical school districts. In a differentiated staffing plan the staff teacher is relieved of semi-professional and clerical duties by employment of the following assistants:

The Academic Assistant

The academic assistant is a skilled paraprofessional, or a teacher intern (associate teacher) from a nearby college or university. He works with students and may instruct in special or skilled areas. He may also maintain physical materials, grade papers, and supervise resource center activities or student study.

The Educational Technician

The educational technician assumes many of the clerical and housekeeping tasks that consume so much professional time in the present organization. The technician keeps records, duplicates material, types, supervises student movement on campus, takes attendance, etc. The technician has little, if any, instructional responsibilities.

The Academic Senate

Teachers are formally involved in school decision making through the organization of an academic senate on each campus. One of the responsibilities of senior teachers is to represent the staff in the establishment of school policies relating to the educational program and its improvement.

The School Manager

In addition, the principal's role is differentiated by establishing a position called school manager. The school manager assumes responsibility for most of the business functions of school operation and thus relieves the principal for attention to the instructional program. It is hoped that eventually the principal will also refurbish his image as a teacher by assuming some direct teaching responsibilities with students. Most principals would find this impossible now, since they too are overburdened with paperwork and administrivia.

This combination of teacher specialists and administrator generalists would provide the school with the best judgments of all the professionals occupied with shaping a dynamic instructional program. School leadership is clearly enhanced with teachers exercising judgment as to how the instructional program should be improved. The principal's role is strengthened, since he can count on the specialized expertise of his senior teachers in the hiring and evaluation of the instructional staff. Teachers are intimately involved in professionalizing and disciplining their own ranks through the academic senate. This is crucial for full-fledged maturity; effective professional regulation can only occur when teachers assume responsibility for each other's performance. Administrators should welcome this desire for more responsibilities and assist their staffs in learning how to develop and exercise the leadership concomitants to fulfill this important professional role.

A discussion of differentiated staffing would not be complete without mentioning some of the problems the district has encountered in studying this concept. Differentiated staffing challenges a basic assumption inherent in the organizational structure of education. The myth that all teachers are equal exercises a powerful influence upon our thinking. The present organizational structure which assumes that one teacher can be all things to all students is a barrier of the first magnitude, especially at the elementary level.

One way of avoiding change and protecting oneself is for the teacher to shut his door and isolate himself with his 30 children. The position of the teacher in his classroom fortress is easier and more secure without the scrutiny of his colleagues. To differentiate teacher roles is contrary to the standard organizational pattern of elementary education for the last 100 years. When teachers perform different functions and assume new responsibilities they cannot be with children all day long. They must have time during the school day to plan with colleagues and conduct studies or meet with individual students. This implies some type of flexible scheduling, plus dual use of instructional models and resource facilities. This in turn means that teachers must delegate to paraprofessionals many nonprofessional responsibilities that do not demand a high degree of skill and training.

We have found a greater resistance at the elementary level to concepts of differentiated staffing than at the secondary. Some teachers fear that team teaching, use of paraprofessionals, resource centers, and flexible scheduling will permanently "damage" their children. They fail to recall that the present organizational structure established in 1870 at the Quincy Grammar School was organized for administrative convenience and that critics pointed out even then that it rather callously ignored the needs of continuous educational progress for each individual student.

Also we noted that a greater proportion of women than men object to teachers assuming a professional disciplinary role with their colleagues. This is especially true at the primary level, where a traditionally protective environment shields both students and teachers from decision making and colleague interaction.

At the secondary level, the idea of differentiated staffing was received more warmly. Here more teachers are men and the tradition of subject area specialization and leadership through department chairmen has been well established. However, some teachers at the secondary level are just as immobilized in their six-period day, self-contained classrooms as their elementary counterparts.

Some administrators will be uncomfortable in sharing the decision-making process with their staffs. Fear of losing status is an important consideration when proposing new roles for teachers. One must remember that almost all other roles in a school district hinge upon that of the teacher. If the teacher

Figure 1
The Proposed Teacher Hierarchy Based on Differentiated
Compensation and Responsibilities*

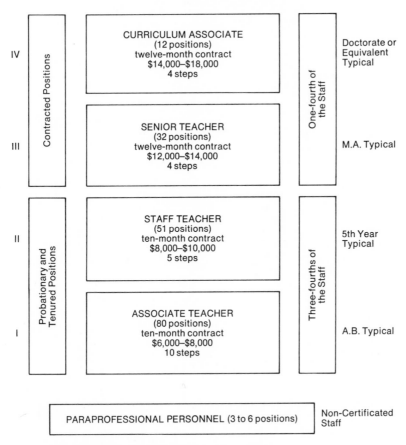

*This model of a differentiated staffing plan was developed by Dwight Allen and was
presented to the California State Board of Education in April, 1966.

base is expanded upward, a shift is required in functions all the way to the superintendent. This means that in the Temple City plan teachers (teaching research associates) will sit with principals in an academic coordinating council headed by the superintendent. This district-wide group plans and anticipates district movement. Teachers (teaching curriculum associates) will also be a part of the curriculum coordinating council headed by the assistant superintendent. This group articulates curriculum development through the grades. Teacher specialists form an integral part of the decision-making machinery with the administrators of the district.

Figure 2

Temple City Unified School District: A Model of Differentiated Staffing*

ACADEMIC ASSISTANT A.A. or B.A. Degree	STAFF TEACHER B.A. Degree plus 1 year	SENIOR TEACHER M.S., M.A., or equivalent	TEACHING CURRICULUM ASSOCIATE M.S., M.A., or equivalent	TEACHING RESEARCH ASSOCIATE Doctorate or equivalent	REGULAR SALARY SCHEDULE PLUS FACTORS
Non-tenure	Tenure	Non-tenure	Non-tenure	Non-tenure	
				3/5's staff teaching responsibilities	Twelve Months ($16,000-20,000)
			3/5's-4/5's staff teaching responsibilities		Eleven Months ($14,000-16,000)
		4/5's staff teaching responsibilities			Ten to Eleven Months ($11,000-14,000)
	100 percent teaching responsibilities				Ten Months ($6,000-11,000)
Some teaching responsibilities					Ten Months ($4,000-5,000)
EDUCATIONAL TECHNICIANS					

*This model of differentiated staffing was developed by Temple City Teachers.
The model is currently being revised to combine the TRA-TCA functions. Salary figures are tentative.

278

The Temple City plan of differentiated staffing offers a way to emancipate the teacher. It changes and enlarges the roles of teachers, increases their autonomy and decision-making powers, offers career advancement, and places them in a position to assume a regulatory function of their own profession. From the point of the administrator it enhances the leadership potential of his staff and builds in some guarantee that the instructional program will indeed remain vital and strong in all areas. A board of education and community should be encouraged when their teachers are willing to assume a corporate responsibility for the quality of education in their schools. The fact that teachers are disciplining themselves, are constantly in the self-renewal process, and have the freedom to rise as teachers to the top of their abilities and willingness to work means that the collective human resources which lie fallow in every organization are more fully tapped. In the short time our project has been operative we have been amazed at the talent which has emerged from our staff.

The most difficult barrier of all is not physical or financial but the subtle limitations in our vision, attitudes, and expectations, conditioned by one organizational structure for over 100 years. The validity of this structure may have been eroded, but its form has been firmly implanted in our psyches. The ability to rise above our own conditioning and previous expectancy levels is the most difficult problem, for solutions cannot be devised until problems are accurately perceived. Perception is limited when assumptions cannot be questioned. Our inability to see that some of our frustrations stem from traditional assumptions is a tragic dilemma. Differentiated staffing is a concept which challenges a whole host of notions about how American education should be organized and operated. At the moment it may be heresy; in a decade it may be practice.

28

The Phantom Nongraded School

WILLIAM P. McLOUGHLIN

Critically taking a look at what Americans call a "nongraded school" system, McLoughlin states that very few schools claiming to be nongraded actually are, and, furthermore, true nongradedness has seldom been tried.

Perhaps you have attended a nongraded school. If so, would you go along with the author's defense of the concept of true nongradedness mainly on the grounds that "the graded school is indefensible"? McLoughlin's views have been presented as a point of departure from which you might pursue your own study of other nongraded schools. By careful consideration of the pros and cons of nongraded schools, you can prepare to assume some degree of leadership when entering the field of education.

FEW PROPOSITIONS for educational change have generated and sustained as much interest as the nongraded school. It is discussed at nearly every major educational conference, and symposiums on the nongraded school are increasing in popularity. Furthermore, the body of available literature is increasing rapidly; most leading professional journals have published several articles on this topic. Through these and other means, educators have learned more of the promises of the nongraded school than they have of its accomplishments.

This is understandable, for nongrading appears to be preached more than practiced and practiced more than appraised. In fact, few dependable estimates on the present status and anticipated growth of the nongraded school are currently available and sound studies on its accomplishments are even more difficult to come by. From what is available one would be hard put to determine just how many schools have nongraded their instructional programs and how many are seriously contemplating the change. If findings in these areas are obscure, the outcomes of the evaluations of existing nongraded programs are even less definitive.

The available estimates of the number of schools with nongraded programs

SOURCE: *Phi Delta Kappan*, Vol. 49, No. 5 (January 1968), pp. 248–250. Reprinted by permission of the publisher.

The author is professor of education at St. John's University in New York City. During a year's leave of absence, he designed and assisted in conducting a study for the New York State Department of Education. Dr. McLoughlin wrote this paper while participating in the study.

fluctuates from 5.5 percent [1] to 30 percent.[2] These, it must be pointed out, are unqualified estimates; they do not consider the quality of the programs purporting to be nongraded. When this element is added, estimates of the number of schools with *truly* nongraded programs shrink considerably. Goodlad, in 1955, estimated that less than one percent of the schools in the country were nongraded [3] and in 1961 he felt there were probably fewer than 125 schools to be found with *truly* nongraded programs.[4]

If uncertainty marks present estimates of the number of schools operating nongraded programs, certainly forecasts for future growth are dubious. In 1958 the NEA reported 26.3 percent of the respondents to its survey saying they intended to nongrade their schools.[5] Five years later, however, this estimate had dwindled to 3.2 percent.[6] On the other hand, the USOE's pollings reverse this trend. Of schools queried in 1958, only 13.4 percent expected to become nongraded,[7] but two years later this estimate doubled and 26.3 percent of the respondents reported considering nongrading their schools.[8] With these conflicting findings it is difficult to know if the nongraded school is coming into its own or passing out of existence.

One thing seems clear from these surveys, however: nongrading is related to district size. Nearly all available surveys confirm this; the larger the district, the more likely it is to have one or more nongraded units. Here we should stress that this does not mean that nongrading is the principal organizational pattern in large school districts. It simply means a nongraded unit is operating in one or more of the district's several elementary schools.[9]

Studies of the influence of nongrading on students are rare, too, and their composite findings somewhat bewildering. Thirty-three empirical studies of

[1] Lillian L. Gore and Rose E. Koury, *A Survey of Early Elementary Education in Public Schools, 1960–61.* Washington, D.C.: U.S. Department of Health, Education and Welfare, 1965.

[2] National Education Association, *Nongraded Schools.* Research Memo 1965-12. Washington, D.C.: Research Division, NEA, May, 1965.

[3] John I. Goodlad, "More About the Ungraded Plan," *NEA Journal,* May, 1955, pp. 295–96.

[4] National Education Association, *Nongrading: A Modern Practice in Elementary School Organization.* Research Memo 1961-37. Washington, D.C.: Research Division, NEA, October, 1961.

[5] National Education Association, *Administrative Practices in Urban School Districts, 1958–1959.* Research Report 1961-R10. Washington, D.C.: Research Division, NEA, May, 1961.

[6] NEA, *Nongraded Schools, op. cit.*

[7] Stuart E. Dean, *Elementary School Administration and Organization: A National Survey of Practices and Policies.* Washington, D.C.: U.S. Department of Health, Education and Welfare, 1963.

[8] Gore and Koury, *op. cit.*

[9] William P. McLoughlin, *The Nongraded School: A Critical Assessment.* Albany, N.Y.: The University of the State of New York, The New York State Education Department, 1967.

the influence of nongrading on student academic achievement have been identified. Not all of these, however, consider the same variables. About half of
them assess the influence of nongrading on reading achievement, while 25
percent look at its influence on arithmetic performance. Only 11 percent of
the studies question the impact nongrading has on the student's development
in language arts. Nine percent report on the total achievement scores of children. The remaining studies are spread so thinly through the other curricular
divisions that a detailed consideration of their findings is hardly profitable.[10]

Judged by these studies, the academic development of children probably
does not suffer from attending a nongraded school; there is some evidence,
admittedly sketchy and tentative, to indicate it may be somewhat enhanced.
One thing is certain; children from graded classes seldom do better on these
measures than children from nongraded classes. More commonly, children
from nongraded classes excell their contemporaries from graded classes.

For example, 15 studies considered the influence of nongrading on the general reading achievement of children. Seven of these report no significant difference between children from graded and nongraded classes. In other words,
nothing is lost by having children attend nongraded classes. But only two
studies found children from graded classes outscoring children from nongraded classes, while six studies found the general reading attainments of
children from nongraded classes superior to that of children in graded classes.

Similar though less distinct outcomes are attained when the reading subskills of comprehension and vocabulary development are examined. Again, the
principal finding of 14 studies is that there are no marked differences in the
accomplishments of children in these areas regardless of the type of organization in which they learn to read. Furthermore, for every study showing
greater gains for children from graded classes, there is an equal number of
studies counterbalancing these findings.

The mirror image of this picture emerges when the arithmetic attainments
of children from graded and nongraded classes are contrasted. Eleven studies
considered the influence of nongrading on children's general arithmetic
achievement, and their findings are inconclusive. Three report differences favoring children from nongraded classes, five found differences favoring children from graded classes,[11] and three found no difference.

But when the arithmetic subskills of reasoning and knowledge of fundamentals are examined, different outcomes appear. Of the 12 published studies
in these areas, one reports differences favoring children from graded classes
but six report differences favoring children from nongraded classes. The remaining five show no real difference in the achievement of children in these
areas, regardless of the type of class organization.

In language arts, too, there is scant evidence to demonstrate that organiza-

[10] *Ibid.*   [11] *Ibid.*

tion influences achievement. Seven of the 10 studies in this area report no true differences in the language skills developed by children from graded and nongraded classes. One reports achievement test scores of children from graded classes as superior to those of children from nongraded classes, while two studies found the observed differences in the achievement of children from nongraded classes indeed significantly superior to that of controls in the graded classes. Apparently, nongraded classes are no more effective in developing language arts skills than are graded classes.

Total achievement test scores, too, seem remarkably immune to change because of changes in organizational pattern. Half of the eight studies using them to measure the efficacy of the nongraded school found no significant differences in the achievements of children from graded and nongraded classes. The remaining studies divide equally: Two reported differences favoring children from graded classes while two found differences favoring children from nongraded classes. So here, once again, the influence of nongrading on the academic development of children is indeterminate.

Better student achievement is not the only claim put forth for the nongraded school. Its advocates maintain, implicitly or explicitly, that superior student adjustment is attained in the nongraded school. Certainly student adjustment and personality development are crucial concerns of educators and, quite reasonably, they are interested in developing learning settings which foster this goal.

Unfortunately, studies assessing the influence of nongrading on student adjustment are even more rare than studies assessing its influence on their academic achievement. Moreover, the diversity of procedures utilized in these studies to measure adjustment lessens their cumulative value. Sociograms, adjustment inventories, anxiety scales, and even school attendance records have all been used as indices of pupil adjustment. But no matter how measured, there is scant evidence to support the contention that superior student adjustment is realized in nongraded schools. On the 32 separate indices of adjustment used in these studies, the overwhelming majority, 26, indicate that there is no significant difference in the adjustment of children from graded and nongraded classes. Only four of the measures (general adjustment, social adjustment, social maturity, and freedom from age stereotypes) showed differences favorable to children from nongraded classes, while the remaining two (social participation and freedom from defensiveness) were favorable to children from graded classes.[12]

Research, then, finds little to impel or impede practitioners interested in nongrading. Under either organization children's adjustment and achievement appear to remain remarkably constant. For those to whom the nongraded school is a magnificent obsession, these findings must come as a numbing dis-

[12] *Ibid.*

appointment. Taken at face value, current research on the nongraded school seems to say that its contribution to the academic, social, and emotional development of children is marginal.

But should these findings be taken at face value? It might be naive to rest the fate of the nongraded school on past research. The validity of these studies should be rigorously tested, for they depend on one tacit but critical assumption: that the experimental schools, those purporting to be nongraded, are *truly* nongraded. If this assumption is not met and the experimental schools are not nongraded, then research has told us nothing about the efficacy of the nongraded school.

Too often, on close inspection, one finds that schools credited with operating nongraded programs are not nongraded at all. Homogeneous grouping and semi-departmentalization of instruction in reading and arithmetic are frequently passed off as nongraded programs. These techniques must be recognized for what they are. They are administrative expediencies developed to make the *graded* school work. They are not nongraded instructional programs.

If these are the "nongraded" programs represented in these studies, then researching their effectiveness is an exercise in futility, for the *experimental* schools are as graded as the control schools and no experimental treatment is being tested. Research has done nothing more than contrast the performances of children from graded schools called graded schools with the performance of children from graded schools called nongraded schools. Essentially, we have simply researched the age-old question: "What's in a name?"

The nongraded school is defensible only because the graded school is indefensible. Its justification flows from its efforts to correct the instructional errors of the graded school. It is reasonably unlikely that any amount of manipulation of the physical arrangements of schools will produce discernible differences in the academic or psycho-social development of children. Every grade label can be cleansed from every classroom door in the school without influencing the school's attainments with children as long as graded instructional practices prevail behind these doors.

Nongrading begins with significant alterations in instructional, not organizational, procedures. As long as schools seek practices designed to group away differences they are *not* nongraded. The nongraded school never held this as a goal, for it is impossible. Rather, nongrading says: "Accept children as they are, with all their differences, and teach to these differences. Don't try to eradicate them!" Until educators develop instructional programs that will meet this challenge they are not nongrading. They are simply masking their old egg-crate schools with a new facade.

29
Opportunities for Enterprise in Education

DONALD D. DURRELL

In the following selection, presented as the annual lecture of the Kappa Delta Phi in 1969, Durrell assumes the right to write an unsolicited policy statement for the new Secretary of Health, Education, and Welfare, proposing that the Office of Education return to its original founding purpose, namely, the pursuit of research for the betterment of schools. Durrell claims that this policy would "bring order out of the chaos of cults and panaceas which clamor for preference in education." In reading this selection, you will doubtlessly ask yourself many questions. Among them might be, "Would the Secretary of Health, Education, and Welfare assume this right in good faith?" "Would he, himself, take such an unsolicited statement seriously?" "Should you?" "Has Durrell made any novel recommendations?" "Is cooperative competition feasible among schools, school systems, and states in the way the author conceived of it?"

Some thought might also be given to the practicality of the provision for individual differences among learners under the conditions Durrell imposes. Could not learning be both relevant and significant without all the elaborate organization of cooperative competition he has described? One final possible question: "Had the author a 'tongue-in-cheek' attitude when making the recommendations, or are they based on his practical experience as a teacher and an educational policymaker?"

I STARTED TEACHING in 1923 as a result of a chance conversation which pointed out that schools were a major source of human suffering. This confirmed my experience and appealed to my altruism. Since that time, my professional life has been a search for ways to improve the conditions of learning, to increase the amount and quality of learning in schools. Originally, I thought that with a reasonable effort the job could be done in twenty years

SOURCE: *Kappa Delta Phi Lectures,* No. 3 (1969), pp. 1–9. Reprinted by permission of the publisher.

Dr. Durrell has had a long and distinguished teaching career in both public schools and universities, interrupted for a two-year period during which he was a research assistant in psychology at the Rockefeller Foundation. Among his many positions, he has served as professor in and Dean of the School of Education of Boston University and as a member of the Research Advisory Council of the United States Office of Education.

and my attention could then be directed toward minor tasks such as the elimination of war, of labor strife, of poverty, of crime, and other social ills.

Certainly I have been given the opportunity to solve education's problems. In the past forty years, few New England teachers have escaped my courses or those taught by my colleagues and former students. In countless extension courses and in more than five hundred classroom-oriented research studies, schools have opened their doors to every project I have proposed. I wish to certify that there is in New England no "establishment resistance" to new ventures in education. I have had the larger opportunities of policy making: As dean of a school of education for ten years and as a member of the research advisory council of the United States Office of Education.

With all of these opportunities, however, I must confess that the problems of education I set out to solve single-handed are still relatively untouched. Since it is the current fashion to turn to the federal government which has the most rigorous taxing power and appears willing to assume the problems of all mankind, I am suggesting that the federal government set up a new program which will encourage widespread competition in the search for improvement of education.

We have a new Republican administration in Washington. As one of the few members of that party in academic circles, I feel a special responsibility to the new administration. In his statements on education thus far, the new Secretary of Health, Education, and Welfare shows the usual confusions of a new man to the business. To set him on the right road, I have written a short statement of one significant educational policy for him. He hasn't asked for this contribution. However, here is what he should say on the topic of educational research: Its title is "Cooperative Competition for Improvement of School Instruction."

"It is the policy of this administration to focus upon the improvement of the amount and quality of learning in elementary and secondary classrooms. Educational service is essentially personal. The learner is always an individual; the quality of his learning depends upon the services he meets in the classroom. The only way to affect the learning of 28 million elementary school children and the 17 million secondary school students is through improving the classroom services offered by 2 million teachers. We will welcome and support educational projects which focus upon classroom services which provide the conditions of effective learning for each American child.

"To further this objective, we will encourage cooperative competitive ventures among schools, school systems, and even states. We recognize that competition is a powerful force in the improvement of goods and services in a free enterprise system. This force we propose to utilize in public education. We shall finance cooperative-competitive ventures in order to discover those components of effective-services in the many areas of curriculum for the wide variety of differing needs among children in American schools.

"Election to engage in such competition will be voluntary; no school system will be forced to enter. Funds will be provided for evaluation of outcomes of the different ventures; the factors to be included in such evaluations will be determined by cooperative planning of those who engage in the competition.

"We suggest two areas for emphasis in these competitions: provision for individual differences among learners, and making learning relevant and significant. It is obvious that we have too much uniform instruction for decidedly un-uniform pupils; bright students suffer from a too meager diet and slow learners fall into frustration. We must seek ways to provide instruction more precisely adjusted to levels and learning rates in each school and classroom. The second need is to make learning significant for the student; many current school offerings appear to the student to have little relevance to his current and future activities.

"This direct approach, utilizing cooperative-competition marks a significant departure from past federal efforts to improve public education. It moves directly into classrooms where success or failure is determined. It opens the doors of comparative research to all who are willing to engage in competition for excellence. It allows unlimited innovation with every school free to search for ways to improve curricula or services. However, it couples the freedom to innovate with the responsibility to evaluate; to discover the relative power of the components of various approaches. It avoids the past programs of noncomparable local ventures which lacked the needed comparative analytical evaluations. It departs from the scattered frenetic approaches of the past, where a favored few institutions skilled in "grantsmanship" absorbed huge sums of money in noncomparable research studies on nebulous projects often remote from classroom learning. It returns the Office of Education to its original founding purpose, the pursuit of research for the betterment of schools."

This ends the statement for the new Secretary of Health, Education, and Welfare. It presents a major approach to bring order out of the chaos of cults and panaceas which clamor for preference in education. It is politically sound, will be understood by members of Congress, and approved by the layman. It opens to all the exciting venture of searching for ways to reach utopia through thousands of ways to improve learning.

There is no shortage of ideas, either great or small, for the improvement of public education. Administrative approaches appeal to many people as solutions to problems of classroom learning. Among the large ideas is that of school control: From Admiral Rickover who would abolish 55 thousand school committees to the present New York City move which would multiply local administrative boards, perhaps having a separate committee for each school. Apparently the thought is that it makes a difference whether ignorance of the needs of children is centralized or fragmented. We have various administrative divisions of pupils: the eight-four plan, the six-three-three plan, the four-three-five plan. Most of these arise from building problems and school crowding, but are justified after the fact by psychological and philosophical rationale. Within the school, we try various methods of body-sorting, with ability grouping the central idea: grouping by subject ability, by vocational objective, by intelligence, with classes for the gifted and for the mentally retarded. There are also the various types of pupil sorting in the myriad forms of teacher-team approaches. Grouping, of course, has no inherent merit; it merely provides the opportunity for adjusting the educational diet. We are attracted to individualized instruction, embodied in the old Winnetka and Dalton plans and reincarnated as ungraded schools, nongraded schools, and continuous progress programs. Unfortunately, such programs are more evident in school publicity than in the classrooms. One major study found more individualization in self-contained classrooms than in schools claiming nongraded programs. There may be value in different types of administrative approaches. Every single idea in the foregoing list has some basic merit; but each needs the cleansing experience of cooperative competition with other approaches.

We are constantly offered solutions through educational gadgetry. Each new audio-visual aid appears to be a potential panacea; overhead projectors, multiple copiers, tachistoscopes, tape recorders, film loops, video taping, movie projectors, teaching machines of various designs, and computer based instruction. We are told that with these devices all that is needed is suitable "software," the lessons to make them work. Agreed: The oldest and most adaptable teaching machine—the textbook—would be highly efficient if it contained suitable "software." Television is another gadget which tempts the educationally naive, to them it appears an instant and inexpensive panacea: Find the master teacher and share him with all pupils, with all noses turned toward Mecca for the standardization of American minds. This device for uniform instruction ignores differences among pupils in ability levels, in learning rates, in subskills needs. It assumes that the mental activity of the teacher outranks the mental activity of the pupil; it forgets that pupil initiative in using knowledge is the key to effective learning.

In meeting individual differences, we will increasingly depend upon self-directing, self-correcting instructional materials, many of which will be the software for the gadgets, but more will appear in textbooks, workbooks, and learning packages. Skills instruction in tool subjects is admirably suited to such instructional packaging. The task is to design materials which approach the high effectiveness of individual tutoring under a skilled teacher. This area is rich with opportunities for inventive minds; we are still in the early pioneering stages of devising self-directing, self-correcting learning materials. As such materials are produced, they should be put to the test of careful component evaluation, in competition with other products designed for the same purpose. We need such free competition among creative teachers, rather than attempting materials production by committee-oriented federally supported curriculum development centers. If federal support continues for purchase of instructional materials, we will find it unnecessary to depart from free enterprise in materials production. Highly promising materials are constantly being developed by superior teachers; we must find ways to get these more widely distributed and to provide royalties to the teachers who produce them. But these materials too, need the test of comparative research.

Let's take a look at teacher education. During the past year the federal government allotted 200 million dollars for "educational personnel development grants." Good! We know that the teacher makes the difference! But again, the plans called for local noncomparable ventures with no research design for comparison of outcomes. Those with the best publicity will be the "winners." But from such projects there is no hope of acquiring assured knowledge of the components of superior teacher education. Schools and colleges of education, in New England at least are ready for cooperative-competitive research in teacher education. It is true that the evaluation of teacher education is highly complex, but only by making the attempt will we discover the effective components of the education of the superior teacher.

I am aware that time grows short for me in this meeting as well as in this incarnation. Let me make ten predictions in relation to education, some major, some minor:

1. Solo learning—lonely individual learning—will be replaced largely by pupil-team learning, in teams of two to five students. In most of our studies, teams have a higher learning yield than solo learning.

2. Skipping of grades will return to favor, with students entering college at a much earlier age. Pressey's research shows a high incidence of intellectual and scientific leadership resulting from this former practice.

3. Coeducation will be discovered to be advantageous to girls, a handicap to boys. We will separate the sexes in large blocks of learning time after third grade and through college.

4. In my own field of reading, better instructional analysis and improved teaching materials will eliminate reading disabilities. Many first grade teachers have already reached this goal. We will no longer study an imaginary condition called "dyslexia" through techniques resembling psychological witchcraft.

5. We will suddenly discover the mental hygiene hazards of an ototverbal curriculum, compounded by ototverbal mass media with its daily dramatizing of social and personal disasters. Major curriculum emphasis will be given to arts, crafts, applied sciences, sports, recreational activities. Even colleges will discover that their most important jobs are to increase variety and depth of interest, and to establish the untold opportunities for personal and professional pioneering.

6. We will learn that class sizes may be increased without hazard to learning yield or personal development objectives when self-directing pupil-team learning materials are more widely utilized. Classes under thirty will be considered uneconomical in many areas of the curriculum.

7. Local parents will take over much of the teaching and other services in el-

ementary and secondary schools, with much of this on a voluntary public service basis. Rising school costs and the increasing militancy of labor-union type "negotiations" followed by teacher strikes will force this change. The amount and quality of learning in schools may possibly be improved.

8. The demand for integrated schools through bussing and redistribution by color will diminish when precisely adjusted and highly motivated learning in schools is available to all children.

9. States and administrative bodies will recognize that most attempts to regulate instructional matters do nothing more than to standardize current ignorance. In regulations prescribed for persistently weak schools which are cited to justify such regulations there will be the addendum: "We encourage departures from this regulation and will offer financial assistance for evaluation of variant practices."

10. We will eventually put into practice the sound ideas contained in Harold Benjamin's Inglis Lecture, titled "Education as the Cultivation of Idiosyncrasy." In New England, at least, the climate is right for the production of independent minds, producing the variant idea from which all progress stems.

EVALUATION

BURTON G. ANDREAS, **An Educational System Analyzed**

1. Andreas states that there is no "process of education," but that formal education is a "subsystem" of an individual's ongoing development.
   (a) What processes does he say constitute an individual's education?

   (b) What two factors does he regard as important contributors to personal intellectual growth?

   (c) In the designing of instruction, how do the two processes contribute to the design?

2. Name the components in Andreas's concept of the triadic nature of individual development.

3. Andreas stresses individual development in education in a systems approach to individualized promotion.
   (a) What six measures or steps does he include?

   (b) On what is his system based?

4. Andreas considers "team teaching" and "learning teams" analogous. Explain how he visualizes the functions of teaching teams with (1) fast learners and with (2) slow learners.

5. In a brief paragraph, state whether or not you agree with this method of teaching and give reasons for your answer.

6. Andreas indicates certain aspects of preschool life and home environment which he believes offer either promise or problems for formal learning. List the four aspects and draw upon one or two illustrations from your own personal experiences or observations in support or in contradiction of the author's viewpoints.

HAROLD S. DAVIS, **Organizing an Effective Team Teaching Program**

7. Davis discusses team teaching as a "phenomenon in American education." Give his definition of team teaching; then, in your own words, explain why the words "regularly" and "purposefully" are key words in his definition.

8. (a) Name and describe the two types of teaching teams Davis discusses.

   (b) Write a statement on each type, making a clear distinction between them.

   (c) Prepare a diagram identifying a schema representing each team and its major functions.

9. (a) List the three most frequently heard reasons for adopting team teaching.

   (b) Using Davis's rationale for team teaching as the basis of your answers, write at least one statement in support of or rejecting each of these three reasons.

10. What does Davis regard as the basic approach to planning instruction for various sized groups of students?

UNITED STATES COMMISSIONER OF EDUCATION, **Differentiated Staffing**

11. Differentiated staffing in schools has become quite common where an adequate supply of qualified teachers cannot be found. According to the article published as part of a 1968 Report by the U.S. Commissioner of Education, on what basis was differentiated staffing initially implemented?

12. In a school where differentiated staffing is conducted, how do staff assignments differ from those generally found in a traditional school?

13. The 1968 Report of the U.S. Commissioner of Education suggests part-time tutors and teacher aides at the lower level of responsibilities in the proposed hierarchy within a school system using a differentiated staffing system and educational specialists at the other end of the scale. On what basis is organization placed in this concept of instruction?

14. What challenges to our prevailing system of education does the author seek as results of differentiated staffing?

15. How does the author believe that these challenges may be satisfactorily met?

JOHN M. RAND and FENWICK ENGLISH, **Towards a Differentiated Teaching Staff**

16. (a) Name the two factors that Rand and English regard as responsible for "unbearable strains upon the present organized structure in education."

    (b) On the basis of your agreement or disagreement with their position, relate the two factors to your own local educational structure and support your own views on these factors and their influence.

17. What evidence have the authors for their contention that there is an increasing dissatisfaction of teachers and "constituent dissatisfaction"?

18. (a) What are teachers demanding in educational decision making and in their professional roles that the authors regard as direct justification for the "dissolution of the single salary schedule"?

    (b) Does this seem to be a logical conclusion?

19. A majority of students have evaluated their teachers at one time or another formally or informally and generally with considerable self-confidence. In the light of Rand and English's statements concerning merit pay, how valid would you regard your evaluation of your teachers?

20. Explain specifically how the authors believe they could avoid fallacies, as they see them, of merit pay for teachers.

WILLIAM P. MCLOUGHLIN, **The Phantom Nongraded School**

21. Prior to Horace Mann's time, American schools were what might be classified as "nongraded." What evidence does McLoughlin present to show there is a noticeable increase of interest in nongraded schools?

22. The first school system reported as a "graded school system" was in Boston, Massachusetts, in 1848. A return to the nongraded school has been sought by many teachers, but McLoughlin claims that nongrading has "been preached more than practiced." What statistics does he give to support this statement?

23. What does McLoughlin conclude regarding nongradedness and the size of a school district? Elaborate on his rationale for this conclusion.

24. Why does McLoughlin defend nongraded schools?

25. How does the author describe nongrading?

26. According to McLoughlin, what is the initial step by which schools might move toward nongradedness?

DONALD D. DURRELL, **Opportunities for Enterprise in Education**

27. (a) What is Durrell's major thesis?

    (b) What two major areas in his educational venture does Durrell emphasize?

28. Does Durrell visualize his proposal for education to be appropriate for adoption in teacher education? Elaborate his views on this point.

29. Where does the author believe the emphasis in learning should be placed for each child?

30. What two major claims does Durrell make to qualify him as a policy-maker in education?

31. (a) What significance does Durrell believe cooperative competition would have in improving public education?

    (b) What does the author regard as the most adaptable teaching machine?

32. (a) What are three administrative alternatives Durrell views as problems of classroom learning?

    (b) Explain each of these approaches briefly.

FOR FURTHER READING

"Science and Technology in Contemporary Society," *Daedalus,* Spring 1962.
A high-level selection indicating the implications for our society that science and technology hold.

Davis, Harold, *Instructional Media Center: Broad New Venture* (Bloomington: Indiana University Press, 1972).
An exciting new book presenting the latest report on what has been done, and what is possible to do, with the media by imaginative, creative teachers.

Dewey, John, "John Dewey Sketches a New Type of School," *Turning Points in American Educational History,* ed. D. B. Tyack (Waltham, Mass.: Blaisdell Publishers, 1967).
Discusses the difficulty of putting the principles of the new education into practice. Dewey also reprimands extreme progressives.

Lierheimer, Alvin P., "Cast Off the Bowline!" *Today's Education* (Washington, D.C.: National Education Association, 1969).
The author is Director of the Division of Teacher Education and Certification in the New York State Education Department. His experience in this office apparently has convinced him that differentiated staffing and performance assessment point the way for casting off the line that has kept the certification sloop circling its moorings for years. You should enjoy this short article, for it offers a number of sound ideas.

Ramo, Simon, "The Limitations of the Systems Approach," *Cure for Chaos* (New York: David McKay Company, 1969).
A thought-provoking analytical study of the currently popular systems approach. Following your study of Andreas's analysis of a systems approach to education, you might find it very interesting to read this selection. It will make you aware of the "other side of the coin."

Trump, J. Lloyd, and Baynham Dorsey, *Focus on Change* (Chicago: Rand McNally & Company, 1961).
An imaginative discussion on a premise for change based on the contention that the world may not long survive as we now know it. The authors report on school projects and offer proposals as their suggestions for action through such practices as the team teaching, planned large- and small-group instruction, teaching assistants, independent study, and tutorial teaching.

Tyler, Ralph, "National Planning and Quality Control in Education," *Modern Viewpoints in the Curriculum,* ed. Paul C. Rosenbloom (New York: McGraw-Hill, 1964).

An excellent outline of planning for education on a nationwide scale. Tyler appropriately considers every possible facet in the process. He leaves you with the thought, "why not quality control education?"

Weismann, Rozanne, "Staff Differentiation," *Florida Education* (NEA Division of Press, Radio and Television Relations, 1968).

Recommending this as a design for a new staffing plan in schools. This proposal calls for new roles for teachers, which give greater responsibility for decision making as well as financial rewards for teachers with broader backgrounds and greater experience. You will ask yourself, "Should teachers be treated alike regardless of their experience, career desires, motivations, talents, or ability to assume additional responsibility?"

Witt, Paul F., ed., *Technology and the Curriculum* (New York: Teachers College, Columbia University, 1968).

The information presented in each of the nine statements in this volume on educational technology and its implications for you as teachers in this technological age cannot be overestimated. They were edited from addresses given at the 1967 Curriculum Conference at Teachers College, Columbia University.

PART THREE

Education as a Career

Teaching is an art, which is to say, it
calls for the exercise of talent and
creativity. But it is also a science,
for it involves a repertoire of techniques,
procedures, and skills, which can be
systematically studied and improved. The
great teacher is the one who adds creativity
and inspiration to that basic repertoire.

CHARLES E. SILBERMAN
"Technology Knocking
at the Schoolhouse Door,"
Fortune, August 1966, p. 124.

Three groups of readings will be found in this part of the book. The first discusses careers in education; the second, teachers and teaching; and the third, teaching as a profession. By no means are the selections intended to be an exhaustive treatment of these topics. For some readers, the greatest value may be found in the information presenting specific suggestions for choosing and preparing for a career in education. For others, the selections on teachers and teaching, with the discussion of technology and communication, may be more appealing. The final group ranges from John Dewey's statements at the turn of the present century to a consideration of educational goals and teacher roles in the 1970's.

Specific requirements for choosing a suitable occupation are given in "Choosing a Career" (Selection 30). A thoughtful study of this statement will help you find their answer to the question, "Is education a career for me?" Following a discussion of six areas of knowledge crucial to making the best choice of a career, some astute observations are made on the occupational flexibility of a career in education in relation to embarking upon several careers within one lifetime. The authors draw some significant conclusions on the basis of occupational trends in society today.

The next two selections give a full coverage of careers at almost all levels of education. In the first (Selection 31), Sylvester Balassi provides job descriptions of six careers in specialized teaching areas and school programs, going into great detail on those careers he considers most unfamiliar to many people. The information on nonteaching professional careers in education is particularly well presented and should serve to interest students who desire to dedicate their lives to education but do not have either the desire or the ability to teach well.

Garda W. Bowman and Gordon J. Klopf discuss careers in education other than professional instruction, administration, and pupil personnel in "Auxiliary School Personnel" (Selection 32). They stress the need for clear differentiation of the roles to be played by the professional and the paraprofessional. As you read this selection, it will interest you to evaluate the effect on education of utilizing paraprofessionals in schools which have differentiated staffing, the subject examined earlier under the heading "Innovations in Education." The NEA statement (Selection 33) on how to prepare for a professional career in education concludes this group of readings. Specific academic requirements, college costs, the process of accreditation and legal requirements for certification clearly present the factors future teachers must consider. Exciting and rewarding careers await future teachers if education follows the imaginative and stimulating ideas found in these readings.

The selections in the section "Teachers and Teaching" were chosen to assist you in confirming your decision for a career in education. They give an overview of what you can expect to find as you involve yourself more and more in the work and activities of the profession. According to John Dewey (Selection 34), the teacher must be a student of the pupil's mind just as the student is a student of subject matter. The professional knowledge Dewey would require of a teacher includes psychology, history of education, and teaching methods. These requisites in professional preparation support the distinction Harold Benjamin makes between training and learning in Selection 35. According to Benjamin, understanding and learning go hand-in-hand if learning is to occur. His definition of teaching is somewhat unusual although not unrealistic.

In "Authentic Teachers" (Selection 36), Sydney J. Harris presents a somewhat austere image of what he describes as an authentic teacher in which he stresses freedom from artificiality. To be true to one's own values and one's own vital personality is what Harris believes is the mystery at the heart of the teaching process and is the quality that enables a teacher to tune in on another's wavelength.

George Gerbner, in "Technology, Communication, and Education" (Selection 37), equates teaching with technology in a very meaningful way. His portrait of teachers will lead you to underlying reasons for the grotesque image teachers have been given by mass media. Gerbner predicts that the survival of education in an industrial culture depends upon institutional remodeling aimed to bring the forces of human history under more reasonable control.

John Dewey wrote a pedagogic creed for teachers (Selection 38) in 1897 which reads like a restatement of his aims for education; in fact, many educational leaders regard it as just that. According to Dewey, education must include both social and individual goals which do not permit neglect or subordination of either the social or the psychological aspects. In "The Teacher as a Member of a Profession" (Selection 39), Grace Graham defines a profession and lists five major characteristics of which it is constituted. Graham's discussion of these characteristics is quite detailed and her elaboration of a professional culture especially significant in light of her statement that "no group ever completely attains its professional goals or measures up the ideal attributes of a profession."

"Professional Organizations" (Selection 40) by Sidney Dorros considers in great detail the subject of professional organizations, their history, their major concerns, and their contributions to the advancement of teaching as a profession. Dorros states their objectives and ways of achieving them, and also outlines the organizational structure and related work of the National Education Association. You will notice that he gives strong support to membership in professional organizations. Since a decision for or against membership must eventually be made by every teacher, this selection is well worth your thoughtful consideration.

Jacques Barzun, in "Profession: Teacher" (Selection 41), defines education as an intangible and unpredictable activity, burdened with doing everything the rest of the world leaves undone. Barzun's major concern appears to be with the retention of competent teachers; he regards this as a serious problem largely accounted for by the existing prejudice against teaching and the absence of respect for teachers. His persuasive pen and obvious personal involvement reflect a deep empathy with those who strive to have teaching respected and recognized as a profession.

"Reordering Goals and Roles: The Teaching Profession in the 1970's" (Selection 42) by T. M. Stinnett is chosen to conclude this book of readings since it not only projects into the immediate future but also reviews recent events in education that the author believes are cause for grave concern in American education. He identifies two disturbing trends, both within and outside the system, which have caused the compulsory school attendance laws to be challenged as well as undermined the potential capability of public schools to continue in existence. Stinnett's prognosis is that professional educators must assume new leadership roles in the nation, and if his predictions for the new roles are sound, the influence of outstanding educators will have a far greater impact than ever before on the history of the United States.

It is a well-known fact that teaching is one of the oldest occupations known to man. It is also one of the most sacred trusts ever given to or accepted by an individual. Assuming both of these statements to be true, a person who has made a decision to enter education and who has committed himself to this career will then need to consider the functions and responsibilities of the profession. These selections in this part are intended first to help in the decision-making process, and second, to discuss those factors that must be considered once the decision is made.

A Career in Education

30

Choosing a Career

NATIONAL EDUCATION ASSOCIATION

Guidelines to assist prospective teachers in making their personal commitment to a career in education are found in this 1968 statement of the National Commission of Teacher Education and Professional Standards (NCTEPS). The statement tells us that the success or failure in making a wise career decision cannot and should not be minimized. This is so whether or not it is the first career in your work experience.

THE FACT that a working lifetime is now likely to include several careers has not reduced the importance of career choice. A second, third, or even fourth career is often built upon or related to the first, and each decision affects those that will follow it. Investment of time and attention in selection of suitable occupations is repaid by career satisfaction throughout a working lifetime.

For those who are selecting a first career, and who therefore know little about the job market or the experience of work, careful study is necessary to prevent errors, which can be costly in both money and time. Selection of a suitable occupation requires accurate knowledge of oneself and of the nature of various kinds of work and the ability to project both of these into the future. Vocational counseling and aptitude testing are available to students in most high schools and colleges, and agencies sponsored by the different levels of government offer this assistance to others. Educational materials on occupations also are readily available from governmental agencies and from organizations connected with specific occupations. The prospective worker can obtain further information on the advantages and disadvantages of specific occupations from employed friends and relations and by personal observation. Well-founded knowledge of his own abilities and of what he wants from his career in terms of remunerations, working conditions, opportunities for

SOURCE: *NEA Journal—1968: Careers in Education*, pp. 27–28. Reprinted by permission of the publisher.

growth, social status, and role is crucially important. Once the prospective worker has decided that a specific kind of work is likely to be suited to his abilities and meet his requirements, a period of temporary employment connected with that occupation is valuable as a test of the decision.

Persons who have had occupational experience usually know something about different kinds of jobs related to their work and have already formulated ideas about their vocational abilities and requirements. If they are contemplating a change to a completely different kind of work, however, it is advisable for them to use all available means of evaluating their knowledge of themselves and of the work that interests them, and to seek some preliminary experience before committing themselves to a new occupation.

The field of education offers the occupational flexibility suitable to a society in which every worker can expect to embark upon several different careers as his abilities and interests mature and the nature of society and employment changes. Because the careers now open in education are numerous and developing rapidly, educators have great opportunity to take on increased or different responsibilities. Because many of these careers require expertise in other fields, it is not difficult, with some additional preparation, for educators to move into these fields or for others to move into education. Additional preparation is available to many educators through in-service training programs and opportunities for summer study.

This flexibility is one feature of educational careers that many people find attractive. Another is the security provided by tenure in many educational positions. Educational occupations are excellent opportunities for persons who want to contribute to human services. The schools offer a wide variety of positions to persons interested in working with young people. Interest in a particular subject matter field leads some people to choose careers in teaching, research, or the combination of both that is encouraged in colleges and universities. Others, with abilities for coordination and management, are drawn to educational administration. Like everything else about education, its attractions as a career are changing. It is a field no longer safe for authoritarians: the successful teacher—or administrator—is frequently one who is willing to challenge and be challenged.

The main characteristic shared by all careers in education is their impact on the future, increasing as the responsibilities of the educational system are broadened. The work of all educators is directed to providing children the most thorough and most relevant possible preparation for adult life. Educators influence all aspects of our national life, from social and economic conditions to breadth of international understanding. They influence all aspects of individual life, from vocational competence to self-respect. They also have an increasing amount of influence on the ways they themselves fulfill their functions and the conditions under which they work. As the demands of the future—and the present—on the schools increase, the demands and rewards of careers in education grow with them.

31
Careers in Education

SYLVESTER J. BALASSI

Dealing directly with specific careers in education, Sylvester Balassi discusses in considerable detail six specialized teaching areas that are not too well known by the general public. He also presents three fields in pupil personnel services and four in the administrative areas of education. This selection reflects the high degree of specialization present in education today. It may prompt you to take another look at existing educational opportunities and help you find a career well suited to your unique talents and interests.

THERE ARE many careers one could pursue within the broad field of education. Whole volumes are devoted to such careers. In this chapter, the author has selected for discussion six rather specialized teaching areas probably not so familiar to the reader: art education, business education, industrial arts education, music education, physical education for women, and speech therapy. These areas were selected not only because of their unfamiliarity as careers, but also because they represent parts of the program of public education that may not be very well understood. For similar reasons the work of three specialists in the area of pupil personnel services will be considered: the school counselor, the school psychologist, and the school social worker. And, because a number of teachers move into administration, that area of careers will also be included. The various areas will be taken up in alphabetical order. . . .

SOURCE: Sylvester J. Balassi, *Focus on Teaching* (Indianapolis, Ind.: The Bobbs-Merrill Co., 1968), Chap. 8. Copyright © 1968 by Western Publishing Co. Reprinted by permission of the publisher.

Dr. Balassi is a member of the faculty of education at Paterson State College in New Jersey. He is the author of *Guide to Introduction to Education* and a contributor to a number of periodicals, including the *National Business Education Quarterly* and the *Journal of Business Education*. Prior to entering the field of education, he held various positions in sales, personnel, and business management. This combination of both business and teaching experience gives Dr. Balassi's analysis of careers a freshness and vitality too often lacking in the writing of those whose experience has been in education alone.

Administration

A number of opportunities are available in public school administration for those with initiative, leadership, and experience. The positions to be discussed here are superintendent, assistant superintendent, principal, and assistant principal. There are a number of other administrative positions, however, that will not be included in this discussion, like departments heads, already discussed in Chapter 4; directors of specific areas or fields such as elementary education or physical education; positions concerned with the business management of the school district and the supervision of buildings and grounds.

School Superintendent [1]

While the superintendent holds the best-paying position in the public schools,[2] his position is also the most difficult and demanding one. The demands and difficulties of his work are apparent in the four principal parts of his job:

1. *Improving educational opportunity.* All aspects of the instructional program are included in this part; such questions as what shall be taught and how it shall be taught are considered here.

2. *Obtaining and developing personnel.* The divisions of the job concerned with recruitment, selection, placement, and promotion of personnel are relevant here. All matters of personnel administration are likewise considered. Pupil personnel problems are considered under this head in addition to matters relating to professional and non-professional personnel.

3. *Maintaining effective relations with the community.* This part of the job is more broadly conceived than mere public relations. It includes interpreting the schools to the public and studying the community so as to further education.

4. *Providing and maintaining funds and facilities.* The business and housekeeping aspects of school administration are included in this part of the job. Included are budget planning, plant maintenance, construction and renovation of buildings, and similar functions.[3]

Attempting to improve educational opportunity has become a major responsibility as schools enroll more and more young people and attempt to do more

[1] Reference in this discussion is to the local superintendent of schools in a school district with a student population of about 20,000.

[2] In systems with enrollments of 25,000 or more, the average maximum salary paid to superintendents was $26,017 in 1966–67; with 6,000–11,999 enrollment, it was $19,387. (National Education Association, Research Division, *Salary Schedules for Administrative Personnel, 1966–67,* Public-School Salaries Series, Research Report 1967-R3 [Washington, D.C.: the Association, 1967], p. 5.)

[3] Daniel E. Griffiths, *The School Superintendent,* The Library of Education (New York: The Center for Applied Research in Education, 1966), pp. 70–71.

and more for them. Now there is concern for nursery school, junior college, and adult education. In short, the superintendent needs to be concerned about educational opportunity for all within his school district.

The superintendent needs assistance in meeting his responsibilities. In arriving at aims and objectives of the schools, for instance, he may utilize a committee composed of teachers, administrators, and lay citizens. He cannot spend his time working directly on the actual improvement of instruction, so these responsibilities are turned over to building principals, supervisors, and consultants. Such activities as construction of student schedules, the keeping of pupil personnel records, and numerous technical functions are turned over to others.[4]

Recruiting, selecting, placing, promoting, and training personnel is a major responsibility of the superintendent as is developing and maintaining high morale among the staff. He needs to establish a sound organization structure and a grievance system. Many personnel problems in today's schools are due partly to faulty organizational structure and the lack of a mechanism by which grievances can be communicated to the administration and the board of education. This need for effective communication is also evident in interpreting the schools to the community. A plan of public relations needs to be developed, and such a plan must provide for two-way communication. Educational needs and the work of the schools must be presented, and the opinions, attitudes, and feelings of the community must be assessed. The community must be involved in the schools if the school system is to be adequately provided with funds and facilities. The function of providing funds and facilities requires much of the time and skill of the superintendent, for preparation of the school budget and the development of long-range plans for the school district are his responsibilities.[5]

It is obvious that the superintendent must be a man of many talents in order to perform effectively and efficiently in all aspects of his work. He must have a deep and broad knowledge of education; he must be able to make sound judgments; he must know and understand human behavior of individuals and groups; and he must have courage and vision. And this is only a partial list of desirable characteristics. It is not surprising then that the American Association of School Administrators recommends at least two years of graduate study in the education of superintendents.[6] Teaching experience, of course, is required for the superintendency. In large school districts, the pattern for reaching the position is usually teacher, principal, assistant or associate superintendent, superintendent. In small communities, the common pattern is teacher, principal, superintendent.[7]

[4] *Ibid.*, pp. 72–74.   [5] *Ibid.*, pp. 75–79.

[6] American Association of School Administrators, *Professional Administrators for America's Schools,* Thirty-Eighth Yearbook (Washington, D.C.: the Association, 1960), p. 177.

[7] Griffiths, *op. cit.,* p. 48.

Assistant Superintendent

The principal function of the assistant superintendent is to aid the superintendent who, in a large district, cannot handle all of the responsibilities by himself. There may, in fact, be assistant superintendents in charge of personnel administration, curriculum, public relations, and business management. Or there may be but one assistant superintendent who takes on such duties as the superintendent may designate. As noted above, assistant superintendents usually come from the ranks of principals and can move on to the superintendency. The position of assistant superintendent is an excellent training ground not only for the superintendency but for other educational positions such as those at the county or state level.

Principal

Principals constitute both the largest group of administrators and the most visible one, for they head the individual school—the unit of education best known to students, parents, and the general public. Teaching principals are found in small schools where their duties include teaching as well as administration. When a principal is in charge of both elementary and secondary schools, he is usually known as a supervising principal. Assistant principals are normally found in large school districts.

A master's degree and successful teaching experience are generally required for the position of principal. Salaries earned are better than those for teachers. For instance, in districts with enrollment of 25,000 or more students in 1966–67, the average salary for senior high school principals was $10,918; for junior high school principals, it was $10,155; and for elementary school principals, it was $9,191.[8] The estimated average salary for elementary teachers in 1966–67, on the other hand, was $6,069; for secondary teachers, the comparable figure was $7,095.[9]

The principal has a multitude of things to do. Ideally, he is responsible for the total educational program of the school and the management of the school's affairs. He is, therefore, concerned with instruction and curriculum. He may take part in the selection of new staff members, the orientation of new teachers, and the further development of the staffs capabilities. The principal will supervise the work of the teachers, the maintenance staff, and perhaps a cafeteria staff. And he must be concerned with textbooks, equipment, and supplies. There is much paper work to be done: correspondence, reports, bulletins, and memorandums. There are many meetings with the su-

[8] National Education Association, Research Division, *Salary Schedules for Administrative Personnel,* Public School Salaries Series, Research Report 1967-R3 (Washington, D.C.: the Association, 1967), p. 10.

[9] National Education Association, Research Division, *Rankings of the States,* Research Report 1967-R1 (Washington, D.C.: the Association, 1967), p. 26.

perintendent, other administrators, the school staff, parents, and community groups to attend. The principal must be concerned with proper pupil behavior, a system of reporting pupil progress to parents, and the health and safety of all in the school. In addition to an active interest in student affairs, the principal must take an active role in community affairs.

Throughout his work, the principal must deal with a variety of groups, many of which will make different demands on him. He is the "man in the middle" because he stands between the central administration and the teaching staff. He must carry out school district policies while meeting the professional and personal needs of the teaching staff. This often can bring about conflict, for policy and teacher needs are not always identical. While the central administration and the teachers may have different expectations for the principal, the community may well have expectations different from both groups. Furthermore, the principal's professional organizations may set expectations conflicting with all of the above groups.[10]

Assistant Principal

Some large elementary schools have assistant principals, but the position is much more common in the secondary school where the title used is frequently "vice-principal." Obviously, the assistant principal "assists" the principal, but the way in which he assists varies. It is the principal's responsibility to define the role of the assistant principal.[11] The principal, however, should delegate authority commensurate with the responsibilities given the assistant principal. Making someone responsible for a particular function without giving him the necessary authority is a poor administrative practice.

In a particular secondary school there may be one or more assistant principals to administer and/or supervise any or all of the following: counseling and guidance, attendance, club programs, student assemblies, school calendar, cafeteria, curriculum improvement, student teachers, and instructional materials. When the principal is absent, the vice-principal is in charge of the school. A position with duties such as the above provides an excellent opportunity for acquiring the necessary knowledge and experience that help to prepare one for the principalship.

[10] Daniel E. Griffiths in the introduction to Samuel Goldman, *The School Principal,* The Library of Education (New York: The Center for Applied Research in Education, 1966), p. vii.

[11] Gareth B. Goddard, "The Assistant Principal—Understudy or Partner in Professional Leadership," *National Association of Secondary School Principals Bulletin,* 46, No. 275:33, September, 1962.

Art Education

Art education opportunities in the public schools consist of such positions as art specialist for the elementary school, secondary teacher of art, department head, and art education supervisor. The art teacher should possess the qualities found in any good teacher, to be sure. Beyond these qualities, however, every art teacher, ideally, should be an active creative artist.[12] Such creative activity can deepen the teacher's understanding of the work his pupils are doing. Certainly, then, if one is considering art education as a career, he should have artistic talent and be interested in pursuing the cultivation of that talent.

The position of art specialist for the elementary school is singled out for attention here because the reader may be less familiar with this position. Furthermore, it is felt that in such work the art teacher can exert a great influence upon developing the expressive capacity of children and educating them to create and respond to art.

Art education in the elementary school is not just "fun" or "play." "Art experience provides opportunity for heightening sensitivity to the physical world, introducing order into sense impressions, and bringing into existence a visible token of imagination and feeling." [13] This kind of art experience is not found in simply tracing, copying, or in other ways producing just what the teacher wants. Such experience brings about mere compliance on the part of children and certainly does not foster creativity. What kinds of things would one find in a good elementary school art program?

The current art program employs a wide variety of materials and procedures. It makes use of both three-dimensional techniques, such as papier mâché, clay modeling, and wood construction, and two-dimensional techniques, such as drawing, painting, printing, and finger painting. It includes abstract and representational art, group and individual projects, and the production of both functional and purely ornamental objects.[14]

These materials and procedures, together with a good art teacher, can make for a fine program.

The art specialist in the elementary school might be an itinerant teacher going to several elementary schools to actually teach art to boys and girls. Or she could be serving as a consultant on call to assist the elementary teachers in planning art activities. In the latter position the art teacher may, for example, conduct workshops for the elementary teachers in anticipation of appropriate art activities for an up-coming holiday observance or special event. In

[12] Hilda Present Lewis, *Art Education in the Elementary School* (Washington, D.C.: National Education Association, 1961), p. 29.
[13] *Ibid.*, p. 3.   [14] *Ibid.*, p. 3.

an ideal situation, the art consultant would work with a classroom teacher in devising art activities to coordinate with a unit of study she was planning. The teacher would plan with the specialist art activities that could be integrated in the unit of study to make the learning more interesting and valuable for the students.

For someone who has the artistic ability, the qualities of a good teacher, and the necessary skill in interpersonal relations a career in art education offers a great challenge and much satisfaction.

Business Education

The teacher of business education at the secondary level is concerned with both general and vocational education. Business education contributes to general education (education that has value for all students), for it helps the student to become a more intelligent consumer of goods and services; it also increases the student's proficiency to function well in the economic aspects of our society. Courses like business arithmetic, general business, advertising, and business law can deal with knowledge and skills of value to all students. Examples of such knowledge and skills are how to borrow money intelligently; how to compute interest and discount; how to manage a checking account; how to complete income tax forms; what constitutes a legal contract; what kind of life insurance to buy; and how to detect false or misleading advertisements.

The vocational aspect of business education (preparing students for entry into the world of work) has always been of importance. This aspect has been given increased emphasis in recent years, however, particularly with the passage of the Vocational Education Act of 1963. This is the first Act to include business and office occupations in federally aided programs. Typewriting, shorthand, bookkeeping, clerical practice, office machines, and other business courses help the student to gain the knowledge, skills, understandings, and attitudes necessary for securing initial employment. Typewriting, which is also a useful general skill, has the largest enrollment of any business subject in the secondary curriculum, 23 percent of high school students.[15]

The business education teacher should have a good collegiate preparation for teaching which includes a concentration on mastery of a variety of business subjects.[16] While some states have only one certificate for business edu-

---

[15] U.S. Department of Health, Education and Welfare, *Summary of Offerings and Enrollments in High School Subjects, 1960–1961* (Washington, D.C.: U.S. Government Printing Office, July, 1964), p. 2.

[16] Frank M. Herndon, "A Career in Teaching the Business Subjects," *Business Education Forum*, 18:9, January, 1964.

cation requiring the candidate to be competent in all business areas, other states grant several certificates, perhaps one for the secretarial area, one for bookkeeping and accounting, and one for general business or social business. Whether business experience is required or not, the prospective teacher of business subjects should have such experience.[17] Furthermore, it is desirable for the business teacher to renew this work experience from time to time in order to keep current with the business world.

Ideally, business education should be an important area of the secondary school program. Too often, it is not. This is due to a number of things. In some schools, business courses have been used by administrators as "dumping grounds" for students who were behavior problems or who could not show satisfactory achievement in other parts of the program.[18] This has tended to give business education, its teachers, and it students "second-class citizenship" in the high school. Another contributing factor has been the inability of college-bound students to fit business courses into their crowded programs, should they be interested in such courses. Some business teachers themselves have not enhanced the position of business education because of their limited view of the field and their work in it. They do not see business education in its broader socio-economic aspects; they see themselves simply as teachers of some basic business skills.

The author certainly does not wish to discourage anyone from considering business education as a teaching career, but he does wish to point out what has sometimes been the "reality" for the business teacher. There is a need for able young people to come into the field. There is now and will continue to be for some time a shortage of well-qualified business teachers.[19] Furthermore, the opportunities for the teacher of business education at the post-secondary level are expanding as the number of community colleges continues to increase.

Industrial Arts

Industrial arts education, as general education, is concerned with a study of our industrial society through laboratory-classroom experiences. The role of industry and technology is viewed in the study of the

[17] Lloyd V. Douglas, James T. Blanford, and Ruth I. Anderson, *Teaching Business Subjects*, Second edition (Englewood Cliffs, N.J.: Prentice-Hall, 1965), p. 11.
[18] Unfortunately, the same situation often prevails for art courses and other so-called nonacademic courses.
[19] C. A. Nolan, Carlos K. Hayden, and Dean R. Malsbary, *Principles and Problems of Business Education*, Third edition (Cincinnati: South-Western Publishing Company, 1967), p. 51.

. . . history, growth, and development of industrial organizations, materials, products, processes and related problems. . . . It provides experiences in developing basic skills and knowledge common to many occupations and professions.[20]

Industrial arts is usually a required subject in the junior high school and is offered as an aspect of general education. Students are introduced to various areas of industry and may study natural and synthetic materials, production methods, and the resulting products. Industrial and technological problems are also explored.

In the senior high school, industrial arts is generally offered on an elective basis. The courses become more technical and specialized and may include subjects such as the following: automotives, ceramics, design, drawing, electricity-electronics, graphic arts, metalworking, plastics, textiles, and woodworking. Though most industrial arts educators do not agree with him, Dr. Conant believes that these courses should develop skills that are marketable, i.e., they should prepare the student for a job and not simply give him a practical acquaintance with the industrial world.[21] This requires a teacher who is both qualified and vocationally oriented.

It must be remembered by the teacher that the students are being trained to get a skilled job and hold it in a competitive world. Not only must the teacher be qualified for the purpose, but the tools must be qualified too.[22]

Trade and industrial education should provide knowledge of good workmanship and design; skill in the use of the tools and machines of production; good work habits and appreciation of efficiency; resourcefulness, self-reliance, and self-discipline; and the ability to work well with others.[23]

While certification requirements vary, the prospective industrial arts teacher should have completed his bachelor's degree in an accredited college with a good program of industrial arts education. Actual experience in industry is a must, if the teacher is to be really well prepared. Furthermore, he needs to be creative and imaginative, to truly enjoy working with students, and to possess organizational abilities. Patience and calmness of disposition are also important, particularly for his work with individuals and small groups who are at the beginning stages of learning.

There is a pronounced need for industrial arts teachers and the opportunities in the field are good.

---

[20] American Industrial Arts Association, *A Career in Teaching Industrial Arts* (Washington, D.C.: the Association, n.d.).

[21] James B. Conant, *Slums and Suburbs* (New York: McGraw-Hill Book Company, 1961), p. 107.

[22] The Institute for Research, *Trade and Vocational Teaching as a Career*, Research Number 231 (Chicago: the Institute, 1966), p. 14.

[23] E. Dale Davis, *Focus on Secondary Education: An Introduction to Principles and Practices* (Glenview, Ill.: Scott Foresman and Company, 1966), p. 146.

Music Education

Music education in the public schools offers positions in teaching at the elementary or secondary level as well as in supervision of the music program. Music education is similar to art education in that in addition to the usual requirements for teaching one needs a special talent—in this case, musical talent. Not only talent and a liking for music are necessary, but also the desire to assist others in sharing in the beauty, joy, and satisfaction of music. The prospective music educator must be willing to develop his talent further so that he has capacity in both vocal and instrumental music. The Music Educators National Conference also recommends functional facility in piano for all music teachers.[24]

The opportunities in music education are good. The field of music education is so broad today that a capable teacher can generally secure a position that enables him to spend his time working with the phase of music that interests him most.[25] He may find that instrumental music interests him most and wish to work with this phase of music. On the other hand, he may want to help others become intelligent appreciators of music and thus work more in a classroom situation with general music. Or he may find that he would like to do several of these things. The music program, though, is not a standardized one and ". . . the teacher's duties in one community can be quite different from those in another."[26]

A good collegiate program of preparation for music teaching will provide experience in all areas of music. Proficiency in vocal and instrumental music will be developed, and opportunities will be afforded in conducting. There will be other music courses such as composition, arranging, harmony, and sight singing. All of this, of course, is in addition to work in general education and professional education.

When the new teacher becomes certified, he may decide to seek a position in elementary school music. Here he may be the special music teacher who actually teaches music to the boys and girls; or he may be the music consultant who assists the classroom teacher in planning her music program; or he may be an instrumental specialist who gives instrumental lessons and conducts the band or orchestra if the school has one.

In the junior high school and the senior high school, the music teacher may do a variety of things or may specialize. There are general and special music

[24] Music Educators National Conference, *A Career in Music Education* (Washington, D.C.: Music Educators National Conference, National Education Association, 1965), p. 11.
[25] *Ibid.*, p. 7.
[26] Ira C. Singleton, *Music in Secondary Schools* (Boston: Allyn and Bacon, 1963), p. 3.

classes as well as instrumental and vocal performing groups. The program will vary with the size of the school. As a matter of fact, in a small school district the music teacher may teach at both the elementary and secondary level. In any event, he will work with individuals and with large and small groups.

It would be fair to say that in a number of school systems music education is not well supported. This is partly due to the cost of a good program, but it is also due to the fact that the purpose of music education is not fully understood. To many, unfortunately, it is just a frill or "fun" and not considered an important part of the curriculum. More needs to be done to help some educators and part of the public to realize the value of music—not only its cultural value, but the good sense of aural beauty it can develop, the creative experience it can provide, and the life-long interest or recreation it can become.

Physical Education for Women

While there is an oversupply of men in physical education, there is a shortage of women in the field. Hence, the opportunities in physical education for women are excellent. This is especially true in the elementary school where there is growing recognition that physical education specialists are needed, particularly in grades 4, 5, and 6.[27] Therefore, attention here is directed to the career possibilities for women in elementary school physical education.

A good physical education program in the elementary school is based upon a thorough knowledge of how physical education can contribute to the overall growth and development of children at each age level. However, too many elementary schools have poor programs or no real program at all:

All too often elementary school physical education is a haphazard affair in which the teacher supervises the choosing of sides or the assembling in formation for playing a game, which has been endorsed as a favorite by the youngsters, and then stands on the sidelines until the ringing of the bell signifies the end of the physical education period. Obviously, while such an activity may be "physical," it is not "education" to any significant degree.[28]

The physical education period should provide systematic learning experiences and is different from recess or after-school play. However, it is not possible to give boys and girls all of the activity they need in one period, since most children should have between three to five hours of vigorous physical exercise each day.[29]

[27] Charles A. Bucher, *Foundations of Physical Education,* Fourth edition (St. Louis: The C. V. Mosby Company, 1964), pp. 553–554.
[28] Hollis F. Fait, *Physical Education for the Elementary School Child* (Philadelphia: W. B. Saunders Company, 1964), p. 3.
[29] Anna S. Espenschade, *Physical Education in the Elementary School* (Washington, D.C.: National Education Association, 1963), p. 19.

The physical education program is concerned with developing good physical fitness, motor skills and coordination, sound attitudes, and knowledge. "Fair play" and "good sportsmanship," taking turns, and abiding by the rules can be learned. Also, the role of play in transmitting the culture has been widely recognized.[30] Many forms of human movement are involved in the program: ". . . games and sports, rhythms and dance, and such exercises as gymnastics, apparatus, stunts, and tumbling." [31] In view of the increasing amount of leisure time available to adults and the value of moderate exercise for people of all ages, children should be encouraged to participate regularly in some form of physical activity and to cultivate interests and habits that can remain throughout life.

Since teachers of physical education frequently have responsibilities involving health education and administrative functions,[32] these areas should be included in the preparation of such teachers. Obviously, they need to be familiar with the methods and materials used in various physical education activities. Any good program to prepare physical education teachers should provide a thorough background, including such courses as anatomy, physiology, kinesiology, and chemistry. An understanding of the child and his growth and development is essential for a good physical education teacher.

The physical education teacher should have the qualities of any good teacher. However, she needs particularly to be in good health, enthusiastic, physically skilled, able in human relations, and capable of being a leader. Her work can bring much satisfaction as she attempts ". . . to help each child develop his capacities, broaden his interests, and find joy in play." [33]

School Counseling

The school counselor, along with the school psychologist and the school social worker, to be discussed later in the chapter, is a member of the pupil personnel services team.[34] Even though the counselor is concerned with the guidance function, the term *pupil personnel services* is used here because there has been a shift away from the term *school guidance*. The latter term has come to be confused and misunderstood, and the shift away from its use reflects a growing awareness that no one person can be all things to all people.[35] Today, the counselor works with a variety of specialists to provide the kinds of services that students need.

The actual work of a particular school counselor is not easy to describe be-

[30] *Ibid.*, p. 18.   [31] *Ibid.*, p. 19.   [32] Bucher, *op. cit.*, p. 433.
[33] Espenschade, *op. cit.*, p. 27.
[34] Richard P. Koeppe and John F. Bancroft, "Elementary and Secondary School Programs," American Educational Research Association, "Guidance, Counseling, and Personnel Services," *Review of Educational Research*, 36: 219, April, 1966.
[35] *Ibid.*, p. 228.

cause of differences among schools and among responsibilities assigned to counseling positions. Edward Roeber, acknowledging these differences, suggested that the secondary school counselor spends about 50–60 percent of his time for direct services to pupils such as counseling and working with large and small groups; 10–15 percent of his time for direct services to parents such as parent conferences and group meetings; 15–20 percent of his time for direct services to teachers and administrators such as individual consultations and case conferences; and 10–20 percent of his time for research and leadership activities such as improving testing plans and records systems and improving relations with community resource groups.[36]

The Commission on Guidance in American Schools has listed four major responsibilities for the school counselor:

a. *counseling [with] students* on matters of self-understanding, decision-making, and planning, using both the interview and group situations;

b. *consulting with staff and parents* on questions of student understanding and student management;

c. *studying changes in the character of the student population* and [making a continuing interpretation of] this information [to] the school [administration] and to curriculum-development committees;

d. *performing a liaison function* between other school and community counseling resources and facilitating their use by teachers and students.[37]

In order to function effectively, the counselor has to be well prepared for his work. To be certified in almost all states, a prospective counselor has to have had teaching experience. Thus, counseling education will be undertaken at the graduate level, and in some institutions the program is a two-year one. The program should include much work in psychology and the social sciences; developing an understanding of educational philosophy and school curriculum patterns; applied or technique courses such as counseling and measurement; supervised experience; developing a basic understanding of research methods; and an introduction to the ethical and legal responsibilities in counseling.[38]

The position of secondary school counselor is fairly well established, but the position of elementary school counselor is a relatively new one. There are some differences of opinion as to just what functions the elementary school counselor should perform. One group sees him as a professional person who will provide services to all pupils and whose education can be similar to that of secondary school counselors; another group sees his major contribution as

[36] Edward C. Roeber, *Orientation to the Job of a Counselor* (Chicago: Science Research Associates, 1961), p. 13.

[37] C. Gilbert Wrenn, *The Counselor in a Changing World* (Washington, D.C.: American Personnel and Guidance Association, 1962), p. 141.

[38] *Ibid.*, pp. 167–168.

that of consulting with teachers, parents, and principals about children who have learning problems. This latter group also feels that the education of the elementary school counselor should be different from that of the secondary school counselor.[39] Furthermore, the Commission on Guidance in American Schools indicated that the elementary school counselor has three specialized capacities: nonverbal communication with children; skills in reading diagnosis and accompanying emotional problems; skill in working with parents individually and in small groups.[40]

Many of the desirable characteristics of a school counselor are similar to those of an effective teacher. He surely must be mature, emotionally stable, and have much self-knowledge and understanding; he must really know, like, and understand young people; he must have good judgment and common sense; he must have leadership qualities and a wholesome philosophy of life; he must have a strong sense of professional ethics and a dedication to his work. All of this he must have, for he works with and influences the growth of human personalities.

School Psychology

School psychology is so new as a profession that its roles are not yet uniformly defined, nor are the services it should provide fully agreed upon. Essentially, school psychologists apply the principles and techniques of psychology to educational problems within the school setting. There are, unfortunately, not enough school psychologists; too many young people do not have access to these specialists.[41]

The school psychologist needs to have preparation in both psychology and education. While most school psychologists are presently trained at the one- or two-year graduate level, the doctorate will surely become the standard of the future.[42] Persons aspiring to work in the field of school psychology should have high intelligence, fine character, maturity, a strong desire to assist young people, and an interest in applying the science of psychology in a school setting. Unable or disinterested people in a number of educational positions can do harm to young people, but probably no position is more dangerous in this sense than the position of school psychologist. Very able and dedicated practitioners are a must in the field of school psychology.

The school psychologist works cooperatively with other school personnel such as the school counselor, the school social worker, reading and speech

---

[39] Koeppe and Bancroft, *op. cit.*, p. 229.   [40] Wrenn, *op. cit.*, p. 150.
[41] Paul E. Eiserer, *The School Psychologist,* The Library of Education (Washington, D.C.: The Center for Applied Research in Education, 1963), pp. 1–5.
[42] *Ibid.*, p. 6.

specialists, the school nurse, administrators, and classroom teachers. His primary roles are those of assessment and remediation. He assesses the abilities, aptitudes, interests, achievements, personality, and adjustment of individual students. Young people are usually referred to the school psychologist because of difficulties in learning, behavior problems in the classroom, or personality disorders. It is his job to diagnose the difficulties and determine remedial steps to be taken. He will make use of all possible data in an intensive study, a *case study,* of a particular youngster and his problem. He may make classroom observations of the student and conduct interviews with the child, his teacher, and perhaps the parents and the principal.

After his study, the school psychologist will probably confer with the child's classroom teacher to discuss remedial steps. The teacher may be an important factor, because remediation usually involves changes in the people and circumstances that brought about the problem as well as changes in the child himself. For younger children, the school psychologist may use play therapy; for older children, a counseling program may be used. Perhaps some sort of group therapy may be utilized.

In his consultant role, the school psychologist works not only with the educational staff but also with parents. Parents can often provide important information about a youngster and assist in a remedial program. Then too, parental problems that are complicating the student's problems can sometimes be identified. His consultant role is expanding in some schools where the school psychologist is helping to improve the functioning of teachers within the classroom. He can bring much knowledge of human growth and development to the teacher as well as knowledge of how groups can function better within the school. He can also assist teachers to function more effectively as persons through increased self-knowledge and insight into their behavior and the behavior of others.

There are other tasks that the school psychologist must undertake. He must complete a number of reports on particular students. Continually, he adds information to the records kept on students. (These records are best if they are cumulative, i.e., if the records contain information about the child's complete school career chronologically.) He frequently is called upon to classify pupils for special education.[43] In the future, the school psychologist will probably be more involved in the research function in both active and consultative roles.[44]

School Social Work

A relatively new member of the pupil personnel services team is the school social worker, who attempts to use the methods of social work to help children ". . . whose problems in school stem from social and emotional causes

[43] These pupils are discussed in Chapter 9 under "Exceptional Children."
[44] Eiserer, *passim.*

within the child, his home, or some other area of his environment." [45] The school social worker searches for the causes of the youngster's difficulties and makes an effort to remedy or at least modify the situation. In doing so, he may often work directly with the child, his teacher, and his parents.

Who are the children and young people to whom the school social worker renders service? They are the emotionally immature; those with poor social adjustments; those who dislike school, are disinterested, and are frequently absent; those who are resentful toward discipline and authority; and others who are not achieving as they should because of social and emotional problems. These problems may be due to the child's attitudes or personality or such factors as an alcoholic parent, a broken home, trouble with the law, or a pregnancy for a high school girl.

The four types of services provided by the school social worker are casework, collaboration, coordination, and consultation.[46] Most of the worker's time, however, is spent on casework and consultation.[47] In casework, he works directly with the child and has frequent conferences with the child's parents and teachers. While regularly scheduled casework interviews are part of the procedure, each youngster and situation may present variations that require different procedures. In his first contact with the home, the worker explains the nature of school social work services and secures the parents' permission to work on the case. Then, in addition to his interviews with the child, he makes use of all the school's records on the youngster and perhaps observes him in a classroom or playground situation. Next, a plan is developed which, it is hoped, will bring about a better school adjustment for the child. The school social worker may well involve other community agencies in the case, if such agencies have been or are presently working with the child or the family.

In consultative cases, the school social worker does not work directly with the child, but he frequently holds conferences with the classroom teacher and other school personnel about the child. Here, the classroom teacher carries the main responsibility for improving the child's adjustment with the assistance of the school social worker. In cooperative cases, the school social worker serves as liaison between the school and other community agencies which have the major responsibility for a case. The school social worker, in supportive cases, ". . . sees the child from time to time for the purpose of supporting him in his school adjustment." [48]

The school social worker needs to have all the qualities of other workers in the field of pupil personnel services such as the school counselor and the school psychologist, previously discussed. He, however, needs particular skill

[45] Joseph P. Hourihan, "School Social Work Services," Frances C. Rosecrance and Velma D. Hayden, *School Guidance and Personnel Services* (Boston: Allyn and Bacon, 1960), pp. 138–139.
[46] Jerry L. Kelley, "Children with Problems: What Does the School Social Worker Do?" *NEA Journal*, 51:57, January, 1962.
[47] Hourihan, *op. cit.*, p. 145.   [48] Hourihan, *loc. cit.*

in interpersonal relations, for almost all of his time is spent in dealing with others. He needs to have the training and experience of both a teacher and a social caseworker; this usually requires two years of graduate study. The work is not without its difficulties and disappointments. The hours may be irregular and may include evening and weekend calls. The school social worker must carry, at times, quite an emotional load in continually working with young people's problems. And he has his share of failures and discouragement. However, he has the opportunity to render real service and to achieve real satisfaction.

Speech Therapy

There is much need for speech therapists to work with the more than two million school children who have impaired speech. The field of speech correction is relatively new in the public schools, the first such program having been established in New York in 1908. But the program has grown greatly and so has the demand for speech clinicians. Speech handicapped children represent the largest group in the area of special education in our public elementary and secondary schools.[49]

What is the work of the speech therapist? What areas come under his responsibility? The speech therapist is responsible for the diagnosis and appraisal of a particular speech handicap; the development of a retraining program; the encouragement of cooperative activity on the part of those involved in the problem (the child, the parents, the speech therapist, the classroom teacher, doctors, nurses, and so forth); the dissemination of information to all those involved; and the interpretation of the profession to the general public.[50]

In addition to the program of speech therapy, a speech improvement program can be instituted for children with minor speech and voice deviations. Such a program can help to decrease the number of children needing speech therapy. The classroom teacher can carry out the speech improvement program with the assistance of the therapist. The therapist thus serves as a consultant and provider of in-service training for teachers, a designer of the speech improvement curriculum, and a coordinator of speech improvement with the regular curriculum and the remedial speech program.[51]

[49] Wendell Johnson and Dorothy Moeller, eds., *Speech Handicapped School Children*, Third edition (New York: Harper & Row, Publishers, 1967), p. 2.

[50] *Ibid.,* p. 451.

[51] Theodore D. Hanley and Frederic L. Darley, "Summary: New Horizons," Research Committee of the American Speech and Hearing Association, "Public School Speech and Hearing Services," *The Journal of Speech and Hearing Disorders,* Monograph Supplement 8, U.S. Office of Education Cooperative Research Project No. 649 (8191), July, 1961, p. 129.

Being a good speech therapist requires much. One has to have a thorough academic preparation at the undergraduate level, and graduate training is desirable; the ability to work with people in individual and group settings; much understanding and an infinite amount of patience; maturity and the ability to work with little supervision; a pleasing personality; and a real desire to help children.

There are difficulties in the work. For one thing, the caseload of children is frequently high. There are many records to keep and reports to make out, both of which are very important. Relations with parents are not always easy or smooth. Some parents may not readily accept the fact of their child's problem, nor may they be fully cooperative. Teachers are not always "happy" to have children leave the classroom for therapy sessions. And administrators and the general public do not always understand the nature of nor the value of a good speech therapy program. However, the work of the speech therapist in the public schools is both important and necessary. Able and dedicated people are needed.

32
Auxiliary School Personnel

GARDA W. BOWMAN AND GORDON J. KLOPF

There are presently increasing numbers of auxiliary personnel employed in the nation's schools. Some of you will have attended schools where teacher aides helped your classroom teachers. The inadequacy of the preparation of these auxiliary school personnel will, in all probability, only become evident as you yourself prepare for a career in professional education. One of the colleges that the federal government has asked to help in its study of auxiliary school per-

SOURCE: This selection is a condensation of the 1966 study entitled *Auxiliary School Personnel: Their Roles, Training, and Institutionalization,* conducted for the Office of Educational Opportunity by the Bank Street College of Education.

Gordon J. Klopf is Provost and Dean of the Faculties at Bank Street College of Education in New York City. He also actively participates in professional organizations and serves as educational consultant to a number of American colleges, the New York State Department of Education, and the Department of Instruction for the Commonwealth of Puerto Rico.

Garda W. Bowman, Program Associate at Bank Street College of Education, was Research Coordinator for the Study of Auxiliary School Personnel in Education, while teaching and also serving as Program Coordinator. Among her other professional pursuits, Dr. Bowman in recent years has served as a member of the National Panel on Career Opportunities Program for the United States Office of Education, while continuing to publish articles on the disadvantaged child and the paraprofessional in education.

sonnel is the Bank Street College of Education in New York City. Here, Bowman and Klopf report on some of the benefits and the foreseeable difficulties of auxiliary personnel in the school. They have also made specific recommendations for consideration of the federal government and agencies responsible for staffing all schools.

THE EMPLOYMENT of teacher aides, teacher assistants, guidance aides, health aides, family workers and other auxiliary personnel in schools increased sharply during the mid-sixties. Often, however, the circumstances under which funds could be secured as well as the urgency of the need required a crash program. The essential component of preparation was therefore lacking, a preparation not only of the nonprofessionals themselves but even more importantly *of the teachers and other professionals with whom they would be working.*

Several convergent forces—social, educational and economic—have contributed to the mushrooming of such employment at a pace which sometimes precluded adequate orientation:

1. The ever-changing and expanding needs for school services;
2. Acute shortages of professionals to meet these needs;
3. New dimensions in education, requiring a more complex and demanding role for teachers;
4. Heightened awareness of the special learning needs of disadvantaged children and youth;
5. Recognition of the communication blocks which often exist between middle-class professionals and lower-class pupils;
6. The plight of undereducated people unable to compete in an increasingly automated economy;
7. The availability of Federal funds for the employment of low-income nonprofessionals in education, through such sources as the Office of Economic Opportunity, the Manpower Development and Training Act and Title I of the Elementary and Secondary Education Act of 1965.

The U.S. Office of Economic Opportunity, alert to this critical situation, requested Bank Street College of Education to conduct a study of auxiliary personnel in education. This study, exploratory and developmental in nature, had three specific areas of inquiry: role development, training and institutionalization of auxiliaries in school systems. One component of the study was the coordination and analysis of fifteen demonstration training programs, eleven of which were conducted during the summer of 1966. The other four started in September, 1966. In these programs professionals and nonprofessionals studied and worked together to increase the effectiveness of auxiliary personnel in various school situations.

The auxiliaries learned specific skills and gained some basic understandings needed to operate in a school setting. The teacher trainees learned in reality situations how to utilize and relate to other adults in a classroom.

The auxiliary trainees in the summer institutes included Navaho Indians from a reservation; low-income whites from Appalachia; Mexican-Americans and Negroes in California; predominantly Negroes in Gary, Indiana, in Jackson, Mississippi, and in Detroit; mothers receiving aid to dependent children in Maine; Puerto Ricans, Negroes and others in East Harlem; Puerto Ricans in disadvantaged sections of Metropolitan San Juan; and a cross-cultural, cross-class group of trainees in Boston.

This chapter, based on the experience thus far in the demonstration programs, considers what seems to help or harm effective utilization of auxiliary personnel in education. It offers: (1) a rationale for the use of auxiliaries in school systems; (2) some difficulties which might be encountered; and (3) some recommendations for coping with these difficulties.

Rationale

The question is often asked, "Should the school system be required to solve all the social problems of our time?" This leads to a second question, "Is the utilization of low-income workers as auxiliary school personnel aimed primarily at creating jobs for the poor, at coping with acute manpower shortage or at helping to meet the needs of pupils?"

To those who conducted demonstration training programs during the summer of 1966, the answer appeared to be that the essential criterion of any innovation in education is whether it helps to meet the learning and developmental needs of children and youth. However, they believed that the learning-teaching process can be truly effective only in relation to the totality of the child's experience. The school, like every other institution, operates within a social context, not in isolation.

The sponsors of the demonstration programs believed that even if there were no shortage of teachers, the quality of education would be enhanced by introducing more adults into the classroom, adults selected on the basis of their concern for children and their potential as supportive personnel rather than primarily on the basis of previous training. They saw, too, great possibilities in the professional-nonprofessional team in enabling the teacher to differentiate the learning-teaching process to meet the individual needs of pupils. They saw, too, in this multilevel team approach, escape from rigid structuring in the classroom, for example, more freedom of movement, more small groupings, more independent activities than would be feasible for one teacher often operating under difficult conditions. In fact, the teacher with this assistance might be able to experiment with innovative techniques which he had long been wanting to inaugurate.

These values are universal, that is to say, they might be realized through the effective utilization of auxiliaries in any classroom regardless of the composition of the school population or the socioeconomic background of the auxiliaries. The proponents of this new development in education saw the possiblity of multiple benefits, in all school situations:

1. *To the pupil,* by providing more individualized attention by concerned adults, more mobility in the classroom and more opportunity for innovation;
2. *To the teacher,* by rendering his role more satisfying in terms of status and more manageable in terms of teaching conditions;
3. *To the other professionals,* by increasing the scope and effectiveness of their activities;
4. *To the auxiliary,* by providing meaningful employment, which contributes at one and the same time to his own development and to the needs of society;
5. *To the school administrator,* by providing some answers to his dilemma of ever-increasing needs for school services coupled with shortage of professionals to meet these needs—*a* solution, not *the* solution, and certainly not a panacea;
6. *To family life,* by giving auxiliaries, many of whom are or may someday become parents, the opportunity to learn child-development principles in a reality situation;
7. *To the community at large,* by providing a means through which unemployed and educationally disadvantaged people may enter the mainstream of productivity.

In addition to these global considerations, there are some specific benefits which may flow from the utilization of indigenous personnel as auxiliaries in schools serving disadvantaged neighborhoods.

The auxiliary who has actually lived in a disadvantaged environment often speaks to the disadvantaged child or youth in a way that is neither strange nor threatening. He may help the new pupil to adjust to the unfamiliar world of the school without undue defensiveness; to fill the gaps, if any, in his preparation for learning; and to build upon his strengths, which may have more relevance to the new situation than the child himself realizes. This cultural bridge is seen as an asset in and of itself.

Moreover, the low-income auxiliary, having faced up to and overcome some of the difficulties and frustrations the children now face, may serve to motivate the child to further effort. His very presence in a role of some status in the school says to the child, "It can be done; it is worth trying to do; you, too, can succeed here." This has far more meaning than the story of a Ralph Bunche or a Felisia de Gautier to one who obviously lacks the exceptional abilities of these great but remote persons.

Naturally, this message would be imparted more forcefully if the faculty, too, were mixed in terms of socioeconomic background. As work-study programs become increasingly available, economic integration may become more frequent in school faculties. Meantime, the low-income auxiliary sometimes provides incentive to poor pupils which would otherwise be lacking.

Further, the auxiliary from the child's own neighborhood may be able to interpret to the middle-class professional some aspects of the behavior of a child who is not responding in school. The auxiliary may, in turn, interpret the goals of the school and the learning-teaching process to both parent and child. To reach the child for a few hours a day without reaching those who influence his mode of living may be of little avail. The parent who doesn't understand a school official sometimes finds helpful a neighbor serving as a school auxiliary.

The fact that low-income auxiliaries may and often do facilitate communication between school and community does not mean that *all* poor people can work effectively with poor pupils and their families. Naturally, any candidate for school employment should be carefully screened for those personal characteristics needed to work with children and youth. However, the demonstration programs have revealed that flexible and imaginative selection may discover potential in poor people that has been overlooked thus far, potential which may be developed as an asset in a school setting.

Possible Difficulties

The difficulties anticipated by each of the groups involved in the demonstration training programs differed widely. For school administrators they were largely "how to" problems, such as the establishment of fiscal policies and the whole process of setting up a new hierarchy of positions with job descriptions, job titles, salaries, increments, role prerogatives and training requirements for advancement. Another "how to" problem for the superintendent was orienting the principals, who in turn were faced with the problem of interpreting the new program to the teachers and other professionals so that they would utilize rather than ignore, reject or resent their would-be helpers. The principals' task was determining who would conduct the training of both professionals and nonprofessionals and how to secure such personnel. Often this had to be accomplished within and in spite of institutional rigidities. Moreover, the school administrator was responsible for involving local institutions of higher learning and the indigenous leadership in the planning, and for interpreting the new program to the Board of Education and to the broader community.

The professionals—teachers, supervisors, guidance counselors, *et al.*— were primarily concerned that professional standards should be maintained. They wondered whether the auxiliaries might try to take over, but they were even more concerned lest the administrators, caught in the bind between increasing enrollment and decreasing availability of professional personnel, might assign functions to the auxiliaries that were essentially professional in nature. The teachers, specifically, believed that teacher aides might sometimes be assigned to a class without the supervision of a certified professional. Teachers, particularly, questioned whether funds that might have been used to reduce the teaching load would be used instead to employ auxiliaries, while increasing rather than decreasing the size of classes.

Teachers and other professionals also doubted that adequate time would be set aside during school hours for *planning* and *evaluating* with the auxiliaries assigned to them. Moreover, many professionals were not accustomed to the new leadership function which they were being asked to perform. Some felt threatened by another adult in the classroom. Others could not envision ways in which to use this new source of assistance effectively. Still others anticipated that the auxiliaries might not speak in standard English and hence might undermine their own efforts to improve the pupils' language skills. A few wondered whether the pupils would respond more easily to the auxiliaries than to themselves and whether they might therefore lose close, personal contacts with their pupils.

The auxiliaries, themselves, had many trepidations. They, too, appeared to be concerned about the differences in their background, values and patterns of speech from those prevailing in the school. While the professionals often considered the effects of such factors upon pupils, the auxiliaries tended to become defensive and uncomfortable because of these differences. On the other hand, some auxiliaries were resentful, particularly in preschool centers, when they observed only the end result of the planning, i.e., what was actually done for pupils and by whom in the classroom. Not understanding the diagnostic skills required of the teacher in designing the program to meet the needs of individual pupils, these auxiliaries were heard to say, "We do the same things as the teachers; why should they be paid more?"

It became evident that the problem of defining and redefining one's own role was only one aspect of the challenge. An even more important task was defining, understanding and accepting the role of the person with whom one was to work. This was equally true of professionals and auxiliaries as they entered into a new, sensitive and complex relationship. In fact, one of the insights gained from the demonstration programs was that many of the doubts and concerns could have been avoided if there had been adequate specification of roles and functions prior to the operation.

In those programs where these possible difficulties were discussed by school administrators, university representatives and community leaders in preplanning sessions, the problems were either ameliorated or prevented. Usually, only the unexpected proves disastrous.

Preliminary Recommendations

In essence, the experiences in the eleven demonstration programs which were operating during the summer of 1966 seemed to indicate that the desired results from the use of auxiliary personnel in a given school situation would not be realized unless certain preconditions were established, so as to avoid or resolve the difficulties listed above.

The specific recommendations that follow, based on the experiences thus far, refer to all types of auxiliaries, not merely to those from low-income groups.

Role Definition and Development

• That role specifications and prerogatives of auxiliaries be clearly defined, in order to prevent either their *underutilization* by unconvinced professionals or their *overutilization* by harried administrators faced by manpower shortages.

• That the functions of individual auxiliaries and of the professionals with whom they work be developed reciprocally in terms of the dynamics of each specific situation.

• That role *definition,* which gives security, be balanced with role *development,* which gives variety and scope to the program.

• That the whole range of teaching functions be re-examined, so as to identify those that might be performed by nonprofessionals, such as monitorial, escorting, technical, clerical and the more important functions directly related to instruction and to home-school relations.

• That teaching functions be further examined to identify the more complex and highly professional functions which should be performed by a teacher alone, such as diagnosis of the learning needs of pupils, planning programs to meet these needs and orchestrating other adults in the classroom in the execution of such programs.

Training

1. Preservice:

• That there be preservice training of auxiliaries to develop communication skills and other concrete skills as well as the basic understanding needed for success during their first work experience, thus bolstering self-confidence and encouraging further effort.

• That the training be differentiated to meet the special needs and characteristics of each group, considering such variables as the age of the trainees and the levels (elementary, middle or secondary) for which they are being trained.

• That there be orientation of both the administrators and the professionals with whom the auxiliaries will be working, including an opportunity for the expression of any doubts or fears which may exist, and for consideration of the new and challenging leadership role of the professionals vis-à-vis the nonprofessionals.

• That institutes for administrators, teachers and auxiliaries be conducted where a common approach to collaborative education can be developed.

• That all preservice training include a field teaching experience where professionals and nonprofessionals can try out and evaluate their team approach under the close supervision of the training staff.

• That training of trainers and supervisors be provided.

2. In-service:

• That there be a comprehensive, continuing, in-depth program of development and supervision of auxiliaries closely integrated with a long-term program of stable, open-ended employment, so that each level of work responsibility will have comparable training available.

• That mechanisms for process observations and feedback be developed with a spirit of openness to suggestion so that dynamic role concepts and relationships may emerge which are relevant to each specific situation.

3. Higher education:

• That the cooperation of two-year and community colleges be sought in the development of programs for auxiliaries who would move into roles requiring more knowledge and skills than at the entry level. For example, library aides might have one or two years' training in the librarian's role.

• That the cooperation of colleges of teacher education and departments of education in institutions of higher learning be sought in two respects, first to provide educational opportunities for auxiliaries who desire to qualify for advancement to the professional level, and second to incorporate into their curricula the expanded role concept of the teacher in collaborative education.

Since the demonstration programs conducted during the summer of 1966 were primarily for purposes of role development and training, the third focus of the study—institutionalization—was not a component of these demonstrations except in the programs conducted by school systems: Detroit, Michigan, Gary, Indiana, and Puerto Rico. However, in every training program, the need for institutionalization was stressed by staff and participants alike. They believed that the anticipated benefits had been realized in their training experience, but they also believed that training for jobs that were not stable or were at best dead-end would be frustrating to the participants. The following recommendations on institutionalization are, in effect, a look into the future rather than a look backwards at the summer institutes. They represent the developments necessary for the optimum effectiveness of auxiliary personnel in American education.

Institutionalization

• That when and if a school system decides to utilize auxiliary personnel, the program be incorporated as an integral part of the school system, not treated as an extraneous adjunct to the system.

• That goals be thought through carefully, stated clearly and implemented by means of definite procedures.

• That there be cooperative planning by the school systems, local institutions of higher learning and the indigenous leadership of the community served by the schools, both before the program has been inaugurated and after it has been institutionalized.

• That each step on the career ladder be specified in terms of functions, salaries, increments and role prerogatives, moving from routine functions at the entry level to functions that are more directly related to the learning-teaching process.

• That professional standards be preserved and that all tasks performed by an auxiliary be supervised by a teacher.

• That encouragement of those who desire to train and qualify for advancement be expressed in such a way that others who prefer to remain at the entry level feel no lack of job satisfaction, status and recognition of the worth of their services; in other words, that there should be *opportunity* but not *compulsion* for upward mobility.

• That time be scheduled during the school day or after school hours with extra compensation [1] for teachers and auxiliaries and other professional-non-

[1] This arrangement would vary according to the pattern established in each school system.

professional teams to evaluate their experiences and plan together for the coming day.

• That the quantity and quality of supervision be re-examined in the light of the needs of this program.

• That the personal needs and concerns of both professionals and auxiliaries be dealt with in counseling sessions as they adjust to a new and sometimes threatening situation.

• That parents be involved in the program both as auxiliaries and as recipients of the services of family workers.

• That contacts be established with professional groups.

• That a continuing program of interpretation among educators and to the broader community be developed, with emphasis upon feedback as well as imparting information.

• That an advisory committee of school administrators, supervisors, teachers, auxiliaries, parents, community leaders and university consultants be established to evaluate and improve the utilization of auxiliaries in each school where such a program is undertaken.

33

Preparation for Careers in Education

NATIONAL EDUCATION ASSOCIATION

This selection, taken from the 1968 statement of the National Commission of Teacher Education and Professional Standards (NCTEPS), presents you with a sound basis on which to plan and prepare for a career in education. You would benefit a great deal at this point in your study by reviewing the selections on teaching in the sections "The Past and the Present" and "Innovations in Education" in Part Two of this book. Those selections not only offer a comparison of the past and present emphases, but they also will direct your evaluation of teachers and what is expected of them in their role. Try to keep in mind

SOURCE: *NEA Journal—1968: Careers in Education,* pp. 21–24. Reprinted by permission of the publisher.

that as the pace of present cultural change increases, it is virtually impossible to prepare specifically for any one role in education. Many new careers have appeared in the past few decades and many more will undoubtedly appear in the future. Will you be ready for your place in education?

THERE ARE many ways to prepare for careers in education. A bachelor's degree is required for almost all of them except auxiliary personnel work. All states require the four-year degree for secondary school teachers; all but five require it for elementary teachers, and, of these, two have provided for the degree requirement by 1969 and 1972 respectively. Increasingly, the master's degree is expected of those considered to be fully qualified teachers, and some states require beginning teachers to obtain this degree within a specific period of time if they are to continue teaching. Many school systems and many education associations provide teachers programs of inservice education to maintain their professional knowledge and skills at the highest level possible.

More preparation is required of those entering the teaching profession at postsecondary levels; a master's degree is generally the minimum preparation for junior college teachers, and four-year colleges and universities seek faculty members who either have doctoral degrees or are working toward them. Professional education careers other than teaching—school or system administration, for example—generally require between one and three years of specialized graduate study, and some teaching experience is valuable in many of them.

The four- or five-year program for teachers consists of general education, specialized education in the fields the student expects to teach, and professional education. This last includes study of the history and philosophy of education and learning; the psychology, growth, and development of children; teaching techniques; classroom guidance; tests and measurements; and curriculum and organization.

An important part of a teacher's professional education is supervised student teaching, usually done in the senior year of college. This offers opportunities for practical application of what the prospective teacher has learned, through actual classroom teaching under the supervision of an experienced teacher. College students are increasingly using opportunities for classroom experience as teacher aides even earlier in their college years. Internships are becoming commonly available, in which students serve as teachers, receive salaries, and work under supervision. These kinds of interaction between the schools and the institutions that train teachers can provide valuable information concerning what the schools need from their teachers and how teacher education programs can provide for these needs.

Teacher education programs are available in 1,200 institutions accredited by their states. Of these, the greatest number by far are private liberal arts colleges (598), universities (305), and public general colleges (207). The others are junior colleges (39), technical schools (31), teachers colleges (19), or unclassified (1). In 1964, 53 percent of the graduates prepared to teach came from private liberal arts or public general colleges; 41.9 percent came from universities; and 5.1 percent, from teachers colleges.*

Preparation for teaching consisting of a bachelor of arts or science degree and a master of arts in teaching (MAT) is a regular degree program through which people with bachelor's degrees in liberal arts can obtain certification as teachers. The MAT program may be one or two years in length and includes education courses, specialized subject matter preparation, and student teaching or internship.

The Teacher Corps, a federal program, and programs like it sponsored by foundations or similar groups and local school districts provide college graduates in fields other than education with training in teaching the disadvantaged, leading to a master's degree and teaching certification. The Teacher Corps also accepts some applicants with only two years' college education. This program provides participants with an intensive preservice course, similar to that offered by the Peace Corps, followed by education courses in a college or university, experience as teacher aides and then as solo teachers or teaching team members, and experience in working with the communities in which their schools are located. Each group of five trainees works with a certificated teacher experienced in teaching the disadvantaged.

The MAT, Teacher Corps, and other programs sponsored by colleges and universities, state departments of education, and local school systems make it possible for persons whose completed education is in other fields to begin careers in education. In some cases, such persons can gain classroom experience while they complete the requirements for certification. Special certification programs are available in some states for specialized groups such as military personnel and Peace Corps returnees. Development has begun of programs to enable persons who are not college graduates to fulfill certification requirements while working part time or alternate terms in the schools.

College Costs

The cost of attending college rises each year, but each year also brings new ways to help students meet their economic needs.

Costs depend on the college chosen and one's personal living habits. Aver-

* The above figures are quoted from the reports of the National Education Association Research Division.

age college expenditures at four-year institutions range from around $1,050 to $3,200 a year. In general, costs to the individual are less at publicly supported universities and colleges than at private schools.

Loans, scholarships, and work-study programs are some of the methods by which students meet educational costs. The best source of information on such matters is the financial-aid officer of the college.

Four programs of federal assistance in financing a college education are administered by the Division of Student Financial Aid, U.S. Office of Education, Department of Health, Education, and Welfare, Washington, D.C. 20202. These programs are college work-study, National Defense Education Act student loans, Educational Opportunity Grants, and guaranteed loans. The details of each program change periodically as Congress enacts new legislation to implement them.

The colleges and universities themselves make available various kinds of scholarships. Many state departments of education offer scholarships or low-cost loans to state residents. Social, civic, and fraternal organizations in some communities offer scholarships or loans. So do local parent-teacher associations, teachers associations, church groups, and industrial groups and corporations.

Students often help finance their college education by working at summer or part-time jobs. College student-aid officers offer assistance to students who wish to find part-time jobs while enrolled in college.

Accreditation

Accreditation is one important factor to consider when choosing a college. Accreditation is a process whereby an agency indicates that a college or a university or a program of study has met certain predetermined qualifications and standards. There are three kinds of accreditation of teacher education institutions—state, regional, and national.

State approval is basic, because it generally assures graduates of approved four-year teacher education programs that they will be eligible for certification to teach in the state.

Regional accreditation indicates the adequacy of the institution as a whole, including faculty, curriculum, and facilities.

Accreditation by the National Council for Accreditation of Teacher Education ensures that an institution has met national standards for its program of teacher education.

The current catalog of a college or university almost always indicates the kinds of accreditation held. Annual lists of approved teacher education institutions within a given state are generally available on request from the state department of education. A list of institutions holding NCATE accreditation for their programs of teacher education can be obtained from the National Council for Accreditation of Teacher Education, 1750 Pennsylvania Avenue, N.W., Washington, D.C. 20006. A complete list of teacher education institutions, showing accreditation and types of programs offered by each, will be found in *A Manual on Certification Requirements for School Personnel in the United States*. This publication is updated every third year by the NEA National Commission on Teacher Education and Professional Standards in cooperation with the National Association of State Directors of Teacher Education and Certification.

Certification

Each of the states defines the legal requirements for various kinds of positions in its public schools. Educators who qualify receive a document called a license, a certificate, or a credential. The requirements vary from state to state and in accordance with job responsibilities—subject or level taught or type of service performed. In most states a certificate not only provides a license to hold a position in the public schools but also specifies any limitations concerning subjects to be taught or other duties.

In recent years it has become easier for a person who is fully qualified in one state to meet certification requirements in other states. For example, approximately 30 states now grant regular initial teaching certificates under most circumstances to out-of-state applicants who have completed approved teacher education programs in institutions accredited by the National Council for Accreditation of Teacher Education.

EVALUATION

NATIONAL EDUCATION ASSOCIATION, **Choosing a Career**

1. In "Choosing a Career," what initial requirements are given for selection of a suitable occupation?

2. (a) What two sources does the selection give for educational materials on occupations?

   (b) Where would one look for vocational counseling and aptitude testing?

3. "Choosing a Career" names six areas of knowledge crucial to a career decision. Name the six.

4. Why does the author equate a career in education with our current kind of society?

5. According to the author, what factors account for several different careers in one lifetime?

SYLVESTER J. BALASSI, **Careers in Education**

6. (a) Name the six teaching careers Balassi discusses.

   (b) How might this selection be significant to a student considering a career in education?

7. What reasons does Balassi give for his choice in discussing these teaching careers?

8. (a) What other two areas of careers in education does he discuss?

   (b) Name the careers in each area.

   (c) What reasons are given for the author's decision to discuss both of these areas?

9. How does Balassi say that the attractions of a career in education are changing?

10. Name four specific areas, according to Balassi, in which an educator has a marked impact on the future.

GARDA W. BOWMAN and GORDON J. KLOPF, **Auxiliary School Personnel**

11. In "Auxiliary School Personnel," Bowman and Klopf identified two components of preparation as essential to the effective placing of auxiliary personnel in the schools. Identify them.

12. The authors have given reasons why adequate orientations for the most effective functioning of paraprofessionals in schools has been precluded by certain rapidly changing social, educational, and economic factors. What are these reasons?

13. (a) How did the Bank Street College of Education become involved in a study of auxiliary personnel in education?

    (b) What was the nature of the study?

    (c) What was its general objective?

14. State the specific objectives for (1) the auxiliaries and (2) the teacher trainees given in "Auxiliary School Personnel."

15. List the various cultural groups and their location as represented by the auxiliary trainees who participated in the eleven 1966 summer demonstration training programs of the Bank Street College studies.

16. One essential criterion of any innovation in education is found to be the answer to those responsible for the summer training programs of this study.
    (a) What is this criterion?

    (b) What other conviction is held by these people in relation to this work for the schools?

17. List the seven advantages (values) regarded as "global" considerations of having auxiliary personnel at work in schools.

18. Name the three focal points of the Bank Street College studies.

19. Sum up the authors' specific recommendations for each of the three focuses given above.

NATIONAL EDUCATION ASSOCIATION, **Preparation for Careers in Education**

20. List the major requirement given in "Preparation for Careers in Education" for elementary and secondary school teachers.

21. What major requirement is generally minimal for teaching in (a) junior colleges, (b) four-year colleges and universities, (c) other professional education careers other than teaching?

22. (a) What is included in the four- or five-year teacher education program under professional education preparation?

    (b) What values in supervised student teaching have been indicated here?

23. (a) In what other two ways have future teachers been getting classroom experience earlier in their college years?

    (b) What two added contributions to education do these kinds of interaction between the schools and teacher training institutions make?

24. What is the MAT program?

25. What is the Teacher Corps?

26. The cost of college education is a major factor when your decision is being made for a career in education.
    (a) Write to two or three colleges in which you may be interested for costs, student-aid assistance information, and latest information on scholarships available to you.

    (b) Write for information on the four programs of federal assistance in financing a college education to the address given in this selection.

    (c) Compare these data and use what you have learned to continue your education if a career in education is now your firm choice.

FOR FURTHER READING

Bowman, Garda W., and Gordon J. Klopf, *New Careers and Roles in the American School* (New York: Bank Street College of Education, 1968).
  A very exacting task well done, which reports "action research" of fifteen demonstration programs using auxiliary personnel in the schools. The authors recognize and recommend new qualifications for careers in education. Truly innovative in our traditionally conservative school systems!

Dennison, George, *The Lives of Children* (New York: Random House, 1969).
  A successful career in education demands deep insights and appreciation of children. This book pictures clearly how children are able to meet their own problems and successfully solve them when they are free to do so.

Greene, Marvin L., *Something Else* (Glenview, Ill.: Scott, Foresman, 1970).
  The teacher who appreciates the need to have a curriculum that reaches the children in the schools will enjoy this book. It is filled with ideas of how the "generation gap" can be closed.

Teachers and Teaching

34

The Function of a Teacher

JOHN DEWEY

In his discussion of the functions of a teacher in the selection that follows, Dewey emphasizes the teacher's need for abundant knowledge as well as for specific preparation of each lesson. Comparing his views with those of Samuel Hall in his lecture to school-masters more than a hundred years ago (Selection 17), we find a similar emphasis on knowledge, for Hall states that a defect in knowledge implies a defect in teaching ability. Dewey distinguishes between two kinds of knowledge—"professional" and "technical"—and his elaboration between them explains much of his pragmatic philosophy.

The Teacher as Leader

THE OLDER TYPE of instruction tended to treat the teacher as a dictatorial ruler. The newer type sometimes treats the teacher as a negligible factor, almost as an evil, though a necessary one. In reality the teacher is the intellectual leader of a social group. He is a leader, not in virtue of official position, but because of wider and deeper knowledge and matured experience. The supposition that the principle of freedom confers liberty upon the pupils, but that the teacher is outside its range and must abdicate all leadership is merely silly.

Fallacious Notions Minimizing His Leadership

In some schools the tendency to minimize the place of the teacher takes the form of supposing that it is an arbitrary imposition for the teacher to pro-

SOURCE: John Dewey, *How We Think* (Lexington, Mass.: D. C. Heath and Company, 1933), pp. 274–277. Copyright 1933 by John Dewey and reprinted by permission of the publisher.

John Dewey (1859–1952) was an institution in American education. Books and hundreds of articles have been written by this highly respected and greatly loved

pose the line of work to be followed or to arrange the situation within which problems and topics arise. It is held that, out of due respect for the mental freedom of those taught, all suggestions are to come from them. Especially has this idea been applied in some kindergartens and primary grades. The result is often that described in the story of a young child who, on arriving at school, said to the teacher: "Do we have to do to-day what we want to do?" The alternative to proposals by the teacher is that the suggestions of things to do come from chance, from casual contacts, from what the child saw on his way to school, what he did yesterday, what he sees the next child doing, etc. Since the purpose to be carried out must come, directly or indirectly, from somewhere in the environment, denial to the teacher of the power to propose it merely substitutes accidental contact with some other person or scene for the intelligent planning of the very individual who, if he has a right to be a teacher at all, has the best knowledge of the needs and possibilities of the members of the group of which he is a part.

His Need of Abundant Knowledge

The practically important question concerns the conditions under which the teacher can really be the intellectual leader of a social group. The first condition goes back to his own intellectual preparation in subject matter. This should be abundant to the point of overflow. It must be much wider than the ground laid out in textbook or in any fixed plan for teaching a lesson. It must cover collateral points, so that the teacher can take advantage of unexpected questions or unanticipated incidents. It must be accompanied by a genuine enthusiasm for the subject that will communicate itself contagiously to pupils.

Some of the reasons why the teacher should have an excess supply of information and understanding are too obvious to need mention. The central reason is possibly not always recognized. *The teacher must have his mind free to observe the mental responses and movements of the student members of the recitation-group.* The problem of the pupils is found in *subject matter;* the problem of teachers is *what the minds of pupils are doing with this subject matter.* Unless the teacher's mind has mastered the subject matter in advance, unless it is thoroughly at home in it, using it unconsciously without the need of express thought, he will not be free to give full time and attention to

teacher of teachers. Among his other accomplishments he was an educational reformer, the recognized founder of the Progressive School Movement, and the Father of Pragmatism. Dewey stressed experience and experimentation over pure reasoning and continuously followed through with applications of his theories and ideas. He devoted his life to teaching and became one of the first American scholars to receive world recognition as the great American philosopher of his age.

observation and interpretation of the pupils' intellectual reactions. The teacher must be alive to all forms of bodily expression of mental condition—to puzzlement, boredom, mastery, the dawn of an idea, feigned attention, tendency to show off, to dominate discussion because of egotism, etc.—as well as sensitive to the meaning of all expression in words. He must be aware not only of *their* meaning, but of their meaning as indicative of the state of mind of the pupil, his degree of observation and comprehension.

His Need of Technical, Professional Knowledge

The fact that the teacher has to be a student of the pupil's mind, as the latter is a student of subject matter in various fields, accounts for the teacher's need for technical knowledge as well as for knowledge in the subjects taught. By 'technical knowledge' is here meant professional knowledge. Why should a teacher have acquaintance with psychology, history of education, the methods found helpful by others in teaching various subjects? For two main reasons: the one reason is that he may be equipped to note what would otherwise go unheeded in the responses of the students and may quickly and correctly interpret what pupils do and say; the other reason is that he may be ready to give proper aid when needed because of his knowledge of procedures that others have found useful.

Unfortunately this professional knowledge is sometimes treated, not as a guide and tool in personal observation and judgment—which it essentially is —but as a set of fixed rules of procedure in action. When a teacher finds such theoretical knowledge coming between him and his own common-sense judgment of a situation, the wise thing is to follow his own judgment— making sure, of course, that it is an enlightened insight. For unless the professional information enlightens his own perception of the situation and what to do about it, it becomes either a purely mechanical device or else a load of undigested material.

Finally the teacher, in order to be a leader, must make special preparation for particular lessons. Otherwise the only alternatives will be either aimless drift or else sticking literally to the text. Flexibility, ability to take advantage of unexpected incidents and questions, depends upon the teacher's coming to the subject with freshness and fullness of interest and knowledge. There are questions that he should ask before the recitation commences. What do the minds of pupils bring to the topic from their previous experience and study? How can I help them make connections? What need, even if unrecognized by them, will furnish a leverage by which to move their minds in the desired direction? What uses and applications will clarify the subject and fix it in their minds? How can the topic be individualized; that is, how shall it be treated so that each one will have something distinctive to contribute while the subject is also adapted to the special deficiencies and particular tastes of each one?

35
What Is Teaching?

HAROLD BENJAMIN

Although Benjamin deals with the same question as Dewey did in the previous selection, Benjamin's answer provides a different emphasis resulting from his view of incidents that occur when learning takes place but no teaching is being done. Benjamin proposes some provocative ideas that help bring into sharper focus the functions of the classroom teacher.

TEACHING is a process of arranging conditions under which the learner changes his ways consciously in the direction of his own goals.

There are three words in this definition that are key words. They are: (1) conditions, (2) consciously, and (3) goals.

When we look, first at this process of arranging conditions for learning, we must never forget that the first and most effective teacher is the learner himself. In education every learner is his own teacher. In training, the trainee is never his own trainer. The rat in the maze, learning to take the right-hand path because the left-hand one leads to an electric shock, is being trained by the electricity and by the psychologist, not by his own conditions. He (Mr. Rat) doesn't know what the conditions are. All he knows about this process is that he does not want to get hurt.

Much of human learning is incidental. There is no teaching involved because the learner's ways are not being changed *consciously*. To have real

SOURCE: J. A. Battle and Robert L. Shannon, eds., *The New Idea in Education* (New York: Harper & Row, 1968), p. 19. Copyright © 1968 by J. A. Battle and Robert L. Shannon. Reprinted by permission of the publisher.

Dr. Benjamin, a native of Oregon, now lives in semiretirement near Glassboro State College, New Jersey. He has been a teacher in public schools and colleges and has received many honors for his work as both a teacher and school administrator. In addition to his earned degrees, he has been awarded numerous honorary degrees.

teaching, therefore, the learner must know what is going on. He must know the score from the outset.

This means, furthermore, that the learning and teaching process is directed toward the learner's own goals. If a learner's ways are being changed in the direction of goals he does not understand and accept, he is merely being trained, not taught.

The professional teacher reaches the heights of his craft when his pupils become their own best teachers, consciously setting up conditions for changing their ways in the direction of their own goals. The good teacher is always trying to work himself out of his teaching role by getting the learners to assume that role for themselves.

36
Authentic Teachers

SYDNEY J. HARRIS

An immeasurable contribution to the teaching process is made by a teacher's personality. Harris succinctly states that knowledge and the need for knowledge are superseded by the need for teachers who possess the ability "to come to terms with their own individuated person." Have you done this? Harris presents his views extremely well, and every future teacher should give them his thoughtful consideration.

DISCUSSING a common school problem, a parent recently asked me, "How is it that some teachers are able to control their classes with a very light rein, and have no disciplinary troubles, while others must shout and plead and threaten and still get nowhere with the trouble-makers?"

I don't think the answer has much to do with teaching techniques or even experience, beyond a certain degree. I think it has almost everything to do with the "authenticity" of the teacher.

SOURCE: *Phi Delta Kappan* (April 1964), back cover. Reprinted by permission of the author, the Chicago *Daily News,* and the publisher.

A highly perceptive commentator on contemporary American life, Mr. Harris is a journalist *par excellence,* having been a syndicated columnist with the Chicago *Daily News* since 1941. British by birth, he has lived in the United States since the age of five. He served for many years as a Leader in the Great Books program at the University of Chicago and is the author, among other books, of *On the Contrary* and *Leaving the Surface.*

Notice I do not say "authority," but "authenticity." For genuine authority, which is more than a matter of official position and the ability to reward or punish, comes out of the depths of the personality. It has a realness, a presence, an aura, that can impress and influence even a six-year-old.

A person is either himself or not himself; is either rooted in his existence, or is a fabrication; has found his humanhood or is still playing with masks and roles and status symbols. And nobody is more aware of this difference (although unconsciously) than a child. Only an authentic person can evoke a good response in the core of the other person. Only a person is resonant to another person.

Knowledge is not enough. Technique is not enough. Mere experience is not enough. This is the mystery at the heart of the teaching process; and the same mystery is at the heart of the healing process. Each is an art, more than a science or a skill—and the art is at bottom the ability to "tune to the other's wavelength."

And this ability is not possessed by those who have failed to come to terms with their own individuated person, no matter what other talents they possess. Until they have liberated themselves (not completely, but mostly) from what is artificial and unauthentic within themselves, they cannot communicate with, counsel, or control others.

The few teachers who meant the most to me in my school life were not necessarily those who knew the most, but those who gave out the fullness of themselves; who confronted me face to face, as it were, with a humanhood that awoke and lured my own small and trembling soul and called me to take hold of my own existence with my two hands.

Such persons, of course, are extremely rare, and they are worth more than we can ever pay them. It should be the prime task of a good society to recruit and develop these personalities for safeguarding our children's futures; and our failure to do so is our most monstrous sin of omission.

37

Technology, Communication, and Education: A Social Perspective

GEORGE GERBNER

The selection that follows offers an exceptional description of teachers and teaching. The equating of teaching with technology and communication underlies Gerbner's ideas. While he gives what may be viewed as a discouraging picture, it seems reasonable and fair to share with prospective teachers his projected "image" of the teacher. It also may help you to be more alert to your own image when and if you do elect to enter the profession.

IT SEEMS TO ME that when most people can be exposed to the same sources of communication, or atomic radiation, the very shape of human affairs has changed. It used to be drawn-out long and thin. Now it seems compressed flat and wide. We pressed time into space. We sliced it into segments, wrapped it in commercials, sold it on television. A hundred years ago most people learned of the attack on Fort Sumter by word of mouth, if at all. Today, with three times the number of people, we're wired for sound, sight, soon even smell. We're wired together tightly enough for a short-circuit to fry us all.

It is obvious that technology has revolutionized the social process. It is less obvious, but equally true, that we cannot make sense of technology in communication, in education, or in anything else, without attempting to fit it into the broadest possible context of relationships and concepts in which it operates.

My purpose is to discuss some elements of that context. In an historical mood, I would like to develop some concepts about the basic humanizing functions of social communication, and list some imperatives the industrial transformation imposes on us. Then we shall focus on a few characteristics of the uneasy relationship between two major systems of human communication

SOURCE: *Tomorrow's Teaching*, pp. 16–25. This book was designed and produced by The Pate Organization, Oklahoma City, Oklahoma, Public Relations Counsel for the Frontiers of Science Foundation of Oklahoma, Inc.

The author is Dean of the Annenberg School of Communications at the University of Pennsylvania. Born in Hungary, he has devoted his professional life to improving education in American schools. He is the author of *Analysis of Communication Content* and *Toward a General Theory of Communication*.

345

—the mass media system and the school system—viewing the two as the informal and the formal educational agencies of industrial culture.

When the last invasion of glaciers began to recede, Homo Sapiens emerged from the Ice Age a pretty accomplished craftsman, artist, scientist, socialite, and communicator. His distant past in damp tropical forests had shaped his forearms into strong, delicate instruments and left them free from carrying the burden of the body. Exceptionally deft manipulation developed literally hand-in-hand with an exceptionally large and complex control system, the human brain. A hundred million years of evolution is compressed in the word "to comprehend." It stems from the expression "to grasp with the forehand."

The more immediate past had put Homo Sapiens to his severest test, at least until today. Huddled in cold valleys, flooded during the warm spells, he was hard-pressed to develop resources of collaboration, community, and communication. In surviving, Homo Sapiens transformed himself into what we recognize—a human.

Collaboration, community, and communication made our kinds of men and women out of members of the species. Communication infuses the other humanizing processes with our most unique capabilities: non-instinctive social organization, art, science and technology.

Speech, chant, song, dance, and the shaping of forms, images, and stories arose from the needs of living and working together. Rhythm was a pace-setter, a system of measurement, a way of easing the monotony of carving wood, of chipping stone, of the long march. Man the artist helped all to share and to bear the hardships of work. Then he came forth to represent, to recreate, to conjure up and to celebrate that great truth. His art made the truths of the tribe, its way of work, and its way of looking at life, believable and compelling.

From the taming of fire to the sowing of seeds man had learned not only the arts of making truths more believable and compelling but also something of the vital significance of making beliefs truer. Man reached out, got burned, and, instead of fleeing in panic, he contemplated an abstract proposition: Which end of a burning stick could be seized with impunity? He was a scientist.

Organized communication of pertinent fact and value—ritual, education, symbolic re-creation of the varieties, limitations and potentials of the human condition—this was, and is, popular culture. It is a source and instrument of social power. Responsibility for its system of organization, for the purpose and nature of its controls, and for the quality and structure of its freedoms, is administrative responsibility. Man the organizer combines the process of government with those of art and science as key functions in communications.

What about technology? Technology is a term of a different order. It is to be judged by the criteria of the others rather than by any criterion of its own. Unlike art, science, and even government, technology is the direct and immediate intervention into the everyday affairs of man. As science is the penetration of the mind into human necessities of existence, technology is the changing of these necessities. Its fruits are all around us. They transform the qualities of life and the uses of the mind. Technology means *change*. It is a most revolutionary and ambivalent force in history. Uncritical or indiscriminate technology is as scientific as slashing around with a scalpel. Science limits technology at the same time it feeds and directs it. The sharp cutting edge of technology is slanted in the direction of our scientific beliefs and values only if its operation in one realm of necessities does not conflict with what we know about another set of human necessities.

The concept of technology vaults us across a span of thousands of years. For the vast majority of mankind, the chief glory of those years is the building of the foundations of world societies resting not on bent-over human backs and frayed human nerves but on the uses of non-human and super-human energy. This is the only major qualitative change in living man has known he learned to raise food from the earth rather than only to pluck it from the wilderness.

For two-thirds of mankind, much of it living in our own back-yard, this change of the ages is only a hope. But not a vain hope. They are driven to supreme sacrifices to bring it off. Some are determined to reach their goal in less time than we did, to reach it by roads and shortcuts *they* see fit, and nothing but bombs can stop them. Barring that act of genocide, the roads taken today will lead in the next century to a world as different from ours as ours is from the world of the Pharaohs'.

There are certain requirements inherent in the logic of industrial technology. These are universal imperatives applicable to all roads to the new transformation. Success in meeting these imperatives will largely determine the power of national or supra-national units to exist as relatively independent and self-governing entities.

The first imperative is the accumulation of massive capital investment. It is the saving rather than spending or wasting of all forms of human and natural energy, the turning of this energy, through technology, into providing the essentials of a human life for all. This requirement places a special burden of development and accommodation on a country which mines 50 per cent of the world's resources to collect 40 per cent of the world's income for 6 per cent of the world's population.

The second imperative is sizeable organization, and the consequent necessity for planning and for the orderly allocation of resources. Industrial society is urban society, planned society, and organized society, whether the organizing is done in public or in private. Industrial man is "the organization man" whether he takes the posture of conformity or rebellion, whether he behaves as a self-styled individualist or a responsibly self-directing individual. The logic of highly organized life should, on the whole, require and produce greater personal responsibility than any other form of life; the consequences of personal judgement and action are much more far-reaching.

The third imperative has to do with the popular culture of society revolutionized through technology. By popular culture I still mean the organized social communication of pertinent fact and value.

The social communication system of industrial culture comes to bear a double burden. One is the requirement for the cultivation of skill, intelligence, and personal responsibility on a totally unprecedented scale. This is the full meaning of the demand for "high level manpower." The degrees of incompetence, incomprehension, and immorality tolerably diminish in geometric proportion as increasingly tightly-knit world societies bid for ever higher stakes.

The second burden is the necessity for free and imaginative exploration of the meanings and opportunities inherent in a life of continuous change. It is the need to help man shape the forces of his own transformation. There is perhaps a third cultural burden related to this one; but let me save that till the end.

The humanizing processes of collaboration, community and communication shift to a high technological gear in industrial society. Man is—or should be —at the wheel. The communications functions of art, science and administration must map his territory and help chart his course.

There are many roads to the industrial transformation. Each road confronts the imperatives in its own way. Our path is the one blazed by the once revolutionary middle class, somewhat deflected from its original course by the once counter-revolutionary intellectual. (I am using these terms merely to symbolize certain characteristic ways of dealing with the imperatives of technological change.)

The conceptual discovery which made the middle class an agent and prime-mover of industrial revolutions was the idea of the market as automatic pilot. Progress along this road was to be self-regulating. The imperatives of capital accumulation, mechanization, organization, and acculturation were to be met through a system of balances inherent in the structure of markets. The market was to govern best when it was governed least. Art and science were to be pursued for their own sake, and yield such fruits as technology could put to efficient and gratifying use in the markets.

For the intellectual, attached to aristocracy and clergy, this was a pretty vulgar and revolting development indeed—at least until it provided *him* with a market to offset the loss of the old patronage. Once a part of the new system, yet having no investment in it beyond his personal talents, he could observe it more objectively. In a world of unprecedented accumulation of riches and enlightenment, and the technical means to share it, deprivation and ignorance could no longer be considered natural. Indeed, all such social degradation is manufactured by the system that provides the means for its abolition. The automatic pilot has a built-in bias. The ride is on a roller coaster. That government is best which governs best. The now revolutionary intellectual was to harness all the humanizing processes of collaboration, community, communication, the functions of art, science, technology, rapid mass training and cultural harmonizing for a hard-driving industrial program along a straight and narrow path. Damn the markets; full speed ahead.

The two cultural offsprings of the industrial revolution grew up side-by-side, playing, as it were, an intricate game of chess. The two siblings are the system of formal secular public education, the schools, and the system of informal secular public education, the mass media.

The mass media system is the direct descendent of technology, mass production, and mass markets. It was ideally suited to the demands of industrial culture, to its need for rapid, standardized reproduction and distribution of commodities to heterogeneous, anonymous, mass audiences too large to interact face-to-face.

Formal education needed more prodding. It is not so easily mechanized, not so cheaply organized, not so readily standardized and not so handily merchandised. But as the paths to industrial transformation crossed and at times even merged before parting again, the cultural imperatives of the road emerged with increasing clarity.

The Founding Fathers tried to protect the integrity of both systems of popular culture from the main threat *they* knew: strong central government. The press by Constitutional commission and education by Constitutional omission escaped centralized public development and control. But although exempt from the laws of the Republic, the mass media were subject to the laws of industrial development from which they sprang. These laws required organization, concentration, mechanization, and control—if not public, then private. By comparison, public schools remained the last folk institution of industrial society.

During the so-called marketing revolution of the 1950's we began to spend more time on mass-produced communications than on paid work, or school, or play, or anything else except sleep (and the "late show" cut into that, too). Television alone demanded one-fifth of the average American's waking life. Comic books sold one billion copies a year at a cost of a 100 million dollars —four times the budget of public libraries, and more than the cost of the book supply for primary and secondary schools. Almost 50 million people still went to movies each week, and the same number stayed home and watched them on TV each night—400 million exposures a week.

Our thirst for information grew likewise. Yet Sputnik came as a surprise. We had been swamped by an avalanche of communications geared to the demands of markets, insulating us from some relevant realities of the day. The "human interest story"—ironically enough—is some cute foible of the race, like the AP wirephoto of last February 16, a heartwarming picture story of boys and girls joined in merry laughter, bearing the caption: "Best kind of bonfire—It's easy to see why these kids are enjoying the fire—the burning building is their school."

It was, in more ways than one. Dollar-for-dollar schools kept up with the mass media. But because of the inherent nature and structure of the formal education system, schools got much less mileage out of their dollar. Major educational responsibility remained relegated to political subdivisions which had less to do with social, economic or even political life than in any other country on earth. What had been designed as protection became invitation to sabotage. Thirty million Americans were on the move each year, but we persisted in the illusion that education in some places costs 2.5 times less than in others. All in all 1 in 9 youths examined by the Armed Forces failed minimum literacy tests. But in one area of seven states 1 out of 3 failed and two-thirds were ruled out for skilled work or advanced training. While television was made available free and equal to all, and while all broadcasting tripled its revenues, our only massive national effort in higher education—the GI bill—came to an end. College degrees declined by one-fourth of the total awarded in the first four years of the decade. Each year a hundred thousand college caliber youth did not go to college for financial reasons. Higher education never got 40 per cent of the top fourth of our high school graduates.

Perhaps in retrospect we shall smile indulgently at the antics of an age in which we could put the Royal Laotian Army on the federal payroll (with dubious results), but considered it interference in the affairs of a state to do the same for the teachers of New Orleans.

True, the typical American school was a bright, cheerful, happy place compared to schools in many lands. A sympathetic visitor from England noted that they were "unmistakably faced with a custodial . . . problem that is unfamiliar in other countries. The difficulty is not that of getting boys and girls ready . . . so that they can help with the national housekeeping; it might be somewhat unkindly described as that of keeping young Americans happily and rather profitably occupied as long as possible before getting them ready. . . . Criticisms of . . . slow progress . . . underestimate the interplay of economic and scholastic considerations." [1]

Despite that interplay, we were somewhat dismayed to find that half of our high schools did not offer a foreign language, a quarter did not teach physics,

[1] Edmund J. King, *Other Schools and Ours,* London: Methuen & Co., 1958, p. 115.

chemistry, or geometry. Math and science subjects took up nearly 40 per cent of the time of every Soviet pupil of the middle school, we were told. Adding to our dismay was the discovery that the Russians were graduating three times as many engineers and two and one-half times as many doctors as we were, and, furthermore, that our supply of engineers and doctors was enough to satisfy the market, even if not the need, for their services. Symptomatic of the situation was that of all professional shortages, the teacher shortage was the most acute, and the supply dwindling in relation to need. One-fifth of our college graduates went into teaching. The Russians returned half of their graduates to teaching every year. Sputnik went into orbit. A rocket hit the moon. There was much talk about a "gap." You might find the gap in the U.N. Statistical Yearbooks for those years. Our education budget was two-tenths of our military budget. The Soviet education budget was seven-tenths of their military budget. The gap is in the ways of meeting the imperatives of the new world industrial transformation.

We had indeed been outflanked. The mass media appeared increasingly to take over democratic national responsibilities for illuminating the realities of today and setting the agenda for our life of tomorrow.

How did they fulfill that responsibility? As well as could be expected, perhaps even better. Being free from public control but lacking guarantees of public support in using that freedom, the mass media must, on the whole, merchandise such gratifications as can be profitably cultivated under the circumstances. And the circumstances did not particularly favor the use of mass communications to meet the cultural imperatives of our age.

The agenda of life's business as seen through the window of the mass media is pretty clouded. Only systematic study can lift the blinders each of us wears as a matter of choice, temperament, or habit. So let me mention two areas of concern in which we have scratched the surface, and which have a direct relation to preparing young people for the life they will live tomorrow. One might be called a success story; the other perhaps a course in failure.

A now classic study of biographies in popular magazines [2] traced the remarkable growth of attention devoted to personal success stories in the first half of the twentieth century. But even more remarkable were the changes in the *kinds* of personalities that symbolized success. Before World War I, three-fourths of these models of achievement came from political life, industry, and the professions. Forty years later the "idols of production," gave way to the "idols of consumption." Aside from the political figures, nine out of ten of the latter-day celebrities' chief claim to fame was stardom in the world of the mass media and of the markets they serve.

[2] Leo Lowenthal, "Biographies in Popular Magazines," in *Reader in Public Opinion and Communication,* edited by Bernard Berelson and Morris Janowitz, Glencoe, Ill.: The Free Press, 1950.

The celebrity cult is not a simple affair. Matt Dillon outdraws the election returns. Several TV stars are more familiar to a test panel of 2,000 viewers than a President of the United States who does not or cannot become a TV star himself. About one out of four magazines on the newsstands can be classified into the fan-romance category. Half of the lives immortalized on "This Is Your Life," 76 per cent of those personalized on "Person to Person," and 69 per cent of those interviewed on "The Mike Wallace Interview" came from entertainment and the mass media. Such celebrities account for over 40 per cent of all paper back biographies in print. The size of the Hollywood press corps just about equals the combined memberships of the education writers' and science writers' associations. *McCall's* much publicized list of the most exciting reading of our time features such famous authors of non-books as Zsa Zsa Gabor, Fred Astaire, Arlene Francis, Keenan Wynn, Jack Paar, Art Linkletter, and Marilyn Monroe. (*This* must have been the last straw for Arthur Miller!) Even as good a series as "Reading Out Loud," by Westinghouse and the American Library Association finds it necessary to enlist "fifteen of the nation's most prominent people" to popularize reading, people who turn out to be two writers, one businessman, three political figures, eight stars, and one TV teacher.

Yes, the TV teacher. Since Sam Levenson quit being a school guidance advisor and became a comedian, he lectures to 150 PTAs a year on child guidance, and employs a staff of two to answer letters asking for advice. Charles Van Doren lectures to no one.

Patrick D. Hazard of the University of Pennsylvania (who collected most of the figures) commented that our "society depends for its continued viability on a bewildering proliferation of exacting roles for which arduous preparation of intellect and imagination is demanded. Yet the media system, largely to facilitate its function as a marketing agency, has made the entertainer in our culture vastly more visible than he has any right to be. This inevitably means that occupational roles and activities much more crucial to the proper functioning of a free society are less noticeable, even invisible. Teenage idols, television and motion picture stars, sports champions, and media-created celebrities crowd out the scientist, educator, legislator, and artist from the vision of the great majority of our people." [3]

Now I am as kindly and even warmly disposed as any man towards the charms of my erstwhile compatriot Zsa Zsa Gabor, or ex-partner in intellectual enterprise Marilyn Monroe. I don't even begrudge a little visibility here and there. What chills me is the idea of a checkmated culture. Some people are worried about our alleged failure to communicate to young people. I am afraid we communicate too well. Some people are alarmed about our "beat-

---

[3] Patrick D. Hazard, "The Entertainer as Hero: The Burden of an Anti-Intellectual Tradition," unpublished paper, read at the Association for Education in Journalism Convention at Pennsylvania State University, August, 1960.

niks" and "youth problems." So am I; but secretly I am heartened to see some of our messages unacceptable to so many.

And now the study in failure. There is one basic ingredient to any formula for attracting young people into teaching. That is to stop doing what keeps them away. Raising salaries is a necessary but not a sufficient condition. The one thing all young people want is to grow up. We have not made that easy. For to grow up means to know the score, to do things that really matter, to be taken seriously. Nothing saps self-respect as much as to encounter in one's culture one's professional image placed high on a pedestal perhaps, but in stature smaller than life. You can fight about a paycheck, or even sulk about it in a perfectly soul-satisfying way. But who can fight or sulk about the lovable Mr. Boynton?

We know that by-and-large the teacher in literature is too often either an inhibited, sexless prune (with apologies to Dr. Dichter and the prune industry), or, as an early study on the subject put it "stooped, gaunt, and gray with weariness. His suit has the shine of shabby gentility and hangs loose from his under-nourished frame." [4] That is, unless class is out and memory rings the school bell, when we say a tearful "Good Morning" to the wonderful, "The Terrible Miss Dove," or bid a nostalgic "Goodbye, Mr. Chips."

But perhaps memory fails us. So we did a study of 81 American movies produced since 1950, portraying teachers in leading or supporting parts. And this is what we found.[5]

The presence of an educator tips the odds 3 to 1 in favor of the movie being a comedy, and 2 to 1 in favor of its being a standard love story. Movies without teachers are more likely to fall into the action-adventure category by a margin of 12 to 1, and into the category of Westerns by 21 to 1. Since most movies involve love, and since love has a peculiar affinity to humanity, a look at love and the teacher will give us a good measure of his human stature.

His opportunities for love were virtually unlimited. Although male teachers outnumber female teachers (this is not surprising in the predominantly male world of the mass media) six out of 10 male and nine out of 10 female teachers were unmarried at the beginning of the picture. Alas, most of them were unmarried also at the end of the picture.

Not that they didn't try. They just didn't try hard enough. With so many unmarried teachers running around, it was inevitable that some would run into recognizable pedagogues of the opposite sex, and vice versa. The clash, five times out of six, had the shattering impact of a popgun.

With all the happy endings, the teacher's chances of success in love with

[4] Arthur Foff, "The Teacher as Hero," in Arthur Foff and Jean Grambs, ed., *Readings in Education,* New York: Harpers, 1956, p. 21.
[5] Jack Schwartz, "The Portrayal of Educators in Motion Pictures, 1950–58," *The Journ. of Educ. Sociology* 34:82-90, October, 1960.

anybody were 50–50. The most common conditions of success in love were (1) that the teacher find a partner without college education, and (2) that the teacher leave the teaching profession. The typical pattern has her quitting a New England high school and a biology teacher fiance to "find herself" and a *man* in New York. Or it has him leaving a dull musical chair at a Western college, along with a straight-laced professor girl friend, to be taught something about music, and love, in Tin Pan Alley.

With such a pattern of romantic success among screen pedagogues, what need be said about failure? Failure in love permitted the teacher to remain fully dedicated to the profession. Blindness to the mature emotional needs of others allowed the others to escape into the stronger, warmer arms of less educated more human creatures.

Enough of love among popular cultural symbols of the education process. On a somewhat more sordid side, we also noted the pattern of the pretty young teacher suspected of carrying on with a precocious high school gorilla. All ends happily when we find out that he only tried to rape her. You couldn't blame her, though, for being somewhat miffed at all this, or her more dynamic male colleague for leaving a field of endeavor where for a while he risked being beaten to pulp every time he turned his back.

The film teacher leaving the profession usually goes to greener pastures. Are there any others? Actually, the still youthful teacher going into another specific occupation knows what it takes to do things that really matter. Five times out of six, he becomes an entertainer.

Semanticists have unwittingly done us a disfavor. Key terms and concepts *should* be fighting words, like technology, with a sharp cutting edge slanted in the direction of our values. I think it was Florence Nightingale who once said that whatever hospitals do, they should not make people sick. Semmelweiss enraged eminent medical practitioners only a hundred years ago with the simple request that they wash the hands that poke inside other people's bodies. Freud was looking forward to the time when "culture will not crush anyone any more." Commenting on the uses of his inventions, Lee De Forest asked, "What have you done with my child?"

So forgive me for not being fair to the bookkeeper's trade, for not balancing all the great *humanizing* functions splendidly performed in our industrial culture with all the dreams that hurt. I am now engaged in a study of the portrayal of teachers and schools in all media of more than half dozen countries. I know there is much on the credit side of the ledger: probably enough to give us a soothing, static sense of equilibrium.

But there is no equilibrium. The once solid ground of supremacy in peace and war buckles under our feet. Electric organs play their canned music in temples and in honky-tonks. The shrieks of the joyride still resound and mingle with wails from the chamber of horrors. Former targets rise to take aim.

It is the end of a whole shooting match. New signs erected in some scattered workshops read "under new management. Check your guns outside. *Man* at *work!*"

There is no equilibrium. The fruit ripens in the forest, birds fatten on it, and scatter the seeds of its destruction. The soil receives the seed. Moisture, minerals, and sunshine turn them into forces of construction.

We are going into a difficult fall and winter. Our basic problems and perplexities do not stem from temporary aberration or accidental neglect. They are rooted in structural characteristics of middle-class society. So is our pride and joy: the most privileged life for the most people ever to inhabit a country of man. Ripe is the fruit along our road toward the imperatives of tomorrow. And so is the worm in the apple.

The revolutionary example of our own dynamic techniques transforms the world—but not to our own image. We can take it, or leave it, or blow it to smithereens. We're well-equipped to blow it. We're too privileged to leave it. But are we prepared to take it?

We can take it and survive, again, through transformation. In glancing at the past, and at *The Future as History,* Robert L. Heilbroner notes that in our society technological progress and penetration "are not facets of human life which we normally subject to 'history-making' decisions. In general we allow these aspects of history to follow their autonomous course. . . . Thus we limit our idea of what is possible in history by excluding from our control the forces of history themselves." It is true, he points out, that "the exercise of such historic control is fraught with risk. *But so is the exercise of non-control.*" (His italics.) And he writes: ". . . Until the avoidable evils of society have been redressed or at least made the target of the wholehearted effort of the organized human community, it is not only premature but presumptuous to talk of the 'dignity of the individual.' The ugly, obvious, and terrible wounds of mankind must be dressed and allowed to heal before we can begin to know the capacities, much less enlarge the vision, of the human race as a whole.

"In the present state of world history the transformations which are everywhere at work are performing this massive and crude surgery. . . ."

And: "There is needed a broad and compassionate comprehension of the history-shaking transformations now in mid-career, of their combined work of demolition and construction, of the hope they embody and the price they will extract. Only from such a sense of historic understanding can come the strength to pass through the gauntlet with an integrity of mind and spirit.

"What is tragically characteristic of our lives today is an absence of just such understanding. . . ."

This comprehension, this new reach of the grasp of our hands and our brain, is the third cultural burden of the imperatives and the logic of the changing world. The twin systems of education in industrial culture can join hands and use technology to that end. But technology means change, and the direction of change requires some institutional remodeling to bring the forces of human history under more responsible human control. There is no other way to survival—and to evolution—in industrial culture. The teacher of tomorrow must have the tools and the support of society to become a full-fledged participant in popular culture, and to grow in stature as big as life—even if not on a pedestal. The old game is up. There is little time to wait for historians of tomorrow to tell us what we should have done today. The humanities need not fear the teaching machine or electronic media any more than they had to fear the original instrument of programmed learning which they also opposed—the book. Not if the teacher of tomorrow, in the classroom or on the screen or on the air, can combine the historic humanizing functions of communication—art, science, and administration—to make our beliefs truer, our truths more believable, and our knowledge freer. Anyway, *these* are the dreams that heal.

EVALUATION

JOHN DEWEY, **The Function of a Teacher**

1. In "The Function of a Teacher," Dewey states that the teacher has a need for abundant knowledge if he is to be the intellectual leader of a social group.
   (a) Does Dewey say he is the leader because of his official position as teacher?
   (b) To what two areas of knowledge does Dewey make specific reference?
   (c) According to Dewey, what accounts for the need of this particular knowledge?

2. (a) What does Dewey mean by "technical" knowledge for a teacher?
   (b) Identify three areas of this knowledge.
   (c) State the two reasons Dewey gives for requiring this technical knowledge.
   (d) What misuse has Dewey indicated might occur? How does he propose that this misuse be avoided?

3. In order for a teacher to qualify as a leader, what responsibility has he in his classes? Why?

HAROLD BENJAMIN, **What Is Teaching?**

4. Explain carefully how Benjamin distinguishes between training, being trained, and being taught?

5. (a) When can learning be taking place without teaching being involved?
   (b) When might it be said a learner is being trained?

6. According to Benjamin, what words must be present in the definition of teaching?

7. Who does Benjamin regard as the most efficient teacher?

8. (a) In learning experiences, how must the learner's ways be changed?

357

(b) Toward what must the learning and teaching process be directed?

(c) When does the author believe a professional teacher reaches the height of his craft?

SYDNEY J. HARRIS, **Authentic Teachers**

9. In "Authentic Teachers," Harris says the most important characteristic of a teacher is "authenticity."
   (a) Define "authenticity" as Harris uses the term.

   (b) How does Harris see that this authenticity enables the teacher to be a better teacher of his students?

10. Give Harris's statement on "the mystery of the teaching process."

GEORGE GERBNER, **Technology, Communication, and Education**

11. In "Technology, Communication, and Education," Gerbner presents what many successful teachers would consider to be a devastating image of teachers. The selection gives, however, a reasonably accurate picture of how teachers have fared due largely to the image of them presented by the mass media. List Gerbner's stated purposes for which the mass media system is ideally suited to serve.

12. Why does the author believe that formal education has not profited by similar ways?

13. What generalized rationale has Gerbner stated as an explanation of why technology has not revolutionized communication and education as it has the social process?

14. State what Gerbner gives as the two cultural offsprings of the industrial revolution, and the two major systems of human communications.

15. What are Gerbner's figures on the percentage of our college graduates and the percentage of Russia's college graduates who go into teaching?

16. (a) What does Gerbner contend to be the one basic ingredient in any formula for attracting young people into teaching?

   (b) What is being done to keep them away?

17. What instructional devices and materials does Gerbner include under mass media?

18. In discussing his viewpoint of the basic humanizing functions of social communications, Gerbner identifies three processes developed by Homo sapiens that account for the human being of today.
    (a) Name these.

    (b) How does he believe these three humanizing processes are related?

19. List the imperatives Gerbner believes the industrial transformation has imposed on us.

20. With the spreading of mass media, television became available to a majority of the American people and broadcasting revenues tripled. What was the status of our national education when this occurred?

21. Gerbner depicts the unattractiveness of teachers in his discussion of "the study of failure."
    (a) What simple solution does he recommend?

    (b) To what does he attribute the unattractive teacher image?

    (c) On the count of love, what chances has the featured teacher for marriage?

    (d) Where is the teacher to find a marriage partner?

    (e) Once a teacher becomes a successful television teacher, what are the odds that he will remain in a teaching career?

22. What does Gerbner regard as "tragically characteristic of our lives today"?

23. Gerbner regards this comprehension as the third cultural burden of the imperatives he previously identified. How else has he described it?

24. How does the author see that education can survive in the industrial culture through the twin systems of education?

FOR FURTHER READING

Rogers, Carl R., *Freedom to Learn* (Columbus, Ohio: Charles Merrill, 1969).
A clearly defined statement supporting those who advocate freedom in learning. Rogers presents three examples of classroom approaches that illustrate his ideas, which will help a teacher to achieve true dialogue in his classroom.

Shipley, C. Morton, and Marjorie M. Cann, *A Synthesis of Teaching Methods* (Toronto: McGraw-Hill, 1968).
A fairly comprehensive discussion of teaching methods applied in elementary schools. This book provides many examples of specific teaching tasks, which are examined in detail.

Teaching as a Profession

38
My Pedagogic Creed

JOHN DEWEY

The story of American history shows the many ways in which professional educators have influenced all aspects of our national life. Readings in this book reflect both their professional hopes and the realizations of many of their dreams. The pedagogic creed of John Dewey, now more than seventy years old, has in essence become the basis for a statement of professional ethics by the National Education Association.

Article One—What Education Is

I BELIEVE that all education proceeds by the participation of the individual in the social consciousness of the race. This process begins unconsciously almost at birth, and is continually shaping the individual's powers, saturating his consciousness, forming his habits, training his ideas, and arousing his feelings and emotions. Through this unconscious education the individual gradually comes to share in the intellectual and moral resources which humanity has succeeded in getting together. He becomes an inheritor of the funded capital of civilization. The most formal and technical education in the world cannot safely depart from this general process. It can only organize it or differentiate it in some particular direction.

The only true education comes through the stimulation of the child's powers by the demands of the social situations in which he finds himself. Through these demands he is stimulated to act as a member of a unity, to emerge from his original narrowness of action and feeling, and to conceive of himself from the standpoint of the welfare of the group to which he belongs. Through the responses which others make to his own activities he comes to know what these mean in social terms. The value which they have is reflected back into

SOURCE: Bernard Johnston, *Issues in Education* (Boston, Mass.: Houghton Mifflin Co., 1964), pp. 213–221. Reprinted by permission of the publisher.

For biographical data on John Dewey, see Selection 34.

them. For instance, through the response which is made to the child's instinctive babblings the child comes to know what those babblings mean; they are transformed into articulate language, and thus the child is introduced into the consolidated wealth of ideas and emotions which are now summed up in language.

This educational process has two sides—one psychological and one sociological—and neither can be subordinated to the other, or neglected, without evil results following. Of these two sides, the psychological is the basis. The child's own instincts and powers furnish the material and give the starting point for all education. Save as the efforts of the educator connect with some activity which the child is carrying on of his own initiative independent of the educator, education becomes reduced to a pressure from without. It may, indeed, give certain external results, but cannot truly be called educative. Without insight into the psychological structure and activities of the individual, the educative process will, therefore, be haphazard and arbitrary. If it chances to coincide with the child's activity it will get a leverage; if it does not, it will result in friction, or disintegration, or arrest of the child-nature.

Knowledge of social conditions, of the present state of civilization, is necessary in order properly to interpret the child's powers. The child has his own instincts and tendencies, but we do not know what these mean until we can translate them into their social equivalents. We must be able to carry them back into a social past and see them as the inheritance of previous race activities. We must also be able to project them into the future to see what their outcome and end will be. In the illustration just used, it is the ability to see in the child's babblings the promise and potency of a future social intercourse and conversation which enables one to deal in the proper way with that instinct.

The psychological and social sides are organically related, and that education cannot be regarded as a compromise between the two, or a superimposition of one upon the other. We are told the psychological definition of education is barren and formal—that it gives us only the idea of a development of all the mental powers without giving us any idea of the use to which these powers are put. On the other hand, it is urged that the social definition of education, as getting adjusted to civilization, makes of it a forced and external process, and results in subordinating the freedom of the individual to a preconceived social and political status.

Each of these objections is true when urged against one side isolated from the other. In order to know what a power really is we must know what its end, use, or function is, and this we cannot know save as we conceive of the individual as active in social relationships. But, on the other hand, the only possible adjustment which we can give to the child under existing conditions is that which arises through putting him in complete possession of all his powers. With the advent of democracy and modern industrial conditions, it is impossible to foretell definitely just what civilization will be twenty years from now. Hence it is impossible to prepare the child for any precise set of conditions. To prepare him for the future life means to give him command of himself; it means so to train him that he will have the full and ready use of all his capacities; that his eye and ear and hand may be tools ready to command, that his judgment may be capable of grasping the conditions under which it has to work, and the executive forces be trained to act economically and efficiently. It is impossible to reach this sort of adjustment save as constant regard is had to the individual's own powers, tastes, and interests—that is, as education is continually converted into psychological terms.

In sum, I believe that the individual who is to be educated is a social individual, and that society is an organic union of individuals. If we eliminate the social factor from the child we are left only with an abstraction; if we eliminate the individual factor from society, we are left only with an inert and lifeless mass. Education, therefore, must begin with a psychological insight into the child's capacities, interests, and habits. It must be controlled at every point by reference to these same considerations. These powers, interests, and habits must be continually interpreted—we must know what they mean. They must be translated into terms of their social equivalents—into terms of what they are capable of in the way of social service.

Article Two—What the School Is

I believe that the school is primarily a social institution. Education being a social process, the school is simply that form of community life in which all those agencies are concentrated that will be most effective in bringing the child to share in the inherited resources of the race, and to use his own powers for social ends.

Education, therefore, is a process of living and not a preparation for future living.

The school must represent life, life as real and vital to the child as that which he carries on in the home, in the neighborhood, or on the playground.

That education which does not occur through forms of life, forms that are worth living for their own sake, is always a poor substitute for the genuine reality, and tends to cramp and to deaden.

The school, as an institution, should simplify existing social life; should reduce it, as it were, to an embryonic form. Existing life is so complex that the child cannot be brought into contact with it without either confusion or distraction; he is either overwhelmed by the multiplicity of activities which are going on, so that he loses his own power of orderly reaction, or he is so stimulated by these various activities that his powers are prematurely called into play and he becomes either unduly specialized or else disintegrated.

As such simplified social life, the school should grow gradually out of the home life; it should take up and continue the activities with which the child is already familiar in the home.

It should exhibit these activities to the child, and reproduce them in such ways that the child will gradually learn the meaning of them, and be capable of playing his own part in relation to them.

This is a psychological necessity, because it is the only way of securing continuity in the child's growth, the only way of giving a background of past experience to the new ideas given in school.

It is also a social necessity because the home is the form of social life in which the child has been nurtured and in connection with which he has had his moral training. It is the business of the school to deepen and extend his sense of the values bound up in his home life.

Much of the present education fails because it neglects this fundamental principle of the school as a form of community life. It conceives the school as a place where certain information is to be given, where certain lessons are to be learned, or where certain habits are to be formed. The value of these is conceived as lying largely in the remote future; the child must do these things for the sake of something else he is to do; they are mere preparations. As a result they do not become a part of the life experience of the child and so are not truly educative.

The moral education centers upon this conception of the school as a mode of social life, that the best and deepest moral training is precisely that which one gets through having to enter into proper relations with others in a unity of work and thought. The present educational systems, so far as they destroy or neglect this unity, render it difficult or impossible to get any genuine, regular moral training.

The child should be stimulated and controlled in his work through the life of the community.

Under existing conditions far too much of the stimulus and control proceeds from the teacher, because of neglect of the idea of the school as a form of social life.

The teacher's place and work in the school is to be interpreted from this same basis. The teacher is not in the school to impose certain ideas or to form certain habits in the child, but is there as a member of the community to select the influences which shall affect the child and to assist him in properly responding to these influences.

The discipline of the school should proceed from the life of the school as a whole and not directly from the teacher.

The teacher's business is simply to determine, on the basis of larger experience and riper wisdom, how the discipline of life shall come to the child.

All questions of the grading of the child and his promotion should be determined by reference to the same standard. Examinations are of use only so far as they test the child's fitness for social life and reveal the place in which he can be of the most service and where he can receive the most help.

Article Three—The Subject Matter of Education

I believe that the social life of the child is the basis of concentration, of correlation, in all his training or growth. The social life gives the unconscious unity and the background of all his efforts and of all his attainments.

The subject matter of the school curriculum should mark a gradual differentiation out of the primitive unconscious unity of social life.

We violate the child's nature and render difficult the best ethical results by introducing the child too abruptly to a number of special studies, of reading, writing, geography, etc., out of relation to this social life.

The true center of correlation on the school subjects is not science, nor literature, nor history, nor geography, but the child's own social activities.

Education cannot be unified in the study of science, or so-called nature study, because apart from human activity, nature itself is not a unity; nature in itself is a number of diverse objects in space and time, and to attempt to make it the center of work by itself is to introduce a principle of radiation rather than one of concentration.

Literature is the reflex expression and interpretation of social experience, hence it must follow upon and not precede such experience. It, therefore, cannot be made the basis, although it may be made the summary of unification.

Once more, history is of educative value insofar as it presents phases of social life and growth. It must be controlled by reference to social life. When taken simply as history it is thrown into the distant past and becomes dead and inert. Taken as the record of man's social life and progress it becomes full of meaning. I believe, however, that it cannot be so taken excepting as the child is also introduced directly into social life.

The primary basis of education is in the child's powers at work along the same general constructive lines as those which have brought civilization into being.

The only way to make the child conscious of his social heritage is to enable him to perform those fundamental types of activity which make civilization what it is.

In the so-called expressive or constructive activities is the center of correlation.

This gives the standard for the place of cooking, sewing, manual training, etc., in the school.

They are not special studies which are to be introduced over and above a lot of others in the way of relaxation or relief, or as additional accomplishments. I believe rather that they represent, as types, fundamental forms of social activity; and that it is possible and desirable that the child's introduction into the more formal subjects of the curriculum be through the medium of these constructive activities.

The study of science is educational insofar as it brings out the materials and processes which make social life what it is.

One of the greatest difficulties in the present teaching of science is that the material is presented in purely objective form, or is treated as a new peculiar kind of experience which the child can add to that which he has already had. In reality, science is of value because it gives the ability to interpret and control the experience already had. It should be introduced, not as so much new subject matter, but as showing the factors already involved in previous experience and as furnishing tools by which that experience can be more easily and effectively regulated.

At present we lose much of the value of literature and language studies because of our elimination of the social element. Language is almost always treated in the books of pedagogy simply as the expression of thought. It is true that language is a logical instrument, but it is fundamentally and primarily a social instrument. Language is the device for communication; it is the tool through which one individual comes to share the ideas and feelings of others. When treated simply as a way of getting individual information, or as a means of showing off what one has learned, it loses its social motive and end.

There is, therefore, no succession of studies in the ideal school curriculum. If education is life, all life has, from the outset, a scientific aspect, an aspect of art and culture, and an aspect of communication. It cannot, therefore, be true that the proper studies for one grade are mere reading and writing, and that at a later grade, reading, or literature, or science, may be introduced. The progress is not in the succession of studies, but in the development of new attitudes towards, and new interests in, experience.

Education must be conceived as a continuing reconstruction of experience; the process and the goal of education are one and the same thing.

To set up any end outside of education, as furnishing its goal and standard, is to deprive the educational process of much of its meaning, and tends to make us rely upon false and external stimuli in dealing with the child.

Article Four—The Nature of Method

I believe that the question of method is ultimately reducible to the question of the order of development of the child's powers and interests. The law for presenting and treating material is the law implicit within the child's own nature. Because this is so I believe the following statements are of supreme importance as determining the spirit in which education is carried on.

The active side precedes the passive in the development of the child nature; expression comes before conscious impression; the muscular development precedes the sensory; movements come before conscious sensations; I believe that consciousness is essentially motor or impulsive; that conscious states tend to project themselves in action.

The neglect of this principle is the cause of a large part of the waste of time and strength in school work. The child is thrown into a passive, receptive, or absorbing attitude. The conditions are such that he is not permitted to follow the law of his nature; the result is friction and waste.

Ideas also result from action and devolve for the sake of the better control of action. What we term reason is primarily the law of order or effective action. To attempt to develop the reasoning powers, the powers of judgment, without reference to the selection and arrangement of means in action, is the fundamental fallacy in our present methods of dealing with this matter. As a result we present the child with arbitrary symbols. Symbols are a necessity in mental development, but they have their place as tools for economizing effort; presented by themselves they are a mass of meaningless and arbitrary ideas imposed from without.

The image is the great instrument of instruction. What a child gets out of any subject presented to him is simply the images which he himself forms with regard to it.

If nine-tenths of the energy at present directed towards making the child learn certain things were spent in seeing to it that the child was forming proper images, the work of instruction would be indefinitely facilitated.

Much of the time and attention now given to the preparation and presentation of lessons might be more wisely and profitably expended in training the child's power of imagery and in seeing to it that he was continually forming definite, vivid and growing images of the various subjects with which he comes in contact in his experience.

Interests are the signs and symptoms of growing power. I believe that they represent dawning capacities. Accordingly the constant and careful observation of interests is of the utmost importance for the educator.

These interests are to be observed as showing the state of development which the child has reached.

They prophesy the stage upon which he is about to enter.

Only through the continual and sympathetic observation of childhood's interests can the adult enter into the child's life and see what it is ready for, and upon what material it could work most readily and fruitfully.

These interests are neither to be humored nor repressed. To repress interest is to substitute the adult for the child, and so to weaken intellectual curiosity and alertness, to suppress initiative, and to deaden interest. To humor the interest is to substitute the transient for the permanent. The interest is always the sign of some power below; the important thing is to discover this power. To humor the interest is to fail to penetrate below the surface, and its sure result is to substitute caprice and whim for genuine interest.

The emotions are the reflex of actions.

To endeavor to stimulate or arouse the emotions apart from their corresponding activities is to introduce an unhealthy and morbid state of mind.

If we can only secure right habits of action and thought, with reference to the good, the true, and the beautiful, the emotions will for the most part take care of themselves.

Next to deadness and dullness, formalism and routine, our education is threatened with no greater evil than sentimentalism.

This sentimentalism is the necessary result of the attempt to divorce feeling from action.

Article Five—The School and Social Progress

I believe that education is the fundamental method of social progress and reform.

All reforms which rest simply upon the enactment of law, or the threatening of certain penalties, or upon changes in mechanical or outward arrangements, are transitory and futile.

Education is a regulation of the process of coming to share in the social consciousness; and the adjustment of individual activity on the basis of this social consciousness is the only sure method of social reconstruction.

This conception has due regard for both the individualistic and socialistic ideals. It is duly individual because it recognizes the formation of a certain character as the only genuine basis of right living. It is socialistic because it recognizes that this right character is not to be formed by merely individual precept, example, or exhortation, but rather by the influence of a certain form of institutional or community life upon the individual, and that the social organism through the school, as its organ, may determine ethical results.

In the ideal school we have the reconciliation of the individualistic and the institutional ideals.

The community's duty to education is, therefore, its paramount moral duty. By law and punishment, by social agitation and discussion, society can regulate and form itself in a more or less haphazard and chance way. But through education society can formulate its own purposes, can organize its own means and resources, and thus shape itself with definiteness and economy in the direction in which it wishes to move.

When society once recognizes the possibilities in this direction, and the obligations which these possibilities impose, it is impossible to conceive of the resources of time, attention, and money which will be put at the disposal of the educator.

It is the business of everyone interested in education to insist upon the school as the primary and most effective interest of social progress and reform in order that society may be awakened to realize what the school stands for, and aroused to the necessity of endowing the educator with sufficient equipment properly to perform his task.

Education thus conceived marks the most perfect and intimate union of science and art conceivable in human experience.

The art of thus giving shape to human powers and adapting them to social service is the supreme art; one calling into its service the best of artists; no insight, sympathy, tact, executive power, is too great for such service.

With the growth of psychological service, giving added insight into individual structure and laws of growth; and with growth of social science, adding to our knowledge of the right organization of individuals, all scientific resources can be utilized for the purposes of education.

When science and art thus join hands the most commanding motive for human action will be reached, the most genuine springs of human conduct aroused, and the best service that human nature is capable of guaranteed.

The teacher is engaged, not simply in the training of individuals, but in the formation of the proper social life.

Every teacher should realize the dignity of his calling; he is a social servant set apart for the maintenance of proper social order and the securing of the right social growth.

In this way the teacher always is the prophet of the true God and the usherer in of the true kingdom of God.

39

The Teacher as a Member of a Profession

GRACE GRAHAM

Treating the topic of the teacher as a member of a profession, Graham presents, in the selection that follows, a realistic yet sometimes idealistic study. It is realistic in that the teacher is well defined and the illustrations are appropriate. However, the selection may also be considered idealistic because Graham's pessimism toward the influence of existing, less-than-ideal conditions in the schools is suggestive of an essentially idealistic attitude. No student considering entry into the profession can afford to miss this enunciation of the aspirations of a true professional.

A PROFESSION is generally defined as a vocation requiring special knowledge of a department of learning or science. In this discussion more specific attributes of a profession are delineated as a basis for judging teaching as a profession and for describing the teacher's role as a professional person.

Ernest Greenwood's article on professionalism, summarized and paraphrased here, will serve as the basis for an evaluation of teaching as a profession.[1] In using polar concepts of professionalism and nonprofessionalism as Greenwood does, one must think in terms of a continuum rather than of discrete entities. That is, some occupations are more nearly professional than others, the range being from the most highly professional occupations to those that have little or no relationship to a profession. Hence the occupations of lawyers, professors, ministers, and physicians contrast sharply in degree of professionalism with those of migratory workers, garbage collectors, and scrubwomen; other vocations fall somewhere in between these extremes.

---

[1] Ernest Greenwood, "Attributes of a Profession," *Social Work*, 2 (July, 1957), 45–55 *passim;* also in Sigmund Nosow and William H. Form, eds., *Man, Work, and Society,* Basic Books, 1962, pp. 206–218.

SOURCE: Grace Graham, *The Public School in the New Society* (New York: Harper & Row, 1963), pp. 354–362. Copyright © 1963, 1969 by Grace Graham. Reprinted by permission of the publisher.

Dr. Graham is professor of education at the University of Oregon. She holds three degrees in education, and her special interest is the role of schools in American society. Among her more than thirty publications dealing with this special interest are clearly evidenced her extensive knowledge and understanding of contemporary problems.

Greenwood isolates the following five characteristics attributed to professions:

Systematic Body of Theory

The difference between a profession and nonprofession does not necessarily lie in the element of skill; a diamond-cutter, for example, has more manual dexterity and infallible expertness than a professor. The crucial distinction is that professional skills "flow from and are supported by a fund of knowledge that has been organized into an internally consistent system, called a *body of theory*." Theory is the "groundwork for practice" in a profession. Since the practices of a profession are based on an acquisition of theory, "preparation for a profession must be an intellectual as well as a practical experience." Professional preparation is therefore more abstract and academic, includes more intellectual content, and requires more formal education than does apprentice training.

Because theory is essential to the development of practice in a profession, much activity within the profession is devoted to "theory construction via systematic research." Professionals test their theories by applying the scientific method to problems of the profession. Their attitude is characterized by rationality: They question existing theories and new conceptualizations. Much of the activity of professional associations involves theoretical considerations. The emphasis upon theory among professional people creates "an intellectually stimulating milieu" that is in marked contrast to the occupational environment of a nonprofessional worker.

In every profession some individuals devote their efforts to expanding knowledge through theoretical research and others put into practice the theory and research findings. Not only is there a division of labor between the theory-oriented and the practice-oriented groups, but also the developing body of theory creates cleavages within the profession by promoting specialties.

Does teaching have a body of theory? There can be little doubt that it does —unsystematized perhaps and sometimes contradictory. The psychological, philosophical, and social foundations of education usually provide the theoretical bases for methodology and research. Experimentalist philosophy, based largely on the theories of John Dewey, and theories of child development have been very influential in American schools, especially in elementary schools. Other theories of recent origin are being tested. For example, Flanders and others hypothesize that a dimension Flanders calls "indirectness" in teacher behavior leads to increased achievement on the part of students. The so-called "discovery method" is predicated on the same theory.

Bruner, B. O. Smith, Ausubel, Gage, Hickey, and Newton theorize similarly with respect to the "cognitive structure" or organization of materials to be learned.[2] New theories of learning are expected to emerge out of biological research now in process.

Many teachers, almost totally unaware of the theoretical assumptions that they make in their daily work, are indifferent to the relationship between theory and practice and are prone to accept current theory as absolute truth. As undergraduates and perhaps as graduate students, they may jeer at professors who discuss theory and not practices and procedures. Professors of education are partly to blame for these attitudes. The professor who knows full well the benefits and limitations of theory is pressed by students for absolutes, for clean-cut, how-to-do-it recipes. If he hedges, the students brand him as incompetent. Finally under pressure what he started to expound as theory sounds like dictum. Any competent professor of education can and should make applications of theory, but if students graduate with only cookbook recipes about how to teach, they have been cheated. If they do not understand the theory and research behind practice, they do not know *why* they teach as they do. Furthermore, they cannot explain an educational program to the public nor develop new and creative approaches to teaching.

Let us take a simple illustration. Methods of helping children learn to read have changed because the theory changed. Traditionally children were taught the alphabet first, then short words and syllables, followed by longer words, and finally sentences. To early theorists this approach seemed logical. Later theorists began to think in terms of perception. Do we recognize a person because we have added together his various features, body structure, coloring, and the like, or do we recognize him at a glance when we see him or even when we see only part of him? Just as we may recognize a person without remembering the color of his eyes, we can recognize a word, a phrase, or a sentence without recalling whether a specific word had an "i" or an "e" in it. A radical change in the method of teaching reading developed from such concepts followed by experimentation. The result is that one widely accepted method of teaching reading today requires that children be taught to read whole phrases and sentences before they discover the alphabet and syllabication. This explanation is, of course, an oversimplification of reading theories, but it illustrates how a change in theoretical assumptions can set off a chain of new developments.

As theories are tested and elaborated and as new and sometimes better theories emerge, better methods of teaching are initiated. Unfortunately many practicing teachers fail to keep up with current theory and research. It is said to take 20 years for proved experimental results to trickle down to the level

[2] Nathaniel L. Gage, "Can Science Contribute to the Art of Teaching," *Phi Delta Kappan, 49* (March, 1966), 399–403.

of common practice. Not all teachers, of course, should be judged by the shortcomings of some teachers. Certainly many professional-minded teachers are well acquainted with recent research, cognizant of theoretical assumptions, active in professional associations and in-service training programs where new research findings are discussed. Nevertheless, teachers probably would not fare well in comparison with some other professionals in their attitudes toward theory. The conclusion might be drawn that although teaching skills are derived from a body of theory, not all members of the teaching profession are fully conversant with the theories.

Professional Authority

The professional educated in the systematized theory of his discipline possesses a body of knowledge that the layman does not have. This knowledge gives the professional an authority in his field. Unlike the customer in a store who decides for himself what he needs, the client of a professional believes that the professional knows what he needs. Because the professional has a "monopoly of judgment," he is constrained by the professional-client relationship to restrict his authority. He cannot use the professional relationship in which his client is dependent upon him to satisfy his own need to manipulate others, to live vicariously, or as a sexual outlet. Extraprofessional relations between client and professional tend to impair professional authority and lessen the professional's effectiveness, as many a doctor has reason to know.

Does the lay public accord teachers a "monopoly of judgment"? Is he considered an authority? The criticisms of the teaching of reading clearly indicate that many people believe that they know how to teach children to read better than teachers do. Similar criticisms of teaching methods and of the knowledge of high school teachers suggest that many people, especially those in the middle class, do not consider the teacher an authority in his field. A factor that weakens the teacher's "monopoly of judgment" is the educator's view that "the schools belong to the people." Educational leadership has tried to draw a line between the public's authority and the teacher's sphere of expertness by pointing out that the community should decide the general policy in respect to what should be taught and the teacher should be responsible for details of content and methodology. But at the local community level the line has not always been held.

Although a teacher is not granted a complete monopoly of expertness, he has considerable discretion, through selection of materials for study, in the content of classwork. State departments of education provide guidelines. The NEA code of ethics warns him to "discuss controversial issues from an objective point of view, thereby keeping his class free from partisan opinions." The publications of professional organizations keep him posted on current issues. The teacher's subculture forbids his introducing discussions of sexual behavior except under certain conditions and prohibits his use of obscenity, profanity, and vulgarity. The teaching norms warn a teacher against extraprofessional relationships with pupils that may weaken his effectiveness as a teacher. The neophyte who becomes an equal and intimate of his pupils soon learns the error of his ways. He loses his equalitarian status among teachers and becomes a competitor or a love object rather than a guide to young people.

Sanction of the Community

The members of each profession try to induce society to recognize their authority by giving them certain powers and privileges. Professional organizations seek to control the admission of persons to the profession, the accrediting of training centers, and the licensing of individuals. Among the privileges members of a profession want is that of "privileged communication," the legal right to keep confidences between professional and client confidential. They want to be judged on technical matters by their colleagues, not by laymen. Such powers and privileges are not easily gained because many people resist strongly the profession's claim to authority. Members of the profession have to persuade lay people that they will benefit by giving them such privileges.

Specifically the profession seeks to prove: that the performance of the occupational skill requires specialized education; that those who possess this education, in contrast to those who do not, deliver a superior service; and that the human need being served is of sufficient social importance to justify the superior performance.[3]

To what extent do teachers have "the sanction of the community?" Teachers as a professional group have little control over who becomes a teacher. Unlike medical professionals who are accused of deliberately limiting the number of applicants to medical schools, teachers cannot prevent almost anybody who can earn a college degree from becoming a teacher. Although a few are eliminated by selection processes in professional schools, many persons who major in liberal arts and take the minimum number of hours in education are never evaluated formally by anyone except a critic teacher, and then only by one person using limited criteria. If they can pass the courses, they get a state credential. In 1946 the NEA created the National Commission on Teacher Education and Professional Standards, and in 1952 several agencies cooperated in founding the National Council for Accreditation of

[3] Greenwood in Nosow and Form, *op. cit.,* p. 212.

Teacher Education. Both of these agencies are working to raise the level of professional education of teachers.

In recent years many persons have entered teaching on emergency credentials at the recommendations of school superintendents and with the approval of the state departments of education. Some teachers on emergency credentials have had little formal college training in either liberal arts or professional education. The teacher shortage seemed to justify emergency credentials, but somehow the "emergency," with little abatement, has lasted for over two decades. The question might be raised as to whether lowering or raising standards is the better way to encourage qualified persons to enter teaching. The number of unqualified teachers who are employed in American schools is undoubtedly a factor in the folk belief that "anybody can teach school."

Martin Mayer, a professional writer who has observed hundreds of teachers, in *The Schools* says that teaching, like journalism, can never become a profession as long as a "gifted amateur" can do the work as well as a professionally educated person. By this criterion few professionals exist. A few years ago a clever impersonator posed as a physician, performed surgery, and served under the surveillance of physicians as a medical doctor in the armed forces. Another posed successfully as a college dean after falsely claiming that he had a doctorate. It is still possible for a gifted and persistent person to read law on his own and pass a state bar examination, and much legal work is done by accountants, law clerks, and auditors who do not hold law degrees. The knowledge of subject matter or the theories upon which teaching skills are based can be learned without formal instruction. To deny that a gifted person can learn without the benefit of formal education would be to deny the very purpose of formal education, but rules are made to cover the usual and not the unusual cases. Clearly the majority of persons benefit from the education required of teachers. Exceptions can then be made for persons who offer equivalences for specific requirements.

Teacher-education programs differ somewhat, however, from state to state because the requirements for a credential are determined in different ways in different states. The power to specify the requirements is divided among legislatures, boards of education, teacher-training institutions, state departments of education, and superintendents of public instruction. The hodgepodge of programs that developed contribute to the layman's belief that there are no theories a person should understand or specific skills that he should acquire before he begins to teach.

Regulative Code of Ethics

Since a professional's monopoly can be abused by malpractice that might cause the community to revoke power and privileges, the profession as a whole adopts a regulative code to compel members to behave ethically. Such a code is in part formal and in part informal. In it the profession pledges itself to social welfare. It specifies that a member of a profession must provide services to anyone who requests them, irrespective of the applicant's income, religion, politics, race, and other such factors. Whether he likes or dislikes the applicant is irrelevant. He must give the best service of which he is capable, even at the sacrifice of personal convenience.

The code further requires that the professional's behavior in relationships with his professional associates shall be "cooperative, equalitarian, and supportive." He shares technical knowledge. He does not compete blatantly for clients. He regards his colleagues as equals and grants professional recognition to those whose performance in practice or whose contributions to theoretical research are superior to his own. He supports his fellow professionals by his words and actions in the presence of those who are not members of the profession.

The code is enforced by pressures upon individual members to exert self-discipline. Through consultation and referral, colleagues become mutually interdependent. When a professional behaves in an unseemly manner, he is excluded from this system of reciprocity. For serious offenses the professional association may censure a member or even bar him from further membership in the association. To be disbarred from the association can be a stigma that may prevent a member from pursuing the profession.

Do public school teachers subscribe to a Code of Ethics? The NEA Code is presumably accepted by NEA members. Over half of the state education associations use the same code or a similar one. This code sets out the obligations of teachers toward pupils, parents, the community, and the school administration.

Among other provisions, it states that the teacher's first obligation is that he "deal justly and impartially with students regardless of their physical, mental, emotional, political, economic, social, racial, or religious characteristics." He is admonished to maintain "a professional level of service." He should "speak constructively of other teachers" and deal with them as he himself wishes to be treated. The provisions spell out ethical conduct for a teacher in respect to securing and honoring contracts, his behavior in a community, and his obligation to respect the basic responsibility of parents for their children.

A professional code is effective to the extent that members of a profession understand and accept the code's principles and abide by them. The severest punishment that can be meted out to one who breaks such a code is the revoking of his membership in the professional association. Expulsion of a member from the NEA is, however, relatively meaningless since almost half of the nation's teachers do not belong to this association. Until the day when teachers must belong to a professional association as a condition of employment, an association's rebuke cannot effectively discipline offenders.

The Professional Culture

All occupations operate through a system of formal and informal groupings. The formal professional groupings are the institutions (universities, hospitals, law offices, public schools and the like) within which professionals give service to clients, the educational and research centers of the profession, and the professional associations. The informal professional groupings consist of cliques of colleagues formed around specialties, professional affiliations, place of work, personal attraction, and perhaps family, religious, and ethnic backgrounds. As a result, a professional culture develops that is quite different from the nonprofessional culture. Each profession also develops its own subcultures or variants of the professional culture.

The content of professional culture is its values, norms, and symbols. The most fundamental of its beliefs is the social value that each subculture attributes to its own contributions to the general welfare. The members of a profession believe that they are far more knowledgeable in their sphere of expertness than are any outsiders. Nevertheless, within the subculture the professional's theory and technical knowledge are often challenged. Subcultural norms are the standards of behavior in social relationships. There are approved modi operandi for obtaining appointments, making referrals, and holding consultations. There are proper ways of relating to clients, peers, superiors, and subordinates. Greenwood defines the symbols of a profession as its "meaning-laden items," such as its distinctive dress, its history and folklore, its heroes and its villains; and its stereotypes of its own members, of its clients, and of laymen.

The professional thinks of his occupation as a career, a calling. His work is not "a means to an end; it is an end itself." He considers his service valuable, and performs it primarily for psychic satisfaction rather than for monetary gain. He is absorbed in his work, both on and off the job. His work is his life. The novice in a profession is not a part of it simply because he has learned its theory and mastered technical skill. He must also accept the subcultural values, norms, and symbols of the subculture. One of the purposes of a professional school is to screen out those who might be deviants. If a neophyte cannot acquit himself acceptably in relationships with clients, laymen, and colleagues, he will be judged unfit, irrespective of his academic qualifications.

A teaching subculture is a reality in the nation and in every community. The most significant element of this subculture is the general belief among teachers that they are serving mankind in an important way. Their chief concern is for the children they teach, and much of their "shop talk," sometimes ridiculed by outsiders, is about their pupils. Most teachers are willing to work overtime at night and on week ends if they believe the welfare of their pupils is thereby advanced. In 1915 Abraham Flexner analyzed a profession as basically practical, organized internally, altruistic, and intellectual, based on great knowlege and having techniques that can be taught and learned. After a careful analysis of these criteria, he almost tossed them away by declaring that:

what matters most is professional spirit. . . . The unselfish devotion of those who have chosen to give themselves to making the world a fitter place to live in can fill social work [or teaching] with the professional spirit and thus to some extent lift it above all the distinctions which I have been at such pains to make.[4]

Most people, like Flexner, believed that a profession is distinguished by its moral behavior and its concern for other human beings.

The teacher's subculture has other distinctive characteristics. Although in many respects teachers are less confident of the expertness of some of their colleagues, less knowledgeable of theory, and therefore less intelligently critical of technical knowledge than might be expected of professionals, they are usually as cooperative and supportive of one another as are any other professionals. They use a specialized vocabulary in discussing school problems, develop patterns of behavior (such as addressing each other as "Miss" or "Mister" in the presence of pupils) deemed appropriate to the institutionalized setting, and maintain standards of dress. Teachers are sometimes hypercorrect in their patterns of speech. One of the unfortunate occupational hazards of teaching, which is perhaps less apparent today than in earlier years, is a habit of speaking with authority even on subjects in which the teacher is not an expert. Another characteristic common among elementary school teachers is a tendency to talk to adults as if they were children. Such practices contribute to the stereotype that a teacher is a didactic person. On her first airplane trip, Miss Dove, the teacher-heroine of novel and film, sat close to the pilot to instruct him in celestial navigation!

The Discrepancy Between Reality and the Ideal

The preceding discussion may convey the impression that teaching does not really meet the criteria for a profession. When other limitations are con-

[4] Abraham Flexner, "Is Social Work a Profession?" *Proceedings of the National Conference of Charities and Correction,* Hildmann, 1915, pp. 576–590.

sidered, such as the number of girls who use teaching as a stepping-stone to marriage, the fact that teachers are public servants, and the number of diverse groups including school administrators that are bunched together as members of the teaching profession, the complexities involved in determining professional status of teachers are compounded. Clearly college and university professors have less ambiguous claims to the status than do public school teachers because they are more knowledgeable of theory, more highly educated in esoteric and difficult bodies of knowledge, and more likely to be accepted as experts in their fields. They have more but not complete control over admission to the profession, training of applicants, and evaluation of performance of colleagues, but they too are institutionalized employees who are imperfectly organized internally and subject to social pressures.

Significant to any discussion of professionalism is an acceptance of the view that professional status is actually an honorific symbol of prestige.[5] No group ever completely attains its professional goals or measures up to the ideal attributes of a profession. The medical profession is perhaps the most powerful of all career groups in such matters as controlling admittance to the profession, but it falls short in many respects. It does not have a monopoly of the knowledge of medicine, for much of the knowledge is known and created by scientists who are not doctors of medicine. The profession shares its social function of healing the sick with osteopaths, chiropractors, Christian Science practitioners, and others. Some physicians apparently place making money above service, and their numbers may be growing because medical students today, according to interest and value tests, are much like businessmen in their attitudes. Laymen do make judgments about doctors and demonstrate their lack of faith in the medical expert by shopping around for a "good" doctor. As in all professions, there are unethical practitioners. Even doctors who are usually ethical may be influenced by what the client wants, prescribing new drugs upon demand, for instance. Many physicians are also employees of institutions in which they are subject to the same bureaucratic pressures as professors and teachers.[6]

If the ideal of complete professionalism is unobtainable, why should an occupational group ever strive toward a professional goal? Becker says, "Symbols are useful things. They help people and groups organize their lives and embody conceptions of what is good and worthwhile. They enhance the possibility of purposeful collective action. They make more likely the realization of ideals held by large segments of society." [7] He suggests, however, that a

[5] See Howard S. Becker, "The Nature of a Profession," in National Society for the Study of Education, 61st Yearbook, part 2, *Education for the Professions*, University of Chicago Press, 1962, pp. 33–46.
[6] See Becker, *op. cit.*, pp. 41–45, for a summary and analysis of research on the medical profession.
[7] Becker, *op. cit.*, p. 45.

symbol with so many dysfunctional elements, such as the monopoly of a sphere of knowledge and failure of clients to accept professional judgment, may need revision. He believes the symbol should fit the realities of the present-day world.

If the symbol of professionalism is to be useful to teachers, it must evoke at least five significant responses. These are great concern and effort on the part of teachers to keep abreast of elaborations of theory and research, participation in professional associations, high standards of competence, wholehearted acceptance of a code of ethics, and a sense of moral responsibility. Only in the last response, which fortunately is of great significance, do teachers compare well with people in other professions. Martin Mayer concludes that teachers are "good people," but he also thinks that most teachers believe themselves to be better teachers than they are in fact. Although Mayer's credentials as a critic might be questioned, his words should give us pause.

With the exception of his participation in national and state professional associations, the test of a teacher as a professional person is his behavior in his own school and community. Is he ethical in his relationships with pupils, colleagues, parents, the administration, and the lay public? Does he know and abide by the ground rules of his profession? Is he interested in improving his competence as a teacher? Does he honestly give the *best* service of which he is capable? Is he fair and unbiased in the classroom? Does he keep the confidences of his students? Is he respected for his skill as a teacher and for his integrity? These are criteria by which a teacher is judged as a professional.

Recent growth in membership of the American Federation of Teachers (AFT), an affiliate of the AFL–CIO, which encourages militancy and espouses teacher strikes under certain circumstances, has led to charges that this organization is unprofessional. If such is the case, does the lack of professionalism lie in AFT's failure to abide by the ground rules? Should they be changed?

40
Professional Organizations

SIDNEY DORROS

*As members of a profession, teachers as well as other career persons in educa-
tion have become associated with their own distinctive professional organizations. This selection (an appropriate one to accompany the following piece by
Jacques Barzun, whose persuasive pen and personal involvement reflect his
deep empathy with those striving to have teaching achieve professional recognition) introduces you to some history of the various professional organizations. Dorros says that young, inexperienced teachers too often choose professional affiliations with no knowledge of their real purposes or the professional
advantages they offer, behavior he regards as inexcusable in a professional.*

GROUP professional responsibilities of teachers are fulfilled through various
agencies in many different ways, but the preceding review of nine areas of
professional concern leaves little doubt that professional organizations are by
far the most important agencies through which teachers do collectively what
is impossible for them to do individually.

Before a teacher can help maintain effective professional organizations he
must decide which organizations to join and support. In some situations this
is a difficult problem and requires much knowledge of the types of organizations and of their objectives, methods, activities, dues, and achievements. Education has more organizations than any other occupational field. There are
over one thousand state, regional, and national organizations in education
and about ten thousand local associations.

Major types of such organizations may be classified as follows: (1) general
purpose, embracing most interests of the teaching profession; (2) special interest, related to subject field, teaching level, or type of position; and (3) honorary or fraternal societies. In addition there are teachers' unions which are
usually classified separately.

General purpose organizations may be further divided into three categories: (1) all-inclusive, enrolling all types of educators—classroom teachers,

SOURCE: Sidney Dorros, *Teaching as a Profession* (Columbus, Ohio: Charles E. Merrill Publishing Company, 1968), pp. 94–116. Reprinted by permission of the publisher.

Dr. Dorros is Director of the Publications Division of the National Education Association, a post he has held since 1957. He has taught school and for many years has
been an active member of the Maryland State Teachers Association. He is the author of
How Good Is Your Child's School? and *Legacy of Honor.*

administrators, and others—in one single organization; (2) all-inclusive, but with departments according to special interests; and (3) separate organizations according to occupational position.

The multiplicity of organizations is not quite as chaotic as it seems when one learns that approximately ninety percent of all public school educators are indirectly associated with the all-inclusive national organization, the National Education Association, through membership in departments and in state and local affiliates of the NEA; and slightly more than half of all public school teachers are directly enrolled as NEA members.

Although many teacher organizations overlap or compete with each other for members, there is little open antagonism except between the American Federation of Teachers and the National Education Association, including its state and local affiliates. In 1966, the AFT had in its membership only seven percent of instructional staff of the public schools in the United States but, with backing of the AFL-CIO, the Federation was actively engaged in trying to win the majority of teachers away from the NEA and its affiliates. In the future it is likely that many teachers will be faced with choosing between the rival organizations. To make a wise choice teachers should be familiar with historical highlights of the development of teacher organizations, their current objectives and status, major issues, and the outlook for the future.

History of Professional Organizations

1. Origins of the National Education Association

a. Local general-purpose teacher associations may be traced back at least to 1794 when the Society of Associated Teachers was organized in New York City. Early local associations of teachers served primarily to provide for fellowship, in-service growth of teachers, improvement of the school curriculum and methods of teaching, and financial assistance to teachers in times of sickness or retirement. There is little evidence of significant influence of local teacher organizations in improving financial support and conditions of teaching until the advent of state teachers' associations.

b. The first state teachers' associations were established in the 1840's. By 1857, eighteen states had established state associations of teachers. The state associations emerged to be the most influential type of organization, partly because the most crucial legislation affecting public education had been at the state level.

c. In 1857, ten state teachers' associations initiated a meeting in Philadelphia at which the NEA was established. It was first called the National Teachers' Association. The name National Education Association of the

United States was adopted in 1906 when it was chartered by act of Congress.

(1) The prime initiators of the national association were relatively humble "practical teachers" rather than well-known or highly placed leaders. The two men primarily responsible for the first meeting were Thomas W. Valentine and Daniel B. Hagar, presidents, respectively, of the state associations of New York and Massachusetts. Valentine was a grammar-school teacher in Brooklyn and Hagar was principal of the Normal School at Salem, Massachusetts. However, famous educational leaders such as Horace Mann and Henry Barnard soon joined and became active in the Association.

(2) The purposes of the National Teachers' Association were stated in its first constitution: "To elevate the character and advance the interests of the profession of teaching, and to promote the cause of popular education in the United States." These basic purposes of what is now the NEA have remained the same until the present.

(3) For at least the first thirty years, the major activity of the National Teachers' Association was the exchange of ideas in speeches and discussions at the annual convention. Although now overshadowed by other activities of the NEA, the annual meetings remain a major educational forum. Recorded in the annual volumes of the NEA *Addresses and Proceedings* are thousands of speeches in which one can read the history of the problems, aspirations, and achievements of American education. Speakers have included almost all presidents of the United States since the last quarter of the nineteenth century as well as such educational greats as Horace Mann and John Dewey.

2. The Era of Influence by Committee Pronouncement

From its founding by forty-three educators in 1857 until the end of World War I, the organization that is now the NEA remained a relatively small organization. By 1917, the NEA had only 8,500 members. Its leadership was dominated by college professors and school and college administrators. During the late nineteenth and early twentieth century the pronouncements of various blue ribbon, special committees had major influence on the development of American education. Some of the most influential committees are listed below:

Committee of Ten on Secondary School Studies, 1892–93
Committee of Fifteen on Elementary Education, 1893–95
Committee of Twelve on Rural Schools, 1895
Committees on College Entrance Requirements, 1899–1911
Commission on Reorganization of Secondary Education, 1913–21

3. The Broadening Base of NEA Membership

a. After 1917, the NEA began a slow change from administrator-domination to classroom-teacher predominance. The influx of classroom teachers into membership swelled membership from 8,500 in 1917 to 53,000 in 1920, 216,000 in 1930, 454,000 in 1950, and about one million members by 1966.

b. Reasons for increasing classroom teacher membership and influence in the NEA include the following:

(1) The extension of political and other equal rights to women established a more favorable climate for participation of women teachers in affairs of the NEA and of state and local associations. The first woman president of the NEA, Ella Flagg Young of Chicago, was elected in 1910. This was accomplished only after a vigorous campaign and a vote from the floor in opposition to the candidate proposed by the majority of the nominating committee.

(2) Higher levels of preparation of teachers enabled many more teachers to hold their own in organizational contacts with administrators.

(3) Problems created by wartime neglect of the schools spurred teachers to attempt to improve their situation through teacher organizations.

(4) Competition of the American Federation of Teachers, organized in 1916, stimulated association leaders to attempt to enroll more teachers in membership and to give them a greater voice in the professional associations.

(5) The establishment of a permanent headquarters and staff of the NEA in Washington in 1917 led to great expansion of the association and increased effectiveness in pursuing goals of interest to classroom teachers.

(6) The creation of the Representative Assembly of the NEA in 1920 as the major governing body of the NEA encouraged widespread teacher interest in the NEA because delegates were selected by state and local associations.

(7) Beginning about 1910, and accelerating rapidly after 1920, the NEA began to play a major role in advancing teacher welfare as well as in the improvement of instruction.

(8) State and local associations increased their teacher membership and effective activities on behalf of teachers after 1910.

c. These listed developments led to the election of the first classroom teacher as president of the NEA in 1928. Classroom teachers have steadily gained in leadership, influence, and membership in the association since that time.

4. Development of State Education Associations

a. Between 1907 and 1925, the percent of eligible educators enrolled in state associations increased from fourteen to seventy-three percent. By 1966, approximately, ninety percent of the instructional staff in the United States was enrolled in state associations.

b. Prior to 1910, the principal activity of most state associations was to hold an annual convention. Only a few states employed staffs or maintained offices.

c. As membership and staffs of state associations grew, they became very effective in lobbying for favorable state legislation. Major legislative concerns and successes in most states included increased funds for all aspects of education, the establishment of state minimum salary laws, teacher tenure laws, teacher retirement provisions, and certification requirements.

5. Development of Local Education Associations

Until fairly recently local teacher organizations have been considered to be the weakest link in the chain of professional organizations.

a. Prior to the 1960's, a few local associations employed staffs. Most had nominal dues, too low to support much of a program.

b. In many large cities which could have supported effective organizations, the splintering of teachers and administrators into many different local organizations rendered the organizations relatively ineffective. In New York City, for example, in the 1950's there were well over 100 different organizations of educators. Teachers were divided by teaching level, subjects taught, and even by religion.

c. Since 1960, many local associations have employed executive secretaries, broadened their programs, and increased cooperation with the state associations and the NEA. This vitalization of local education associations seems to be due in part to competition of teacher unions seeking to become exclusive bargaining agents for teachers. But even in school systems where there is no direct competition from teacher unions, local associations have been stimulated by success of strong, unified associations in winning increased support for education, improved teacher welfare, and better teaching conditions.

6. Development of Departments of the NEA

a. The development of NEA departments serving special interests of the teaching profession dates back to 1870. In that year the National Association of School Superintendents and the American Normal School Association merged with the National Teachers' Association to form the National Educational Association. The two groups became the first departments of the NEA.

b. Since 1870, a number of new departments were added to cover almost every major interest in education. Most departments were first established outside the NEA and later applied for admission. In some cases the NEA sponsored and subsidized new departments in fields where they seemed to be needed.

7. History of the American Federation of Teachers

a. The American Federation of Teachers was organized in 1916 and affiliated the same year with the American Federation of Labor (AFL, now AFL-CIO). It was initiated by a few local organizations that had previously affiliated individually with organized labor.

b. From its beginning the AFT differed from the NEA in at least three ways:

(1) The AFT did not admit superintendents into membership and accepted principals and supervisors only under specified conditions.

(2) It adopted many of the tenets of organized labor such as labor-management (teacher-administration) conflict of interests, and it adopted union procedures to achieve its objectives.

(3) The AFT concentrated almost exclusively on teacher welfare and teaching conditions, while the NEA worked for improvement of instruction, professional standards, research, and professional ethics as well as for teacher welfare.

c. Beginning with about 2,400 members in 1917, AFT membership spurted to 10,000 by 1920. However, membership dropped to 3,500 by 1925. This drop was caused in part by revitalization of program and vigorous recruitment activities of the NEA.

d. Teacher union membership grew slowly after 1925 to reach about 61,000 by 1961. This membership constituted slightly less than 4 percent of the instructional staff of public schools.

e. Beginning in the 1950's, the AFT began to get considerable help in money, manpower, and advice from the AFL-CIO, particularly the Industrial Union Department. This assistance was part of a comprehensive union drive to organize white collar workers, technicians, government employees, and salaried professional workers.

f. In 1961 the AFT achieved the greatest gain in its history. In that year the United Federation of Teachers, an AFT affiliate, won an election giving it the right to engage in collective bargaining with the school board on behalf of over 40,000 New York City teachers. This led to a gain of over 20,000 members in New York City alone by 1965.

(1) The New York City representation election was a psychological blow to the NEA, which supported a hastily and loosely organized coalition of dozens of non-union teacher organizations opposed to the AFT in the election.

(2) In the few years following the victory in New York City, AFT affiliates challenged NEA affiliates in a number of cities for the right to represent teachers in bargaining with school boards. In terms of numbers of elections won the NEA affiliates came out far ahead, but the AFT won most of the elections in the very largest city school systems where the NEA had not been very strong.

(3) By 1966, AFT locals had won representation rights in Detroit, Cleveland, and Boston and were engaged in an all-out war with NEA affiliates in a number of other cities. In that year total AFT membership reached 120,000.

8. Accomplishments of Teacher Organizations

a. . . . . Practically every advance of the teaching profession has been led, stimulated, or supported by professional associations.

b. The AFT has not been large enough or powerful enough to build a record of accomplishment that can be evaluated at this time. But Federation spokesmen have declared that the very threat of unionization of teachers has stimulated administrators and school boards to improve teacher welfare and conditions of work and has stimulated professional associations to more militant activity.

Current Status of Professional Organizations

1. Purposes and Activities of the National Education Association

The NEA is the largest professional organization in the world. It serves almost all members of the teaching profession and works for improvement of almost all aspects of education, many of which have been described in this book. It would take more space than is available here even to list the complete variety of concerns and activities of the NEA and its affiliates. The scope of objectives of the NEA may be found in the Platform and Resolutions adopted each summer by the NEA Representative Assembly. These policy guidelines, details of the purposes and activities of the various national units and departments of the NEA, and a complete list of all state and local affiliates, are to be found in the latest edition of the annually-revised *NEA Handbook for Local, State, and National Associations*. Much of the following information is from the *NEA Handbook*. To organize one's concept of the NEA without getting lost in detail, it may be useful to consider the following outline of types of objectives of the NEA and means of achieving them.

a. Basic objectives of the NEA include:

(1) High quality instruction
(2) Favorable teaching conditions
(3) Teacher welfare
(4) Protection of rights of teachers
(5) Professional standards
(6) Active public support of education
(7) Adequate facilities and materials

b. Major means the NEA uses to achieve its objectives include:

(1) Research
(2) Publications
(3) Press, radio, and television
(4) Field services
(5) Conventions
(6) Legislative lobbying
(7) Professional negotiation
(8) Investigation reports
(9) Sanctions

2. Membership in the NEA

In 1966, there were approximately one million individual regular members of the NEA. The members include all types of educators—classroom teachers, school administrators, college professors and administrators, and specialists in schools, colleges, and educational agencies, both public and private. An estimated eighty-five to ninety percent of all regular NEA members are classroom teachers. In addition to regular members (active, associate, life, and retired) the NEA membership includes about 120,000 student members. Annual dues for active members were $10 in 1966.

3. NEA Services to Members

a. All types of members receive nine issues of the *NEA Journal* annually and about twelve issues of the *NEA Reporter.*

(1) The *NEA Journal* contains articles to help improve instruction, improve teacher welfare, raise professional standards, and to keep up with new developments in education from kindergarten through college.

(2) The *NEA Reporter* is a professional newspaper that reports plans and activities of the NEA and its affiliates.

b. NEA members who are also members of their state association are entitled also to participate in money-saving optional economic welfare benefits made possible by the large size of the NEA membership. These programs include the following:

(1) Group life insurance
(2) Accident insurance
(3) Mutual investment fund
(4) Tax-sheltered annuities

c. Active members may serve on NEA committees and commissions, participate in conferences, workshops, and the annual convention, receive consultant help by mail or in person, serve as delegates to the NEA from their local and state education associations, and directly, or through their representatives, have a voice in determining NEA policies.

d. The indirect benefits to the teaching profession and society stemming from NEA activities are probably even more significant than the direct benefits to members. NEA research, publications, films and filmstrips, conferences, press releases, radio and television programs establish a general climate favorable to education and provide specific information and stimulation used by local and state associations, colleges and universities, school boards, lay organizations, and governmental bodies. Many of the gains in advancing the status of the teaching profession and the cause of education, although directly achieved by other agencies, could not come to pass without the services available from the NEA.

4. How NEA Policy Is Determined

In effect, the NEA is governed by representatives of its state and local affiliates. Following are descriptions of the governing bodies:

a. Representative Assembly. The Representative Assembly is composed mainly of approximately 6,500 delegates sent by affiliated local and state associations to the annual meeting of the NEA. Delegates are allocated on the basis of the number of NEA members in each association. The budget, resolutions, recommendations, reports of officers and committees, and amendments to the Bylaws must be presented to the Representative Assembly for approval. The annual resolutions of this body establish policies which outline the general program and guide the activities of the officers and staff throughout the year. The Representative Assembly also elects the president and other major officers of the NEA.

b. Board of Directors. The Board of Directors is charged with looking after many aspects of Association affairs between meetings of the Representative Assembly and with making reports and recommendations to the Assembly. Each state is entitled to choose one or more directors, depending upon the number of NEA members in the state. State directors promote NEA membership and program in their respective states.

c. Executive Committee. The Executive Committee acts on behalf of the Board of Directors between meetings of the Board. The eleven-member Committee is composed of the major officers of the Association, the chairman of the Board of Trustees, two members elected by and from the Board of Directors, at least one of whom must be a classroom teacher, and four members elected at large by the Representative Assembly, at least two of whom must be classroom teachers.

d. Board of Trustees. The trustees' responsibilities are limited to appointment of the executive secretary of the Association and management of the permanent funds and properties of the Association.

5. Organizational Structure of the NEA

The NEA structure at the national level includes four types of permanent units: commissions (and council), committees, departments, and divisions. In addition, special projects of relatively short duration focus attention and action on crucial current problems. See the NEA Organizational Chart for the abbreviated names and relationships of these units.

a. Commissions and Council. Five commissions and one council operate in large areas of professional interest under the general supervision of the Executive Committee. These units conduct investigations, formulate proposed policies, recommend standards, disseminate information, build support for better programs of education, and work for safeguards necessary to protect freedom of teaching and learning.

b. Committees. Six standing committees of the NEA carry on continuous programs of study, interpretation, and action in the fields of citizenship,

Organization Chart of the National Education Association, August 1967

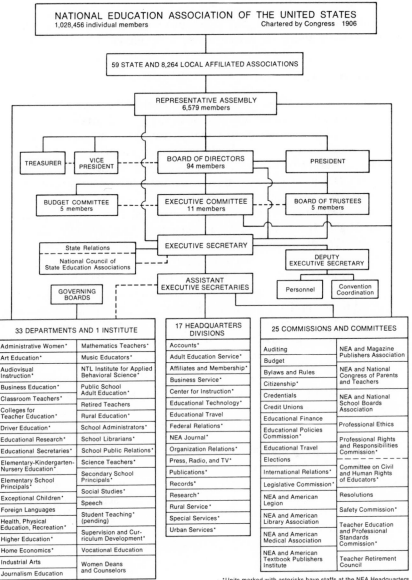

NATIONAL EDUCATION ASSOCIATION OF THE UNITED STATES
1,028,456 individual members   Chartered by Congress   1906

59 STATE AND 8,264 LOCAL AFFILIATED ASSOCIATIONS

REPRESENTATIVE ASSEMBLY
6,579 members

TREASURER | VICE PRESIDENT | BOARD OF DIRECTORS 94 members | PRESIDENT

BUDGET COMMITTEE 5 members | EXECUTIVE COMMITTEE 11 members | BOARD OF TRUSTEES 5 members

EXECUTIVE SECRETARY

State Relations
National Council of State Education Associations

DEPUTY EXECUTIVE SECRETARY

ASSISTANT EXECUTIVE SECRETARIES

Personnel | Convention Coordination

GOVERNING BOARDS

33 DEPARTMENTS AND 1 INSTITUTE

Administrative Women*	Mathematics Teachers*
Art Education*	Music Educators*
Audiovisual Instruction*	NTL Institute for Applied Behavioral Science*
Business Education*	Public School Adult Education*
Classroom Teachers*	Retired Teachers
Colleges for Teacher Education*	Rural Education*
Driver Education*	School Administrators*
Educational Research*	School Librarians*
Educational Secretaries*	School Public Relations*
Elementary-Kindergarten-Nursery Education*	Science Teachers*
Elementary School Principals*	Secondary School Principals*
Exceptional Children*	Social Studies*
Foreign Languages	Speech
Health, Physical Education, Recreation*	Student Teaching* (pending)
Higher Education*	Supervision and Curriculum Development*
Home Economics*	Vocational Education
Industrial Arts	Women Deans and Counselors
Journalism Education	

17 HEADQUARTERS DIVISIONS

Accounts*
Adult Education Service*
Affiliates and Membership*
Business Service*
Center for Instruction*
Educational Technology*
Educational Travel
Federal Relations*
NEA Journal*
Organization Relations*
Press, Radio, and TV*
Publications*
Records*
Research*
Rural Service*
Special Services*
Urban Services*

25 COMMISSIONS AND COMMITTEES

Auditing	NEA and Magazine Publishers Association
Budget	
Bylaws and Rules	NEA and National Congress of Parents and Teachers
Citizenship*	
Credentials	NEA and National School Boards Association
Credit Unions	
Educational Finance	Professional Ethics
Educational Policies Commission*	
Educational Travel	Professional Rights and Responsibilities Commission*
Elections	
International Relations*	Committee on Civil and Human Rights of Educators*
Legislative Commission*	
NEA and American Legion	Resolutions
NEA and American Library Association	Safety Commission*
NEA and American Medical Association	Teacher Education and Professional Standards Commission*
NEA and American Textbook Publishers Institute	Teacher Retirement Council

*Units marked with asterisks have staffs at the NEA Headquarters

credit unions, educational travel, international relations, professional ethics, and educational finance. Six additional committees function in connection with the annual convention: Audit, Budget, Bylaws and Rules, Credentials, Elections, and Resolutions.

c. Joint Committees. The joint committee is one form of cooperation between the NEA and other organizations with mutual interests in specific problems.

d. Departments.

(1) Through thirty-three departments, the NEA meets many of the special needs of educators, as well as the general needs of education. Most departments fall into one of three categories: subject field, such as social studies or science; school level, such as elementary or higher education; and type of position, such as classroom teacher or administrator.

(2) Departments choose their own officers, plan their special-interest programs, and adopt policies which apply to their specialization. Except for the Department of Classroom Teachers and the National Association for Higher Education, all departments levy dues to support their programs. The departments receive free housing and other services from the NEA. All departments promote and urge NEA membership on the part of their members. Many of them require NEA membership.

(3) After a department has decided what ought to be done with respect to any problem in which it is especially interested, it may receive help in implementation from the NEA or other departments. Most of the relationships between the NEA and departments are voluntary and informal and depend to a great degree upon mutual interests and cooperation.

e. Divisions. Eighteen NEA divisions provide basic services such as research and publications for members, affiliates, and other NEA units and departments.

f. Special Projects. Special projects involving intensive programs of short duration focus NEA resources on selected programs of high current concern. Projects of recent years have dealt with juvenile delinquency, the academically talented, urban problems, instruction, time to teach, English composition, automation, and NEA development. Some of these projects have been financed in whole or part by philanthropic foundations. In addition, many special projects have been conducted by departments in their fields of interest.

g. Consultants. Several NEA consultants, who work with state and local associations and school systems and with individuals, operate directly from offices of some assistant executive secretaries of the NEA. Included are general field workers and consultants for such concerns as the improvement of instruction and salaries. However, most consultant services are provided by the staffs of departments and other units listed above.

   h. Regional NEA Offices. Small staffs man regional field offices to bring NEA services closer to the membership and affiliated state and local associations. In 1966, there were such offices in or near Atlanta, Boston, Indianapolis, St. Paul, San Francisco, and Trenton. In addition, the Urban Services Division employs several field workers at these and other locations to render special help to large urban associations.

   i. DuShane Defense Fund and Fund for Teacher Rights. These two funds are administered separately from the units described above. Requests for use of these funds to aid individual teachers are usually made through local and state associations.

6. Staff of the NEA

   The NEA and its affiliated departments employ over 1,100 persons, most of whom work in or from the NEA Headquarters Building in Washington, D.C. Many of the professional personnel on these staffs are former teachers. In addition many are specialists in functions such as writing and editing, public relations, statistics and research, curriculum, and business management. The chief administrative officer of the Association is the executive secretary, appointed by the Board of Trustees for a term of four years.

7. State Education Associations

   a. There are statewide professional associations of teachers in every state, territory, commonwealth, and in the District of Columbia. They hold conferences and conventions, work for favorable legislation, issue publications, assist local education associations—all in terms of the needs of education and the profession within their respective states. They elect their officers, approve policies, and manage their own affairs. Their affiliation with the NEA permits them to send delegates to the NEA Representative Assembly, to receive various kinds of assistance from the NEA, and to cooperate closely in advancing education and the interests and goals of all professional teachers.

   b. State associations, even when they are called "teachers' associations," include all kinds of educators in their membership. Many have active department programs. The annual conventions or district conventions of most state associations are considered to be so valuable in the in-service education of teachers that schools are closed for one or two days to allow teachers to attend.

c. Many state associations offer free or low-cost liability insurance and low-cost automobile, life, and other types of insurance.

d. The effectiveness of state associations varies greatly for a variety of reasons. One indication of great differences in programs is the great variation in annual dues which range from $4 to $39 annually.

e. In 1966, a total of about 1300 persons were employed on the full-time staffs of state associations. About 450 of these may be classified as professional personnel. In addition, literally thousands of teachers work on committees, as officers, or in other leadership capacities.

8. Local Associations Affiliated with NEA

More than 8200 local education associations were affiliated with the NEA in 1966. These range in size from a single school faculty to large city or county associations enrolling many thousands of teachers. Following are some of the characteristics of such associations.

a. The pattern of organization varies greatly and is not prescribed by the NEA. Some are all-inclusive, others include separate departments within an all-inclusive organization, and some are separate organizations of groups such as classroom teachers and principals. Relationships of local organizations with state associations range from complete independence to complete structural integration as a unit of the state association.

b. The scope of activity and effectiveness of local associations varies greatly from very narrow, ineffective programs to extremely broad and influential associations concerned with improving education as well as the welfare of teachers. Dues vary likewise from almost nothing to $35 or more per year.

c. In negotiating with school boards for improved conditions, the local association is the key agency, although it may receive considerable assistance and support from the state association and the NEA.

d. A growing number of larger local associations are employing full-time executive secretaries and other staff. In 1966, about 90 local associations employed a total of over 200 persons.

e. Over ninety percent of all public school teachers in the United States belong to a local education association.

9. Independent Special Interest Organizations

Although most teaching subjects, levels, and types of educational positions are served by some NEA department or unit, there are some sizeable independent special-interest organizations. Some overlap with NEA departments and a few have no counterparts in the NEA. Some of the most significant independent national organizations are listed below, in alphabetical order.

American Association of University Professors
American Personnel and Guidance Association
American Vocational Association
Association for Childhood Educational International
National Council of Teachers of English

10. The American Federation of Teachers

Many educators do not consider the AFT to be a "professional associa-tion" and, indeed, the AFT to date has not assumed more than a few of the professional responsibilities described in this book. Nevertheless, the AFT avows broad objectives not greatly different from those of the NEA. The major differences are in the pattern of organization, methods of achieving objectives, scope of program, and affiliation with organized labor. Major aspects of the status of the AFT follow.

   a. Membership is concentrated in relatively few large urban centers.

   (1) New York City alone accounted for about one-fourth of the esti-mated national membership of 120,000 in 1966.

   (2) About half of the total national membership is concentrated in eight cities: Chicago, Cleveland, Detroit, Gary, Los Angeles, Milwaukee, New York, and Philadelphia.

   (3) Nationwide there were about 600 locals in 1966.

   b. The organizational structure of the AFT is tightly unified. When a teacher joins a local unit he automatically becomes a member of the national and state federation if there is one in his state, and, indirectly, a member of the AFL-CIO Industrial Union Department.

   c. Total annual dues ranged in 1966 from $18 to $60. The national AFT share was set at $12 effective in 1967.

   d. The weakest level in the AFT structure is the state federation. Only about twenty-seven states had state federations at all in 1966, and most of these were relatively inactive.

   e. The major means by which the AFT pursues its objectives are collective bargaining and strikes.

   f. The AFT is pledged to support labor unions. In return the AFL-CIO and some constituent unions provide financial assistance, manpower, advice, and political influence on behalf of the AFT.

11. Professional Fraternities, Sororities, and Societies

Several professional fraternities, sororities, and societies contribute toward advancement of the teaching profession as well as toward fellowship. Some publish journals and other publications, conduct professional programs and conferences, and stimulate the conduct of research and dissemination of its findings.

a. The largest and most influential is the 60,000-member fraternity Phi Delta Kappa. Its journal, the *Phi Delta Kappan,* is noted as a forum for discussion of controversial issues in education. In addition it fosters the conduct of research through special publications, conferences, and other means.

b. Kappa Delta Pi, an honorary society, publishes the periodical, *Educational Forum.*

c. The best-known woman's organization is the Delta Kappa Gamma Society.

d. The National Society for the Study of Education is a small but influential group composed primarily of college professors. Its major acitivity is preparation of scholarly yearbooks.

12. World Confederation of Organizations of the Teaching Profession

The WCOTP is an international organization devoted to improvement of education, teacher status, and international understanding. It is comprised of national teacher organizations of about eighty-five countries of the world. State and local associations may affiliate on an associate basis.

Problems and Issues in Professional Organizations

1. Lack of Adequate Unity of Teachers

The unity of the teaching profession varies greatly among states and school systems. Generally organizations are more successful in advancing the morale, status, and welfare of teachers and the quality of education where most educators are members of the same general purpose organizations. The ability of educators to achieve maximum possible advancement of their status is probably hampered by the following divisive factors:

a. The struggle between the AFT and NEA affiliates in some school systems

b. The lack of fully unified membership and program of the NEA-related associations in many states and at the national level

c. The large number of independent organizations, some overlapping and competing with each other

d. The differences that exist among elementary school teachers, secondary school teachers, and those at the college level

e. The great diversity of professional, social, political, and intellectual backgrounds and outlook among individuals in the teaching profession

f. The lack of adequate provision in some all-inclusive organizations for balance of influence and interests of different groups of educators within the organization, particularly classroom teachers and administrators

g. The lack of an all-inclusive organization at all in some school systems

h. The "freeloaders" who do not join or support any of the organizations working on their behalf.

2. Lack of Adequate Numbers of Trained Association Leaders and Staff

The rapid growth of teacher organizations has outstripped the supply of qualified leaders and staff specialists. Brief leadership programs and staff workshops have been conducted by teacher organizations, but in 1966, there was not a single college or university program to specifically prepare persons for organization work, except for some short-term workshops on professional negotiations and collective bargaining.

3. Is It Desirable for Teachers to Be Affiliated with Unions?

a. Arguments for affiliation with labor unions declare that:

(1) Labor union policies and practices are applicable to teachers because they work for fixed remuneration from employers.

(2) Labor unions generally support the extension and improvement of public education.

(3) Teacher unions receive direct support from other unions.

(4) Support of the labor union movement is a desirable social objective.

(5) Labor unions win greater gains in money and teaching conditions than do professional associations.

b. Arguments against affiliation with labor unions declare that:

(1) Teaching is a unique profession to which labor union philosophy does not apply. In most school systems there is less difference in the outlook of teachers and administrators than between workers and management in industry.

(2) Education serves all segments of society. Affiliation with organized labor may, in the long run, reduce school support by the general public.

(3) The interests of labor unions may run counter to the interests of education and teachers. Labor unions have often opposed taxes needed for school support.

(4) Support of strikes by other unions can interfere with education. For example, in 1965 and 1966, the AFT conducted an active campaign to boycott some major textbooks and encyclopedias because they were produced in a plant struck by a printers' union.

(5) In the past decade, NEA-affiliated associations have won greater salary gains than has the AFT in its areas of predominance and greater gains than won by most industrial unions.

4. Should Teachers Strike?

Although most teachers and other citizens do not favor strikes by teachers under any circumstances, a number of local teacher organizations have resorted to brief work stoppages when frustrated in achieving their objectives.

a. The following are arguments in favor of teacher strikes.

(1) Strikes by organized labor have been successful in industry in winning representation rights, economic benefits, and other advances.

(2) Strikes are invoked only under extreme circumstances.

(3) Gains won by strikes outweigh possible harm to the students and the public image of the teacher.

(4) Brief strikes do less harm to the educational program than the possible alternative of long-term sanctions of a school system.

b. The following are arguments against teacher strikes.

(1) Strikes by teachers are usually illegal or unethical.

(2) Teacher strikes are upsetting to students.

(3) Strikes build public ill will and loss of respect for teachers.

(4) In the long run measures such as public-information programs, political action, and, in extreme cases, professional sanctions, achieve greater gains than strikes.

The Outlook for Teacher Organizations

1. Growing Importance of Associations

Teacher organizations will likely play an even more important role in the future than in the past. One reason is the likelihood that most school systems will have some kind of negotiation agreement with local teacher organizations. Teacher associations also seem to be pointing toward greater activity in improving instruction.

2. Expanded Roles of Local and National Associations

Although state associations will remain important, the roles of local and national organizations will be more significant than in the past because of:

a. The urbanization and consolidation of school systems
b. The employment of staffs by large local associations
c. The increasing national interest in and financial support of education.

3. Continuation of AFT-NEA Struggle

The competition of the NEA and AFT for the allegiance of teachers will probably continue during the foreseeable future.

a. The AFT will probably continue to gain members in areas dominated economically and politically by labor unions but is not likely to enroll more than a small part of teachers nationwide.
b. Competition for membership will make the AFT and NEA more like each other, with teacher unions seeking to expand their programs beyond teacher welfare and NEA and affiliates pursuing teacher welfare with greater militancy.
c. A higher proportion of teachers will belong to and participate in professional organizations.

4. Reorganization of NEA

The NEA is likely, as it has several times in its history, to reorganize in response to changing conditions. It will probably tighten unity and relationships with its local, state, and departmental affiliates to achieve greater efficiency and effectiveness. Merger in 1966, of the NEA with the formerly all-Negro American Teachers Association will probably stimulate accelerated unification of the remaining racially-segregated state and local associations in some southern states.

5. Expanding Need for Association Staff Members

The increased activities of teacher organizations are likely to stimulate planned preparation for professional association work as a recognized career field.

What Teachers Can and Should Do About Professional Organizations

1. Choose Organizations to Join

To make a wise choice of organizations teachers should evaluate the philosophy, objectives, program, and achievements of each organization he considers.

2. Participate Actively

If democratic values and professional status of teachers are to be maintained and advanced, each teacher needs to do more than merely pay dues. He should become familiar with current organizational programs and problems; attend meetings and help to frame policies; and serve on committees or in other capacities if called upon to do so.

3. Suggest and Support Necessary Changes

No human institution is perfect. Also, it is common for organizations to lag behind rapidly changing conditions. Rather than condemn, or blindly support all aspects of the status quo, teachers need to continually evaluate, initiate, support or help implement necessary changes in organizational structure and program.

4. Prepare for Leadership Roles

Increasing numbers of teachers should seek informal and formal preparation for positions of leadership or full-time employment in professional organizations.

41

Profession: Teacher

JACQUES BARZUN

An interesting contrast to the views expressed by the two previous authors is presented here by Barzun. He distinguishes between teaching and education, stating that education is "a lifelong discipline of the individual himself," while teaching is "the business of the parent and teacher" and "concerns many matters of human knowledge which affect our lives from the three R's to electronics." Barzun remains with the contemporary scene, adding a light touch to what might otherwise have been dull reading. One illustration of his humor is his statement that "apparently education is to do everything the rest of the world leaves undone." He suggests that this has become the state of affairs in education to the extent that respect and regard for teaching has become a lost tradition.

> The bore of all bores was the third. His subject had no beginning, middle, nor end. It was education. Never was such a journey through the desert of the mind, the Great Sahara of intellect. The very recollection makes me thirsty.
>
> T. L. PEACOCK

EDUCATION is indeed the dullest of subjects and I intend to say as little about it as I can. For three years past, now, the people of this country have knitted their brows over the shortcomings of the schools; at least that is the impression one gets from newspapers and periodicals. And by a strange necessity, talk about education never varies. It always seems to resolve itself into undeniable truths about "the well-rounded man" and "our precious heritage." Once in a while, in a fit of daring, the man who lectures you about education points out that the phrase "liberal arts" means "liberating." Then he

SOURCE: Jacques Barzun, *Teacher in America* (Boston: Little, Brown and Company, 1944), pp. 3–13. Copyright 1944, 1945 by Jacques Barzun. Reprinted by permission of the publisher.

The author, born in France, received his education at Columbia University, where he has taught history and is currently Dean of Faculties and Provost, posts he has held since 1958. He has published extensively in the fields of history, science, music, and education: among his books are *Darwin, Marx, Wagner; The House of Intellect; God's Country and Mine;* and, most recently, *The American University: How It Runs, Where It Is Going.*

is off on a fine canter about freedom of the mind and democracy. Or again, hypnotized by your glazed eyeballs, he slips into the old trap of proclaiming that "education" comes from the Latin word meaning to "lead out." Alas! the Latin root has nothing to do with "leading out"; it means simply—to educate. But no matter, it is all in a good cause: "Education should be broadening." Of course! "It should train a man for practical life." Of course again! "Education should be democratic—but nothing radical, naturally. Education must be thorough, but rapid too. No waste of precious time conning over our precious heritage." Those for whom these fundamental principles are rehearsed never argue: they are too drowsy.

This narcotic state is not due merely to the fact that we have latterly had too much educational discussion. After all, we have also been chewing the cud of peace plans, labor problems, and expert strategy. No. I am convinced that at any time brooding and wrangling about education is bad. It is as bad as it would be to perpetually dig around the roots of government by talking political theory. Both political and educational theory are for the rare genius to grapple with, once in a century. The business of the citizen and the statesman is not political theory but politics. The business of the parent and the teacher is not education but Teaching. Teaching is something that can be provided for, changed, or stopped. It is good or bad, brilliant or stupid, plentiful or scarce. Beset as it is with difficulties and armed with devices, teaching has a theory too, but it is one that can be talked about simply and directly, for it concerns the many matters of human knowledge which affect our lives, from the three R's to electronics. To deal with it in that fashion is in fact what I am going to do. . . .

Education is obviously something else, something intangible, unpredictable. Education comes from within; it is a man's own doing, or rather it happens to him—sometimes because of the teaching he has had, sometimes in spite of it. When Henry Adams wrote *The Education of Henry Adams*, he gave thirty pages out of five hundred to his schooling. Common usage records the same distinction. No man says of another: "I educated him." It would be offensive and would suggest that the victim was only a puppy when first taken in hand. But it is a proud thing to say "I taught him"—and a wise one not to specify what.

To be sure, there is an age-old prejudice against teaching. Teachers must share with doctors the world's most celebrated sneers, and with them also the world's unbounded hero-worship. Always and everywhere, "He is a schoolteacher" has meant "He is an underpaid pitiable drudge." Even a politician stands higher, because power in the street seems less of a mockery than power in the classroom. But when we speak of Socrates, Jesus, Buddha, and "other great teachers of humanity," the atmosphere somehow changes and the politician's power begins to look shrunken and mean. August examples show that no limit can be set to the power of a teacher, but this is equally true in the other direction: no career can so nearly approach zero in its effects.

The odd thing is that almost everybody is a teacher at some time or other during his life. Besides Socrates and Jesus, the great teachers of mankind are mankind itself—your parents and mine. First and last, parents do a good deal more teaching than doctoring, yet so natural and necessary is this duty that they never seem aware of performing it. It is only when they are beyond it, when they have thoroughly ground irremediable habits of speech, thought, and behavior into their offspring that they discover the teacher as an institution and hire him to carry on the work.

Then begins the fierce, secret struggle out of which education may come— the struggle between home and school, parent and child, child and teacher; the struggle also that lies deep within the parent and within society concerning the teacher's worth: Is this man of knowledge to be looked up to as wise and helpful, or to be looked down on as at once servile and dangerous, capable and inglorious, higher than the parent yet lower than the brat?

Most people meet this difficulty by alternately looking up and looking down. At best the title of teacher is suspect. I notice that on their passports and elsewhere, many of my academic colleagues put down their occupation as Professor. Anything to raise the tone: a professor is to a teacher what a cesspool technician is to a plumber. Anything to enlarge the scope: not long ago, I joined a club which described its membership as made up of Authors, Artists, and Amateurs—an excellent reason for joining. Conceive my disappointment when I found that the classifications had broken down and I was now entered as an Educator. Doubtless we shall have to keep the old pugilistic title of Professor, though I cannot think of Dante in Hell coming upon Brunetto Latini, and exclaiming "Why, Professor!" But we can and must get rid of "Educator." Imagine the daily predicament: someone asks, "What do you do?"—"I profess and I educate." It is unspeakable and absurd.

Don't think this frivolous, but regard it as a symbol. Consider the American state of mind about Education at the present time. An unknown correspondent writes to me: "Everybody seems to be dissatisfied with education except those in charge of it." This is a little less than fair, for a great deal of criticism has come from within the profession. But let it stand. Dissatisfaction is the keynote. Why dissatisfaction? Because Americans believe in Education, because they pay large sums for Education, and because Education does not seem to yield results. At this point one is bound to ask: "What results do you expect?"

The replies are staggering. Apparently Education is to do everything that the rest of the world leaves undone. Recall the furore over American History. Under new and better management that subject was to produce patriots —nothing less. An influential critic, head of a large university, wants education to generate a classless society; another asks that education root out racial intolerance (in the third or the ninth grade, I wonder?); still another requires that college courses be designed to improve labor relations. Once man, otherwise sane, thinks the solution of the housing problem has bogged down—in the schools; and another proposes to make the future householders happy married couples—through the schools. Off to one side, a well-known company of scholars have got hold of the method of truth and wish to dispense it as a crisis reducer. "Adopt our nationally advertised brand and avert chaos."

Then there are the hundreds of specialists in endless "vocations" who want Education to turn out practised engineers, affable hotelkeepers and finished literary artists. There are educational shops for repairing every deficiency in man or nature: battalions of instructors are impressed to teach Civilian Defense; the FBI holds public ceremonies for its graduates; dogs receive short courses in good manners, and are emulated at once by girls from the age of seven who learn Poise and Personality. Above and beyond all these stand the unabashed peacemakers who want Kitty Smith from Indiana to be sent to Germany, armed with Muzzey's *American History,* to undo Hitler's work.

These are not nightmarish caricatures I have dreamed but things I have recently seen done or heard proposed by representative and even distinguished minds: they are so many acts of faith in the prevailing dogma that Education is the hope of the world.

Well, this is precisely where the use of the right word comes in. You may teach spot-welding in wartime and indeed you must. But Education is the hope of the world only in the sense that there is something better than bribery, lies, and violence for righting the world's wrongs. If this better thing is education, then education is not merely schooling. It is a lifelong discipline of the individual by himself, encouraged by a reasonable opportunity to lead a good life. Education here is synonymous with civilization. A civilized community it better than the jungle, but civilization is a long slow process which cannot be "given" in a short course.

No one in his senses would affirm that Schooling is the hope of the world. But to say this is to show up the folly of perpetually confusing Education with the work of the schools; the folly of believing against all evidence that by taking boys and girls for a few hours each day between the ages of seven and twenty-one, our teachers can "turn out" all the human products that we like to fancy when we are disgusted with ourselves and our neighbors. It is like believing that brushing the teeth is the key to health. No ritual by itself will guarantee anything. Brushing won't even keep your teeth clean, by itself. There is no key to health and there is none to education. Do you think because you have an expensive school system there shall be no more spelling mistakes? Then why suppose that you can eradicate intolerance more easily?

Free compulsory "education" is a great thing, an indispensable thing, but it will not make the City of God out of Public School No. 26.

The whole mass of recrimination, disappointment, and dissatisfaction which this country is now suffering about its schools comes from using the ritual word "Education" so loosely and so frequently. It covers abysses of emptiness. Everybody cheats by using it, cheats others and cheats himself. The idea abets false ambitions. The educator wants to do a big job in the world, so he takes on the task of reorienting Germany and improving human relations. The public at large, bedeviled as it is with these "problems," is only too glad to farm them out, reserving the right of indignant complaint when the educator breaks down or the Institute for Human Relations fails to reduce appreciably the amount of wife beating.

Dissatisfaction remains, and not unmixed with ill will. For in this vast side-show of illusions and misplaced effort, educators find an opportunity to be-labor one another in clans: College teachers cry out, "Why can't high school boys write decent English?" The Deans exclaim, "Why can't our college grad-uates speak foreign languages and be ready to serve in wartime? Look at what the Army is doing!" Up and down the line others say, "Discipline is the thing—the Navy knows more about training boys than we do." And the rhe-torical questions continue, answered by the askers themselves: "Why is there so much juvenile delinquency?"—"It's the schools." "Why did army doctors find so many neurotics?"—"It's the colleges." "Educators are Confused," read one front-page headline a couple of years ago, and down below the ex-planation was: "It's the fault of our Higher Education."

This is certainly looping the loop. Like the jurymen in *Alice in Wonder-land,* the parents, the children in high schools, the men and women in col-leges, are bewildered by claims and counter-claims. They are stunned by solicitations to follow this or that course, for this or that imperative reason. And like the jurymen, they repeat "Important," "Unimportant," while mak-ing futile motions with their forefingers. Inside the academic precincts, plans, curriculums, and methods whirl by with newsreel speed. Labels change; the Progressives become Conservative, the Conservatives Progressive, while the Classicals form a Third Party with adherents and attackers in every camp. From a distance the academic grove looks remarkably like Chaos and Old Night.

Happily there is something stable and clear and useful behind this phantas-magoria of Education—the nature of subject matter and the practice of teaching.

The word helps us again to the idea. The advantage of "teaching" is that in using it you must recognize—if you are in your sober senses—that practical limits exist. You know by instinct that it is impossible to "teach" democracy, or citizenship or a happy married life. I do not say that these virtues and benefits are not somehow connected with good teaching. They are, but they occur as by-products. They come, not from a course, but from a teacher; not from a curriculum, but from a human soul.

It is indeed possible so to arrange school and college work that more play is given to good human influences than in other conceivable arrangements. But it is not possible by fiddling with vague topics to insure or even to increase the dissemination of virtue. I should think it very likely that a course in Democracy would make most healthy students loathe the word and all its associations. And meanwhile the setup (no other word will better express my contempt) takes the room and time and energy which should legitimately be used to teach somebody something teachable—English or History, Greek or Chemistry. . . .

Meanwhile I dwell on the necessity of teaching, that is to say on the need for teachers. There are never enough. Statistics tell us that at this moment we are one hundred thousand short—one in ten. This does not include men fighting or putting their special skill at the war plant's disposal. One hundred thousand have simply jumped at the chance for higher pay. That is their right and in a competitive system they must be free from blame. Nevertheless we have here an estimate of the number who are normally in teaching for want of better jobs. The "call" cannot be strong if a teacher will leave the classroom to floor-walk in a department store. Doctors are poor too, but they stick to their rounds and their patients.

But in truth, American schoolteachers as such may well be forgiven their recent desertion—or what looks like it—when we remember how so many college and university administrators acted under the emergency of war. In a twinkling, all that they had professed to believe in for thirty years was discarded as useless. Subjects, schedules, principles, were renounced, with tossing of caps in the air and whoops of joy. Naturally and fortunately, there were notable exceptions to this stampede and much indignation within the ranks. But the bandwagon pressure was great and solid institutions found it hard to resist. One wonders what would have happened if we had been blitzed like England—where no such academic jamboree ensued—or economically hampered like Canada—where academic calm has continued to reign.

I am inclined to think . . . that this excitement signaled a release from long pretense. With us many people who pass as professional teachers are merely "connected with education." They live on the fringes of the academic army—campus followers, as it were—though too often it is they who have the honors and emoluments while the main body lives on short rations. Dislocation by war naturally mixes up the doers with the drones and produces the academic riot that our newspapers depict. To judge fairly, it would be well to draw a veil over the scene since Pearl Harbor and say that on that day the United States suspended all serious educational projects—excepting of course the people's wise award of a traveling fellowship to Mr. Wendell Willkie. Looking at the situation in this way would give us perspective, and something like a fresh start—again from the base of teaching as against Education. For if anything is more alarming than the demand for education as a cure-all, it is the chuckle-headed notion that many educators have of teaching. . . .

Teaching is not a lost art but the regard for it is a lost tradition. Hence tomorrow's problem will not be to get teachers, but to recognize the good ones and not discourage them before they have done their stint. In an age of big words and little work, any liberal profession takes some sticking to, not only in order to succeed, but in order to keep faith with oneself. Teaching is such a profession. . . .

42
Reordering Goals and Roles: The Teaching Profession in the 1970's

T. M. STINNETT

Here is a projected view of the profession as Stinnett believes it might be in the 1970's. Two major areas of concern are expressed. The first concern is for "erosion in the quality of public education"; the second is the need for achieving a greater degree of autonomy in the management of the affairs of the teaching profession. While Stinnett's broad experience in professional development and welfare on the national level undoubtedly qualifies him to appraise the existing state of affairs more ably than many educational leaders, it might also restrict his vision to exclude possible benefits to be derived from the business world. A careful study of this proposal is especially recommended for

SOURCE: *Phi Delta Kappan,* Vol. 52, No. 1 (September 1970), pp. 1–3. Reprinted by permission of the author and publisher.

Dr. Stinnett, a visiting professor at Texas A and M University, was for many years assistant executive secretary for the National Education Association in charge of the office of Professional Development and Welfare. Besides contributing to the *Encyclopedia of Educational Research* and *Saturday Review,* he has written many books on teachers, their professional organizations, and their problems, among them *The Profession of Teaching, Professional Problems of Teachers,* and *Teacher Dropout.*

those readers who are moving toward more extensive involvement in the profession.

THE BASIC THRUST of the symposium, "Unfinished Business of the Teaching Profession in the 1970's," is twofold.

First, how can the teaching profession deal with erosion in the quality of public education?

Second, how can the teaching profession achieve a greater degree of autonomy in the management of its affairs?

No attempt is made in this introduction to define "the teaching profession" precisely. In general, the phrase alludes to practitioners in the public schools. This limitation is regrettable, but it is a fact of life. Teachers in higher education tend to disassociate themselves from public school practitioners. There is separatism even among the specialties in the lower schools. The plural in the title of the Education Professions Development Act reflects this diversity.

Such status schisms exist in few if any other professions. Although every profession has a multitude of specializations, the practitioners manage to be associated together and to operate in a unified manner. Are public school practitioners to acquiesce meekly to these status differences—a condition that means, among other things, preparation of members of the teaching profession by members of other professions?

Both education and the teaching profession are in a serious state of disarray. The decade of the 70's will bring more turmoil. Any thoughtful observer of the current education scene in the United States is bound to be disturbed by two discernible trends.

One trend is the ferment in education—the frantic search for innovations accompanied by attempts to bring order out of chaos. The second trend involves the adverse impact on the teaching profession of criticism from many sources.

Public school criticism has reached such proportions as to elicit predictions of utter collapse and at least partial abandonment of the public schools.

There is no denying the seriousness of the situation. To many critics, the problems of the inner-city schools appear insoluble. Discipline problems have reached alarming proportions. Mounting disorder, disruption, and violence in the high schools have bred proposals that compulsory attendance laws be repealed, at least for youngsters who have finished elementary school.

Inability of the public schools to adjust quickly to the need for a changed curriculum and new procedures, plus the need for more effective teaching and learning processes, encourage those who contend that the public schools are failing. Some critics say that the quality of education in the public schools is deteriorating so rapidly that other options must be provided. Thus there are moves to establish more private schools as an escape valve for parents who feel that their children are being shortchanged in the public schools. This trend, certainly, will tend to escalate movements for state support of nonpublic schools. Already at least four states (Ohio, Pennsylvania, Rhode Island, and Connecticut) have made appropriations for salary and other payments to teachers in parochial schools. (These moves have been sustained by the courts in Pennsylvania and overturned in a test case in Maine.) In addition, there are laws providing some form of aid to parochial schools in 23 other states; and a drive is on for direct public aid in about half the states. Another proposal which will undoubtedly give momentum to the movement to establish nonpublic schools is the voucher plan, which is being offered in various forms. The common feature is a voucher issued to parents by the government to pay education costs in schools of their choice.

The thesis being developed is that it is constitutional for states to buy public services from private institutions. There are many precedents in higher education. For example, as early as 1659, Harvard received grants from the Massachusetts General Court. The thesis will eventually be tested in the U.S. Supreme Court. Whatever the outcome there, expansion in the number of private schools will probably continue.

Still another factor in widespread discontent with the public schools is a series of court decisions, based on the Bill of Rights and other amendments to the Constitution, establishing the rights of students.

These decisions have convinced many parents that certain time-honored controls embodied in the *in loco parentis* principle have been effectively destroyed. They believe it is now virtually impossible for teachers and administrators to maintain the measure of discipline essential to quality instruction and learning. It may of course be argued that this is not so, that the public schools need only to adapt to the new interpretations of student rights. In any case, the generation gap is involved here. Parents, having grown up under the traditional notion of what constitutes order and proper discipline in the public schools, have difficulty in adapting to the new interpretations. They prefer to blame the public schools for the new order of things; and they tend to seek recourse in private schools where, it is assumed, the old authoritarian order can be maintained. But can it? Will not the courts, in time, apply the same rulings to nonpublic schools? This seems especially likely if nonpublic schools receive tax support.

Disarray in the Profession

Former U.S. Commissioner James E. Allen recently warned a group of educators that the public school establishment is being elbowed out of the educational mainstream by performance-minded industry and government, dissatisfied parents and students, and educational TV producers. He asserted that there was a very real possibility that leadership and decision making in education could be taken out of the hands of educators if they fail to spearhead needed changes.

There is little question that shifts in the education power structure are under way. It cannot be predicted with any degree of certainty what structure, what groups or combination of groups, will become predominant. We can be certain that the Nixon Administration will vigorously emphasize performance and accountability, either for the purpose of demonstrating efficiency in education or as an excuse for putting the brakes on increases in school expenditures. Administration sloganeering will have great appeal and the profession may well be intimidated by it.

Can the Teaching Profession Survive?

One of the basic marks of a profession, at least in the United States, is that it is largely autonomous. In some professions, particularly the private ones, these controls are vested in the profession by legislative enactments. In others, controls are assumed through informal, quasi-legal cooperative arrangements among the practitioners, the preparing institutions, and state authorities. In still other professions, such as teaching in the public schools, the arrangement is a basically legal responsibility of the respective states, with the profession having broad advisory powers. Some professional organizations supplement the legal license by membership requirements that, in effect, certify to competence in areas of specialization.

Generally, autonomy for a profession consists of control over accreditation, through determining the standards of preparation; licensure, through setting of requirements to undergird the preparation; continuance in practice, through measurement of performance and professional growth; and disciplining, through developing and enforcing codes of ethics.

During the decade 1950–1960, educators moved vigorously to develop standards cooperatively, involving all segments of the profession. There was constant and cooperative study and refinement of teacher education programs. There was cooperative development and widespread acceptance of a national professional accrediting agency for teacher education. State certification procedures were refined. A "Code of Ethics for the Education Profession" was cooperatively developed and widely accepted.

The profession appeared to be on the way to an unprecedented degree of self-determinism.

Then came the 1960's. For the first time in the United States, teachers took strong collective action to gain welfare benefits and significant roles in school policy making. This decade saw a deterioration in the so-called partnership approach between teachers and administrators. The repercussions were felt throughout the structure of teachers' professional organizations.

Moreover, this was the decade of an awakening national conscience. The public was made painfully aware of the plight of certain minority groups and their neglected children. Inadequacies of public school curricula and teaching were exposed. Exposed also was the obsolescence of much of teacher education, at least insofar as minority group children were concerned.

Colleges and universities are now reaping their fair share of criticism for their failure to prepare teachers to function effectively in large inner-city schools among children of minority cultures.

These developments raise the serious question of the restructuring of teacher education. Can higher education institutions change their programs quickly enough, and appropriately enough, to survive current criticism? William Kottmeyer, superintendent of St. Louis schools, has proposed that the large cities establish or reestablish their own teachers colleges.[1] Already, some big cities have developed their own teacher preparation programs, taking liberal arts graduates for one-year internships and professional orientation.

Out of all this ferment arises the larger question: Can the teaching profession survive as it is? If it can, will it be elbowed out of any control over standards for admission, preparation, licensure, professional growth, and continuance in practice? There is cause for apprehension that teachers in the public schools will become merely technicians.

Disarray in Public Relations

There are signs of a public revolt against the teaching profession. There are demands for assessment of performance. There is a growing trend to vote down school bond proposals and even school levies. There is also strong agitation to repeal legislation providing tenure and other forms of job security. There are pressures to apply performance criteria to teachers as a prerequisite to continuing certification and service. These, I assume, arise in part from public anger stirred up by the profession's insistence upon collective negotiations and the right to strike, legally or illegally.

The recent upsurge in voter rejection of proposed tax increases for school purposes is particularly painful evidence of deterioration in the schools' relations with the public. In Ohio, such voter action has forced several districts to shorten terms or to close schools for a month or more. In Los Angeles and

[1] William A. Kottmeyer, "A Tale of Two Cities." *Your AASA in 1969*. Official Report. Washington, D. C.: American Association of School Administrators, 1969, p. 62.

Houston, voters have forced cutbacks in school services. In the spring of 1969, voters turned down school budgets in 137 of New York State's 700 districts. This rejection rate, nearly 20%, was the highest in the state's history. In Long Island more than 40% of the districts' budgets were rejected.

How does one account for these new negative attitudes? In this country, throughout our history, we have believed that every American was endowed by birth with a passport to the possible. As De Tocqueville wrote more than a century ago, "To the American everything is possible. What he has not yet accomplished is only that which he has not attempted."

Something has gone sadly awry. On every hand the quality of life is diminished by blight, pollution, noise, and overcrowding. Our streams are fouled, our soils eroded, our forests cut down, our traffic snarled. As one quipster put it, "Not only is there no God, but try getting a plumber on weekends."

Man may walk on the moon in safety and security, but not on the streets and in the parks of our big cities. There is hunger in the midst of plenty; poverty abrades the nation's conscience. Riots, violence, pickets, marches, and dissent mar our days and our nights. We seem suddenly to have come upon visions of our limitations; earlier visions of better tomorrows seem now obscured or jaded. The infinity of our powers and possibilities seems, at least momentarily, to be giving way to frustration. We despair that there are no more mountains to climb, no more rivers to cross, no more virgin forests to devastate. Above all, we have lost our identity in the anonymity of the mob. The individual is only a number in the soulless conscience of an error-prone computer.

Chaos in the Cities

The much-ballyhooed American goal of uninterrupted, eternal growth—in GNP, in even bigger cars, in income, in larger cities, in population—is proving to be a delusion. The price of bigness is too big to pay. Our cities are becoming unlivable and ungovernable. Population growth, already outrunning our natural resources, is still climbing dangerously. We can no longer believe in the gospel of growth. Faith in the miracles of technology has sustained our giddiness. But technology cannot defy the limitations of nature. For every technological advance there have been corresponding adverse effects—fouled air, polluted waters, impossible transportation problems.

The boasted efficiency of business is crumbling under the overload. The telephone system in New York City and elsewhere is a shambles, the overburdened and inefficient postal service is little better than the pony express. Power failures are becoming epidemic; brown-outs, lowered voltage, and blackouts chase one another across the land at dangerous speeds. Even the power companies in many of the big cities are pleading with customers not to install new air conditioning equipment.

The cliché of the business community ("If business were run like schools, there would be no business") now has a hollow ring. It may be that schools must turn away from both the bigness and the "efficiency" of business. There is a point in school size beyond which the quality of education deteriorates rapidly. There is a practical limit to the value of technology in teaching and learning.

All these emerging elements put together seem to foretell still greater turbulence for public schools and teachers in the 1970's.

What directions must the profession pursue in the coming decade?

This is the major query of "Unfinished Business of the Teaching Profession," theme of the ensuing symposium. We have dealt with eight major topics, as follows: state and professional licensure of educational personnel; reconstruction of teacher education and professional growth programs; accreditation of teacher education institutions and agencies; expanding roles of laboratory schools; the meaning and application of performance criteria in teacher education, certification, and professional growth; the meaning and application of differentiated staff in teaching; the profession's quest for responsibility and accountability; and the developing program of self-determinism in Canada.

EVALUATION

JOHN DEWEY, **My Pedagogic Creed**

1. In what way does Dewey believe all education proceeds?

2. (a) When does Dewey say a person's unconscious education begins?

   (b) State the five ways in which this process educates.

   (c) What is the function of formal and technical education as Dewey sees it?

3. (a) Name the two sides or aspects Dewey identifies in the educational process.

   (b) Which does he say is more essential?

   (c) Which does he say is the basis of the process?

   (d) Without insight into this aspect, what would education be like?

4. (a) What reason does Dewey give for the need of a knowledge of social conditions in this discussion of the educational process?

   (b) According to this reasoning, how do we learn what a child's instincts and tendencies mean?

   (c) What illustration is given by Dewey to support this contention?

5. Dewey states: "In order to know what a power really is we must know what its end, use, or function is." How does he see this in relation to a child?

6. Why does Dewey believe it is impossible to prepare a child for any precise set of conditions?

7. (a) How does Dewey consider social progress and school to be related?

   (b) What is his concluding remark on this relationship in regard to education?

8. Dewey states that the school is primarily a social institution.
   (a) How is the school defined in Dewey's Creed?

   (b) Give his definition of education.

   (c) What should schools do as an institution?

(d) Why does Dewey believe that present education fails?

(e) What are Dewey's views on (1) the teacher's place and work in the school, (2) discipline of the school, and (3) grading and promotion?

9. What does Dewey regard as (1) the basis of correlation in a child's growth and (2) the true center of correlation on the school subjects and activities?

10. What does Dewey believe subject matter should do?

11. What does Dewey regard as the primary basis of education?

12. Dewey says "language is the device for communication." How does he elaborate on this?

13. How does Dewey define progress in education?

14. Briefly state Dewey's views on the process and goals of education and give the rationale for his views.

15. What was the simple artifice to which Dewey reduced the method of teaching?

16. List the views held by Dewey in regard to the nature of method on (1) the development of the child's nature, (2) ideas, (3) the image in instruction, (4) interests, and (5) the emotions.

17. How does Dewey relate the school and social progress?

18. Explain Dewey's view of education (a) as a process in social progress and (b) as an adjustment of individual activity.

19. How does Dewey's Creed place the teacher uniquely in the social consciousness of the human race?

GRACE GRAHAM, The Teacher as a Member of a Profession

20. What is Graham's major thesis?

21. How has she approached this thesis?

22. List the five major characteristics to be found in the professional spirit of a profession discussed by the author.

23. Within each of the five major characteristics Graham identifies as being present in the professional spirit of a profession, list the sequence of points she makes.

24. Graham states that "no group ever completely attains its professional goals or measures up to the ideal attributes of a profession." She then lists five responses of significance if the symbol of professionalism is to be useful to teachers. What are these?

25. Why does the author believe that college and university professors have less ambiguous claims to "professional" status?

SIDNEY DORROS, **Professional Organizations**

26. Dorros identifies three general types of organizations found in the educational field. Name them.

27. List and briefly describe the three categories given for general purpose organizations in education.

28. What knowledge does the author believe a teacher needs in order to make a wise choice of membership in a professional organization?

29. What does Dorros indicate the primary services of the early associations of teachers were?

30. (a) What was the name originally given to the organization now known as the National Education Association?

    (b) When and where was it established?

    (c) State the basic purpose of the original organization.

31. Outline the beginnings of early educational organizations in America between the years 1794 and 1916 as Dorros gives them.

32. What five major concerns of state education organizations have received legislative support as a direct result of effective lobbying?

33. What conclusion does Dorros draw in regard to practically every advance of the teaching profession?

34. Give the seven stated basic objectives of the NEA.

35. What major means are given as the way the NEA attempts to achieve its objectives?

36. Name the four governing bodies of the NEA as of 1966.

37. Name the five permanent units of the NEA at the national level.

38. What four major differences distinguish the NEA from the American Federation of Teachers (AFT)?

39. What two major problems exist in professional organizations?

40. What does Dorros think teachers can and should do about professional organizations?

JACQUES BARZUN, **Profession: Teacher**

41. How does Barzun define education?

42. How does he define teaching?

43. What does Barzun suggest to aid retention of competent teachers in our schools?

44. (a) According to Barzun what does the remark "he is a school teacher" imply?

    (b) How does the author support his statement that a politician stands higher than a school teacher?

45. (a) Barzun advocates that we can and must get rid of the term "educator." He further states that dissatisfaction is the keynote to the American state of mind about education. Give his reasons for this point of view.

    (b) What results does Barzun say we expect from education?

46. In his concluding remarks Barzun identifies what he believes will be a major educational problem in the future. Briefly state this problem.

T. M. STINNETT, **Reordering Goals and Roles: The Teaching Profession in the 1970's**

47. What two disturbing trends does Stinnett see in the American educational scene in 1970?

48. What evidence does the author give to support his contention that criticism of the public schools has created a serious situation?

49. What three factors does Stinnett see as clear evidence of the adverse effect of public school criticism?

50. (a) Explain the "voucher system" used in providing education for some children in Stinnett's projections for the 1970's.

    (b) How might the voucher system legally lend support to nonpublic schools?

51. What did former U.S. Commissioner James E. Allen predict as a possible outcome in education if educators fail to spearhead needed change?

52. Stinnett identifies four discernible signs of a public revolt against the teaching profession. What are they?

53. According to Stinnett, what serious splits exist within the teaching profession?

54. What detrimental effects of the existing schisms might be expected to result from these status discriminations?

55. What are Stinnett's thoughts on (1) school size and (2) the value of technology?

56. In a study of "Unfinished Business of the Teaching Profession," what are the eight main topics presented in position papers concerned with the direction the teaching profession will pursue in the 1970's?

FOR FURTHER READING

Broudy, Harry S., "Criteria for the Professional Preparation of Teachers," *School, Society, and the Professional Educator,* ed. F. H. Blackington III and R. S. Patterson (New York: Holt, Rinehart, and Winston, 1968).
  Points out the need for specialty foundations, professional content, technological concerns, and research as part of the preparation of teachers. Since these four areas often are a basis of controversy for inclusion in teacher education programs, a student needs to be informed of their potential contribution and also to consider any factor unfavorable to their inclusion in the preparation of teachers.

Burrup, Percy E., "The Teacher and Professional Organizations," *The Teacher and the Public School System,* 2d ed. (New York: Harper & Row, 1967).
  An interesting contrast to the Dorros selection from the point of view of its focus on the autonomy of a teacher. The author shows concern for and apparent dedication to excellence in education.

Conant, James B., "The Theory and Practice of Teaching," *The Education of American Teachers* (New York: McGraw-Hill, 1963).
  In both the preface and the chapter on teaching theories and practices, the author makes penetrating observations on education in contemporary times.

Kimball, Solon T., and James E. McClellan, "Education and Commitment," *Teaching: Essays and Readings,* ed. K. Yamamoto (New York: Random House, 1952).
  A statement on the radical difference between commitment in our culture and commitment in other cultures. It should be required reading for anyone who truly aspires to be a professional educator.